JANUA LINGUARUM

STUDIA MEMORIAE
NICOLAI VAN WIJK DEDICATA

edenda curat

C. H. VAN SCHOONEVELD

Indiana University

Series Maior, 77

SPEECH ERRORS
AS
LINGUISTIC EVIDENCE

edited by

VICTORIA A. FROMKIN
University of California, Los Angeles

1973

MOUTON

THE HAGUE · PARIS

LIBRARY OF CONGRESS CATALOG CARD NUMBER 73-78443

Printed in The Netherlands

To the memory of
Mark Fromkin, 1950-1966

ACKNOWLEDGMENTS

I would like to express my gratitude to the authors of the papers included in this volume. I particularly wish to thank Anthony Cohen and Sieb Nooteboom who encouraged me to edit this collection. The publishers who granted me permission to reprint the papers are also gratefully acknowledged, including the New American Library, *The Yale Scientific Magazine*, the *British Journal of Disorders of Communication Zeitschrift für Phonetik*, *Language*, *Neuropsychologia*, and Mouton and Co.

While most of the errors included in the Introduction and the Appendix were noted by myself, I am grateful to Peter Ladefoged and Ilsa Lehiste who tuned in their linguistic/phonetic ears to note many errors for me.

In addition I would like to express my deepest appreciation to Peter Ladefoged who continues to serve as my teacher and as an inspiration in all of my work.

I am of course indebted to all those who inadvertently provided the data for this book. They include many of the UCLA Linguistics Department students and faculty as well as other personal friends. They will undoubtedly recognize their particular contributions. Besides acting as a source of data, their many useful comments, suggestions, and criticisms have helped to clarify my own thinking. The fact that they do not run when they see me approaching with my 'little black book' is a tribute to their patience and intellectual honesty.

Special mention must be noted of the time and effort contributed by Donald MacKay of the UCLA Department of Psychology in his many discussions with me on this topic.

The typing of the manuscript by Renee Wellin is also gratefully acknowledged.

The work reported here was supported in part by UCLA intramural research funds and in part by grants from the National Science Foundation, The National Institutes of Health, and the Office of Naval Research.

Finally, I would like to thank my husband, Jack, for his encouragement and his ability to overlook or excuse my constant 'errors'.

CONTENTS

INTRODUCTION

VICTORIA A. FROMKIN

The collection of papers in this volume in many ways represents an opposite trend in the field of linguistics from that exemplified by Bloomfield (1922) when he stated: "we are casting off our dependence on psychology, realizing that linguistics ... must study its subject-matter in and for itself ... We must study the way people talk – without bothering about the mental processes that we may conceive to underlie or accompany these habits." These papers are concerned with just such "mental processes" using "the way people talk" as a window into the human mind. In addition, it is assumed here that one cannot understand "the way people talk" without reference to their linguistic knowledge.

It was once thought that "the linguistic processes of the 'mind' are ... simply unobservable (and we therefore) have no right to guess about the linguistic workings of an inaccessible 'mind'" (Twaddell 1935). If the scope of science had been limited to what is directly observable our understanding of the laws of nature would be severely curtailed. Just as there is evidence for such unobservable physical entities as atoms and electrons, there is evidence for unobservable linguistic units and grammatical rules, as is shown in these papers.

Since the onset of transformational theory (Chomsky 1957), linguists working within this paradigm have been concerned with constructing a theory of language that can account for and explain more than just the observable end result of the speech production process. A viable linguistic theory, they maintain, must be able to account for the 'creative aspect' of language use, i.e. the fact that knowing a language means being able to produce and understand novel utterances. The theory also has to account for the speakers' tacit knowledge of structural ambiguities, related sentence types, grammatical vs. nongrammatical sentences, possible vs. impossible (or improbable) 'words', etc. Such a theory would represent a set of general constraints on all human languages, and a grammar of a particular language would represent a model or theory of a speaker's linguistic competence.

In addition, the grammar constructed by the linguist is to represent 'psychological reality' a view put forth earlier by Sapir (1933). In other words it is not enough for the linguist's grammar to be formally elegant and account for the data; rather it "aims at finding a true theory or description (of linguistic knowledge)... which shall also be an explanation of the observable facts" (Popper 1963). What is being sought is a 'God's truth' rather than a 'hocus pocus'theory. This view, then, stands on the side of Galileo and opposed to the scientific philosophy of Andreas Osiander who, in his preface to Copernicus's *De revolutionibus*, stated that "There is no need for these hypotheses to be true, or even to be at all like the truth; rather, one thing is sufficient for them – that they should yield calculations which agree with the observations." (as quoted by Popper 1963).

If there is a need for these hypotheses to be true, and if they concern "the linguistic workings of an inaccessible 'mind'" we are faced with the problem of finding the ways to test the hypotheses, since any hypotheses which are not in principle testable belong to the realm of metaphysics rather than science.

This is not an easy task when viewed in the light of one description of modern linguistic theory:

(Halle and Chomsky's) aim is like that of the physicist who writes a set of differential equations that anyone riding a bicycle must satisfy. No physicist claims that a person need know, let alone be able to solve, such differential equations in order to become a competent cyclist. Neither do Halle and Chomsky claim that humans know or knowingly obey the rules (that) ... govern language behavior. Halle and Chomsky also strive, as do physical theorists, to identify the constants and parameters of their theories with components of reality. (Weizenbaum 1972).

If a cyclist does not 'obey the rules' (the differential equations representing the physical laws) he will fall off the bicycle. A speaker of a language can also break the laws which constitute his linguistic knowledge. Like the bicycle rider he would 'know' that he had broken the rules. It is this knowledge that has provided most of the evidence for the posited grammatical rules, i.e. speakers' intuitive judgements representing their knowledge as opposed to the actual utterances they produce.

With this separation between linguistic competence (knowledge of the rules) and performance (use of the grammar) the testing of the linguistic 'constants and parameters' has been, for the most part, based on intuitive judgements and formal arguments.

Rosenblith (1967) has suggested that

The kind of things that the rational man can say about language ... the kinds of deep structures, the abstract operations, he can concatenate in some sense today – are still untestable. And they are untestable precisely because we do not have as yet a technology of what I might call his cognitive measurement ... (A)s far as (the linguists) are concerned, their freedom and the lack of constraints on making of theories and making of models are restricted only by their own intelligence. I hope that they won't exploit that position by turning away from the laboratories instead of turning towards them. (95–97)

If "turning towards the laboratories" means attempting to find empirical verification for cognitive linguistic processes, a number of papers in this volume attempt to do just that.

The papers represent a number of different linguistic and psychological viewpoints. They are, however, all concerned with the ways in which spontaneously produced speech errors (i.e. utterances which in some way deviate from the intended or target utterances) provide insights into the nature of language and language behavior, and serve to test putative hypotheses.

This is not to imply that all aspects of grammatical theory are testable in this way. In fact, for the most part, such data can at most provide support for some of the units and rules of grammar put forth by linguists, with the assumption that if such constructs are found necessary to explain linguistic performance there is little reason to doubt their existence as part of grammars, particularly when their grammatical 'existence' is necessitated by other linguistic evidence.

This position is supported by Fry[1] who states that speech errors "cannot be accounted for except by attributing to speakers a knowledge of a language system certainly similar to and even in many details coincident with that constructed by linguists".

Speech error data have of course even greater significance in the construction of performance models. A performance model will have to incorporate the theory of competence but will have to deal with many other psychological and physiological factors. As is shown in the papers of Cohen, Boomer and Laver, Laver, Fry, Nooteboom, MacKay, Hill, and Fromkin, and as will be discussed further below, speech error data are invaluable in such a task.

This view is not necessarily the position held by the authors of the collected papers, some of whom would sharply differ with the theoretical position of the editor. But all of the papers are concerned with the importance of speech errors for linguistic theory, in one way or the other.

This linguistic interest in speech errors can be traced back to Hermann Paul (1886) who, according to Meringer (1895), was the first linguist to suggest that an examination of speech errors might reveal a natural cause of certain types of linguistic change. Meringer also notes that Delbrück (1887) suggested that speech error data was of value to linguistics.[2]

Meringer (1895, 1908) may be considered, however, as the 'father' of the linguistic interest in speech errors, if for no other reason than that his published collection of over eight thousand speech, reading, and writing errors has provided the data for other researchers. (See MacKay and Celce-Murcia papers in this volume.) Meringer's view of the mechanisms involved in such 'deviant' utterances – an unconscious mechanical breakdown of the articulatory process – differed from the view put forth by Freud. Freud's interest was in how unconscious 'slips of the tongue' reveal underlying, repressed thoughts. In this sense his aims differed from most of the authors in this volume, but his interest in the mental constructs which can be deduced from speech

---

[1] The papers included in this volume will not be referenced as to publication date, i.e. if no publication is cited the reference refers to the author's included paper.
[2] The references to Paul and Delbrück were brought to my attention by Celce-Murcia.

behavior data is shared by many linguists. His view of speech errors as outward manifestations of repressed sub-conconscious thoughts is discussed to some extent by Hockett, Wells, and Hill.

Besides the enormous corpus of errors published by Meringer, one other small collection of about one hundred errors was published by Bawden, an American psychologist, in 1900. Then in 1917 Sturtevant followed up Meringer's interest in the relationship between speech errors and linguistic change. He notes:

Fortunately the more permanent changes of linguistic form furnish an indirect record of many other mistakes in pronunciation; for we have seen that all of the former which are not due to dialect mixture originated in a momentary variation in the speech of an individual. We may therefore use as illustrations mistakes involved in secondary linguistic change (32).

According to Sturtevant, errors made in speaking are non-random and predictable. This view is reiterated in the Wells article.

Jakobson's 1941 monograph on child language and aphasia refers to Meringer's and Sturtevant's interest in speech errors as related to linguistic change. But the importance of speech error data for a general theory of language and language behavior was most notably shown in Lashley's paper on "The Problem of Serial Order in Behavior" (1951). It is interesting to note that this leading physiological psychologist had planned to undertake an extensive study of linguistics hoping that this would help him find answers to the problem of brain function, which was his main concern. His unfortunate death in 1957 prevented him from doing this, but his insights remain as important today as when he projected them more than twenty years ago.

Lashley was concerned with presenting an alternative theory to the mechanistic behaviorism which dominated much of psychology (and linguistics). He aimed, by using "speech (as) ... the only window through which the physiologist can view the cerebral life" (Fournie 1887, quoted by Lashley) to show that an associative stimulus/response chain theory can not account for the "multiplicity of integrative processes" underlying the production of an utterance. He proposed "a series of hierarchies or organization: the order of vocal movements in pronouncing the word, the order of words in the sentence, the order of sentences in the paragraph ..." The disordering which may occur at any stage or level in the hierarchy would account for the variety of observed speech errors. Lashley's ideas are further elaborated in the MacKay paper.

1951 was also the year in which Wells published his paper "Predicting Slips of the Tongue". This is a pioneering effort in using speech error evidence in linguistics. It remains an important contribution to our understanding of language and linguistic performance.

Hockett has had a continuing interest in speech errors as important linguistic data (1955, 1958, 1967). His last, most extensive treatment on the subject, is included in this collection as are eight papers of other researchers written from 1966 to the present.

There have been more papers utilizing speech error data written by linguists and psycholinguists in the last five years than in all the previous years of linguistic history.

It seems that speech errors have become legitimitized. This collection is published in an attempt to show why.

It is not my aim in this introduction to play the role of critic, evaluating all the papers which follow. They have been included because they are interesting and insightful, despite the fact that in many cases the views expressed differ from my own. The aim is rather to discuss some of the requirements for a model of linguistic performance in light of speech error data. If, however, the view that "A theory of performance will have to incorporate the theory of competence – the generative grammar of a language – as an essential part" (Chomsky 1972) is correct, then it is necessary to view the 'constants and parameters' of such a theory in relation to a performance model.

Most of the linguistic analyses of speech errors deal with 'phonological' errors. The discreteness of such phonological units has been assumed in all linguistic theories and in all the papers that follow. Despite the semi-continuous nature of the speech signal wave form, such segments are 'real'. Without such discrete units one cannot account for speech errors in which single 'segments' are anticipated, perseverated, are transposed, added, or deleted. Furthermore, there are errors which appear to be solely phonological in nature, thus suggesting a partial independence of phonology from other grammatical components. Even Freud recognized that phonetic influences may account for certain kinds of contaminations, particularly in accelerated speech. However, in his effort to discount the importance of such influences he goes so far as to say:

Among the examples of the mistakes in speech collected by me, I can scarcely find one in which I would be obliged to attribute the speech disturbance simply and solely to ... 'contact effect of sound'. Almost invariably I discover besides this a disturbing influence of something outside of the intended speech. The disturbing element is either a single unconscious thought, which comes to light through the speech-blunder ... or it is a more general psychic motive, which directs itself against the entire speech.

Hill's suggestion that spoonerisms seldom if ever produce non-existent words would seem to support Freud's contention. But many spontaneous errors do result in nonexistent words and can easily be explained as phonological in origin as is shown by the examples under (1).[3]

(1) (a) group three → greep three
    (b) my money is running out → my runny is munning out
    (c) felony → fenoly
    (d) Rabelais → Ralebais
    (e) skip one stage → stip one skage
    (f) hash or grass → hass or grash
    (g) bank of America → mank of aberica
    (h) yesterday's lecture → lesterday's yecture
    (i) weak and feeble → feak and weeble

[3]   The intended utterance appears to the left of the arrow and the error on the right in all examples in the introduction.

In fact, it is the 'conscious word-play' that so often produces spoonerisms with amusing meaning, such as those attributed to the good Reverend Spooner himself as in (2) (Robbins 1966).

(2) (a) light a fire → fight a liar
    (b) it's pouring rain → it's roaring pain
    (c) leave it at the house → heave it at the louse
    (d) wasted a whole term → tasted a whole worm
    (e) you missed my history lecture → you hissed my mystery lecture
    (f) humming birds → bumming herds
    (g) dear old queen → queer old dean
    (h) enjoying the sun with some old folks → enjoying the sun with some old soaks.

In the *snovelling show* for *shovelling snow* error cited by Hill, the intrusion of *sniffling* may have had the influence he suggests. Similarly, the speaker who, in a discussion of animal sterilization, produced *pat copulation* for *cat population* may have been influenced by "a more general psychic motive". Equally plausible is the possibility that these are both examples of disordering of initial consonants.

Hill's conclusion was probably due to his admittedly small corpus. Freud's, however, may have been due to his own unconscious 'filter'. In this regard his observation that "Mistakes in speech are in a great measure contagious" is of interest. This 'virulence' is observed by anyone working with these data. On a number of occasions, after presenting papers concerned with speech errors at professional meetings, the subsequent speakers seemed to produce a rash of such errors. This produced amusement and strange looks directed toward me, as if I had special psychic powers manipulating the audience to provide support for my contentions. Freud stated that he knew "no reason for this psychic contagiousness". But Hill presents one possible explanation when he suggests "that we all have a sort of internal editing mechanism which enables us to correct a speaker's error without noticing that an error has occurred". Cohen underscores this point: "Very often errors went undetected by both the speaker himself and the average listener. Only in cases where the meaning was obviously deviant from the speaker's intentions could one be fairly sure of detection."

In the course of listening to speech we are concerned with the message. Once our attention is directed to other aspects of the speech signal, such as errors, we begin to be aware of them. This situation is parallel to that of a phonetician when he is speaking and listening to speech without his 'phonetician's hat' on. He is often consciously unaware of phonetic differences unless he is 'tuned in' to them.

The 'contagion' may therefore only be a greater awareness of errors which continually occur. If we are concerned with certain kinds of errors we will fail to notice others. Freud was obviously not interested in purely phonetic or phonological errors and failed to notice them.

Freud and Hill are however both correct in their suggestion that many errors do produce unintended but real words. This question will be discussed below. What must be emphasized here however is that there is a hierarchy of errors, just as there is a hierarchy of stages in the speech process, as pointed out by Lashley. Errors, primarily phonological in nature, must occur at a different stage than other slips, and one cannot explain their occurrence without recognizing the reality of the phonemic/phonetic sized segmental unit.

Yet the complexities of language and language behavior require more than a single phonological unit. In my paper in this volume I suggest that there are other errors which can only be accounted for if the segment is viewed as a composite of semi-independent features. Nooteboom notes that "in significantly more cases than is to be expected in a random distribution the two elements involved in a substitution error are phonetically similar to one another" which provides some support to the independence of features. MacKay suggests that "other explanations are possible ... (e.g.) a partial fusion of phonemes in natural speech". Hockett states, "Blending can yield a pronunciation with a phoneme (a simultaneous bundle of components) not present in either of the contributing forms: *bubbles* and *tough* yielding /bəvɨlz/. Here the voicing of the /v/ is from the medial /b/ of *bubbles*, while its degree of aperture is from the final /f/ of *tough*."

Whether one calls such errors 'blending' or 'fusion', what is apparent is that specific and distinct properties or features of phonemes are involved in certain errors as independent elements. Celce-Murcia provides a number of examples from Meringer's corpus which can best (or only) be explained in terms of features rather than whole segments. She states: "Feature switches such as those exemplified by *0, Du Saukramer* for *0, Du Grausamer*, in which a voiced /g/ is uttered as a voiceless /k/ bothered Meringer. He had no way of explaining the change of voicing and he tried to develop ad hoc arguments to account for such errors."

One can of course provide ad hoc explanations for all errors including those given in (3). (See also Appendix, Section L.)

(3) (a) Dick Carter is a musician → Nick Carter is a musician (nasality anticipation)
   (b) the party will go on all night → the marty will go on all tight (nasality reversal)
   (c) sit all day → zit all day (voicing anticipation)
   (d) big and fat → pig and vat (voicing reversal)
   (e) a nasal infix → a navel infix (labiality anticipation)
   (f) flipping his lid → flipping his lib (Labiality perseverance)
   (g) Zwicky is getting skinny → Zwicky is getting skwinny (rounding perseverance or /w/ perseverance)

Such errors are less rare than has been suggested. And when they are combined with the great percentage of errors, classified as segmental unit errors, in which only one feature is involved it seems strange to question the validity of independent features in speech production. This is particularly true when we know that features do play a role in phonological rules and in historical change where classes of sounds defined by a single feature are involved.

It would be more surprising if such features did not 'show up' in slips of the tongue. But MacKay is correct in asserting:

> ... the possibility of phoneme reversals is not eliminated even if feature reversal were demonstrable. The relevance of distinctive features no more disproves the Phonetic Unit Hypothesis for speech production than the relevance of distinctive features to speech perception disproves the importance of phonemes in speech perception.

What speech errors show is that both segments and features are real elements in performance.

Besides the evidence for features and segments as necessary phonological elements, a number of investigators suggest the need for a larger syllabic unit. MacKay's statistical analysis provides evidence for what he calls the "Syllabic Similarity Hypothesis" which states that "The syllabic position of reversed phonemes was almost invariably identical, indicating that syllables must be a unit in speech production." These findings are corroborated by Boomer and Laver, Cohen, Nooteboom, and Fromkin.

Up until recently, however, linguists working within the framework of generative phonology have answered in the negative the question posed by Anderson (1969): "Are there ... phonological rules which can be stated more appropriately in terms of the syllable than in terms simply of segments?" Hoard (1971), Hooper (1972) and Vennemann (1972) have however shown that not only will the use of a syllabic unit (or boundary) permit "a more appropriate" statement of phonological rules, but more importantly that significant generalizations can be made in certain cases only if the syllabic unit in phonology is recognized.

This is not surprising for those of us who have recognized the need for a syllable unit in a performance model. Performance factors again and again are shown to influence or constrain phonological (and syntactic) systems. In fact, since the syllable unit is an important one in the speech process, it is understandable that there are languages which utilize this unit in their grammars.

Assuming then that syllable units are psychologically real, the structure of the syllabic unit is of interest. The findings noted above suggest that at some stage in the production process the segments which make up a syllabic unit must have a sequential order imposed. The phonological evidence shows that at least in some languages (and probably all) morphemes are stored with syllabic boundaries represented. The suggestion that there is an imposed order on the concatenated string of segments or feature bundles is directly contrary to a model proposed by Wickelgren (1969a, b). (See MacKay article for arguments against Wickelgren's model.) Wickelgren suggests that the arguments raised by Lashley and others against a chain association theory for explaining the serial order of behavior, and speech in particular, are arguments only against a context-free association theory. That is, if the representation of a word such as *struck* is in terms of phonemes, e.g. /strʌk/, then order must be imposed. But he says that a "context-sensitive chain association" model in which an utterance is "represented" by an unordered set of "context-sensitive allophones" requires no ordering. He illustrates his model by stating that "the spelling of the immediate constituents of the word *struck*"would be as in (4).

$$_\#S_t, \; _st_r, \; _t\Lambda_r, \; _r\Lambda_k, \; _\Lambda k_\# \tag{4}$$

The unordered 'spelling' of the phrase or noun compound *deep structure* would then be presumably as in (5), if we add the syllable boundary symbol (using $ as suggested by Vennemann 1972).

$$_\$\underline{d}_i, \; _d\underline{i}_p, \; _iP_\$, \; _p\underline{\$}_s, \; _\$S_t, \; _s\underline{t}_r, \; _t\underline{r}_\Lambda, \; _r\Lambda_k, \; _\Lambda k_\$, \; _k\$_{\check c}, \; _\$\check c_\vartheta, \; _{\check c}\vartheta_r, \; _\vartheta r_\$ \tag{5}$$

Instead of uttering the above, however, the speaker produced the utterance *steep dructure* which would be represented in Wickelgren's schema as (6).

$$_\$S_t, \; _s\underline{t}_i, \; _t\underline{i}_p, \; _iP_\$, \; _p\underline{\$}_d, \; _\$\underline{d}_r, \; _d\underline{r}_\Lambda, \; _r\Lambda_k, \; _\Lambda k_\$, \; _k\$_{\check c}, \; _\$\check c_\vartheta, \; _{\check c}\vartheta_r, \; _\vartheta r_\$ \tag{6}$$

Notice that none of the underlined 'context-sensitive allophones' in (5) occur in the actual utterance (6) and the underlined 'context-sensitive allophones' in (6) are 'unrepresented' in the intended utterance. Using the syllable boundaries the model may explain how the syllable initial '$_\$ S_t$' was disordered, but given this associative chain model one would have no explanation for why '$_s t_r$' did not follow, nor where the 'unrepresented' allophones came from.

If, on the other hand, *deep structure* is represented by phonemic segments, the error is shown to be one of disordering of units as shown in (7).

$$/\underline{d}\,i\,p\,\#\,\underline{s\,t\,r}\,\Lambda\,k\,\$\,\check c\,\vartheta\,r/ \rightarrow /\underline{s\,t}\,i\,p\,\#\,\underline{d\,r}\,\Lambda\,k\,\$\,\check c\,\vartheta\,r/ \tag{7}$$

This of course requires that the units which represent morphemes be ordered which is a more complex requirement than Wickelgren's. But language behavior, and other human and animal behavior is complex; the model should reveal the real complexities. The order complexity is somewhat countered by the fact that the inventory of sounds which are concatenated in the language is simplified, i.e. phonemes rather than context sensitive allophones are required. All allophonic variants can be explained by recognizing the 'reality' of physiological coarticulation phenomena (e.g. nasalization of vowels before nasal consonants occurring because the velum moves slower than do other articulators [Ohala 1971]) and of phonological rules which constrain articulation and the realization of abstract phonemes.

The feature matrices posited by linguists to represent formatives, where the columns of such matrices representing segments composed of features are serially ordered, seem to be as necessary for a performance model as for a competence grammar.

Both MacKay and Hockett however suggest that there is more structure imposed on syllables than simply the ordering of consonantal onsets, vocalic nuclei, and consonantal codas. MacKay's statistical analysis of the spoonerisms found in Meringer's corpus leads him to support Hockett's proposed phonetic IC structure of English (syllables) which it is proposed consist "of two immediate constituents: the consonantism (even if zero) at its beginning, and all that follows". This IC structure is supported by MacKay because he found that final consonants are rarely reversed and initial consonants frequently reversed. He also found that "vowel reversals occurred about as infrequently as final consonant reversals" which MacKay explains by the fact that "final consonants form a subgroup with the vowels". In addition, he found that "exchanges of consonant clusters were quite frequent, as were exchanges of single consonants and consonant clusters. However, reversals rarely broke up consonant clusters".

My own data agree with these findings up to a point. Reversals, anticipations and perseverations involve initial consonants more often than final segments. Cohen, however, found that 32 % of phonological errors involved vowels, and Nooteboom's figures show that 31 % of the phonemic errors were vowel errors. They do not present a breakdown of initial as opposed to final consonants. Their figures are not restricted to spoonerisms which may account for the different frequencies, and their corpus consisted of errors in Dutch rather than German.

Whatever the frequency, final consonants are involved in errors and consonant clusters are split (see Fromkin, and Appendix, Sections D, G). Neither Hockett nor MacKay would deny that clusters are concatenations of segments whatever their cohesiveness.

While it is important to account for the statistical frequencies, and use these frequencies in a speech production model, the 'noise' in any collection of speech errors may skew the quantitative picture. No 'collector' ever writes down all errors he hears. I doubt whether even Meringer did. This is not to deny the possibility of the $C_0 + VC_0$ syllabic structure. It is, however, likely that at the stage when phonological units are mapped on to motor or acoustic targets, i.e. at the 'motor control' stage, the syllable is a more cohesive unit, possibly THE articulatory unit.

As of now, such a syllabic structure does not appear to be needed in the construction of individual grammars. That is, while syllabic boundaries have been demonstrated to play a role in phonological rules, no one has as yet found the need to utilize such an internal syllable boundary. This does not, however, argue against such a boundary in a model of performance.

While the evidence for three kinds of phonological elements – syllable, segment, feature – seems clear, the question of the nature of these elements as specifications of morphemes is of interest, particularly in relation to a continuing debate among linguists concerning the degree of abstraction in a grammar. Both formal and substantive arguments have been advanced for and against representing lexical formatives by totally abstract segments, i.e. those which never surface phonetically. (See, for example, Kiparsky 1968, Kisseberth 1969, Hyman 1970a, b, Anderson 1969, and Crothers 1971.) This is also somewhat related to the question of whether the phonological representation of morphemes can include non-fully specified segments, e.g. archiphonemes, and the representation of grammatical morphemes. All sides agree that 'this is an empirical issue'.

Speech error data provide some support for the reality of highly abstract phonolo-ical segments. This is discussed in my paper in this collection, but will be further re-viewed here because of the importance of the question. The examples under (8) are fairly straightforward. They all illustrate the split of nasal-stop clusters.

(8) (a) The bank [bæŋk] will pay [pej] 5.6 % interest → the ban [bæn] will [pejk] 5.6 % interest.

([ŋk] → [n], ∅ → [k])

(b) The rank [ræŋk] order of the subjects → the rand [rænd] orker of the sub-jects

([ŋk] ... [rd] → [nd] ... [rk])

(c) The red tide will stink [stɪŋk] up the sea → the red tide will stin [stɪn] up the [sijk]

Example (8a) shows that when the final *k* is deleted (or moved) the nasal which re-mains is an alveolar [n] rather than the expected velar [ŋ]. This suggests that under-lying the [ŋk] in *bank* is /nk/. It also attests to the reality of the homorganic nasal rule in English phonology which must operate in the production process after (or in parallel with) the misordering of units.

The second example supports this hypothesis in a more ambiguous way, since if all examples were like (8b) one could conclude that the homorganic rule was opera-tive but that *rank* was stored as /ræŋk/; the reversal of the /k/ and /d/ would change the velar nasal to an alveolar. But (8c) further attests to the underlying /n/ in phonetic [ŋk] sequences.

The examples under (9) also involve velar nasals, but ones in which the intended utterances do not include phonetic clusters.

(9) (a) swing and sway [swɪ̆ŋ] and [swej] → [swɪ̆n] and [swejg]
    (b) sing for the man [sɪ̆ŋ ... mæn] → [sɪg ... mæ̃ŋ]
    (c) Springtime for Hitler → sprig time for hintler
        [sprɪ̆ŋ] [hɪtlər] → [sprig] [hɪ̆ntlər]

(For further examples see Appendix, Section I).

Errors that produce a phonetic [g] which does not occur in the intended phonetic utterances support the proposal made by Sapir [1925], Chomsky and Halle (1968) and others, for deriving the phonetic [ŋ] from an underlying sequence of /ng/ in English.

Some of the examples above may be alternatively explained by suggesting that these errors involve feature anticipations and reversals. (9b), for example, may result from a denasalization of the [ŋ] in *sing* following the nonnasal [s], and the perseverance of the velarity feature i.e. [ŋ] → [g]; [n] → [ŋ].

The examples (9a) and (9c) however are not so 'easily' explained. To suggest that what occurs in the process of producing '[swɪ̃n] and [swejg]' is that the velar nasal becomes alveolar in *swing* and in addition a non-nasal velar stop is added to *sway* may describe the result but does not explain the mechanism by which it occurs. (9c) is equally complex without positing an underlying /ng/. If on the other hand we assume that prior to the articulatory stage the phonological representation of *swing* is /swɪŋg/, and the phonological representation of *spring* is /sprɪŋg/, then the errors are similar to others in which a cluster is broken up, or a single segment is disordered. This is illustrated in (10).

(10) (a) /swɪŋg/ and /swej/ → /swɪnØ/ and /swejg/
      (b) /sprɪŋg/time for /hɪtlər/ → /sprɪØg/ .... /hɪntlər/

The errors cited under (9) are more plausibly explained by assuming the existence of the /ng/. Such errors also provide 'behavioral' support for the English rule (11).

(11) g → Ø/N -- #

Since the [g] emerges if the nasal is deleted or transposed during speech production, the /g/ must be present at some stage in the production process. Should this hypothesis be accepted it shows that the homorganic nasal constraint must occur after or in parallel with the error in serial ordering since the nasal in *swing* is alveolar rather than velar. The fact that the nasalization of the vowels depends on whether or not the nasal is present (i.e. [sĩŋ] → [sɪg]) also shows that vowel nasalization occurs 'by rule' and that no nasal vowels occur in lexical representation, redundantly or otherwise.

These errors reveal, in addition, the extent to which abstract generalizations are constructed in acquiring a language. While *swing* is never heard as *[swɪŋg] (nor even as *swinger* *[swɪŋgər]) in most dialects of English by 'analogy' with *long* [lɔ̃ŋ] and *longer* [lɔ̃ŋgər] and by recognizing the distributional constraints of both [ŋ] and all nasal clusters, general rules are devised which account for all the data. Some might suggest that these rules (and the underlying forms) are only posited after the speaker has learned to spell. Even if this is the case, the result of the spelling system, together with the phonological facts of the language, can combine to permit the storage of abstract segments never heard phonetically.

While it appears, therefore, that grammars should permit abstract segments which are never realized phonetically, this provides for a very strong grammatical device, probably too strong a one. There must be some constraints on grammars, i.e. some way of arriving at just those grammars which do model the internalized grammars of the speakers. It is possible that there are a set of such grammars rather than one unique grammar. Non-formal empirical evidence should be sought whenever abstract (absolutely neutralized) units are posited. I am not suggesting that only those segments which 'surface' in speech errors are 'real'. The fact that one would hardly expect the posited /x/ in the lexical representation of *right* i.e. /rixt/ (Chomsky and Halle 1968) to show itself, even in a phonetically possible form, is not the only reason such representations can be questioned. Other evidence, experimental and observational and formal, is pertinent.

The anthropologist Sherzer (1970) provides a different kind of evidence for abstract underlying representation from a language game played by the Cuna Indians. The game is similar to Pig Latin, and consists of moving the first syllable of a word to the end of the word. He notes that "speakers sometimes gave differing outputs (suggesting) that there are alternative models or grammars actually in use for the same dialect of Cuna". This game supports the 'reality' of highly abstract underlying representations in children's and adult's grammars.

I will cite just one of the many examples Sherzer provides. In Cuna, stress regularly falls on the penultimate syllable. There are some words however which seem to violate this rule, as is shown in the word [bíriga] 'year'. If one posits a vowel epenthesis rule, which breaks up /rg/ clusters, and in addition, an ordering of the rules such that the stress is assigned prior to the epenthesis rule, then stress is absolutely predictable as is shown in the following derivation:

(12) underlying representation /birga/
    stress rule bírga
    vowel epenthesis rule bíriga

A phonological theory which disallows rule ordering[4] and abstract representation would have to represent this non-alternating form as /biriga/ and complicate the stress rule so that it would assign penultimate stress except where the second syllable is /ri/ followed by a /g/ initial final syllable. The proponents of such a solution would argue that the complexities are real and therefore should be included in the grammar.

All speakers of Cuna, however, produce, in the language game, [gabir] not *[rigabi]. This strongly supports the reality of the abstract representation and, in addition, the rule ordering proposal.

M. Ohala (1972) conducted a number of experiments with native speakers of Hindi which also support the contention that one's grammar is not determined solely by surface phonetic forms or alternations.

Turning to 'the laboratory' thus may decide between alternative linguistic hypotheses.

Speech errors also permit unambiguous solutions to other kinds of representation problems. There was a time when certain linguists believed (and some probably do today) that in clusters of two obstruents in English it was arbitrary as to whether the second stop consonant is represented as voiceless or voiced since the voicing distinction is neutralized in this context. Some proposed that after an /s/ there exists an archiphoneme. Pattern symmetry and morpheme structure constraints have been used by others to propose that after a syllable initial /s/ only the voiceless obstruents may occur. Speech errors provide evidence against the 'archiphoneme' solution and in favor of the morpheme structure condition (Stanley 1967) which restricts such clusters to voice-

---

[4] In this example if both the stress and vowel epenthesis are applied simultaneously one might possibly do away with ordering. But the literature is filled with other cases where simultaneous rule application of all rules will not work.

less segments. If an archiphoneme occurs in this context one would expect with equal probability that when such clusters were split the voiced segments would occur. The examples given under (13) show that this is not the case. (See also Appendix, Section G.) No slips reported in the literature or in my corpus reveal the voiced obstruants.

(13) (a) long and strong → trong and slong (not *drong)
　　　(b) steak and potatoes → [spejk] and tomatoes, (not *domatoes)
　　　(c) stick in the mud → smuck in the tid (not *did)
　　　(d) speech production → peach seduction (not *beach)

It is of course true that in (b) for example the reversals of the intended [t] and [pʰ] produced [p] and [tʰ]. This illustrates what Wells calls "The First Law" which states: "A slip of the tongue is practically always a phonetically possible noise." From his examples it is clear that he means 'phonologically possible' in the particular language. The de-aspiration of the voiceless stop cluster reveals the phonological rules which constrain the output even after a misordering occurs, in keeping with the system of the language.

Not only do errors provide support for particular P-rules or sequential constraints; they may also show the direction of historical change and may in fact show that certain earlier constraints no longer hold. The following examples either contradict Wells's 'law' or a proposed morpheme structure condition for English.

(14) (a) short lady → short shlady [šlejdij]
　　　(b) shut his mouth → shmut his mouth
　　　(c) pot shot → shpot shot.

(For further examples, see Appendix, Section N.)

Most linguists have generally agreed that "the first segment of an initial consonant cluster (in English) must be [s] if the second segment is a true consonant" (Chomsky and Halle 1968: 171). In addition, except for [šr] as in *shrew*, [š] is not supposed to be permitted in other initial clusters, i.e. *[šm] *[šl]. The errors cited above point to the possibility that these restrictions no longer occur in the Grammar of English. The introduction of Yiddish words into the English vocabulary, e.g. *shmuck*, *shtick* (and the German *Schlitz*) may have led to a simplification of the above rule thereby permitting [š] in all clusters where formerly [s] was the only segment allowed. Al Capp's invention of the Shmoo would support this grammatical change, since it isn't often the case, if ever, that new words are constructed either by cartoonists or Madison Avenue that violate phonological constraints of the language. After noting the above errors I conducted an informal test in an introductory linguistics class composed of approximately 80 freshmen and sophomores who had never had any linguistics prior to the class and who had not yet been exposed to these phonological constraints in the class. A number of non-English words were read to them; they were told that some were English words which they had probably never heard and some were foreign words and they were asked to mark 'English' or 'foreign' on the marking sheet. Both *shpot* and *shling* were on the list. More than 50% of the students considered these 'words' as English. This was a very uncontrolled test; I have no idea about the religious, geographic or cultural background of these students. One might predict that the students who considered these as English words could make errors such as those above and students who had not yet changed their grammars would, by 'editing' or 'monitoring' in the process of speaking, not produce such errors.

The point is that no investigators of speech errors have reported the occurrence of initial [ŋ] (except for Hockett's child and he gives no age for when this occurred) or sequences such as initial [ps][rd] in initial position. The fact that [š] should occur in initial clusters in errors is possible evidence that the constraint is an incorrect one for many speakers of English.

All the papers in this volume attest to Wells's 'law' to some extent. Hockett, however, suggests that

Phonological constraints are for the most part not absolute ... blending can yield a pronunciation with constituent sounds that stand outside the 'normal' phonological system of the language, as, by way of an invented example, *sugar sack* yielding [čugir+sæx] with the degree of aperture of the initial and final consonants interchanged. Observing instances of this sort is difficult: the hearer, we suppose, usually interprets the result as though it did not deviate, or else the speaker has gotten his speech organs so entangled that he backs up and starts over again.

The last point suggests that it is the physiological habits acquired by the speaker which prevents the 'breaking' of phonological rules. This further suggests that there is a hierarchy of constraints, some of which can be 'broken' and others which cannot. It might be the case that at any one historical stage in a language only those 'breakable' constraints are candidates for historical changes.

Ladefoged (personal communication) has heard utterances which demonstrate that low level rules do not have to be applied in a certain class of errors, namely, blends. (15) is an example of those he has noted.

(15) in twenty minutes I'm going to be released [rəlist]/
relieved [rəli:vd] → ... to be [rəli:st]

The long *i* [i:] was phonetically similar to this vowel quality found only before voiced segments. The rarity of such examples is probably due to the fact that "the hearer ... usually interprets the result as though it did not deviate" even including phoneticians when they are engaged in conversation. That Ladefoged did note such errors may show the integrity of his non-split personality. He suggests that such examples probably only occur in blends. It would be of interest to find out whether the duration of vowels before voiced segments in errors where in the intended utterance the segment was voiceless is shorter than the duration of vowels before voiced segments in a morpheme without the occurrence of an error. Chen (1970) and others found that in some languages the increased duration of vowels before voiced segments exceeds what can be explained by physiological causes. MacNeilage (1972) suggests, "Findings of this kind make it necessary to postulate that an inherent mechanical constraint on speech production has in some sense 'triggered' differences in vowel duration in some languages which exceed the immediate effect of the constraint itself, and can in some cases achieve perceptual significance." In English, at "the sensory-motor level of the cortex, which is where phonetic units are encoded for the production of speech" duration must be in someway specified. Despite the fact that vowel duration is a 're-dundant' feature in English, one must posit that such length contrasts are 'prepro-grammed'. This preprogramming may be due to the redundant length feature specified in the lexicon (as the Ladefoged example seems to suggest) or to the operation of P-rules. But since P-rules would apply across morpheme boundaries it would be dif-ficult to explain why such errors seem to occur only in blends and not when disordering of segments takes place. The lack of data prevents any solution at this time. It would not be surprising, however, given the occurrence of errors which break this 'low level' rule, and assuming that this would occur only in languages where the vowel duration is not solely due to physiological constraints, if in the process of language change such languages would begin to use vowel length 'phonemically' with a neutralization of the voiced/ voiceless contrast of obstruents in final position arising. We would ex-pect to find this rarer in languages where the duration difference does not exceed the 27 ms reflecting the greater rate of lower lip movement in voiceless stops, where such a difference does not provide enough of a perceptual contrast.

There are of course rules which are not phonetic or strictly phonological in charac-ter which also apply in the speech production process. These are often referred to as 'morphophonemic rules'. Hill presents some evidence from rhymes in particular, for "the internal reality of sounds, rather than of morphophonemes". Yet our knowledge of the phonetic representation of words does not negate the possibility that we also know the morphophonemic structure of formatives and the morphophonemic rules which produce the 'correct' phonemic output. The errors involving the velar nasal discussed above give some indication that our knowledge is far more abstract than phonetic or even phonemic knowledge. Rhymes may very well depend in some cases on the phonetics. Errors do attest to the application of morphophonemic rules. This is not to say that Hill is wrong in suggesting that grammatical morphemes are stored in some phonological shape. It is the nature of this representation which is of interest. He discusses this question in relation to the error which changed the order of *bubble* and *pricked* in *his bubble would be pricked* to produce *his prick would be bubbled*. The /−d/, /−t/ and /−əd/ participial ending is realized as /−t/ in the intended *pricked* and as /−d/ in the produced *bubbled*. Hill states that this 'sound' is "capable of being mod-ified as needed to accomodate itself to the new form to which it was to be attached". This modification is not strictly phonological, however, as is illustrated by the following examples.

(16) (a) the tie dropped [drap+t] out of the bag →
     the drop tied [tay+d] out of the bag
  (b) bloody students [stuwdɨnt +s] → bloodent studies [stuwdij +z]
  (c) cow tracks [træk+s] → track cows [kæw+z]

(For further examples see Appendix, Section S.)

In all three examples the intended voiceless forms of the grammatical morphemes become voiced in the errors. But the voiceless forms are phonologically possible, e.g. *tight* [tajt], *fleece* [flijs], *house* [hæws]. However the grammatical morphemes are stored, the fact that they are grammatical suffixes must be represented in the intended utterance, or as part of Hill's "internal message" prior to the disordering, and the 'adjustment' which occurs must specify the phonological shape prior to any phonological or phonetic 'adjustments' or rules. As to what the correct dictionary representation of these morphemes is cannot be answered by these data alone. But such errors may provide clues as to how such morphemes are represented in storage.

The *a/an* variation of the indefinite article in English is another example of a 'higher-order' constraint which is not strictly phonological as shown in my article and as exemplified briefly in (17). (For further examples, see Appendix, Section T.)

(17) (a) a system → an istem
  (b) an interesting fact about clinical work → a clinical fact about interesting work

Since a schwa followed by a vowel is an allowable phonological string (e.g. *Rosa is*) and a word final consonant followed by a word initial consonant is also permitted (e.g. *Roman court*) the changes from *a* to *an* and from *an* to *a* in the above errors depend solely on the grammatical features of the morpheme and on the application of a morphophonemic rule. The rule must apply after the errors in ordering have occurred or in parallel.

These errors also show that it is sometimes the case that one error in the production process may be 'overlooked' by the 'scanning' or 'monitoring' mechanism at a particular level. (See Laver's paper in this volume for fuller discussion on the monitoring mechanism.) Such errors are usually not compounded. (18) illustrates the failure to apply the *a/an* morphophonemic rule.

(18) (a) an anniversary celebration → a anniversary celebration
  (b) an occurrence → a occurrence

These errors were produced by speakers who usually apply the rule in question. The examples support the proposal that the 'phonological shape' of the indefinite article is /a/ rather than /æn/. It is possible of course that the lack of examples of *an* followed by a consonant initial noun merely represents a gap in the corpus. Until such errors are noted, however, these errors provide evidence for the correctness of Vennemann's

(1971) arguments that in the synchronic grammar /æn/ (which historically derives from *one*) has been reanalyzed as /a/.

Celce-Murcia presents other examples involving German Umlaut and Ablaut rules, where morphophonemic rules were misapplied or failed to apply.

A number of sentences which are grammatically deviant can be explained by this kind of rule-application breakdown, as shown in (19).

(19) (a) when a person grows old → when a person grow old
    (b) Theo comes up with → Theo come up with
    (c) the last I knew about it → the last I knowed about it
    (d) he had to have it → he haved to have it
    (e) if he swam in the pool nude → if he swimmed ...
    (f) how jealous he is → how jealous he am

(19) f) may be the result of a 'Freudian slip' contaminated by *How jealous I am.* The other examples are more appropriately accounted for by errors in rule application. (a) and (b) show the failure to apply the 'third person singular present tense' agreement rule. (They may, of course, simply be the result of segment deletion.) (c), (d), and (e) are more interesting in that the errors produced non-occurring past tense forms. That is, the regular past tense formation rule was wrongly applied to irregular verbs. These three utterances were not spoken by a child who had not yet learned that *know, have,* and *swim* are idiosyncratic. Such errors are very common for children to make but then they are not really errors at all when viewed in terms of the child's grammar.

If (d) is explained simply by word anticipation, i.e. the anticipation of the phonological form *have,* (c) and (e) cannot be accounted for in this way.

Fry provides other examples of errors in which "the wrong morpheme or word inserted into the string is not obviously linked with another item which is about to occur or has occurred in the same or a neighboring sequence". He suggests, "This probably means only that it is difficult to see the connection or that the link is with some alternative programme which is not implemented in actual speech. Whatever the basis for the error, the result is the selection of the wrong item from the store." To illustrate this he says that (20) was probably confounded with *She became, didn't she.* He provides no context or explanation for (21).

(20) Didn't she become → didn't she became

(21) I forget who suggested → I forget whom suggested

It is clear that (19c) and (19e) cannot be due to "the selection of the wrong item from the store" since *knowed* and *swimmed* are not "in the store". Fry himself provides a better explanation when he states that such examples "indicate that word and morpheme encoding have some degree of independence from each other, for no English speaker will find ready-made in his word store the forms 'thoughting' 'introduct' or 'complexibility' ". The last three 'words' occur in other examples he provides.

There are numerous examples that indicate that roots and derivational and grammatical morphemes "have some degree of independence". (See Appendix, Sections R and S.) That being the case, the errors under (19) and those cited by Fry can be better explained as errors in rule application.

In the case of *knowed* a plausible explanation for what occurred is that *know + past* was operated on by the regular past-tense rule. This may have occurred if, when *know* was selected and put in the storage buffer (prior to the articulatory stage) the feature marking it as belonging to a special class of verbs was 'erased', thus making it subject to the regular rule. It may also have occurred because the wrong rule was accidentally selected.

The fact that lexical formatives are often 'moved' or 'reversed' without their suffixal (derivational or grammatical) endings, and that prefixes and suffixes may be involved in errors independently is well attested. Nooteboom illustrates such errors and concludes: "These errors constitute an interesting class in that they show the various ways of word derivation as psychological processes separate from the actual forms to which they are applied."

Such examples illustrate that speech errors involve more than the disordering of units of all sizes and types, although disordering does seem to account for a large percentage of observed slips. (22) cannot be explained by disordering.

(22) you're in a better position → you're in a more better position.

The comparative can be phonologically represented either as *more* as in *more beautiful* (**beautifuller*) or as *-er* as in *taller* (*?more tall, *He's more tall than Mary*). *Good* is, of course, an exception, and requires an idiosyncratic comparative form. To account for (22) it is plausible to suggest that in addition to the correct selection of the idiosyncratic *better*, the COMPARATIVE node in the string was not erased and the 'Comparative → more' rule was wrongly applied.

Fry's examples in which "an error in lexical encoding fails to disturb the proper arrangement of bound morphemes" further attest to the sequencing of morphophonemic rule operation after disordering of morphemes, or, in parallel process. They further provide evidence that formatives are stored in a basic form and that their derived phonological shape is determined by the syntactic structure of the intended utterance. It would be nice if such errors could help decide between the lexicalist/transformationalist controversy. They can't however, since no one suggests that transformations are actually applied in the production of an utterance, and, in addition, the lexicalist position would not deny the existence of separately stored roots and affixes as part of a derivational component of the lexicon. However, when one finds words such as *motionly* and *perceptic* occurring in speech errors, it should not be surprising to find *John's easiness to please*. Yet such 'syntactic errors' have not been noted, despite the wide variety that occur.

Fry further states, "Lexical encoding is a matter of word selection and is wholly dependent on the semantic programme, morpheme encoding is only partly dependent on the lexical programme and is in part dictated by the selection of sentence form and syntactic rules.''

I think there is evidence to suggest that both the lexical encoding and the morpheme encoding is dependent on "the selection of sentence form and syntactic rules". Unless the syntactic structure is already constructed, word selection would not be constrained to proper word classes. That is, there are different ways of expressing the same message as may be illustrated in (23):

(23) (a) Last night I dreamed that the war went on forever
     (b) Last night I had a nightmare that the war went on forever.

The *dream* that was *dreamt* may well have been a *nightmare*. The selection must depend to some extent on the syntactic structure.

(24) *Last night I nightmared that the war went on forever.

If we heard (24) we would say a speech error had occurred in which the noun *nightmare* was incorrectly selected as a verb, or that two phrases were blended.

In Fry's model there is no provision made for the storing of such syntactic structures or the operation of such rules. It is not improbable to suggest that Fry would be willing to include these units and stages in his model in keeping with his purpose "to show that errors of different kinds are made in the generation of speech and they are all of such a nature as to indicate that speakers are operating with a linguistic system essentially similar to that arrived at by linguistic analysis".

Nooteboom argues, "The very fact that a mistakenly selected word always or nearly always belongs to the same word class as the intended word indicates that the grammatical structure of the phrase under construction imposes imperative restrictions on the selection of words." As in example (23) above it would be difficult to explain the actual generation of speech without positing that the selection of the syntactic structures occurs prior to the lexical insertion or selection. This also implies, of course, that formatives are 'listed' or 'stored' with syntactic as well as semantic features as part of their representation.

Nooteboom also notes, "The errors involving whole words as units show the peculiar feature that the two words involved in all cases belong to the same word class." In my collection the great majority of word reversals and substitutions do involve the same syntactic class. (See Appendix, Sections P and V.) A large percentage of the errors involving more than one 'word class' are errors in which the formatives may function in either class as is shown in (25).

(25) (a) my throat is sore → my sore is throat
     (b) there are a lot of people I'd pass up but not students with packs on their
         backs → ... people I'd pack up but not students ...
     (c) cashed a check → checked a cash
     (d) a plus nasal segment → a plus segment nasal.

There are also cases where, when different syntactic classes are involved, the syntactic rules cause a change to correct a syntactically deviant utterance as in (26).

(26) (a) I'm in terrible trouble about the terminology →
           I'm in terrible terminological trouble –– trouble about ...
      (b) I think it's reasonable to measure with care →
           I think it's careful to measure with reason
      (c) chicken livers → living chickens
      (d) the gardener has to pull up the dead flowers →
           the gardener has to die (dye?) the pulled up flowers

The data showing the 'monitoring' of utterances at different stages in the process which prevent compounding of errors show syntactic rules at work, just as the errors which reveal a breakdown in the monitoring mechanism do. The errors under (27) show the breakdown in the corrective mechanisms, where disordering violates syntactic rules.

(27) (a) a card that I just sent him → . . . that I just sent him to
      (b) how much do you want for this → . . . do you want this for
      (c) people tend to make up words → . . . tend up to make words
      (d) how old are you? → how old you are?

The fact that there are errors which show that syntactic structure is not maintained does not argue against the syntactic constraints imposed at other stages.

Another argument for suggesting that syntactic structures are part of the string in the buffer storage is provided by errors involving units larger than morphemes or words. When more than one word is involved in a tongue slip they seem to belong to the same syntactic phrase, as illustrated in (28).

(28) (a) I'd like to speak to you about this matter → . . . to speak to this matter about
           you
      (b) a difference in the syntactic behavior of gerunds →
           a difference in the gerunds of syntactic behavior
      (c) If you'll stick around you'll meet him → if you'll meet him you'll stick around
      (d) when you apply the P-rule to the underlying string → when you apply the
           underlying string to the P-rule

Despite all the disordering that occurs there are no errors that anyone has recorded which totally disrupts the syntactic structures of the utterances. *Furiously sleep ideas green colorless* and *A the Seymour with sliced salami knife* are not possible errors. This may be explained by the constant 'monitoring' which goes on preventing, as stated above, for the most part more than one or two errors in order or rule application.

There are some very 'strange' utterances which may be explained if it is the case that morphemes are stored with syntactic features as well as phonological features in the matrices. (Semantic features will be discussed below.) The independence and existence of grammatical nodes in the strings to be produced must also be recognized as is illustrated by (29).

(29) Rosa always dated shrinks → Rosa always date shranks

(30) gives the intended surface structure of (29).

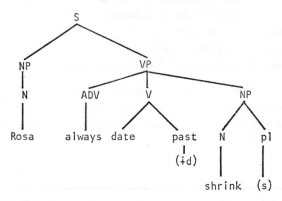

First of all, it is clear that the 'past tense node' had to be moved (disordered) prior to the 'spelling' out of the morpheme. In the lexical selection process, *date*, which is marked both [+Verb] and [+Noun] is selected as the verb, and *shrink* which is similarly marked is selected as the noun. It is possible that in the selection process *shrink* is entered into the string with both its syntactic features. The past tense node is disordered and attached to *shrink* ('primed' because of its [+V] feature). As a verb, *shrink* is also marked as an exception to the regular past-tense rule and thus is operated on to become *shrank*; in addition since *shrink* is also [+N] the rule which provides the phonological shape of the plural also operates thereby producing *shranks*.

MacKay (1972) would possibly explain this error by suggesting that the features were incompletely specified, rather than overspecified, thus permitting the disordering of grammatical nodes and the application of the past tense rule to the incompletely specified *shrink*.

While this explanation may seem far-fetched, the utterance itself is far-fetched and requires a complex mechanism to explain it.

The independence of such syntactic nodes is also shown by many syntactic errors involving the Negative, as is illustrated under (31). (See also, Appendix, Section Z.)

(31) (a) I regard this as *imp*recise → I *dis*regard this as precise[5]
     (b) It's *not* possible that he's going → it's possible that he's *not* going – it's *not* possible that he's *not* going – I mean, it's *imp*ossible that he's going
     (c) people agree that it is *not* well formed → people *don't* agree that it's well formed

[5]   This error was noted by Roland Hausser. I would like to thank him, in addition, for his stimulating insights regarding errors of this type.

The examples under (31) demonstrate that in producing a negative sentence a speaker must first generate an abstract NEGATION element which is independent of any particular word in the string. In non-deviant sentences this element is placed in a specified place. But just as segments or features may be disordered, so may such syntactic elements.

The intended surface structure and the surface structure of the actual utterance containing the error of (31a) are given in (32).

(32) (a) Surface Structure of Intended Utterance

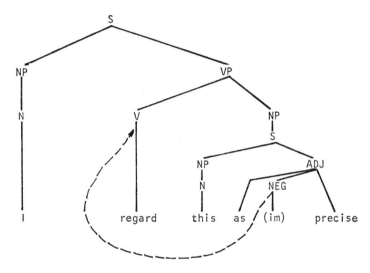

(32) (b) Surface Structure of Spoken Utterance

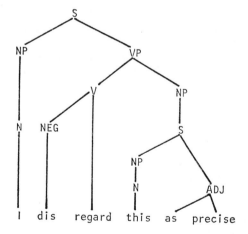

In the intended utterance, the negation occurs in the embedded sentence, while in the deviant spoken utterance the negation occurs in the higher sentence. One cannot explain this error by a performance model which posits a Markovian process of word selection. Such errors provide further evidence of Lashley's hypothesis concerning a hierarchy of structures in the serial order of behavior.

These examples also show that the morphophonemic rules which produce the phonological and final phonetic realizations of negation must occur after (or in parallel with) the Negative element has been moved, that is, NEGATIVE+*precise* → *imprecise* while NEGATIVE+*regard* → *disregard*.

As is shown in (31b) NEG+*possible* may alternatively become *not possible* or *impossible* under certain conditions, just as NEG +*restricted* may occur as *unrestricted*. (See Appendix, Section Z.)

Example (31c) also illustrates the existence of an abstract syntactic rule. The intended utterance has no *do* form, i.e. the present tense of the verb *agree* in the affirmative has no phonetic expression. The *do* insertion must occur after the NEG is disordered. (33) shows the intended surface structure and the disordered surface structure (before the *do* is inserted).

(33)

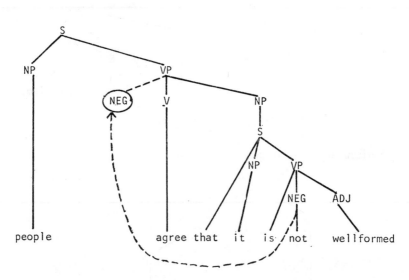

What was said was not *People not agree that it is well formed* but *People* DON'T *agree that it is well formed.*

Since *do* does not occur in the intended utterance, it must be inserted after the NEG element is disordered in keeping with the syntactic rules of the language, and before the contraction rule operates.

I am not claiming that syntactic rules can not be broken. Speech errors reveal those rules which either fail to apply in the production of an utterance or where misordering results in ungrammatical sentences, as discussed above. Other kinds of syntactically deviant utterances are exemplified in (34).

(34) (a) it seems like all the dogs bury their bones → ... bury its bones
    (b) the city has a personality of its own → of his own
    (c) I've begun to change my mind → I've began ...
    (d) she was so drunk when she called him → ... so drank ...
    (e) they forgot to wake me up → forgot to woke me up
    (f) the doctor said you should have been dead 20 years ago → ... you should be dead twenty years ago
    (g) I didn't know he could do it → ... he could did it

Some of these errors show selection of pronouns which disagree with the number or gender of the referent noun, or incorrect tense application etc. Again we find a breakdown in the 'monitoring' mechanism. But the examples under (31) show that a corrective process is at work during production. This aspect of a performance model is discussed at some length by Laver. Such monitoring is not foolproof or no errors would occur. But, as stated earlier, the 'overlooking' of one error does not preclude the 'correction' of other aspects of syntax or phonology. Thus, when NEG is moved incorrectly, the *do* insertion rule may 'correct' another possible syntactic error.

In Hill's discussion of the speech process he suggests that "to select the intonation pattern is to select the type of sentence to be spoken". In the model included in my paper in this volume I suggest rather that the sentence type, i.e. the syntactic structure, is selected or constructed first which in turn determines the intonation contour generated. Nooteboom (personal correspondence) also suggests "that the choice of a particular syntactic structure may be influenced by the intonation pattern chosen". The data collected do not seem to decide between these two possibilities. However, it seems more likely to me that the semantic intent or meaning to be conveyed will, in a number of instances, dictate the particular syntactic structure upon which the intonation depends. The sentences in (35) illustrate this with the italicized words representing primary stress or accent.

(35) (a) It's *John* who's going.
    (b) The one who's going is *John*.

Both (a) and (b) may be answers to the questions *Who's going?* or *Is Bill going?* It seems more plausible to assume that the intonation contour of these sentences depends on a prior selection of syntactic structure rather than the reverse.

More data are needed to decide this question. However, that syntactic structures are represented prior to articulation and prior to many disordering errors is clear.

Some of the examples which Hill discussed concerning phrase and word stress do however suggest that intonation contours and stress are semi-independent and can also be disordered. He cites the example where an incorrect stress on *forest fires* produces the main stress on *fires* rather than on *forest*. This need not be explained by "the suspicion ... that the utterance was a blend of 'forest fires' with some such other phrase as 'terrible fires'". Errors such as this one, and those under (36) can be accounted for by the same mechanisms responsible for segmental errors, i.e. a disordering of the elements.

(36) (a) Jìm Wèst Nìght gáme → Jìm Wèst níght gàme –– I mean –– Jìm Wèst Nìght gáme

   (b) I was supíne → I was súpine – supíne

   (c) símilarly → [siməlǽrəlij]

In (c) note that when the stress is shifted the vowel quality also changes. It is of course possible that this is a blend of *similarly/similarity*. (For further examples, see Appendix, Section O.)

Furthermore, as Fromkin, and Boomer and Laver point out in their papers, the fact that a disordering of words in many cases does not result in change in the intended intonation contour argues for the independent generation of such contours. (See Appendix, Section P.)

There are other kinds of errors which can not be accounted for by the proposed disordering of various sized units or incorrect rule application. These are errors which produce 'blends' and word substitutions. The kinds of word substitutions and the semantic features of the blended words also reveal something about the grammar which a speaker uses in producing speech.

In Wells's discussion of blends he notes that "in all these ... the two original words are synonyms." He than adds "... this fact is of no concern to the linguist as such ... it is to be classified as psychological rather than linguistics". This view reflects the particular paradigm which dominated linguistics at the time of his paper. The fact that so often the substituted or blended words share semantic features requires explanation and must be accounted for in a performance model. In the examples cited by Wells, the blended *shaddy* (from *shabby* and *shoddy*) or *frowl* (from *frown* and *scowl*) share both 'formal' similarities (these, according to Wells are phonological and word class similarities) and semantic features. Wells states that "formal similarity ... by definition does not include similarity or other relationship of meaning". Jakobson once said that "language without meaning is meaningless". If one is attempting to explain what a speaker knows and how he uses that knowledge in producing utterances then the meanings of morphemes and of sentences must be accounted for in both competence and performance models. One can formally deal with semantic features and similarities or differences of meaning just as one deals with syntactic or phonological similarities. We do not store morphemes devoid of such semantic features. And blends of the sort cited by Wells reveal that each word or morpheme is represented by a set of semantic features which together constitute its 'meaning'. Where two words have the same set of features, or closely overlapping sets it is more likely that blends will occur since a choice is involved by the speaker in attempting to verbalize his message.

We have already seen that nouns are blended with (or substituted for, or transposed with) nouns, verbs with verbs etc. This fact implies that our knowledge of the language includes knowledge of the syntactic features of each formative, and, in addition, that these features are part of the stored representation of each morpheme. Furthermore, as previously discussed, the syntactic structure of the sentence to be uttered determines the proper selection.

The fact that "the wrongly chosen word is semantically related to the intended word" and that "this semantical relation may be of several kinds ... semantic opposite ... switches of dimension ..." is accounted for by Nooteboom by suggesting that "a word may be mistakenly selected as a result of the contextual probability induced by one or more of the adjacent words".

I am not sure that "contextual probability" can account for word substitutions such as those in (37). (See also Appendix, Sections V. and W.)

(37) (a) blond hair → blond eyes
     (b) bridge of the nose → bridge of the neck
     (c) under the sun → under the world
     (d) when my gums bled → when my tongues bled
     (e) dachshund → Volkswagen

The "wrongly chosen words would [not] have a great chance of being generated if the speakers were asked to guess the word on the basis of the adjacent words" as Nooteboom suggests.

The errors are accounted for, however, by the further observation of Nooteboom: "The fact that we find selectional mistakes in the semantic field as distinct from selectional mistakes in the formal field might be taken as an indication that the selection of a word meaning in the construction of an utterance must be distinguished as a separate process from the selection of a word form ... Perhaps we might speak of semantic fields in a very real sense."

The examples in (37) attest to such 'semantic fields' and to the fact that words are stored with a set of semantic features. Thus in (e) one may assume that both the intended *dachshund* and the substituted *Volkswagen* are specified in the lexicon as [+German, +small]. These features may have been preprimed prior to going to the specific address of the word to be selected.

While many of the substitutions and blends involve words which are phonologically similar (see below for a discussion on this question) there are many cases of blends which are primarily due to a sharing of semantic features as shown in (38). (See also Appendix, Section U.)

(38) (a) minor/trivial → minal [majnəl]
     (b) spank/paddle → spaddle
     (c) velars/dentals → dentars
     (d) wow/flutter → [flæw]
     (e) before/first → beforst
     (f) clarinet/viola → clarinola

The observation of Wells, however, that many substituted or blended words are phonologically similar also requires explanation. And, in addition, a viable model must account for the fact that even errors which may be explained in simple phonological terms seem to involve some kind of an association mechanism. (39) illustrates such errors.

(39) (a) Nick watered, and Sue weeded the garden → Nick watered, and sea weeded the garden
(b) it spread like wild fire → ... like wild flower
(c) deep phrase marker → deep freeze marker
(d) sesame seed crackers → Sesame Street crackers
(e) I'm going to die young, but I'll die less young → ... I'll die yes lung
(f) he made head lines → he made hairlines (referring to a barber)
(g) the art of the fugue → the arg of the flute
(h) if someone steals my proto-Miwok, you and David are automatic suspects → ... are automatic suffixes

(a) may be simply an example of vowel anticipation. But the resulting utterance does show the 'contextual' contamination Nooteboom discusses. (b) and (c) are similar. In (d) although *seed* and *street* have initial consonants and vowels in common, and dental consonants differing only in the voicing feature, the resulting *Sesame Street* is certainly a stored noun compound and its existence as such appears to have influenced the error. These errors may be accounted for by suggesting either phonological disorderings or selections of the wrong addresses for the inserted words. But the particular utterances (and many others like them) do appear to be the result of a more complex cause. Particularly when these errors are related to (e), (f), (g), and (h) is this seen.

(e) was spoken by someone who had just announced that he had quit smoking. The metathesis of the [y] and [l] may be all that is involved. The particular error, however, may also have been influenced or contaminated by what Freud may have called an unconscious wish, and what I would call an intrusion of a parallel idea which in someway effected the serial ordering of the segments in the string.

In (f) since the speaker was referring to a barber, it would appear that this influenced the selection of *hairline* as opposed to *headline*. The phonological similarity of the two words combined with the semantic association may have 'triggered' the wrong selection.

(g) was spoken by a flute player who was to play the flute in the performance. *Art of the Fugue* must have been phonologically represented in the buffer prior to the substitution of the word *flute* for *fugue* because of the change of *art* to *arg*; that is, the /g/ of /fjug/ was anticipated prior to the substitution of *flute* for *fugue* or both words were selected simultaneously and readied. Again, one cannot discount the phonological similarity of the two words. Had the speaker been a violin player the error might have been *Art of the Violin* (a possible error) but the preponderance of errors of this sort which involve similar sounding words suggests that both phonological and semantic associations contributed to the actual error.

(h) similarly represents an intrusion of a 'thought' external to the intended utterance, since proto-Miwok is a language with a complex suffixal system. And once more it is likely that the phonological similarity of the initial syllables contributed to the surfacing of the intruding word.

Nooteboom's conclusion is thus well taken: "It seems evident ... that by the same token (that we talk of semantic fields) we may talk about formal fields since we see that word forms may be easily evoked by similar forms."

Hill discusses this question in relation to the intrusion of 'taboo' words as a reflection of 'internal stimuli'. That speech errors so often produce unintended but meaningful utterances makes them strong candidates for humor. This is exemplified in the Herb Caen column of the March 7, 1972 San Francisco Chronicle: "The Tuck-Fortner Report (newscasts) is off Channel 2, much to the relief of those who worry about Spoonerisms. Oddly enough, it was Mike Tuck who committed the only near miss in the history of the program, introducing Banker Fortney Stark as 'Fartney Stork'."

The examples in (40), in addition to the ones cited by Hill, support his contention that 'taboo' words may have some influence in producing slips.

(40) (a) back vowels → vack bowels
　　 (b) broke the crystal on my watch → broke the whistle on my crotch
　　 (c) cut the string → cunt the strig
　　 (d) don't take this as a rejection on my part → don't take this as an erection on my part
　　 (e) White Anglo Saxon Protestant → White Anglo Saxon prostitute
　　 (f) hot under the collar → hot under the belt
　　 (g) speech production → preach seduction
　　 (h) we'll start on Friday → we'll fart on Friday

The psychological aspects of Freud's analysis is not the concern here. His observations, however, combined with the examples given in (38), (39) and (40) support his contention that "the mechanism which connects together sounds and words for the reciprocal influence of their articulation [and] the influence outside of the same sentence or context [may] suggest the probable laws of the formation of speech".

The model of speech production proposed in my article in this volume does not account for such semantic or phonological associations. To that extent it is certainly deficient. Laver is obviously correct in suggesting that "the planning function activates more items from storage than it finally selects for the neurolinguistic program" and in "treating ideation as a separate function from neurolinguistic program-planning". He also states that a separation of the "ideation function from the planning function is not to imply that the latter may not influence the former". Unfortunately, no model proposed to date formally and explicitly provides the mechanisms by which ideational and formal associations effect the verbal output.

MacKay (1972) in an interesting unpublished paper, proposes a model to explain word substitutions by an Incomplete Specification Hypothesis whereby "errors result whenever output occurs before the entire feature hierarchy for a word has been filled in". He points to the fact that an analysis of Meringer's corpus shows that "unmarked forms usually intrude on marked forms and rarely vice versa". (e.g. singular form instead of plural, present tense instead of past, etc.) He also suggests that

The procedure or routine for generating a word involves a hierarchically ordered series of choices or coding operations. If this coding process is stopped short due to lack of time, then the required word will not be exactly specified, but a whole class of words which are similar within the limits of the specification reached. Erroneously substituted words would come from this class, the result of incomplete specification at the phonological level.

As the examples above show, many of the phonologically similar substitutions are words which are not similar in semantic class but which are, or seem to be 'triggered' by some parts of the phonological string. One cannot simply account for the substitution of *deep freeze* for *deep phrase* by suggesting that *freeze* was selected because of incomplete specification at the phonological level. To suggest that the substitution of 'unmarked' forms for 'marked' forms occurs because of 'incomplete specification' implies that all such forms are stored. This cannot account for errors in which incorrect, i.e. ungrammatical, forms are substituted, such as *knowed* and *swimmed* for *knew* and *swam*, respectively. The Incomplete Specification Hypothesis does account for a number of aspects of both normal and deviant speech in an interesting way, although it fails to cover all variety of speech errors, even some of those it is purported to handle.

MacKay is deeply concerned about the testability of hypotheses in a model as we all should be. He suggests that "the notion of unconscious wishes seems untestable" and so excludes any consideration of this problem. This, of course, depends on what one considers a 'test'. The incomplete specification of semantic features cannot explain why *flute* is substituted for *fugue* (by a flutist) or why *hairline* is substituted for *headline* (in reference to a barber). Nor can incomplete specification of the phonology explain why just these particular relevant words were substituted. Without reference to the intrusion of ideas external to the intended utterances these errors would be random errors which MacKay himself states is "untenable under the generally accepted principle of determinism". Such errors are evidence for unconscious thoughts and serve to test the hypothesis that such thoughts play a role in producing errors of this kind.

Hill suggests that the "errors which result ... from responses to stimuli which are themselves linguistic seem ... very important for the light [they] throw on internal language activity". One can agree that "internal language activity can be the stimulus for further language activity (which) makes it possible to understand thinking and day-dreaming in language". He concludes that "a preexistent message which is encoded into language is an entity not necessary for a coherent picture of sentence formation". The question of whether thinking can occur without language is not a new one. Blends however seem to suggest that an idea is generated which may have a number of possible linguistic realizations, i.e. that the message is first encoded in some non-linguistic shape. Evidence from data other than speech errors also strongly supports the idea that conceptualization can occur without linguistic form. Split brain patients, who have had their corpus collosum severed due to severe epilepsy are able to point out objects when, for example, olfactory stimuli are presented to their right (non-linguistic) hemisphere but are unable to name the objects. (Gordon et al. 1969) If they can 'match' the odor of an onion or a rose with the objects themselves, without access to the linguistic representation of these concepts, one may conclude that ideation is not dependent upon language but rather that language is but one means of representing thought. For linguistic and extra-linguistic reasons, then, most models of speech production start with the generation of a message in semantic or ideational form.

The translation of this idea into linguistic form constitutes the main stages in a performance model. Just as a speaker does not think of individual ideas one after the other, so the speaker does not produce a string of words one by one. Hockett, in relating speech to reading aloud suggests that "the speaker first construct(s) a 'text' somewhere inside himself and then read(s) it off, sometimes inaccurately". Since the inaccuracies are of various kinds the construction of the 'text' must be in various stages and an internal 'reader' may produce inaccuracies all along the way. To refer to an earlier example, the inaccuracy which produces the disordering of grammatical morphemes or of lexical morphemes must occur prior to the phonological specification of the affixes to account for the morphophonemic 'editing' which occurs which editing is not constrained phonologically by P-Rules of the language.

The size of the 'text' which is constructed and stored prior to articulation has interested a number of writers. Hill suggests that there is some longest distance between segments in a string involved in an error and that "this in turn (may) ... tell us much about the length of lag between perfected message and articulation." Others have also suggested a maximum utterance length involved in errors. Nooteboom states, "The distance between origin and target does not generally exceed seven syllables". Cohen also suggested as a maximum the magic number seven. The errors given in (41) suggest that the 'encoding' process, or the text which is constructed and stored prior to articulation involves a string which may be larger than seven syllables, but usually not longer than seven words.

(41) (a) I think it's reasonable to measure with care →
　　　　I think it's careful to measure with reason
　　(b) that the students should acknowledge the department's wishes →
　　　　that the department should acknowledge the students' wishes
　　(c) Hey, Mike, have you heard the joke about ... →
　　　　Hey, Joke, have you heard the Mike about
　　(d) Bach distinguishes three different types →
　　　　Bach distinguishes three different bipes.

The errors involving stretches of speech as long as those in (41) are certainly rare. Most phonological errors involve units which do not exceed seven syllables, and are usually much closer in distance from each other. MacKay discusses this 'proximity' question to some extent in his paper.

The errors which involve more than two words or constructions, although rarer, do occur providing further evidence that whole structures and strings are 'encoded' and articulated prior to the clearing of this part of the program. There are some people who seem to have a special 'talent' for mangling an utterance as illustrated in (42).

(42) (a) whole second half → soul hecond path
    (b) I hate long hair in hot weather → I hate hot wair [wer] in long heather
    (c) loose leaf notebook → [nows nijf luwf] book
    (d) three toed sloth → slee throwed toth
    (e) using the feature flat and plain → using the peature plat and flain
    (f) are there any corrections to the minutes of the last meeting → are there any collections to the [mijnɨts] of the mast leeting
    (g) when the Japanese attacked Pearl Harbor → when the Jakanese attapped curl harbor

One question which no one writing on speech errors as evidence in the construction of performance models has discussed is the 'intrusion' in the intended message of interjections, filled pauses etc. Van Lancker (1972) suggests that there is good evidence from aphasia cases, split brain patients, lesions etc. that although most of language is 'stored' and 'processed' in the left hemisphere, there is a subset of 'language' which is bilaterally represented. She further suggests that phrases like *you know* [jə now] or *I mean* are not constructed or, rather, that they are stored as whole units like idioms. During a pause, then, such expressions may be 'automatically' selected from this language sub-set. Such expressions occur only in these fixed forms and she further suggests that they will not be subject to the mechanisms creating speech errors. That is, *you know* will not be uttered as *know you* or [nuw jow] or [nə jów] and will not contaminate or influence other elements in the utterance. While it may be possible for a Grammar to ignore these 'phrases', that is, the grammatical rules need not generate as a possible grammatical string a sentence like (43), a model of speech production must in some way account for such an utterance.

(43) I'm you know going to – like – San Francisco – uh – you know – home.

The fillers of filled pauses are usually idiosyncratic in that one individual may say *er*, another *you know*, another *uh*, or, as I was informed by a Frenchman, [œ]. The model of speech production should then include at various stages (or possibly only before the articulatory stage) a program interrupt for a pause break at which point one of these 'automatic utterances' is inserted into the string.

The discussion so far has suggested that in the process of speech production there is a hierarchy of ordered structures and elements represented at different stages in the generation of an utterance: semantic concepts and syntactic structures are generated, intonation contours are assigned to such structures, lexical and grammatical morphemes are inserted into the structures, these morphemes are represented as ordered matrices of segmental units with phonological, syntactic, and semantic features specified, and grammatical rules of all kinds (syntactic, morphophonemic, phonological) 'monitor' (in Laver's terms) the output at different stages. Fry suggests that these 'programmes' are "running continuously in the speaker's brain" and this seems more likely than a series of steps which are disconnected. It is also suggested that the morphemes and phonological elements together with the 'rules' represent the grammar which is utilized during the production (and perception) of an utterance.

Hockett believes "this view is unmitigated nonsense" and suggests instead that all utterances can be accounted for by "a set of habits – that is analogies". In other words, the error which produced *knowed* would, I suppose, be due to a conflicting 'analogy' But calling this an 'analogy' or a 'habit' does not explain what an 'analogy' is. Nor does it explain that the speaker 'knows' (if he catches the error or it is pointed out to him) that he has produced a non-grammatical sentence. One cannot account for a speaker's knowledge and his utterances without an internalized grammar which he uses in speech production and perception.

In the 'Utterance Generator' diagram presented in my article, the Grammar influences the syntactic structure generator and to some extent overlaps with the Lexicon, the Morphophonemic Rules, and the Phonetic Rules. The model should include syntactic rules, in addition, to account for, as an example, the *do* insertion after the disordering of the Negative element, as well as other syntactic 'corrections'.

The model is also deficient in suggesting no way in which ideas external to the intended utterance can contaminate the intended sentence. There must also be a mechanism by which the selection of one lexical item, such as *deep phrase* may 'trigger' the selection of another which is similar either semantically or phonologically, i.e. *deep freeze*. It is clearly the case, then, that there must be a direct route from the 'idea generator' to the lexicon and from the lexicon to the idea generator, bipassing syntactic construction etc. In other words the selection of *deep phrase*, prior to being put into the short term memory buffer (or simultaneously, to explain the *arg of the flute* error) acts as a stimulus to the ideational process which directly generates or 'selects' *deep freeze* from the lexicon. In fact a whole network of 'monitoring' devices as suggested by Laver is required.

The flow chart presented in my article is obviously too simple and too schematic to represent the complexities of the utterance generator, even with the revisions suggested above. Parallel processing is continual which is not revealed in such a diagram. The production of an error itself may 'feedback' into the first stage of the process and stimulate a deliberate 'new error' as suggested by Hockett. As MacKay has stated, "The questions raised by the present research are perhaps as numerous as those answered." This is in the best tradition of science. It is difficult at this stage of our knowledge to be too sanguine about forthcoming answers. Speech error data do however provide us with a 'window' into linguistic mental processes and provide, to some extent, the laboratory data needed in linguistics.

BIBLIOGRAPHY

Anderson, J. M.
 1969 "Syllabic and Non-syllabic Phonology", *Journal of Linguistics* 5: 136-142.
Anderson, S. R.
 1969 "West Scandinavian Vowel Systems and the Ordering of Phonological Rules", unpublished M.I.T. Ph.D. dissertation.
Bawden, H. H.
 1900 "A study of Lapses", *Psychological Monographs* 3: 1-121.
Bloomfield, L.
 1922 Review of *Language* by E. Sapir, *The Classical Weekly* 15.
Chen, M.
 1969 "Vowel Length Variation as a Function of the Voicing of the Consonant Environment", *Project on Linguistic Analysis* 9 (Univ. of California, Berkeley: Phonological Laboratory).
Chomsky, N.
 1957 *Syntactic Structures* (=*Janua Linguarum*, series minor 4) (The Hague: Mouton).
 1972 *Language and Mind*, enlarged edition (New York: Harcourt Brace Jovanovich, Inc.).
Chomsky, N. and M. Halle
 1968 *The Sound Pattern of English* (New York: Harper and Row).
Crothers, J.
 1971 "On the Abstractness Controversy", *POLA Reports* 12 (University of California, Berkeley: Department of Linguistics, Phonology Laboratory).
Delbrück, B.
 1887 "Amnestische Aphasie", *Vgl. Sitzungsberichte der Jenaischen Gesellschaft für Medizin und Naturwissenschaft.*
Gordon, W. W. and R. W. Sperry
 1969 "Lateralization of Olfactory Perception in the Surgically Separated Hemispheres of Man", *Neuropsychologia* 7: 111–120.
Hoard, J. E.
 1971 "Aspiration, Tenseness and Syllabification in English", *Language* 47: 133–140.
Hockett, C. F.
 1955 *A Manual of Phonology* (=*Indiana University Publications in Anthropology and Linguistics II*).
 1958 *A Course in Modern Linguistics* (New York: Macmillan).
Hooper, J.
 1972 "The Syllable in Phonological Theory", *Language* 48: 525–540.
Hyman, L.
 1970a "How Concrete is Phonology?", *Language* 46: 58–76
 1970b "The Role of Borrowing in the Justification of Phonological Grammars", *Studies in African Linguistics* 1: 1–48.
Jakobson, R.
 1941 *Child Language, Aphasia, and Phonological Universals*, 1968 edition (The Hague: Mouton).
Kiparsky, P.
 1968 "How Abstract is Phonology?", unpublished paper, M.I.T.
Kisseberth, C. W.
 1969 "On the Abstractness of Phonology: the Evidence from Yawelmani", *Papers in Linguistics* 1: 248–282.
Lashley, K. S.
 1951 "The Problem of Serial Order in Behavior", in: *Cerebral Mechanisms in Behavior*: *The Hixon Symposium*, ed. by L. A. Jefferess (New York: Wiley).
MacKay, D. G.
 1972 "Hierarchic Specification of Words: Evidence from Paradigmatic Speech Errors", unpublished paper, U.C.L.A.

MacNeilage, P. F.
1972 "Speech Physiology", paper prepared for the Conference on *Speech Production and Percep-
      tion; their Relation to Cortical Function*, Vancouver, B.C., April 12–14, 1972, to appear in
      Proceedings ed. by John Gilbert (Academic Press).
Meringer, R.
1908 *Aus dem Leben der Sprache: Versprechen, Kindersprache, Nachahmungstrieb* (Berlin: Behr's
      Verlag).
Meringer, R. and K. Mayer
1895 *Versprechen und Veriesen: Eine Psychologisch-Linguistische Studie* (Stuttgart: Göschensche
      Verlagsbuchhandlung).
Ohala, J.
1971 "The Role of Physiological and Acoustic Models in Explaining the Direction of Sound
      Change", *POLA* 15: 25–40 (University of California, Berkeley: Phonology Laboratory).
Ohala, M.
1972 "Topics in Hindi-Urdu Phonology", unpublished U.C.L.A. Ph.D. Dissertation.
Paul, H.
1886 *Prinzipien der Sprachgeschichte* (Halle).
Popper, K. R.
1963 *Conjectures and Refutations: The Growth of Scientific Knowledge* (New York: Basic Books).
Robbins, R. H.
1966 "The Warden's Wordplay: Toward a Redefinition of the Spoonerism", *Dalhouse Review*
      46: 457–465.
Rosenblith, W. A.
1967 "Comments", in: *Brain Mechanisms Underlying Speech and Language* ed. by F. L. Darley
      and C. H. Millikan (New York and London: Greene and Stratton).
Sapir, E.
1925 "Sound Patterns in Language", *Language* 1: 37–51.
1933 "The Psychological Reality of Phonemes", reprinted in: *Selected Writings of Edward Sapir
      in Language, Culture, and Personality*, ed. by D. G. Mandelbaum, (Berkeley and Los Angeles:
      U.C. Press, 1949).
Sherzer, J.
1970 "Talking Backwards in Cuna: the Sociological Reality of Phonological Descriptions",
      Southwestern Journal of Anthropology 26: 343–353.
Stanley, R.
1967 "Redundancy Rules in Phonology", *Language* 43: 393–436.
Sturtevant, E. H.
1917 *Linguistic Change* (Chicago: University of Chicago Press).
Twaddell, W. F.
1935 "On Defining the Phoneme", *Language Monograph* 16.
Van Lancker, D.
1972 "Language Lateralization and Grammars", paper presented to the Second California
      Linguistics Conference, U.C.L.A., May, 1972.
Vennemann, T.
1970 "The German Velar Nasal: a Case for Abstract Phonology", *Phonetica* 22: 65–81.
1971 "Rule Inversion", unpublished paper, U.C.L.A.
1972 "On the Theory of Syllabic Phonology", *Linguistische Berichte* 18: 1–18.
Wickelgren, W. A.
1969a "Context-Sensitive Coding, Associative Memory, and Serial Order in (Speech) Behavior",
      Psychological Review 76: 1–15.
1969b "Context-Sensitive Coding in Speech Recognition, Articulation, and Development", in:
      Information Processing in the Nervous System ed. by K. N. Leibovic (New York: Springer-
      Verlag): 85–95.
Weizenbaum, J.
1972 "On the Impact of the Computer on Society", *Science* 176: 609–614.

SLIPS OF THE TONGUE*[1]

SIGMUND FREUD

The ordinary [linguistic] material which we use for talking in our native language appears to be protected against being forgotten; but it succumbs all the more frequently to another disturbance, which is known as a 'slip of the tongue'. The slips of the tongue that we observe in normal people give an impression of being the preliminary stages of the so-called 'paraphasias' that appear under pathological conditions.[2]

This is a subject on which I find myself in the exceptional position of being able to acknowledge the value of a previous work. In 1895 Meringer and C. Mayer published a study on 'Slips in Speaking and Reading'. Their lines of approach differ widely from my own. One of the authors, who acts as spokesman in the text, is in fact a philologist, and it was his linguistic interests which led him to attempt to discover the rules that govern the making of slips of the tongue. He hoped to be able to conclude from these rules that there exists "a certain mental mechanism, in which the sounds of a word, or of a sentence, and the [whole] words as well, are mutually linked and connected in a quite peculiar way" (10).[3]

The examples of slips of the tongue collected by the authors are first grouped by them in purely descriptive categories. They are classed as TRANSPOSITIONS (e.g. *the Milo of Venus* instead of *the Venus of Milo*); PRE-SONANCES or ANTICIPATIONS (e.g. *es war mir auf der Schwest ... auf der Brust so schwer*);[4] POST-SONANCES or PERSEVE-RATIONS (e.g. *ich fordere Sie* AUF, AUF *das Wohl unseres Chefs* AUFzustossen instead of

---

* Reprinted from *Psychopathology of Everyday Life* (first German edition 1901), translated by A. A. Brill (New York: New American Library, Mentor, 1958), ch. V.

[1] With the exception of two paragraphs on pp. 47–48, and Example 8 on p. 54, the whole of the earlier portion of this chapter (up to p. 56) dates back to 1901.

[2] Freud had discussed 'paraphasia' as a symptom of organic brain disorders in his book on aphasia; but he had also pointed out there that the SYMPTOM of paraphasia in such disorders "does not differ from the incorrect use and the distortion of words which the healthy person can observe in himself in states of fatigue or divided attention or under the influence of disturbing affects".

[3] Page references in this chapter, unless otherwise specified, are to Meringer and Mayer (*Versprechen und Verlesen*).

[4] The intended phrase was: 'it lay so heavily on my breast (*Brust*).' The substituted *Schwest* is a non-existent word. This instance is further discussed and explained below, p. 65.

ANzustossen);[5] CONTAMINATIONS (e.g. *er setzt sich auf den Hinterkopf*, combined from *er setzt sich einen Kopf auf* and *er stellt sich auf die Hinterbeine*);[6] and SUBSTITUTIONS (e.g. *ich gebe die Präparate in den Briefkasten*' instead of '*Brütkasten*')[7]. There are in addition to these main categories a few others which are less important (or less significant from our own point of view). In the above arrangement into groups it makes no difference whether the transposition, distortion, amalgamation, etc., is concerned with single sounds in a word, with syllables, or with complete words forming part of the intended sentence.

To explain the various kinds of slips of the tongue he had observed, Meringer postulates that different spoken sounds have a different psychical valency. When we innervate the first sound in a word or the first word in a sentence, the excitatory process already extends to the later sounds and the following words, and in so far as these innervations are simultaneous with one another they can exercise a modifying influence on one another. The excitation of the sound that is psychically more intense anticipates other excitations or perseverates after them, and in this way disturbs the less valent process of innervation. The question has therefore to be decided which sounds in a word have the highest valency. Here is Meringer's view: "If we want to know which sound in a word has the highest intensity, we must observe ourselves when we are searching for a forgotten word, e.g. for a name. Whichever [sound] is the first to come back into consciousness is in every case the one that had the greatest intensity before the word was forgotten" (160). "The sounds which are of high valency are the initial sound in the root syllable, and the initial sound in the word, and the accentuated vowel or vowels" (162).

I cannot help contradicting him here. Whether the initial sound of the name is one of the elements of highest valency in a word or not, it is certainly untrue that in a forgotten word it is the first to return to consciousness. The rule stated above is therefore inapplicable. If we observe ourselves while searching for a forgotten name, we are comparatively often obliged to express a conviction that it begins with a particular letter. This conviction proves to be unfounded just as often as not. Indeed, I should like to assert that in the majority of cases the initial sound which we announce is a wrong one. In our example of *Signorelli*, in fact, the substitute names had lost the initial sound and the essential syllables: it was precisely the less valent pair of syllables – *elli* – which returned to memory[8] in the substitute name Botticelli.

How little attention[9] is paid by the substitute names to the initial sound of the missing name may be learned, for instance, from the following case:

One day I found it impossible to recall the name of the small country of which

---

[5] 'I call on you to *hiccough to* the health of our Principal' instead of '*drink to*'. This instance is referred to again below, p. 66.

[6] 'He stands on the back of his head' (a meaningless phrase) combined from 'He is obstinate' (literally, 'he puts on a head') and 'He gets on his hind legs'.

[7] 'I put the preparation into the letter-box' instead of 'incubator', literally 'hatching-box'.

[8] In the editions before 1924: "to consciousness".

[9] This paragraph and the next were added in 1907.

Monte Carlo is the chief town. The substitute names for it ran: *Piedmont, Albania, Montevideo, Colico. Albania* was soon replaced in my mind by *Montenegro*; and it then occurred to me that the syllable *Mont* (pronounced 'Mon') was found in all the substitute names except the last. Thus it was easy for me, starting from the name of Prince Albert [the ruling Prince], to find the forgotten name *Monaco. Colico* gives a pretty close imitation of the sequence of syllables and the rhythm of the forgotten name.[10]

If we allow ourselves to suppose that a mechanism similar to that which has been demonstrated for the forgetting of names could also play a part in the phenomena of slips of the tongue, we are led to form a more deeply based judgement of instances of the latter. The disturbance in speaking which is manifested in a slip of the tongue can in the first place be caused by the influence of another component of the same speech – by an anticipatory sound, that is, or by a perseveration – or by another for-mulation of the ideas contained within the sentence or context that it is one's inten-tion to utter. This is the type to which all the above examples borrowed from Merin-ger and Mayer belong. The disturbance could, however, be of a second kind, anal-ogous to the process in the Signorelli case; it could result from influences OUTSIDE this word, sentence or context, and arise out of elements which are not intended to be uttered and of whose excitation we only learn precisely through the actual distur-bance. What these two ways in which slips of the tongue arise have in common would be the simultaneity of the interfering excitation; what differentiates them would be the position of the excitation inside or outside the sentence or context. The difference does not at first appear great in so far as it concerns certain deductions that can be made from the symptomatology of slips of the tongue. It is clear, however, that only in the former case is there any prospect of drawing conclusions from the phenomena of slips of the tongue about a mechanism which links sounds and words with one another so that they mutually influence their articulation – conclusions, that is, such as the philologist hoped to arrive at from studying slips of the tongue. In the case of interference from influences *outside* the same sentence or context of what is being said, it would be above all a matter of getting to know what the interfering elements are – after which the question would arise whether the mechanism of this disturbance, too, can reveal the supposed laws of speech formation.

Meringer and Mayer cannot be said to have overlooked the possibility that distur-bances of speech may be the result of 'complicated psychical influences', of elements outside the same word, sentence or sequence of spoken words. They were bound to observe that the theory which asserts that sounds are of unequal psychical valency is strictly speaking only adequate for explaining sound-disturbances, together with sound-

---

[10]   This example was used later by Freud in the sixth of his *Introductory Lectures* (1916–1917). He states there (in a slightly different and perhaps more lucid account of the episode) that the replacement of *Albania* by *Montenegro* was probably due to the contrast between black and white; and that it was thoughts connected with *Munich* – which is also *Monaco* in Italian – which had caused him to forget the name.

anticipations and perseverations. Where word-disturbances cannot be reduced to sound-disturbances (as, for instance, in substitutions and contaminations of words), they have not hesitated to look OUTSIDE the intended context for the cause of the slip – a procedure which they justify by some good examples. I quote the following passages:

Ru. was speaking of occurrences which, within himself, he pronounced to be "*Schweinereien* [disgusting, literally, piggish]". He tried, however, to express himself mildly, and began: "But then facts came to '*Vorschwein*' ..."[11] Mayer and I were present and Ru. confirmed his having thought "*Schweinereien*". The fact of this word which he thought being betrayed in "Vorschwein" and suddenly becoming operative is sufficiently explained by the similarity of the words. (62).

Just as in contaminations, so also – and probably to a much higher degree – in substitutions an important role is played by "floating" or "wandering" speech images. Even if they are beneath the threshold of consciousness they are still near enough to be operative, and can easily be brought into play by any resemblance they may have to the complex that is to be spoken. When this is so they cause a deviation in the train of words or cut across it. "Floating" or "wandering" speech images are often, as we have said, stragglers following after speech processes which have recently terminated (perseverations). (73)

Resemblance can also cause a deviation when another, similar word lies a short way below the threshold of consciousness, *without a decision to speak it having been reached.* This is the case with substitutions. – Thus I hope that my rules will of necessity be confirmed when they are tested. But for this it is necessary (if the speaker is someone else) *that we should obtain a clear notion of everything that was in the speaker's thoughts.*[12] Here is an instructive case. Li., a schoolmaster, said in our presence: "Die Frau würde mir Furcht ein*l*agen."[13] I was taken aback, for the *l* struck me as inexplicable. I ventured to draw the speaker's attention to his slip in saying "ein*l*agen" for "ein*j*agen", upon which he at once replied: "Yes, the reason was that I thought: I should not be in der *Lage* ['in a position'], etc."

Here is another case. I asked R. von Schid. how his sick horse was getting on. He replied: "Ja, das *draut* ... dauert vielleicht noch einen Monat."[14] I could not understand the "*draut*", with an *r*, for the *r* in "*dauert*" could not possibly have had this result. So I drew his attention to it, whereupon he explained that his thought had been: "das ist eine *traurige* Geschichte ['it's a *sad* story']." Thus the speaker had two answers in his mind and they had been intermixed. (97)

It is pretty obvious that the consideration of 'wandering' speech images which lie below the threshold of consciousness and are not intended to be spoken, and the demand for information about everything that had been in the speaker's mind, are procedures which constitute a very close approach to the state of affairs in our 'analyses'. We too are looking for unconscious material; and we even look for it along the same

---

[11] Ru. intended to say "came to *light*" and should have used the word *Vor*SCHEIN. Instead he used the meaningless word *Vor*SCHWEIN.
[12] My italics.
[13] He intended to say: "The lady would strike (*einjagen*) terror into me". But instead of *einjagen* he said *einlagen*, which is a non-existent verb – though *Lage* is a familiar noun meaning 'position'.
[14] What he intended to say was: "Well, it will last (*dauert*) another month perhaps." Instead of *dauert* he used the meaningless word *draut*.

path, except that, in proceeding from the ideas that enter the mind of the person who is being questioned to the discovery of the disturbing element, we have to follow a longer path, through a complicated series of associations.

I shall dwell for a moment on another interesting process, to which Meringer's examples bear witness. The author himself holds that it is some sort of similarity between a word in the sentence intended to be spoken and another word not so intended which permits the latter to make itself felt in consciousness by bringing about a distortion, a composite figure, or a compromise-formation (contamination):

jagen,	dauert,	Vorschein
lagen,	traurig,	. . . schwein.

Now in my *Interpretation of Dreams* I have demonstrated the part played by the work of CONDENSATION in forming what is called the manifest dream-content out of the latent dream-thoughts. A similarity of any sort between two elements of the unconscious material – a similarity between the things themselves or between their verbal presentations – is taken as an opportunity for creating a third, which is a composite or compromise idea. In the dream-content this third element represents both its components; and it is as a consequence of its originating in this way that it so frequently has various contradictory characteristics. The formation of substitutions and contaminations which occurs in slips of the tongue is accordingly a beginning of the work of condensation which we find taking a most vigorous share in the construction of dreams.[15]

In a short essay designed for a wider circle of readers Meringer has claimed that a special practical significance attaches to particular cases in which one word is put for another – viz. to those cases in which a word is replaced by another that has the opposite meaning. "You probably still recall", he writes,

The way in which the President of the Lower House of the Austrian Parliament *opened* the sitting a short while ago: "Gentlemen: I take notice that a full quorum of members is present and herewith declare the sitting *closed*!" His attention was only drawn by the general merriment and he corrected his mistake.[16] In this particular case the explanation no doubt was that the President secretly *wished* he was already in a position to close the sitting, from which little good was to be expected. But this accompanying idea, as frequently happens, broke through, at least partially, and the result was "closed" instead of "open" – the opposite, that is, of what was intended to be expressed. Now extensive observations have taught me that words with opposite meanings are, quite generally, very often interchanged; they are already associated in our linguistic consciousness, they lie very close to each other and it is easy for the wrong one to be evoked.[17]

It cannot be said that in all cases where words are replaced by their opposites it is

---

[15]   Cf. Section A of Chapter VI of *The Interpretation of Dreams* (1900), *Standard Ed.*, 4: 279 ff.
[16]   This example was later quoted by Freud in the second of his *Introductory Lectures* (1916–1917) and again in his posthumously published paper, "Some Elementary Lessons in Psycho-Analysis" (1940), which was written in 1938.
[17]   Cf. Freud's own later paper on "The Antithetical Meaning of Primal Words" (1910).

as easy as in this instance of the President to show the probability of the slip being a consequence of a contradiction arising in the speaker's mind against the uttered sentence. We found an analogous mechanism in our analysis of the *aliquis* example. There the internal contradiction expressed itself in a word being forgotten, instead of its being replaced by its opposite. But in order to soften the distinction we may note that the word *aliquis* is in fact incapable of having an opposite like 'to close' and 'to open', and that 'to open' is a word that cannot be forgotten as it is too familiar a part of our vocabulary.

If the last examples of Meringer and Mayer show that the disturbance of speech can arise on the one hand from the influence of anticipatory or perseverating sounds and words of the same sentence which are intended to be spoken, and on the other hand from the effect of words outside the intended sentence WHOSE EXCITATION WOULD NOT OTHERWISE HAVE BEEN REVEALED, the first thing we shall want to know is whether the two classes of slips of the tongue can be sharply divided, and how an example of one class can be distinguished from a case of the other. At this point in the discussion one must however bear in mind the views expressed by Wundt, who deals with the phenomena of slips of the tongue in the course of his comprehensive discussion of the laws of the development of speech.

According to him, a feature that is never missing from these and other related phenomena is the activity of certain psychical[18] influences.

First of all they have a positive determinant in the form of the uninhibited stream of *sound-associations* and *word-associations* evoked by the spoken sounds. In addition there is a negative factor in the form of the suppression or relaxation of the inhibitory effects of the will on this current, and of the attention which is also active here as a function of the will. Whether this play of association manifests itself by a coming sound being anticipated, or by the preceding sounds being reproduced, or by a habitually practised sound being intercalated between others, or finally by quite different words, which stand in an associative relation to the sounds that are spoken, having an effect upon them – all these indicate only differences in the direction and at the most in the scope of the associations taking place, and not differences in their general nature. In some cases, too, it may be doubtful to which form a certain disturbance is to be assigned, or whether it would not be more justifiable, *in accordance with the principle of the complication of causes*,[19] to trace it back to a concurrence of several motive forces. [Cf. below, p. 65.]

I consider these observations of Wundt's fully justified and very instructive. Perhaps it would be possible to emphasize more definitely than Wundt does that the positive factor favouring the slip of the tongue (the uninhibited stream of associations) and the negative factor (the relaxation of the inhibiting attention) invariably achieve their effect in combination, so that the two factors become merely different ways of regarding the same process. What happens is that, with the relaxation of the inhibiting

---

[18]   This word is in fact italicized by Wundt.
[19]   My italics. Freud was no doubt regarding this as equivalent to his own concept of 'overdetermination'.

attention – in still plainer terms, AS A RESULT OF this relaxation – the uninhibited stream of associations comes into action.

Among the slips of the tongue that I have collected myself, I can find hardly one in which I should be obliged to trace the disturbance of speech simply and solely to what Wundt calls the "contact effect of sounds". I almost invariably discover a disturbing influence in addition which comes from something OUTSIDE the intended utterance; and the disturbing element is either a single thought that has remained unconscious, which manifests itself in the slip of the tongue and which can often be brought to consciousness only by means of searching analysis, or it is a more general psychical motive force which is directed against the entire utterance.

(1) My daughter had made an ugly face when she took a bite of an apple, and I wanted to quote to her:

> Der Affe gar possierlich ist,
> Zumal wenn er vom Apfel frisst.[20]

But I began: "Der Apfe ..." [a non-existent word]. This looks like a contamination of *Affe* ['ape'] and *Apfel* ['apple'] (a compromise-formation), or it might be regarded as an anticipation of the word *Apfel* that was in preparation. The circumstances were, however, more precisely as follows. I had already begun the quotation once before and had not made a slip of the tongue the first time. I only made a slip when I repeated it. The repetition was necessary because the person I was addressing had had her attention distracted from another quarter and she had not been listening to me. I must include the fact of the repetition, together with my impatience to have done with my sentence, among the motives of the slip which made its appearance as a product of condensation.

(2) My daughter said: "I am writing to Frau Schresinger ..." The lady's name is Schlesinger. This slip of the tongue is probably connected with a trend towards making articulation easier, for an *l* is difficult to pronounce after a repeated *r*. I must add, however, that my daughter made this slip a few minutes after I had said "*Apfe*" for "*Affe*". Now slips of the tongue are in a high degree contagious, like the forgetting of names – a peculiar fact which Meringer and Mayer have noticed in the case of the latter. I cannot suggest any reason for this psychical contagiousness.

(3) "I shut up like a *Tassenmescher* [a non-existent word] – I mean *Taschenmesser* ['pocket-knife']", said a woman patient at the start of the hour of treatment. Here again a difficulty in articulation (cf. *Wiener Weiber Wäscherinnen waschen weisse Wäsche* ['Viennese washer-women wash white washing'], *Fischflosse* ['fish-fin'] and similar tongue-twisters) could serve as an excuse for her interchanging the sounds. When her attention was drawn to her slip, she promptly replied: "Yes, that's only because you said *Ernscht* to-day." I had in fact received her with the remark: "To-day we shall really be in earnest [*Ernst*]" (because it was going to be the last session before

---

[20] The ape's a very comic sight, When from an apple he takes a bite.

the holidays), and had jokingly broadened *Ernst* into *Ernscht*.[21] In the course of the hour she repeatedly made further slips of the tongue, and I finally observed that she was not merely imitating me but had a special reason for dwelling in her unconscious on the word *Ernst* in its capacity as a name [*Ernest*].[22]

(4) "I've got such a cold, I can't *durch die Ase natmen* – I mean, *Nase atmen*",[23] the same patient happened to say another time. She knew immediately how she had come to make the slip. "Every day I get on the tram in Hasenauer Street, and while I was waiting for one to come along this morning it struck me that if I was French I should say *Asenauer*, as the French always drop their aitches at the beginning of a word." She then brought a series of reminiscences about French people of her acquaintance, and came in a very roundabout manner to a memory of having played the part of Picarde in the short play *Kurmärker und Picarde*[24] when she was a girl of fourteen, and of having spoken broken German in the part. The chance arrival at her boarding house of a guest from Paris had awoken the whole series of memories. The interchanging of the sounds was therefore the result of a disturbance by an unconscious thought from an entirely different context.

(5) A slip of the tongue had a similar mechanism in the case of another woman patient, whose memory failed her in the middle of reproducing a long-lost recollection of childhood. Her memory would not tell her what part of her body had been grasped by a prying and lascivious hand. Immediately afterwards she called on a friend with whom she discussed summer residences. When she was asked where her cottage at M. was situated she answered: "on the *Berglende* ['hill-thigh']" instead of *Berglehne* ['hill-side'].

(6) When I asked another woman patient at the end of the session how her uncle was, she answered: "I don't know, nowadays I only see him *in flagranti*." Next day she began: "I am really ashamed of myself for having given you such a stupid answer. You must of course have thought me a very uneducated person who is always getting foreign words mixed up. I meant to say: *en passant*." We did not as yet know the source of the foreign phrase which she had wrongly applied. In the same session, however, while continuing the previous day's topic, she brought up a reminiscence in which the chief role was played by being caught *in flagranti*. The slip of the tongue of the day before had therefore anticipated the memory which at the time had not yet become conscious.

(7) At a certain point in the analysis of another woman patient I had to tell her

---

[21] An uneducated way of pronouncing the word.

[22] In fact she turned out to be under the influence of unconscious thoughts about pregnancy and contraception. By the words *shut up like a pocket-knife*, which she uttered consciously as a complaint, she wanted to describe the position of a child in the womb. The word *Ernst* in my opening remark had reminded her of the name (S. Ernst) of a well known Viennese firm in the Kärntnerstrasse which used to advertise the sale of contraceptives.

[23] She meant to say: "I can't breathe through my nose." Her actual last two words, *Ase natmen*, have no meaning.

[24] A *Singspiel* by the Berlin dramatist, Louis Schneider (1805–1878).

that I suspected her of having been ashamed of her family during the period we were just then concerned with, and of having reproached her father with something we did not yet know about. She remembered nothing of the kind and moreover declared it was unlikely. However, she continued the conversation with some remarks about her family: "One thing must be granted them: they are certainly unusual people, they all possess *Geiz* ['greed'] – I meant to say *Geist* ['cleverness']." And this was in fact the reproach which she had repressed from her memory. It is a frequent occurrence for the idea one wants to withhold to be precisely the one which forces its way through in the form of a slip of the tongue. We may compare Meringer's case of *zum Vorschwein gekommen* [p. 49]. The only difference is that Meringer's speaker wanted to keep back something that was in his consciousness, whereas my patient did not know what was being kept back, or, to put it in another way, did not know she was keeping something back and what that something was.

(8)[25] The next example of a slip of the tongue is also to be traced back to something intentionally withheld. I once met two old ladies in the Dolomites who were dressed up in walking clothes. I accompanied them part of the way, and we discussed the pleasures and also the trials of spending a holiday in that way. One of the ladies admitted that spending the day like that entailed a good deal of discomfort. "It is certainly not at all pleasant", she said, "if one has been tramping all day in the sun and has perspired right through one's blouse and chemise." In this sentence she had to overcome a slight hesitation at one point. Then she continued: "But then when one gets *nach* HOSE and can change ..." No interpellation, I fancy, was necessary in order to explain this slip. The lady's intention had obviously been to give a more complete list of her clothes: blouse, chemise and *Hose* ['drawers']. Reasons of propriety led her to suppress any mention of the third article of linen. But in the next sentence, with its different subject-matter, the suppressed word emerged against her will, in the form of a distortion of the similar word *nach* HAUSE ['home'].

(9) "If you want to buy carpets", a lady said to me, "you must go to Kaufmann [a proper name, also meaning 'merchant'] in the Matthäusgasse [Matthew Street]. I think I can give you a recommendation there. ""At Matthäus ...", I repeated, "I mean Kaufmann's." My repeating one name in the other's place looks like a result of my thoughts being distracted. They really were distracted by what the woman said, for she diverted my attention to something much more important to me than carpets. As a matter of fact, the house in which my wife lived when she was my fiancée was in the Matthäusgasse. The entrance to the house was in another street, and I now noticed that I had forgotten its name and could only make it conscious in a round-about way. The name Matthäus, which I was lingering over, was therefore a substitute name for the forgotten street-name. It was more suitable for this purpose than the name Kaufmann, for Matthäus is exclusively a personal name, while Kaufmann is not, and the forgotten street also bears the name of a person: Radetzky.

[25] This example was added in 1917. It had previously been used by Freud in the fourth of his *Introductory Lectures* (1916–1917).

(10) The following case could just as appropriately be included in the chapter below on "Errors", but I quote it here since the phonetic relations, which were the basis of one word being put in place of another, are quite unusually clear. A woman patient told me a dream: A child had resolved to kill itself by means of a snake-bite. It carried out its resolution. She watched it writhing in convulsions, and so on. She had now to find the impressions of the previous day which the dream had taken as its starting point. She immediately recalled that on the previous evening she had listened to a public lecture on first aid for snake-bites. If an adult and a child were bitten at the same time, the child's injury should be attended to first. She also remembered what the lecturer had prescribed by way of treatment. It would very much depend, he had said, on what kind of snake caused the bite. I interrupted at this point and asked: Surely he must have said that we have very few poisonous kinds in these parts and he must have told you which are the dangerous ones? "Yes, he particularly mentioned the *Klapperschlange* ['rattlesnake'].'' My laughter drew her attention to her having said something wrong. She did not correct the NAME, but took back her statement: "Yes, of course, they aren't found here; he was talking of the viper. How can I have got the idea of the rattlesnake?" I suspected it was due to interference by the thoughts which had hidden behind her dream. Suicide by means of a snake-bite could hardly be anything other than an allusion to the beautiful Cleopatra [in German: *Kleopatra*]. The great similarity between the sound of the two words, the occurrence in both of the same letters *Kl* ... *p* ... *r* in the same order, and of the same stressed *a*, was unmistakable. The close connection between the names *Klapper*schlange and *Kleopatra* resulted in her judgement being momentarily restricted, so that she saw no objection to asserting that the lecturer had given his audience in Vienna instructions on how to treat rattlesnake bites. In the ordinary way she knew as well as I did that that species of snake is not among the fauna of our country. We will not blame her for her equal lack of hesitation in transferring the rattlesnake to Egypt, for it is usual for us to lump together everything which is non-European and exotic, and I had myself to reflect for a moment before declaring that the rattlesnake is confined to the New World.

The continuation of the analysis brought further confirmation. On the previous day the dreamer had for the first time inspected the Mark *Antony* monument by Strasser, which stood in the vicinity of her home.[26] This then was the second exciting cause of the dream (the first having been the lecture on snakebites). In the continuation of the dream she was rocking a child in her arms. This scene reminded her of Gretchen.[27] Further ideas which occurred to her brought reminiscences of *Arria und Messalina*.[28] From the fact that the names of so many plays made their appearance in the dream-thoughts we may already have a suspicion that in her earlier years the dreamer had cherished a secret passion for the profession of actress. The beginning of the dream –

[26] A bronze group in Vienna representing the Triumph of Mark Antony by the Austrian sculptor Artur Strasser (1854–1927).
[27] In Goethe's *Faust*.
[28] A tragedy by the Viennese playwright Adolf Wilbrandt (1837–1911).

"A child had resolved to put an end to its life by means of a snake-bite" – had in fact no other meaning than that when she was a child she had made up her mind to become a famous actress one day. Finally, from the name *Messalina* the path of thoughts branched off which led to the essential content of the dream. Certain recent events had made her apprehensive that her only brother might make a socially unsuitable marriage, a *mésalliance* with a non-*Aryan*.

(11)[29] I will reproduce here an entirely innocent example (or perhaps one whose motives were insufficiently elucidated), because it displays a transparent mechanism.

A German who was travelling in Italy needed a strap to tie up his damaged trunk. For 'strap' [*Riemen*] the dictionary gave him the Italian word *coreggia*. It will be easy, he thought, to remember the word by thinking of the painter *Correggio*. After that he went into a shop and asked for "*una ribera*".

He had apparently not been successful in replacing the German word by the Italian one in his memory, but his efforts were nevertheless not entirely unsuccessful. He knew he had to keep in mind the name of a painter, and in this way he hit upon the name not of the painter who sounded much the same as the Italian word, but of another one who resembled the German word *Riemen*.[30] I could of course have quoted the present case just as appropriately as an example of the forgetting of a name rather than of a slip of the tongue.

When I was collecting slips of the tongue for the first edition of this book I proceeded by subjecting to analysis every case I was able to observe, and accordingly included the less impressive ones. Since then a number of other people have undertaken the amusing task of collecting and analysing slips of the tongue, and have thus enabled me to select from a richer material.

(12) A young man said to his sister: "I've completely fallen out with the D.'s now. We're not on speaking terms any longer." "Yes indeed!" she answered, "they're a fine *Lippschaft*".[31] She meant to say "*Sippschaft* ['lot, crew']", but in the slip she compressed two ideas: viz. that her brother had himself once begun a flirtation with the daughter of this family, and that this daughter was said to have recently become involved in a serious and irregular *Liebschaft* ['love-affair'].

(13)[32] A young man addressed a lady in the street in the following words: "If you will permit me, madam, I should like to *begleit-digen* you." It was obvious what his thoughts were: he would like to *begleiten* ['accompany'] her, but was afraid his offer would *beleidigen* ['insult'] her. That these two conflicting emotional impulses found expression in one word – in the slip of the tongue, in fact – indicates that the young man's real intentions were at any rate not of the purest, and were bound to seem, even to himself, insulting to the lady. But while he attempted to conceal this from

---

[29]   This example and the following one (12) were added in 1907.
[30]   Ribera, the well-known seventeenth century Spanish painter.
[31]   A non-existent word.
[32]   This example was added in 1912. Freud later alluded to it in the second and third of his *Introductory Lectures* (1916–1917).

her, his unconscious played a trick on him by betraying his real intentions. But on the other hand he in this way, as it were, anticipated the lady's conventional retort: "Really! What do you take me for? How dare you *insult* me" (reported by O. Rank).

I will next quote a number of examples[33] from an article by Stekel, entitled "Unconscious Admissions", in the *Berliner Tageblatt* of January 4, 1904.

(14) An unpleasant part of my unconscious thoughts is disclosed by the following example. I may start by stating that in my capacity as a doctor I never consider my remuneration but only have the patient's interest in mind: that goes without saying. I was with a woman patient to whom I was giving medical attention in a period of convalescence after a serious illness. We had been through hard days and nights together. I was happy to find her improved; I painted a picture for her benefit of the delights of a stay in Abbazia, and concluded by saying: "If, as I hope, you will *not* leave your bed soon ... " This obviously owed its origin to an egoistic motive in the unconscious, namely that I should be able to continue treating this well-to-do patient some time longer – a wish that is entirely foreign to my waking consciousness and which I would indignantly repudiate.

(15) Here is another example from Stekel.

My wife was engaging a French governess for the afternoons, and after agreement had been reached on the terms, wanted to retain her testimonials. The Frenchwoman asked to be allowed to keep them, giving as her reason: *Je cherche encore pour les après-midis, pardon, pour les avant-midis* [I am still looking for work in the afternoons – I mean, in the forenoons]. She obviously had the intention of looking round elsewhere and perhaps finding better terms – an intention which she in fact carried out.

(16) From Stekel:

I had to give a stiff lecture to a wife; and her husband, at whose request I did it, stood outside the door listening. At the end of my sermon, which had made a visible impression, I said: "Good-bye, sir". To any well-informed person I was thus betraying the fact that my words were addressed to the husband and that I had spoken them for his benefit.

(17) Stekel reports of himself that at one time he had two patients from Trieste in treatment whom he always used to address the wrong way round. "Good morning, Herr Peloni", he would say to Askoli, and "Good morning, Herr Askoli" to Peloni. He was at first inclined not to attribute any deeper motive to this confusion but to explain it as being due to the numerous points of resemblance between the two gentlemen. However it was easy for him to convince himself that the interchanging of the names corresponded in this case to a kind of boastfulness: he was able in this way to let each of his Italian patients know that he was not the only visitor from Trieste who had come to Vienna in search of his medical advice.

(18) Stekel reports that during a stormy General Meeting he said: "We shall now *streiten* ['quarrel']" (instead of *schreiten* ['proceed']) "to point four on the agenda."

(19) A professor declared in his inaugural lecture: "I am not *geneigt* [inclined]" (instead of *geignet* ['qualified']) "to describe the services of my most esteemed predecessor."[34]

[33] These examples (14–20) were added in 1907.
[34] Quoted by Freud in the second of his *Introductory Lectures* (1916–1917).

(20) To a lady whom he suspected of having Graves' disease Stekel said: "You are about a *Kropf* [goitre]" (instead of *Kopf* ['head']) "taller than your sister."

(21)[35] Stekel reports: "Someone wanted to describe the relationship of two friends and to bring out the fact that one of them was Jewish. He said: 'They lived together like Castor and Pollak.'[36] This was certainly not said as a joke; the speaker did not notice the slip himself until I drew his attention to it."

(22) Occasionally a slip of the tongue takes the place of a detailed characterization. A young woman who wore the breeches in her home told me that her sick husband had been to the doctor to ask what diet he ought to follow for his health. The doctor, however, had said that a special diet was not important. She added: "He can eat and drink what *I* want."[37]

The following[38] two examples given by Reik (1915) have their origin in situations where slips of the tongue occur especially easily – situations in which more must be kept back than can be said.

(23) A gentleman was offering his condolences to a young lady whose husband had recently died, and he intended to add: "You will find consolation in 'devoting' [*widmen*] yourself entirely to your children." Instead he said "*widwen*".[39] The suppressed thought referred to consolation of another kind: a young and pretty widow [*Witwe*] will soon enjoy fresh sexual pleasures.

(24) At an evening party the same gentleman was having a conversation with the same lady about the extensive preparations being made in Berlin for Easter, and asked: "Have you seen today's display [*Auslage*] at Wertheim's?[40] The place is completely *decollated*." He had not dared to express his admiration for the beautiful lady's *décolletage*, while the word *Auslage* ['display'] was used unconsciously in two senses.

The same condition applies to another case, observed by Dr. Hanns Sachs, of which he has tried to give an exhaustive account:

(25) A lady was telling me about a common acquaintance. The last time she saw him, he was, she said, as elegantly dressed as ever: in particular he was wearing strikingly beautiful brown *Halbschuhe* [low shoes]. When I asked where she had met him she replied: "He rang at the door of my house and I saw him through the blinds, which were down. But I didn't open the door or give any other sign of life, as I didn't want him to know I was already back in town." While I was listening to her I had an idea that she was concealing something from me, most probably the fact that her reason for not opening the door was that she was not alone and not properly dressed to receive visitors; and I asked her somewhat ironically: "So you were able to admire his *Hausschuhe* [house shoes] – *Halbschuhe* [low shoes], I mean – through the blinds when they were drawn?" In *Hausschuhe* I was giving expression to the thought of her *Hauskleid* [lit. house dress, i.e. *négligée*] which I had refrained from uttering.

---

[35]   This and the following example (22) were added in 1910.
[36]   Castor and Pollux were the 'heavenly twins' of Greek mythology. Pollak is a common Jewish name in Vienna.
[37]   Quoted by Freud in the second of his *Introductory Lectures* (1916–1917).
[38]   This paragraph and (23)–(26) were added in 1917.
[39]   A non -existent word.
[40]   A well-known department store.

There was on the other hand a temptation to get rid of the word *"Halb* [half]" for the reason that it was precisely this word which contained the core of the forbidden answer: "You are only telling me *half* the truth and are hiding the fact that you were *half* dressed." The slip of the tongue was encouraged by the additional circumstance that we had been talking directly before about this particular gentleman's married life, about his *häuslich* [domestic] happiness; this no doubt helped to determine the displacement [of *"Haus"*] on to him. Finally, I must confess that envy on my part may perhaps have contributed to my placing this elegant gentleman in the street in house shoes; only recently I myself bought a pair of brown low shoes, which are certainly not "strikingly beautiful" any longer.

Times of war like the present produce numerous slips of the tongue which there is not much difficulty in understanding.

(26) "What regiment is your son with?" a lady was asked. She replied: "With the 42nd Murderers " [*Mörder* – instead of *Mörser*, 'Mortars'].

(27)[41] Lieutenant Henrik Haiman writes from the front (1917): "While I was reading an absorbing book, I was torn away to act temporarily as reconnaisance telephone operator. When the artillery post gave the signal to test the line I reacted with: 'Duly tested and in order; *Ruhe.*'[42] According to regulations the message should have run: 'Duly tested and in order; *Schluss* [end (of message)]'. My aberration is to be explained by my annoyance at being interrupted while I was reading."

(28)[43] A sergeant instructed his men to give their people at home their correct addresses, so that *"Gespeckstücke"* should not go astray.[44]

(29) The following exceedingly fine example, which is also significant in view of its most unhappy background, I owe to Dr. L. Czeszer, who observed it while he was living in neutral Switzerland during the war and who analysed it exhaustively. I quote his letter verbatim with some inessential omissions:

I am taking the liberty of sending you an account of a slip of the tongue of which Professor M. N. of O. University was the victim in one of the lectures that he gave on the psychology of feelings during the summer term which has just ended. I must start by saying that these lectures took place in the Aula of the University before a great crowd of interned French prisoners-of-war as well as of students, most of whom were French-Swiss whose sympathies lay strongly on the side of the *Entente*. In the town of O., as in France itself, *"boche"* is the name in universal and exclusive use for the Germans. But in public announcements, and in lectures and the like, senior public servants, professors and other persons in responsible positions make an effort, for the sake of neutrality, to avoid the ominous word.

Professor N. was in the middle of discussing the practical significance of affects, and intended to quote an example illustrating how an effect can be deliberately exploited in such a way that a muscular activity which is uninteresting in itself becomes charged with pleasurable feelings, and so made more intense. He accordingly told a story – he was, of course, speaking in French – which had just then been reproduced in the local papers from a German one. It concerned a German schoolmaster who had put his pupils to work in the garden, and

---

[41]   This example was added in 1919.
[42]   'Quiet'; often used as an exclamation: 'Silence!'
[43]   This example, and (30) and (31) were added in 1920; (29) was added in 1919.
[44]   He meant to say *"Gepäckstücke"* ('parcels'). *Gespeckstücke* is a non-existent word; but *Speckstücke* would mean 'bits of bacon'. The vowel after the p has practically the same sound in each case (whether written e or ä).

in order to encourage them to work with greater intensity invited them to imagine that with every clod of earth that they broke up they were breaking a French skull. Every time the word for "German" came up in the course of his story N. of course said "*allemand*" quite correctly and not "*boche*". But when he came to the point of the story he gave the school-master's words in the following form: *Imaginez-vous qu'en chaque moche vous écrasez le crâne d'un Français.* That is to say, instead of *motte* [the French word for 'clod'] – *moche*!

One can see very clearly how this scrupulous scholar took a firm grip on himself at the beginning of his story, to prevent himself from yielding to habit – perhaps even to temptation – and from permitting a word that had actually been expressly proscribed by a federal decree to fall from the rostrum of the University Aula! And at the precise moment at which he had successfully said "*instituteur allemand* [German schoolmaster]" with perfect correctness for what was the last time, and was hurrying with an inward sigh of relief to the conclusion, which seemed to offer no pitfalls – the word which had been suppressed with so much effort caught hold of the similar-sounding "*motte*", and the damage was done. Anxiety about committing a political indiscretion, perhaps a suppressed desire to employ the usual word in spite of everything – the word that everyone expected – and the resentment of one who was born a republican and a democrat at every restriction on the free expression of opinion – all these interfered with his main intention of giving a punctilious rendering of the illustration. The interfering trend was known to the speaker and he had, as we cannot but suppose, thought of it directly before he made the slip of the tongue.

Professor N. did not notice his slip: at least he did not correct it, which is something one usually does quite automatically. On the other hand the slip was received by the mainly French audience with real satisfaction and its effect was exactly as though it had been an intentional play upon words. I myself followed this seemingly innocent occurrence with real inner excitement. For although I had for obvious reasons to forego asking the professor the questions prompted by the psychoanalytic method, I nevertheless took his slip of the tongue as conclusive evidence of the correctness of your theory about the determining of parapraxes and the deep-lying analogies and connections between slips of the tongue and jokes.

(30) The following slip of the tongue, which was reported by an Austrian officer, Lieutenant T., on his return home, also had its origin among the melancholy impressions of war-time:

For several months of the time that I was a prisoner-of-war in Italy I was one of two hundred officers accommodated in a small villa. During this time one of our number died of influenza. The impression made by this event was naturally a deep one, for the circumstances in which we found ourselves, the lack of medical assistance and the helplessness of our condition at the time made it more than probable that an epidemic would break out. – We had laid out the dead man in a cellar-room. In the evening, after I had taken a walk around our house with a friend, we both expressed a wish to see the dead body. The sight which greeted me on entering the cellar (I was the one in front) startled me violently, for I had not expected to find the bier so near the entrance and to be confronted at such close quarters with a face transformed by the play of the candlelight into something set in movement. While the effects of this scene were still on us we continued our walk around the house. When we came to a place from where there was a view of the park bathed in the light of a full moon, a brightly-lit meadow and beyond it a thin veil of mist, I described the picture that it conjured up; it was as if I saw a ring of elves dancing under the fringe of the neighbouring pine trees.

The next afternoon we buried our dead comrade. The course of our walk from our prison to the cemetery of the small neighbouring village was both bitter and humiliating for us; for a mocking, jeering crowd made up of shouting half-grown lads and rough, noisy villagers took advantage of the occasion to give open vent to their emotions, which were a mixture of curiosity and hatred. My feeling that even in this defenceless condition we could not escape insults and my disgust at the demonstration of coarseness overwhelmed me with bitterness until the evening. At the same hour as on the previous day and with the same companion, I began to walk along the gravel path around our house, just as I had done before; and as we passed by the grating of the cellar behind which the dead body had lain I was seized by the memory of the impression which the sight of it had made on me. At the place where the brightly lit park once more lay before me, in the light of the same full moon, I stopped and said to my companion: "We could sit down here in the *grave* ['*Grab*'] – grass ['*Gras*'] and *sink* ['*sinken*'] a serenade." My attention was not caught until I made the second slip; I had corrected the first one without having become conscious of the meaning it contained. I now reflected on them and put them together: "in the grave – to sink!" The following pictures flashed through my mind with lightning rapidity: elves dancing and hovering in the moonlight; our comrade lying on his bier, the impression of movement; some scenes from the burial, the sensation of the disgust I had felt and of the disturbance of our mourning; the memory of some conversations about the infectious illness that had appeared, and the forebodings expressed by several of the officers. Later I remembered that it was the date of my father's death; in view of my usually very poor memory for dates I found this striking.

Subsequent reflection brought home to me the sameness of the external circumstances on the two evenings: the same time of day and lighting conditions, the identical place and companion. I recalled my uneasy feelings when there had been an anxious discussion of the possibility of the influenza spreading; and I remembered at the same time my inner prohibition against letting myself be overcome by fear. I also became conscious of the significance attaching to the order of the words "we could – in the grave – sink",[45] and I realized that only the initial correction of "grave" into "grass", which had taken place unobtrusively, had led to the second slip ("sink" for "sing") in order to ensure that the suppressed complex should have its full expression.

I may add that I suffered at the time from alarming dreams about a very close relative. I repeatedly saw her ill and once actually dead. Just before I was taken prisoner I had received news that the influenza was raging with particular virulence in her part of the world, and I had expressed my lively fears to her about it. Since then I had been out of touch with her. Some months later I received news that she had fallen a victim to the epidemic a fortnight before the episode I have described!"

(31) The next example of a slip of the tongue throws a flash of light on one of those painful conflicts which fall to the lot of a doctor. A man whose illness was in all probability a fatal one, though the diagnosis had not as yet been confirmed, had come to Vienna to await the solution of his problem, and had begged a friend whom he had known since his youth, and who had become a well-known physician, to undertake his treatment. This the friend had with some reluctance finally agreed to do. It was intended that the sick man should stay in a nursing home and the doctor proposed that it should be the 'Hera' sanatorium. "Surely", objected the patient, "that is a home for a special type of case only (a maternity home)." "Oh no!" replied the doctor hastily, "in the 'Hera' they can *umbringen* ['put an end to'] – I mean, *unterbringen* ['take in'] – every type of patient." He then violently disputed the interpretation of his slip. "Surely you won't believe I have hostile impulses against you?" A quarter of an

---

[45]   *Wir könnten ins Grab sinken* – 'we could sink in the grave'. The order of the words, on which the present point turns, is different in English and in German.

hour later, as the doctor was going out with the lady who had undertaken to nurse the invalid, he said: "I can't find anything, and I still don't believe in it. But if it should be so, I am in favour of a strong dose of morphia and a peaceful finish." It emerged that his friend had stipulated that he (the doctor) should shorten his sufferings by means of a drug as soon as it was confirmed that he was past helping. Thus the doctor had in fact undertaken to put an end to his friend.

(32)[46] Here is a quite especially instructive slip of the tongue which I should not like to omit, although according to my authority it is some twenty years old. A lady once advanced the following opinion at a social gathering – and the words show that they were uttered with fervour and under the pressure of a host of secret impulses: "Yes, a woman must be pretty if she is to please men. A man is much better off; as long as he has his *five* straight [*fünf gerade*] limbs he needs nothing more!" This example allows us a good view of the intimate mechanism of a slip of the tongue that results from CONDENSATION or from a CONTAMINATION (cf. p. 47). It is plausible to suppose that we have here a fusion of two turns of phrase with similar meanings:

> as long as he has his *four straight limbs*
> as long as he has his *five wits* about him.

Or the element *straight* [*gerade*] may have been common to two intended expressions which ran:

> as long as he has his *straight* limbs
> to treat all *five(s)* as *even numbers*[47]

There is nothing in fact to prevent us from assuming that BOTH turns of phrase, the one about his five wits and the one about 'the even number five', played their separate parts in causing first a number, and then the mysterious five instead of the simple four, to be introduced into the sentence dealing with the straight limbs. But this fusion would certainly not have come about if, in the form that appeared in the slip of the tongue, it had not had a good meaning of its own – one expressing a cynical truth which could not of course be admitted to undisguised, coming as it did from a woman. – Finally we should not omit to draw attention to the fact that the lady's remark, as worded, could pass just as well for a capital joke as for an amusing slip of the tongue. It is simply a question of whether she spoke the words with a conscious or an unconscious intention. In our case the way the speaker behaved certainly ruled out any notion of conscious intention and excluded the idea of its being a joke.

How closely[48] a slip of the tongue can approximate to a joke is shown in the following case, reported by Rank (1913), in which the woman responsible for the slip actually ended by herself treating it as a joke and laughing at it.

---

[46]   This example was added in 1910.
[47]   'Alle *fünf gerade* sein lassen.' The German *gerade* means both 'straight' and 'even'. The meaning of the phrase, literally translated in the text, is: 'To close one's eyes to irregularities.'
[48]   This paragraph and Example 33 were added in 1917.

(33) A recently married man, whose wife was concerned about preserving her girlish appearance and only with reluctance allowed him to have frequent sexual intercourse, told me the following story which in retrospect both he and his wife found extremely funny. After a night in which he had once again disobeyed his wife's rule of abstinence, he was shaving in the morning in the bedroom which they shared, while his wife was still in bed; and, as he had often done to save trouble, he made use of his wife's powder-puff which was lying on the bedside table. His wife, who was extremely concerned about her complexion, had several times told him not to, and therefore called out angrily: "There you go again, powdering *me* [*mich*] with *your* [*deiner*] puff!" Her husband's laughter drew her attention to her slip (she had meant to say: "you are powdering *yourself* [*dich*] again with *my* [*meiner*] puff") and she herself ended by joining in his laughter. *To powder* [*pudern*] is an expression familiar to every Viennese for 'to copulate'; and a powder-puff is an obvious phallic symbol.

(34)[49] In the following example, too – supplied by Storfer – it might be thought that a joke was intended:

Frau B., who was suffering from an affection of obviously psychogenic origin, was repeatedly recommended to consult a psycho-analyst, Dr. X. She persistently declined to do so, saying that such treatment could never be of any value, as the doctor would wrongly trace everything back to sexual things. A day finally came, however, when she was ready to follow the advice, and she asked: "Nun gut, wann *ordinärt* also dieser Dr. X.?"[50]

(35)[51] The connection between jokes and slips of the tongue is also shown in the fact that in many cases a slip of the tongue is nothing other than an abbreviation:

On leaving school, a girl had followed the ruling fashion of the time by taking up the study of medicine. After a few terms she had changed over from medicine to chemistry. Some years later she described her change of mind in the following words: "I was not on the whole squeamish about dissecting, but when I once had to pull the finger-nails off a dead body, I lost my pleasure in the whole of – *chemistry*."

(36)[52] At this point I insert another slip of the tongue which it needs little skill to interpret. "In an anatomy lesson the professor was endeavouring to explain the nasal cavities, which are notoriously a very difficult department of enterology. When he asked whether his audience had understood his presentation of the subject, he received a general reply in the affirmative. Thereupon the professor, who was known for his high opinion of himself, commented: "I can hardly believe that, since, even in Vienna with its millions of inhabitants, those who understand the nasal cavities can be counted *on one finger*, I mean on the fingers of one hand."

(37) On another occasion the same professor said: "In the case of the female geni-

---

[49] Added in 1924.
[50] What she meant to say was: "All right, then, when does this Dr. X. have his consulting hours?" She should have used the word *ordiniert* for 'has his consulting hours'. Instead she said *"ordinärt,"* which is a non-existent word. *Ordinär*, however, means 'common', 'vulgar'.
[51] Added in 1920.
[52] This example and the following one (No. 37) were added in 1912. They were quoted by Freud in the third and second of his *Introductory Lectures* (1916–1917).

tals, in spite of many *Versuchungen* ['temptations'] – I beg you pardon, *Versuche* ['experiments'] ..."

(38)[53] I am indebted to Dr. Alfred Robitsek of Vienna for drawing my attention to two slips of the tongue which were recorded by an old French writer. I reproduce them without translating them:

Brantôme (1527–1614), *Vies des Dames galantes*, Discours second:

> Si ay-je cogneu une très-belle et honneste dame de par le monde, qui, devisant avec un honneste gentilhomme de la cour des affaires de la guerre durant ces civiles, elle luy dit: "J'ay ouy dire que le roy a faict rompre tous les c ... de ce pays là." Elle vouloit dire *les ponts*. Pensez que, venant de coucher d'avec son mary, ou songeant à son amant, elle avoit encor ce nom frais en la bouche; et le gentilhomme s'en eschauffa en amours d'elle pour ce mot.
>
> Une autre dame que j'ai cogneue, entretenant une autre grand' dame plus qu'elle, et luy louant et exaltant ses beautez, elle luy dit après: "Non, madame, ce que je vous en dis, ce n'est point pour vous *adultérer*"; voulant dire *adulater*, comme elle le rehabilla ainsi: pensez qu'elle songeoit à adultérer.[54]

(39)[55] There are of course more modern examples as well of sexual *doubles entendres* originating in a slip of the tongue. Frau F. was describing her first hour in a language course. "It is very interesting; the teacher is a nice young Englishman. In the very first hour he gave me to understand *durch die Bluse* ['through the blouse'] – I mean, *durch die Blume* [literally, 'through flowers', i.e. 'indirectly'] that he would rather take me for individual tuition." (From Storfer.)

In the psychotherapeutic procedure[56] which I employ for resolving and removing neurotic symptoms I am very often faced with the task of discovering, from the patient's apparently casual utterances and associations, a thought-content which is at pains to remain concealed but which cannot nevertheless avoid unintentionally betraying its existence in a whole variety of ways. Slips of the tongue often perform a most valuable service here, as I could show by some highly convincing and at the same time very singular examples. Thus, for instance, a patient will be speaking of his aunt and, without noticing the slip, will consistently call her "my mother"; or another will refer to her husband as her "brother". In this way they draw my attention to the fact that they have 'identified' these persons with one another – that they have put them into a series which implies a recurrence of the same type in their emotional life. – To give

---

[53] Added in 1910.

[54] Thus I knew a very beautiful and virtuous lady of the world who, discoursing with a virtuous gentleman of the court on the affairs of the war during those civil disturbances, said to him: "I have heard tell that the king had a breach made in all the c ... of that region". She meant to say the 'ponts' ('bridges', which rhymes with the missing French word). One may suppose that, having just lain with her husband, or thinking of her lover, she had this word freshly on her tongue; and the gentleman was fired with love of her on account of this word.

Another lady whom I knew, entertaining another lady of higher rank than herself, and praising her and extolling her beauties, she said after to her: "No, madame, what I say to you is not in order to *adulterate* you"; meaning to say *adulate*, as she clad the word thus anew, one may suppose that she was thinking of adultery.

[55] Added in 1924.

[56] Except where otherwise indicated, the whole of what follows down to p. 68 dates back to 1901.

another example:[57] a young man of twenty introduced himself to me during my consulting hours in these words: "I am the father of So-and-so who came to you for treatment. I beg your pardon, I meant to say I am his brother: he is four years older than I am." I inferred that he intended this slip to express the view that, like his brother, he had fallen ill through the fault of his father; that, like his brother, he wished to be cured; but that his father was the one who most needed to be cured. – At other times an arrangement of words that sounds unusual, or an expression that seems forced, is enough to reveal that a repressed thought is participating in the patient's remarks, which had a different end in view.

What I find, therefore, both in grosser disturbances of speech and in those more subtle ones which can still be subsumed under the heading of 'slips of the tongue', is that it is not the influence of the 'contact effects of the sounds' [p. 52] but the influence of thoughts that lie outside the intended speech which determines the occurrence of the slip and provides an adequate explanation of the mistake. It is not my wish to throw doubt on the laws governing the way in which sounds modify one another; but by themselves these laws do not seem to me to be sufficiently effective to disturb the process of correct speaking. In the cases that I have studied and explored in some detail these laws represent no more than the preformed mechanism which a more remote psychical motive makes use of for its convenience, though without becoming subject to the sphere of influence of these [phonetic] relations. IN A LARGE NUMBER OF SUBSTITUTIONS [p. 47] RESULTING FROM SLIPS OF THE TONGUE SUCH PHONETIC LAWS ARE COMPLETELY DISREGARDED. In this respect I find myself in full agreement with Wundt, who assumes as I do that the conditions governing slips of the tongue are complex and extend far beyond the contact effects of the sounds.

If I accept these 'remoter psychical influences' (as Wundt calls them [cf. above, p. 51]) as established, there is nothing, on the other hand, to prevent me at the same time from allowing that, in situations where speaking is hurried and attention is to some extent diverted, the conditions governing slips of the tongue may easily be confined within the limits defined by Meringer and Mayer.[58] For some of the examples collected by these authors a more complicated explanation nevertheless seems more plausible. Take, for instance, one of those quoted above [p. 46]: *Es war mir auf der* SCHWEST ... BRUST *so schwer.*

Was what happened here simply that the sound *schwe* forced back the equally valent sound *bru* by 'anticipating' it? The idea can hardly be dismissed that the sounds making up *schwe* were further enabled to obtrude in this manner because of a special relation. That could only be the association *Schwester* ['sister'] – *Bruder* ['brother']; perhaps also *Brust der Schwester* ['sister's breast'], which leads one on to other groups of thoughts. It is this invisible helper behind the scenes which lends the otherwise innocent *schwe* the strength to produce a mistake in speaking.

There are other slips of the tongue where we may assume that the true disturbing

---

[57] This example was inserted in 1907.
[58] I.e. may be confined to phonetic factors. Cf. p. 46.

factor is some similarity in sound to obscene words and meanings. Deliberate distortion and deformation of words and expressions, which is so dear to vulgar minds, has the sole purpose of exploiting innocent occasions for hinting at forbidden topics; and this playing with words is so frequent that there would be nothing remarkable in its occurring even when not intended and against one's wishes. To this category no doubt belong such examples as *Eischeissweibchen* (for *Eiweissscheibchen*),[59] *Apopos Fritz* (for *à propos*),[60] *Lokuskapitäl* (for *Lotuskapitäl*),[61] etc.; and perhaps also the *Alabüsterbachse* (*Alabasterbüchse*)[62] of St. Mary Magdalen.[63] – "Ich fordere Sie auf, auf das Wohl unseres Chefs *auf*zustossen" [see p. 46] can hardly be anything other than an unintentional parody which is a perseveration of an intended one. If I were the Principal who was being honoured at the ceremony to which the speaker contributed this slip, I should probably reflect on the cleverness of the Romans in permitting the soldiers of a general who was enjoying a Triumph openly to express in the form of satirical songs their inner criticisms of the man who was being honoured. – Meringer relates that he himself once said to someone, who by reason of being the eldest member of the company was addressed familiarly by the honorific title of *Senexl*[64] or *altes* ['old'] *Senexl*: "*Prost* ['Your health!'], *Senex altesl!*" He was himself shocked at this mistake (Meringer and Mayer 1895: 50). We can perhaps interpret his emotion if we reflect how close *Altesl* comes to the insulting phrase *alter Esel* ['old ass']. There are powerful internal punishments for any breach of the respect due to age (that is, reduced to childhood terms, of the respect due to the father).

I hope that readers will not overlook the difference in value between these interpretations, of which no proof is possible, and the examples that I have myself collected

---

[59]   A meaningless term (literally: 'egg-shit-female'), for 'small slices of white of egg'.

[60]   *Apopos* is a non-existent word; but *Popo* is the nursery word for 'buttocks'.

[61]   A meaningless word, literally: 'W.C. capital', for 'lotus capital', an architectural term.

[62]   A non-existent word (though the middle part of it *Büste* means 'breast') for 'alabaster box'.

[63]   Making slips of the tongue was a symptom of a woman patient of mine which persisted until it was traced back to the childhood joke of replacing *ruinieren* ('ruin') by *urinieren* ('urinate'). – (*Added* 1924:) The temptation to employ the artifice of a slip of the tongue for enabling improper and forbidden words to be freely used forms the basis of Abraham's observations on parapraxes "with an overcompensating purpose". A woman patient was very liable to duplicate the first syllable of proper names by stammering. She changed the name *Protagoras* to 'Protragoras", shortly after having said "A-alexander" instead of *Alexander*. Inquiry revealed that in childhood she had been especially fond of the vulgar joke of repeating the syllables *a* and *po* when they occurred at the beginnings of words, a form of amusement which quite commonly leads to stammering in children. (*A-a* and *Popo* are the German nursery words for 'faeces' and 'buttocks'.) On approaching the name *Protagoras* she became aware of the risk that she might omit the *r* in the first syllable and say "Po-potagoras". As a protection against this danger she held on firmly to this *r*, and inserted another *r* in the second syllable. She acted in the same way on other occasions, distorting the words "*Parterre*" (ground floor) and "*Kondolenz*" ('condolence') so as to avoid *Pater* ('father') and *Kondom* ('condom') which were closely linked to them in her associations. Another of Abraham's patients confessed to an inclination to say "Angora" every time for *angina* – very probably because of a fear of being tempted to replace *angina* by *vagina*. These slips of the tongue owed their existence therefore to the fact that a defensive trend had retained the upper hand instead of the distorting one; and Abraham justly draws attention to the analogy between this process and the formation of symptoms in obsessional neurosis.

[64]   This is the affectionate Austrian form of diminutive applied to the Latin *senex*, 'old man'.

and explained by means of an analysis. But if I still secretly cling to my expectation that even apparently simple slips of the tongue could be traced to interference by a half-suppressed idea that lies OUTSIDE the intended context, I am tempted to do so by an observation of Meringer's which is highly deserving of attention. This author says that it is a curious fact that no one is ready to admit having made a slip of the tongue. There are some very sensible and honest people who are offended if they are told they have made one. I would not venture to put it so generally as does Meringer in saying "no one". But the trace of affect which follows the revelation of the slip, and which is clearly in the nature of shame, has a definite significance. It may be compared to the annoyance we feel when we cannot recall a forgotten name, and to our surprise at the tenacity of an apparently indifferent memory; and it invariably indicates that some motive has contributed to the occurrence of the interference.

The twisting round of a name when it is intentional amounts to an insult; and it might well have the same significance in a whole number of cases where it appears in the form of an unintentional slip of the tongue. The person who, as Mayer reports, said "Freuder" on one occasion instead of *Freud* because he had shortly before mentioned Breuer's name (Meringer and Mayer), and who another time spoke of the 'Freuer-Breudian' method of treatment (ibid., 28), was probably a professional colleague – and one who was not particularly enthusiastic about that method. In the chapter below on slips of the pen I shall report an instance of the distortion of a name which certainly cannot be explained in any other way.[65]

[65] Footnote added 1907: It can in fact be observed that members of the aristocracy in particular are prone to distort the names of the doctors they consult. We may conclude from this that inwardly they despise them, in spite of the courtesy they habitually show them. – [*Added* 1912]: I quote here some pertinent observations on the forgetting of names which come from an account of our subject written in English by Dr. Ernest Jones, at that time in Toronto:

Few people can avoid feeling a twinge of resentment when they find that their name has been forgotten, particularly if it is by some one with whom they had hoped or expected it would be remembered. They instinctively realize that if they had made a greater impression on the persons's mind he would certainly have remembered them again, for the name is an integral part of the personality. Similarly, few things are more flattering to most people than to find themselves addressed by name by a great personage where they could hardly have anticipated it. Napoleon, like most leaders of men, was a master of this art. In the midst of the disastrous Campaign of France, in 1814, he gave an amazing proof of his memory in this direction. When in a town near Craonne he recollected that he had met the mayor, De Bussy, over twenty years ago in the La Fère regiment; the delighted De Bussy at once threw himself into his service with extraordinary zeal. Conversely there is no surer way of affronting some one than by pretending to forget his name; the insinuation is thus conveyed that the person is so unimportant in our eyes that we cannot be bothered to remember his name. This device is often exploited in literature. In Turgenev's *Smoke* the following passage occurs. "So you still find Baden entertaining, M'sieu – Litvinov.' Ratmirov always uttered Litvinov's surname with hesitation, every time, as though he had forgotten it, and could not at once recall it. In this way, as well as by the lofty flourish of his hat in saluting him, he meant to insult his pride." The same author in his *Fathers and Sons* writes: "The Governor invited Kirsanov and Bazarov to his ball, and within a few minutes invited them a second time, regarding them as brothers, and calling them Kisarov." Here the forgetting that he had spoken to them, the mistake in the names, and the inability to distinguish between the two young men, constitute a culmination of disparagement. Falsification of a name has the same significance as forgetting it; it is only a step towards complete amnesia. [Quoted by Freud in German; here given in the original English.]

In these cases the disturbing factor which intervenes is a criticism which has to be set aside since at the moment it does not correspond to the speaker's intention.

Conversely,[66] replacing one name by another, assuming someone else's name, identification by means of a slip over a name, must signify an appreciative feeling which has for some reason to remain in the background for the time being. An experience of this kind from his schooldays is described by Sándor Ferenczi:

When I was in the first form at the *Gymnasium* [Secondary School] I had, for the first time in my life, to recite a poem in public (i.e. in front of the whole class). I was well prepared and was dismayed at being interrupted at the very start by a burst of laughter. The teacher subsequently told me why I had met with this strange reception. I gave the title of the poem "Aus der Ferne [From Afar]" quite correctly, but instead of attributing it to its real author I gave my own name. The poet's name is Alexander (Sándor [in Hungarian]) Petöfi. The exchange of names was helped by our having the same first name; but the real cause was undoubtedly the fact that at that time I identified myself in my secret wishes with the celebrated hero-poet. Even consciously my love and admiration for him bordered on idolatry. The whole wretched ambition-complex is of course to be found as well behind this parapraxis.

A similar identification by means of an exchange of names was reported to me by a young doctor. He had timidly and reverently introduced himself to the famous Virchow[67] as "Dr. Virchow". The professor turned to him in surprise and asked: "Ah! is your name Virchow too?" I do not know how the ambitious young man justified the slip of the tongue he had made – whether he relied upon the flattering excuse that he felt himself so small beside the great name that his own could not fail to slip away from him, or whether he had the courage to admit that he hoped one day to become as great a man as Virchow, and to beg the Professor not to treat him so contemptuously on that account. One of these two thoughts – or perhaps both of them simultaneously – may have confused the young man while he was introducing himself.

From motives of an extremely personal nature I must leave it open whether a similar interpretation is applicable to the following case as well. At the International Congress at Amsterdam in 1907 my theory of hysteria was the subject of lively discussion.[68] In a diatribe against me one of my most vigorous opponents repeatedly made slips of the tongue which took the form of putting himself in my place and speaking in my name. For example, he said: "It is well known that Breuer and *I* have proved ..." where he could only have meant "... Breuer and *Freud* ..." My opponent's name bears not the least resemblance to my own. This example, together with many other cases where a slip of the tongue results in one name replacing another, may serve to remind us that such slips can entirely dispense with the assistance afforded by similarity in sound [cf. p. 65] and can come about with no more support than is provided by hidden factors in the subject-matter.

---

[66]   The next four paragraphs were added in 1910.
[67]   The celebrated pathologist (1821–1902).
[68]   The First International Congress of Psychiatry and Neurology, Amsterdam, September, 1907. The 'opponent" was Aschaffenburg. See Jones.

In other, far more significant, cases[69] it is self-criticism, internal opposition to one's own utterance, that obliges one to make a slip of the tongue and even to substitute the opposite of what one had intended. One then observes in astonishment how the wording of an assertion cancels out its own intention, and how the slip has exposed an inner insincerity.[70] The slip of the tongue here becomes a mode of mimetic expression – often, indeed, for the expression of something one did not wish to say: it becomes a mode of self-betrayal. This was the case, for instance, when a man who did not care for what is called normal sexual intercourse in his relations with women broke into a conversation about a girl who was said to be a flirt, [*kokett*] with the words: "If she had to do with me, she'd soon give up her *koëttieren* [a non-existent word]." There is no doubt that it can only have been another word, namely *koitieren* ['to have coitus'], whose influence was responsible for making this change in the word that was intended, *kokettieren* ['to flirt, coquette']. – Or take the following case: "We have an uncle who for months past had been very much offended because we never visited him. We took his move to a new house as an occasion for paying him a long overdue visit. He seemed very glad to see us, and as we were leaving he said with much feeling: 'I hope from now on I shall see you still *more seldom* than in the past.'"

When the linguistic material happens to be favourable,[71] it often causes slips of the tongue to occur which have the positively shattering result of a revelation, or which produce the full comic effect of a joke. – This is the case in the following example observed and reported by Dr. Reitler:

"That smart new hat – I suppose you *aufgepatzt* [instead of *aufgeputzt* ('trimmed')] it yourself?" said one lady in a voice of admiration to another. She could proceed no further with her intended praise; for the criticism she had silently felt that the hat's trimmings [*Hutaufputz*] were a *Patzerei* ['botch'] had been indicated much too clearly by the unfriendly slip of the tongue for any further phrases of conventional admiration to sound convincing.[72]

The criticism contained in the following example[73] is milder but none the less unambiguous:

A lady who was visiting an acquaintance became very impatient and weary at her tedious and long-winded conversation. When at last she succeeded in tearing herself

---

[69] The first part of this paragraph, down to the words *mode of mimetic expression*, dates back to 1901. The next two and a half sentences were added in 1907, and the final section (beginning: *Or take the following case*) in 1920.

[70] Slips of the tongue of this type are used, for instance, by Anzengruber (the Viennese dramatist (1839–1889) in his *Der G'wissenswurm* to expose the character of the hypocritical legacy-hunter.

[71] This and the following paragraph were added in 1907.

[72] Quoted by Freud in the second of his *Introductory Lectures* (1916–1917). – In the editions of 1910 and 1912 only, the following paragraphs appeared in the text at this point.

"The same is to be found in a case reported by Dr. Ferenczi:

" 'Come *geschminkt* ('painted', i.e., 'with make-up on')' (instead of *geschwind* 'quickly'), said one of my [Hungarian] women patients to her German-speaking mother-in-law. By this slip she gave away precisely what she wanted to conceal from her: namely, her irritation at the old lady's vanity."

It is by no means rare for someone who is not speaking his mother tongue to exploit his clumsiness for the purpose of making highly significant slips of the tongue in the language that is foreign to him."

[73] Added in 1920.

away and taking her leave she was detained by a fresh deluge of words from her companion, who had meanwhile accompanied her into the front hall and now forced her, as she was on the very point of departing, to stand at the door and listen once more. At last she interrupted her hostess with the question: "Are you at home in the front hall [*Vorzimmer*]?" It was not till she saw the other's astonished face that she noticed her slip of the tongue. Weary of being kept standing so long in the front hall she had meant to break off the conversation by asking: "Are you at home in the mornings [*Vormittag*]?", and her slip betrayed her impatience at the further delay.

The next example,[74] which was witnessed by Dr. Max Graf, is a warning that one should keep a watch on oneself.

At the General Meeting of the Concordia, the Society of Journalists, a young member who was invariably hard-up made a violently aggressive speech, and in his excitement spoke of the "*Vorschussmitglieder*" ['lending members'] (instead of "*Vorstandsmitglieder*" ['officers']" or "*Ausschussmitglieder*" ['committee members']"). The latter have the authority to sanction loans, and the young speaker had in fact put in an application for a loan.

We have seen[75] from the example of '*Vorschwein*' [p. 49] that a slip of the tongue can easily occur if an effort has been made to suppress insulting words. In this way one gives vent to one's feelings:

A photographer who had made a resolution to refrain from zoological terms in dealing with his clumsy employees, addressed an apprentice – who tried to empty out a large dish that was full to the brim and in doing so naturally spilt half the contents on the floor – in the following words: "But, man, *schöpsen Sie*[76] some of it off first." And soon after this, in the course of a tirade against a female assistant who had nearly spoilt a dozen valuable plates by her carelessness, he said: "Are you so *hornverbrannt*...?"[77]

The next example[78] shows how a slip of the tongue resulted in a serious self-betrayal. Certain details in it justify its repetition in full from the account given by Brill in the *Zentralblatt für Psychoanalyse*, Volume II.[79]

I went for a walk one evening with Dr. Frink, and we discussed some of the business of the New York Psychoanalytic Society. We met a colleague, Dr. R., whom I had not seen for years and of whose private life I knew nothing. We were very pleased to meet again, and on my invitation he accompanied us to a café, where we spent two hours in lively conversation. He seemed to know some details about me, for after the usual greetings he asked after my small child and told me that he heard about me from time to time from a mutual friend and

---

[74] This was added in 1907; it was later quoted by Freud in the third of his *Introductory Lectures* (1916–1917).

[75] This and the following paragraph were added in 1920.

[76] He meant to say 'draw', which would have been *schöpfen Sie*. Instead he used *schöpsen Sie*, which is meaningless. The word *Schöps*, however, means 'sheep' or 'silly fellow'.

[77] Here he meant to say *hirnverbrannt*, 'idiotic', literally 'with your brain (*Hirn*) burnt up'. The word he used instead, a non-existent term, would mean 'with your horn (*Horn*) burnt up'. The word *Hornvieh*, literally 'horned cattle', is used in the sense of 'fool'.

[78] Added in 1912.

[79] In the *Zentrallblatt* the paper was ascribed in error to Ernest Jones. [The version given here is the one to be found in Brill (1912), slightly modified].

had been interested in my work ever since he had read about it in the medical press. To my question as to whether he was married he gave a negative answer, and added: "Why should a man like me marry?"

On leaving the café, he suddenly turned to me and said: "I should like to know what you would do in a case like this: I know a nurse who was named as co-respondent in a divorce case. The wife sued the husband and named her as co-respondent, and *he* got the divorce.[80] I interrupted him, saying: "You mean *she* got the divorce." He immediately corrected himself, saying: "Yes, of course, *she* got the divorce", and continued to tell how the nurse had been so affected by the divorce proceedings and the scandal that she had taken to drink, had become very nervous, and so on; and he wanted me to advise him how to treat her.

As soon as I had corrected his mistake I asked him to explain it, but I received the usual surprised answers: had not everyone a right to make a slip of the tongue? it was only an accident, there was nothing behind it, and so on. I replied that there must be a reason for every mistake in speaking, and that, had he not told me earlier that he was unmarried, I would be tempted to suppose he himself was the hero of the story; for in that case the slip could be explained by his wish that he had obtained the divorce rather than his wife, so that he should not have (by our matrimonial laws) to pay alimony, and so that he could marry again in New York State. He stoutly denied my conjecture, but the exaggerated emotional reaction which accompanied it, in which he showed marked signs of agitation followed by laughter, only strengthened my suspicions. To my appeal that he should tell the truth in the interests of science, he answered: "Unless you wish me to lie you must believe that I was never married, and hence your psycho-analytic interpretation is all wrong." He added that someone who paid attention to every triviality was positively dangerous. Then he suddenly remembered that he had another appointment and left us.

Both Dr. Frink and I were still convinced that my interpretation of his slip of the tongue was correct, and I decided to corroborate or disprove it by further investigation. Some days later I visited a neighbour, an old friend of Dr. R., who was able to confirm my explanation in every particular. The divorce proceedings had taken place some weeks before, and the nurse was cited as co-respondent. Dr. R. is to-day thoroughly convinced of the correctness of the Freudian mechanisms.

The self-betrayal is equally unmistakable in the following case,[81] reported by Otto Rank:

A father who was without any patriotic feelings, and who wished to educate his children so that they too should be free from what he regarded as a superfluous sentiment, was criticizing his sons for taking part in a patriotic demonstration; when they protested that their uncle had also taken part in it, he replied: "*He* is the one person you should not imitate: he is an *idiot*." On seeing his children's look of astonishment at their father's unusual tone, he realized that he had made a slip of the tongue, and added apologetically: 'I meant to say *'patriot'*, of course."

Here is a slip of the tongue[82] which was interpreted as a self betrayal by the other party to the conversation. It is reported by Stärcke, who adds a pertinent comment, though it goes beyond the task of interpreting the slip.

[80] In the German version of Brill's paper the following footnote appeared at this point: "By our laws a divorce cannot be obtained unless it is proved that one party has committed adultery; and in fact the divorce is granted only to the innocent party."
[81] Added in 1912.
[82] This example and the two following ones (i.e. down to the middle of the next page) were added in 1917.

A woman dentist promised her sister that she would have a look some time to see if there was *Kontakt* ['contact'] between two of her molars (that is, to see if the lateral surfaces of the molars were touching each other so that no fragments of food could lodge in between). Her sister finally complained about having to wait so long for this inspection, and jokingly said: "She's probably treating a colleague at the moment, but her sister has to go on waiting." The dentists eventually examined her, found there was in fact a small cavity in one of the molars, and said: "I didn't think it was in such a bad way – I thought it was merely that you had no *Kontant* [ready money] – I mean *Kontakt*." "You see?" laughed her sister; "your greed is the only reason why you made me wait so much longer than your paying patients!"

(Obviously I should not add my own associations to hers or base any conclusions on them, but when I heard of this slip of the tongue it at once sprang to my mind that these two pleasant and gifted yound ladies are unmarried and have in fact very little to do with young men, and I asked myself whether they would have more *contact* with young people if they had more *ready money*.)

In the following example, too, reported by Reik (1915), the slip of the tongue amounts to a self-betrayal:

A girl was to become engaged to a young man whom she did not care for. To bring the two young people closer together, their parents arranged a meeting which was attended by the parties to the intended match. The young girl possessed sufficient self-control to prevent her suitor, who behaved in a very on-coming manner towards her, from detecting her antipathy to him. But when her mother ashed her how she liked the young man she answered politely: "Well enough. He's most *liebenswidrig!*"[83]

Equally self-revealing is the following, which Rank (1913) describes as a "witty slip of the tongue".

A married woman, who enjoyed hearing anecdotes and who was said not to be altogether averse to extra-marital affairs if they were reinforced by adequate gifts, was told the following time-honoured story, not without design on his part, by a young man who was eager to obtain her favours. One of two business friends was trying to obtain the favours of his partner's somewhat prudish wife. In the end she consented to grant them to him in exchange for a present of a thousand gulden.[84] When, there-fore, her husband was about to start on a journey, his partner borrowed a thousand gulden from him and promised to pay them back next day to his wife. He then, of course, paid the sum to the wife, implying that it was the reward for her favours; and she supposed she had been caught at last when her husband on his return asked for the thousand gulden and thus found insult added to injury. When the young man reached the point in his story at which the seducer says: "I'll *repay* the money to your wife tomorrow", his listener interrupted with the highly revealing words: "Let me see, haven't you *repaid* me that – I'm sorry – I mean *told*[85] me that already?" She could hardly have given a clearer indication, without actually putting it into words, of her willingness to offer herself on the same terms.

---

[83]   She intended to say *liebenswürdig*, 'agreeable' (literally 'worthy of love'). The word she actually used, *liebenswidrig*, would mean literally 'repelling to love'.

[84]   About £80 or $400.

[85]   There is no resemblance between the two German words for 'repaid' and 'told.'

A good example[86] of this kind of self-betrayal, which did not lead to serious consequences, is reported by Tausk under the title of 'The Faith of our Fathers'. "As my fiancée was a Christian", Herr A related,

and was unwilling to adopt the Jewish faith, I myself was obliged to be converted from Judaism to Christianity so that we could marry. I did not change my religion without some internal resistance, but I felt it was justified by the purpose behind it, the more so because it involved abandoning no more than an outward adherence to Judaism, not a religious conviction (which I had never had). Notwithstanding this, I always continued later on to acknowledge the fact of my being a Jew, and few of my acquaintances know I am baptized. I have two sons by this marriage, who were given Christian baptism. When the boys were sufficiently old they were told of their Jewish background, so as to prevent them from being influenced by anti-semitic views at their school and from turning against their father for such a superfluous reason. Some years ago I and my children, who were then at their primary school, were staying with the family of a teacher at the summer resort in D. One day while we were sitting at tea with our otherwise friendly hosts, the lady of the house, who had no inkling of her summer guests' Jewish ancestry, launched some very sharp attacks on the Jews. I ought to have made a bold declaration of the facts in order to set my sons the example of having the courage of one's convictions, but I was afraid of the unpleasant exchanges that usually follow an avowal of this sort. Besides, I was alarmed at the possibility of having to leave the good lodgings we had found and of thus spoiling my own and my children's in any case limited holiday period, should our hosts' behaviour towards us take an unfriendly turn because of the fact that we were Jews. As however I had reason to expect that my sons, in their candid and ingenuous way, would betray the momentous truth if they heard any more of the conversation, I tried to get them to leave the company by sending them into the garden. I said: "Go into the garden, *Juden* ['Jews']", quickly correcting it to "*Jungen* ['youngsters']". In this way I enabled the 'courage of my convictions' to be expressed in a parapraxis. The others did not in fact draw any conclusions from my slip of the tongue, since they attached no significance to it; but I was obliged to learn the lesson that the 'faith of our fathers' cannot be disavowed with impunity if one is a son and has sons of one's own.

The effect produced by the following slip of the tongue,[87] which I would not report had not the magistrate himself made a note of it for this collection during the court proceedings, is anything but innocent:

A soldier charged with housebreaking stated in evidence: "Up to now I've not been discharged from military *Diebsstellung*;[88] so at the moment I'm still in the army."

A slip of the tongue[89] has a more cheering effect during psycho-analytic work, when it serves as a means of providing the doctor with a confirmation that may be very welcome to him if he is engaged in a dispute with the patient. I once had to interpret a patient's dream in which the name *Jauner* occurred. The dreamer knew someone of that name, but it was impossible to discover the reason for his appearing

---

[86] Added in 1919.

[87] Added in 1920.

[88] He meant to say *Dienststellung*, 'service', literally 'service [*Dienst*] position [*Stellung*]'. Instead he said "*Diebstellung*", which would mean literally 'thief position'.

[89] This paragraph and the following one were added in 1907. The 'Jauner' slip was also quoted by Freud in his late paper on "Constructions in Analysis" (1937).

in the context of the dream; I therefore ventured to suggest that it might be merely because of his name, which sounds like the term of abuse *Gauner* ['swindler']. My patient hastily and vigorously contested this; but in doing so he made a slip of the tongue which confirmed my guess, since he confused the same letters once more. His answer was: "That seems to me too *jewagt* [instead of *gewagt* ('far-fetched')]".[90] When I had drawn his attention to his slip, he accepted my interpretation.

If one of the parties involved in a serious argument makes a slip of the tongue which reverses the meaning of what he intended to say, it immediately puts him at a disadvantage with his opponent, who seldom fails to make the most of his improved position.

This makes it clear[91] that people give slips of the tongue and other parapraxes the same interpretation that I advocate in this book, even if they do not endorse theoretically the view I put forward, and even if they are disinclined, so far as it applies to themselves, to renounce the convenience that goes along with tolerating parapraxes. The amusement and derision which such oral slips are certain to evoke at the crucial moment can be taken as evidence against what purports to be the generally accepted convention that a mistake in speaking is a *lapsus linguae* and of no psychological significance. It was no less a person than the German Imperial Chancellor Prince Bülow who protested on these lines in an effort to save the situation, when the wording of his speech in defence of his Emperor (in November 1907) was given the opposite meaning by a slip of the tongue. "As for the present, the new epoch of the Emperor Wilhelm II, I can only repeat what I said a year ago, namely that *it would be unfair and unjust to speak of a coterie of responsible advisers round our Emperor ...*" (loud cries of 'irresponsible') "*... irresponsible advisers*. Forgive the *lapsus linguae*." (Laughter.)

In this case, as a result of the accumulation of negatives, Prince Bülow's sentence was somewhat obscure; sympathy for the speaker and consideration for his difficult position prevented this slip from being put to any further use against him. A year later another speaker in the same place was not so fortunate. He wished to appeal for a demonstration 'with no reserves' [*rückhaltlos*] in support of the Emperor, and in doing so was warned by a bad slip of the tongue that other emotions were to be found within his loyal breast. Lattmann (German National Party): "On the question of the address our position is based on the standing orders of the Reichstag. According to them the Reichstag is entitled to tender such an address to the Emperor. It is our belief that the united thoughts and wishes of the German people are bent on achieving a *united demonstration* in this matter as well, and if we can do so in a form that takes the Emperor's feelings fully into account, then we should do so *spinelessly* [*rückgratlos*] as well." (Loud laughter which continued for some minutes.) "Gentlemen, I should have said not *rückgratlos* but *rückhaltlos* ['unreservedly']" (laughter), "and at this

---

[90]   In vulgar speech, particularly in North Germany, *g* at the beginning of a word is often pronounced like the German *j* (English *y* instead of like the hard English *g*).

[91]   This paragraph and the two following ones were added in 1910.

difficult time even our Emperor accepts a manifestation by the people – one made without reserve – such as we should like to see".[92]

The [social-democratic paper] *Vorwärts* of November 12, 1908, did not miss the opportunity of pointing to the psychological significance of this slip of the tongue:

Probably never before in any parliament has a member, through an involuntary self-accusation, characterized his own attitude and that of the parliamentary majority towards the Emperor so exactly as did the anti-Semitic Lattmann, when, speaking with solemn emotion on the second day of the debate, he slipped into an admission that he and his friends wished to express their opinion to the Emperor *spinelessly*. Loud laughter from all sides drowned the remaining words of this unhappy man, who thought it necessary explicitly to stammer out by way of apology that he really meant '*unreservedly*'.

I will add a further instance,[93] in which the slip of the tongue assumed the positively uncanny characteristics of a prophecy. Early in 1923 there was a great stir in the world of finance when the very young banker X. – probably one of the newest of the *nouveaux riches* in W., and at any rate the richest and youngest – obtained possession, after a short struggle, of a majority of the shares of the – Bank; and as a further consequence, a remarkable General Meeting took place at which the old directors of the bank, financiers of the old type, were not re-elected, and young X. became president of the bank. In the valedictory speech which the managing director Dr. Y. went on to deliver in honour of the old president, who had not been re-elected, a number of the audience noticed a distressing slip of the tongue which occurred again and again. He continually spoke of the *expiring* [*dahinscheidend*] president instead of the *outgoing* [*ausscheidend*] president. As it turned out, the old president who was not re-elected died a few days after this meeting. He was, however, over eighty years old. (From Storfer.)

A good example of a slip of the tongue[94] whose purpose is not so much to betray the speaker as to give the listener in the theatre his bearings, is to be found in [Schiller's] *Wallenstein* (*Piccolomini*, Act I, Scene 5); and it shows us that the dramatist, who here availed himself of this device, was familiar with the mechanism and meaning of slips of the tongue. In the preceding scene Max Piccolomini has ardently espoused the Duke's [Wallenstein's] cause, and has been passionately describing the blessings of peace, of which he has become aware on the course of a journey while escorting Wallenstein's daughter to the camp. As he leaves the stage, his father [Octavio] and Questenberg, the emissary from the court, are plunged in consternation. Scene 5 continues:

QUESTENBERG   Alas, alas! and stands it so?
                What friend! and do we let him go away
                In this delusion – let him go away?
                Not call him back immediately, not open
                His eyes upon the spot?

[92] Freud later alluded to this slip in the fourth of his *Introductory Lectures* (1916–1917).
[93] Added in 1924.
[94] Added in 1907.

OCTAVIO (*recovering himself out of a deep study*)

> He has now open'd mine,
> And I see more than pleases me.

QUEST.   What is it?
OCT.   Curse on this journey!
QUEST.   But why so? What is it?
OCT.   Come, come along, friend! I must follow up
> The ominous track immediately. Mine eyes
> Are open'd now, and I must use them. Come!
> (*Draws Q. on with him*)
QUEST.   What now? *Where* go you then?
OCT.   To her herself.
QUEST.   TO –
OCT.   (*correcting himself*)   To the Duke. Come let us go.

[Coleridge's translation.]

The small slip of saying *to her* instead of *to him* is meant to reveal to us that the father has seen through his son's motive for espousing the Duke's cause, while the courtier complains that he is "talking absolute riddles" to him.[95]

Another example[96] in which a dramatist makes use of a slip of the tongue has been discovered by Otto Rank (1910) in Shakespeare. I quote Rank's account.

A slip of the tongue occurs in Shakespeare's *Merchant of Venice* (Act III, Scene 2),which is from the dramatic point of view extremely subtly motivated and which is put to brilliant technical use. Like the slip in *Wallenstein* to which Freud has drawn attention, it shows that dramatists have a clear understanding of the mechanism and meaning of this kind of parapraxis and assume that the same is true of their audience. Portia, who by her father's will has been bound to the choice of a husband by lot, has so far escaped all her unwelcome suitors by a fortunate chance. Having at last found in Bassanio the suitor who is to her liking, she has cause to fear that he too will choose the wrong casket. She would very much like to tell him that even so he could rest assured of her love; but she is prevented by her vow. In this internal conflict the poet makes her say to the suitor she favours:

> I pray you tarry; pause a day or two,
> Before you hazard: for, in choosing wrong,
> I lose your company; therefore, forbear awhile:
> There's something tells me (*but it is not love*)
> I would not lose you...
>
>   ... I could teach you
> How to choose right, but then I am forsworn;
> So will I never be; so may you miss me;
> But if you do you'll make me wish a sin,
> That I have been forsworn. Beshrew your eyes,
> They have o'erlooked me, and divided me;
> *One half of me is yours, the other half yours, –*
> *Mine own, I would say*; but if mine, then yours,
> And so all yours.

[95]   Octavio realizes that his son's motive springs from love of the Duke's daughter. – This example and the next were quoted by Freud in the second of his *Introductory Lectures* (1916–1917).
[96]   Added in 1912.

The thing of which she wanted to give him only a very subtle hint, because she should really have concealed it from him altogether, namely, that even before he made his choice she was *wholly* his and loved him – it is precisely this that the poet, with a wonderful psychological sensitivity, causes to break through openly in her slip of the tongue; and by this artistic device he succeeds in relieving both the lover's unbearable uncertainty and the suspense of the sympathetic audience over the outcome of his choice.[97]

In view of the interest that is lent to our theory of slips of the tongue by support of this nature from great writers, I feel justified in citing a third such instance which has been reported by Ernest Jones[98] (1911):

In a recently published article Otto Rank drew our attention to a pretty instance of how Shakespeare caused one of his characters, Portia, to make a slip of the tongue which revealed her secret thoughts to an attentive member of the audience. I propose to relate a similar example from *The Egoist*, the masterpiece of the greatest English novelist, George Meredith. The plot of the novel is, shortly, as follows: Sir Willoughby Patterne, an aristocrat greatly admired by his circle, becomes engaged to a Miss Constantia Durham. She discovers in him an intense egoism, which he skilfully conceals from the world, and to escape the marriage she elopes with a Captain Oxford. Some years later Patterne becomes engaged to a Miss Clara Middleton, and most of the book is taken up with a detailed description of the conflict that arises in her mind on also discovering his egoism. External circumstances, and her conception of honour, hold her to her pledge, while he becomes more and more distasteful in her eyes. She partly confides in his cousin and secretary, Vernon Whitford, the man whom she ultimately marries; but from loyalty to Patterne and other motives he stands aloof.

In a soliloquy about her sorrow Clara speaks as follows: "If some noble gentleman could see me as I am and not disdain to aid me! Oh! to be caught out of this prison of thorns and brambles. I cannot tear my own way out. I am a coward. A beckoning of a finger[99] would change me, I believe. I could fly bleeding and through hootings to a comrade ... Constantia met a soldier. Perhaps she prayed and her prayer was answered. She did ill. But, oh, how I love her for it! His name was Harry Oxford ... She did not waver, she cut the links, she signed herself over. Oh, brave girl, what do you think of me? But I have no Harry Whitford; I am alone ..' The sudden consciousness that she had put another name for Oxford struck her a buffet, drowning her in crimson."

The fact that both men's names end in "ford" evidently renders the confounding of them more easy, and would by many be regarded as an adequate cause for this, but the real underlying motive for it is plainly indicated by the author. In another passage the same *lapsus* occurs, and is followed by the spontaneous hesitation and sudden change of subject that one is familiar with a psycho-analysis and in Jung's association experiments when a half-conscious complex is touched. Sir Willoughby patronisingly says of Whitford: "False alarm. The resolution to do anything unaccustomed is quite beyond poor old Vernon.'" Clara replies: "But if Mr Oxford-Whitford ... your swans, coming sailing up the lake, how beautiful they look when they are indignant! I was going to ask you, surely men witnessing a marked admiration for someone else will naturally be discouraged?" Sir Willoughby stiffened with sudden enlightenment."

[97] In reproducing this in the second of his *Introductory Lectures*, Freud added a further comment of his own.
[98] This example – also added in 1912 – appears in Freud's book in a German translation. We here give the original English.
[99] Note by the [German] translator [J. Theodor von Kalmar]: I had originally proposed to translate the English words *beckoning of a finger* by *leiser Wink* ['slight hint'] till I realized that by suppressing the word *finger* I was robbing the sentence of a psychological subtlety.

In still another passage, Clara by another *lapsus* betrays her secret wish that she was on a more intimate footing with Vernon Whitford. Speaking to a boy friend, she says: "'Tell Mr. Vernon – tell Mr. Whitford.'"[100]

The view[101] of slips of the tongue which is advocated here can meet the test even in the most trivial examples. I have repeatedly been able to show that the most insignificant and obvious errors in speaking have their meaning and can be explained in the same way as the more striking instances. A woman patient who was acting entirely against my wishes in planning a short trip to Budapest, but who was determined to have her own way, justified herself by telling me that she was going for only three days; but she made a slip of the tongue and actually said "only three *weeks*". She was betraying the fact that, to spite me, she would rather spend three weeks than three days there in the company which I considered unsuitable for her. – One evening I wanted to excuse myself for not having fetched my wife home from the theatre, and said: "I was at the theatre at ten past ten." I was corrected: "You mean ten *to* ten." Of course I meant ten *to* ten. *After* ten o'clock would have been no excuse. I had been told that the theatre bills said the performance ended before ten. When I reached the theatre I found the entrance-hall in darkness and the theatre empty. The performance had in fact ended earlier and my wife had not waited for me. When I looked at the clock it was only five to ten. But I decided to make my case out more favourable when I got home and to say it had been ten to ten. Unfortunately, my slip of the tongue spoilt my plan and revealed my disingenuousness, by making me confess more than there was to confess.

This leads on to those speech-disturbances which cannot any longer be described as slips of the tongue because what they affect is not the individual word but the rhythm and execution of a whole speech: disturbances like, for instance, stammering and stuttering caused by embarrassment. But here too, as in the former cases, it is a question of an internal conflict, which is betrayed to us by the disturbance in speech. I really do not think that anyone would make a slip of the tongue in an audience with his Sovereign, in a serious declaration of love or in defending his honour and name before a jury – in short, on all those occasions in which a person is heart and soul engaged. Even in forming an appreciation of an author's style we are permitted and accustomed to apply the same elucidatory principle which we cannot dispense with in tracing the origins of individual mistakes in speech. A clear and unambiguous manner of writing shows us that here the author is at one with himself; where we find a forced and involved expression which (to use an apt phrase) is aimed at more than one target, we may recognize the intervention of an insufficiently worked-out, com-

---

[100] [*Footnote added* 1920:] Other instances of slips of the tongue which the writer intends to be taken as having a meaning and usually as being self-revealing can be found in Shakespeare's Richard II (Act II, Scene 2), and in Schiller's *Don Carlos* (Act II, Scene 8; a slip made by Princess Eboli). There would doubtless be no difficulty in extending this list.

[101] This paragraph was added in 1907; the one which follows dates back to 1901.

plicating thought, or we may hear the stifled voice of the author's self-criticism.[102]

Since this book first appeared [103] friends and colleagues who speak other languages have begun to turn their attention to slips of the tongue which they have been able to observe in countries where their language is spoken. As was to be expected they have found that the laws governing parapraxes are independent of the linguistic material; and they have made the same interpretations that have been exemplified here in instances coming from speakers of the German language. Of countless examples I include only one:

Brill (1909) reports of himself: "A friend described to me a nervous patient and wished to know whether I could benefit him. I remarked: 'I believe that in time I could remove all his symptoms by psycho-analysis because it is a *durable* case' – wishing to say *curable*!'[104]

In conclusion,[105] for the benefit of readers who are prepared to make a certain effort and to whom psycho-analysis is not unfamiliar, I will add an example which will enable them to form some picture of the mental depths into which the pursuit even of a slip of the tongue can lead. It has been reported by Jekels.

On December 11, a lady of my acquaintance addressed me (in Polish) in a somewhat challenging and overbearing manner, as follows: "Why did I say to-day that I have twelve fingers?" At my request she gave an account of the scene in which the remark was made. She had got ready to go out with her daughter to pay a visit, and had asked her daughter – a case of dementia praecox then in remission – to change her blouse; and this she in fact did, in the adjoining room. On re-entering, the daughter found her mother busy cleaning her nails, and the following conversation ensued:

---

[102] *Footnote added* 1910:   Ce qu'on conçoit bien
                                   S'announce clairement
                                   Et les mots pour le dire
                                   Arrivent aisément.

                                   [What is well thought out
                                   Presents itself with clarity,
                                   And the words to express it
                                   Come easily.]
                                          Boileau: *Art poétique.*

[In a letter to Fliess of September 21, 1899, Freud applied a criticism of this precise kind to what he felt was his own unsatisfactory style in *The Interpretation of Dreams*. The passage will be found quoted in *Standard Ed.*, 4, xx.

[103] This paragraph and the example that follows were added in 1912.

[104] This example is given in English in the original. – In the 1912 edition only, the following passage appeared in the text at this point: An extremely instructive instance of the way in which a simple slip of the tongue may be made use of in a psycho-analysis has been reported by Stekel (1910):

' "A patient suffering from agoraphobia said during the analysis: 'If I start on a subject I keep "*dablei*" [for "*dabei*", "at it"] with some obstinacy.' When his attention had been drawn to his slip, he went on: 'I have done what children do and said "l" instead of "ı" – "blei" instead of "brei" ', so making a second slip of the tongue.

' "This slip was obviously of great significance. The syllables 'bei – brei – blei' [in German: 'at', 'broth', 'lead'] carried important associations."

[105] The rest of the chapter was added in 1917.

Daughter: "There! I'm ready now and you're not!"

Mother: "Yes, but you have only one blouse and I have *twelve nails*."

Daughter: "What?"

Mother (impatiently): "Well, of course I have; after all, I have *twelve fingers*."

A colleague who heard the story at the same time as I did asked what occurred to her in connection with *twelve*. She answered equally quickly and definitely: "Twelve means nothing to me – it is not the date of anything (of importance)."

To *finger* she gave the following association after a little hesitation: "Some of my husband's family were born with six fingers on their feet (Polish has no specific word for 'toe'). When our children were born they were immediately examined to see if they had six fingers." For external reasons the analysis was not continued that evening.

'Next morning, December 12, the lady visited me and told me with visible excitement: "What do you suppose has happened? For about the last twenty years I have been sending congratulations to my husband's elderly uncle on his birthday, which is to-day, and I have always written him a letter on the 11th. This time I forgot about it and had to send a telegram just now."

I myself remembered, and I reminded the lady, how positive she had been the evening before in dismissing my colleague's question about the number twelve – which was in fact very well fitted to remind her of the birthday – by remarking that the twelfth was not a date of importance to her.

She then admitted that this uncle of her husband's was a wealthy man from whom she had in fact always expected to inherit something, quite especially in her present straitened financial circumstances. Thus, for instance, it was he, or rather his death, that had immediately sprung to her mind a few days before when an acquaintance of hers had predicted from cards that she would receive a large sum of money. It flashed through her mind at once that the uncle was the only person from whom money could possibly come to her or her children; and this same scene also instantly reminded her of the fact that this uncle's wife had once promised to remember the lady's children in her will. But in the meanwhile she had died intestate; had she perhaps given her husband appropriate instructions?

The death-wish against the uncle must clearly have emerged with very great intensity, for she said to the friend who made the prophecy: "You encourage people to make away with others." In the four or five days that elapsed between the prophecy and the uncle's birthday she was constantly looking at the obituary columns in the newspapers from the town where the uncle lived. Not surprisingly, therefore, in view of the intensity of her wish for his death, the event and the date of the birthday he was about to celebrate were so strongly suppressed that not only was a resolution which had been carried out for years forgotten in consequence, but even my colleague's question failed to bring them to consciousness.

In the slip "twelve fingers" the suppressed "twelve" had broken through and had helped to determine the parapraxis. I say "*helped* to determine", for the striking association to "finger" leads us to suspect the existence of some further motivations. It also explains why the "twelve" had falsified precisely this most innocent phrase, "ten fingers". The association ran: "Some members of my husband's family were born with six fingers on their feet." Six toes are a sign of a particular abnormality. Thus six fingers mean *one* abnormal child and twelve fingers *two* abnormal children. And that was really the fact in this case. The lady had married at a very early age; and the only legacy left her by her husband, a highly eccentric and abnormal person who took his own life shortly after their marriage, were two children whom the doctors repeatedly pronounced to be abnormal and victims of a grave hereditary taint derived from their father. The elder daughter recently returned home after a severe catatonic attack; soon afterwards, the younger daughter, now at the age of puberty, also fell ill from a serious neurosis.

The fact that the children's abnormality is here linked with the death-wish against the uncle, and is condensed with this far more strongly suppressed and psychically more powerful element, enables us to assume the existence of a second determinant for the slip of the tongue, namely a *death-wish against the abnormal children.*

But the special significance of twelve as a death wish is already indicated by the fact that the uncle's birthday was very intimately associated in the lady's mind with the idea of his death. For her husband had taken his life on the 13th – one day, that is, after the uncle's birthday; and the uncle's wife had said to the young widow: "Yesterday he was sending his congratulations, so full of warmth and kindness – and to-day ...!"

I may add that the lady had real enough reasons as well for wishing her children dead; for they brought her no pleasure at all, only grief and severe restrictions on her independence, and she had for their sake renounced all the happiness that love might have brought her. On this occasion she had in fact gone to exceptional lengths to avoid putting the daughter with whom she was going to pay the visit in a bad mood; and it may be imagined what demands this makes on anyone's patience and self-denial where the case is one of dementia praecox, and how many angry impulses have to be suppressed in the process.

The meaning of the parapraxis would accordingly be:

"The uncle shall die, these abnormal children shall die (the whole of this abnormal family, as it were), and I will get their money."

This parapraxis bears, in my view, several indications of an unusual structure:

(a) Two determinants were present in it, condensed in a single element.

(b) The presence of the two determinants was reflected in the doubling of the slip of the tongue (twelve nails, twelve fingers).

(c) It is a striking point that one of the meanings of "twelve", viz., the twelve fingers which expressed the children's abnormality, stood for an indirect form of representation; the psychical abnormality was here represented by the physical abnormality, and the highest part of the body by the lowest.

PREDICTING SLIPS OF THE TONGUE*

RULON WELLS

A professor comparing the record of Scholars of the House with other Yale students was heard to speak of their "overall battering average". Another man telling his wife about a party reported that "the conversation slagged slightly." One time I was giving my opinion of a certain person and said, "He knows nothing at ever." A radio announcer predicted that the day's weather would be "coldy and winder", and a housewife hearing this announcement decided to call off her planned trip to the "shoe-shore".

These were slips of the tongue. The professor meant to say "batting average"; the other man intended to say "the conversation lagged slightly." When I came out with "He knows nothing at ever", I was wavering between "nothing at all" and "nothing whatever". The phrase "coldy and winder" is a lapse for "colder and windy"; and the word "shore" in "shoe-shore" is an ingenious blend of "shop" and "store".

All the world knows that Sigmund Freud found great significance in lapses such as these. He spectacularly showed how slips of the tongue or pen, as well as forgettings, slight or major accidents, and other lapses might reveal deeply hidden intentions on the part of the person committing them. These instances of the "psychopathology of everyday life" could be as illuminating as dreams for diagnostic purposes. Freud's *Interpretation of Dreams* (1900) was a great triumph; but in a way the *Psychopathology of Everyday Life* (1901) was even more brilliant. Dreams had always been noticed, studied, and interpreted, but slips of the tongue and other lapses had either been ignored or, at best, drawn passing attention as amusing quirks. Freud saw what everybody had seen, but he saw it with new eyes; he saw the meaning of it. Like Galton's insight into the use of fingerprints and Douglass's perception that tree-rings could be used to date archeological remains, Freud's grasp of the diagnostic value of lapses was a great idea, whether or not his own particular theory ultimately stands up.

There are several things that a scientist might do with lapses. First of all, he might simply classify them. As for slips in speaking, writing, and reading, this had already been done in 1895 by a Viennese colleague of Freud's, the linguist Rudolf Meringer. But Freud was not content with mere DESCRIPTION of the facts; he wanted to EXPLAIN

* Reprinted from *The Yale Scientific Magazine* XXVI(3): 9–30 (1951).

them. He shared the general view of scientists then and today that an explanatory science is more advanced and more satisfying, because it is more powerful, than a merely descriptive science. And so Freud gave a causal explanation of lapses in terms of his general theory.

Now it is generally agreed that an explanatory science will do three things at once. First, it will explain certain phenomena. Second, it will treat those phenomena as signs or symptoms of other phenomena. And third, it will predict phenomena that have not been observed at the time it makes its prediction.

Freud analyzed many cases of lapses, and explained them by his theory of the unconscious. And he treated these lapses as symptoms, having diagnostic value. But he paid relatively little attention to the third aspect, i.e., to prediction. Successful prediction is regarded as the final proof of a theory, and it has been a stock criticism of Freudianism that it is in large part incapable of this rigorous proof. However that may be, it is a striking fact that in his monograph on the psychopathology of everyday life Freud explains and diagnoses many lapses, but does not record any attempts at predicting them.

"BATTLE-SCARRED, BOTTLE-SCARRED VET"

In fact, Freud's theory as it stands could not predict any concrete, specific slips of the tongue, and I shall argue that this is partly because of his neglect of the linguistic factor. The neglect is deliberate; Freud was perfectly familiar with Meringer's work, and indeed drew many of his examples from it. But he dismissed Meringer's approach. It would be pointless to defend Meringer; what is important is to take up where Meringer left off, with the hope of rendering a service both to psychology and to linguistics. Freud's writings convey the strong impression, even if they never come right out and say it, that slips of the tongue, like forgettings and other lapses, are mere vehicles, whose particular character is quite incidental and unimportant. About forgettings he does say just this (*A General Introduction to Psychoanalysis* [Garden City Publishing Company, N. Y., 1943: 51]), and cites the following example among others to prove his point. "Ernest Jones relates that he once allowed a letter to lie on his writing desk for several days for some unknown reason. At last he decided to post it, but received it back from the dead-letter office, for he had forgotten to address it. After he had addressed it he took it to post but this time without a stamp." Where linguistic lapses are concerned – slips of the tongue or pen, and mistakes in reading and in hearing – the analogous situation would be that a certain revelation would come to light, would find linguistic expression somehow or other; it is idle to try to prevent it, just as there is no sense in patching an old shirt, because if you stop the shirt from ripping in one place it will give way somewhere else.

In some cases Freud's implicit view is not hard to maintain. If the presiding officer of a legislature says, "Gentlemen, I declare a quorum present and herewith declare the session closed", Freud can plausibly comment: "The President wished himself in a position to close this session, from which he had little good to expect, and the thought broke through at least partially" (*Psychopathology of Everyday Life*, ch. 5). Language offered no obstacle, the president could have substituted *closed* for *opened* in any language. But what of the newspaper that described a famous general as a "battle-scared veteran"; then corrected this – with apologies – to read "bottle-scarred veteran"? These two slips could not be translated into most languages; they depend on

A GOOD "BATTERING AVERAGE"

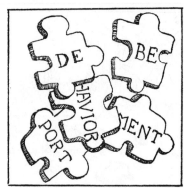

BLENDS – THE SIMPLEST SLIP

the accident that in English there is a word meaning 'frightened' and spelled very much like *scarred*, and another word meaning 'flask, vessel' and spelled very much like *battle*. Is there any evidence that, without the help of these two accidents, the newspaper's typesetter could have found other means (consciously or unconsciously) of nearly and briefly expressing contempt for the general? To answer yes would be like saying that any thought can be expressed in poetry in any language.

To explain and predict slips of the tongue, we need to take two kinds of factors into account: the psychological factors, that dispose one to make a certain kind of slip, and the linguistic factors, that make such a slip easy, difficult, or impossible. Freud gave a great impetus to the study of the former. Let us see what linguistic science can teach us about the latter.

II

The predictions that linguistic science can make today about slips of the tongue have two limitations: they are conditional and they are alternative. Linguistics doesn't enable us to predict: "This professor is about to say 'the overall battering average'"; it enables us to predict conditionally: "IF this professor is going to make a slip of the tongue in the phrase 'the overall batting average', it will be ..." And as a rule, linguistics doesn't predict just one slip; it gives two or more possibilities, and assigns a rough probability to each, for example: "If this professor is going to make a slip of the tongue in the phrase 'the overall batting average', it will most probably be 'the overall battering average'; less probably, 'the overall battering avage'; still less probably, 'the overall avering battage'; ..." The linguistic prediction typically sets up a hierarchy of probabilities.

At the worst, linguistics cannot yet pick out any one of the alternatives as more probable than the others. For example, given that a speaker is hesitating between "I think I'll drop past his house" and "I think I'll drop by his house," and that he will form a blend between the words *past* and *by*. As we shall see in a moment, linguists are in a position to say that there are just two blends of these two words that are at all probable: *bast* and *py*; but they are not today in a position to rate one of these as more probable than the other. As a matter of fact, in the case that I actually heard and recorded the speaker said "drop py".

Blends are the simplest kind of slip of the tongue, so it is a good idea to begin with them. A blend is a word formed from two other words (very rarely more than two) by dividing each of the two original words into two parts, and combining one part from each original word into the new word called the blend. Here are some examples: "behortment" (*behavior+deportment*); "drig a well" (*drig: drill+dig*); "ebvious" (*evident+obvious*); "shaddy" (*shabby+shoddy*); "frowl" (*frown+scowl*); "refudiating" (*refuting+repudiating*). It happens that in all of these examples the two original words are synonyms. However, this fact is of no concern to the linguist as such. It is true that hesitation between synonyms is one very frequent factor in causing slips of the tongue, but it is to be classified as psychological rather than linguistic. On the other hand it is linguistically relevant that in each of these examples the two original words are FORMALLY similar. Formal similarity includes phonetic similarity (e.g. *behavior* and *deportment* both have three syllables, and are both accented on the second syllable) and grammatical similarity (*behavior* and *deportment* are both nouns, *drill* and *dig* are both verbs, *evident* and *obvious* are both adjectives), but by definition does not include similarity or other relationship of meaning.

Now, what about prediction? Given that a blend is to be formed from *past* and *by*, there are a number of apparently possible blends. *Past* can be broken up into two parts in three ways: *p-ast*, *pa-st*, and *pas-t*; *by* can be broken up in only one way: *b-y*. (In this word the letter *y* spells a sound which is phonetically complex, being a diphthong, but which always behaves as a unit.) So there are six apparently possible blends:

(1) *p-y*; (2) *pa-y*; (3) *pas-y*; (4) *b-ast*; (5) *b-st*; (6) *b-t*. Spelling is treacherous here; it is to be borne in mind that throughout our discussion of this example the letter *a* has the value that it has in *past*, and *y* has the value that it has in *by*.

Of these six apparent possibilities, three can be ruled out at once. Nos. (2), (5) and (6) are ruled out by what I shall call

The First Law. A SLIP OF THE TONGUE IS PRACTICALLY ALWAYS A PHONETICALLY POSSIBLE NOISE.

The notion of phonetic possibility is most easily explained by examples. There are lots of noises that could perfectly well be English words, though they are not: *scrin, scring, scrill, scriffly, sny, mip*, and so on. Then there are a lot of noises that could not be English words, either because they contain un-English sounds (e.g. *loef* – with *oe* pronounced as in French *l'oeuf* or German *Loeffel*) or because they contain English sounds but in un-English combinations (e.g. *ktin, pmip, ksob*, where none of the letters are silent). It is extremely important to realize that phonetic possibility varies from language to language. In ancient Greek words can begin with *kt* but cannot end with *kt*; in English just the opposite is true.

A few exceptions to this First Law have been recorded; but exceptions are so exceedingly rare that in the present state of linguistics they may be disregarded.

Our task of prediction has become simplified. There remain only three apparently possible blends of *past* and *by* to reckon with. And of these, number (3) is rendered quite unlikely by

The Second Law. IF THE TWO ORIGINAL WORDS ARE RHYTHMICALLY SIMILAR, A BLEND OF THEM WILL, WITH HIGH PROBABILITY, RHYTHMICALLY RESEMBLE BOTH OF THEM.

Two words are rhythmically similar if they have the same number of syllables and are accented on corresponding syllables. For example, *behavior, deportment*, and their blend *behortment* are rhythmically similar: each has three syllables and each is accented on the second syllable. *Adequate* is not rhythmically similar to these three words because although it has three syllables, it is accented on the first syllable rather than on the second.

Now possibility (3), *pas-y*, is not rhythmically similar to the monosyllables *past* and *by*, and consequently is not likely to be uttered as a blend of these two words. This leaves only (1) *py* and (4) *bast*; and in the present state of linguistic theory we are not in a position to rate either of these as more likely to occur than the other.

To further illustrate the linguistic approach, I will mention one more law governing slips of the tongue:

The Third Law. IF THE TWO ORIGINAL WORDS CONTAIN THE SAME SOUND IN THE SAME POSITION, A BLEND OF THEM WILL CONTAIN THAT SOUND IN THAT POSITION.

The sound may be simple or complex; it may be a vowel, a consonant, a sequence of two consonants, a vowel followed by a consonant, or any other phonetically possible combination. The two words *frown* and *scowl* have the same sound in the same position: "ow", in the middle of the word. The speaker who wavered between speaking of a graduate student's *essay* and his *dissertation* and finally said "essertation" conformed to the Third Law; the two original words both contain the sound spelled *ss*, and both of them contain it immediately after the first vowel of the word. The speaker who wavered between *more removable factors* and *more maneuverable factors* also conformed to the Third Law when he finally said "removerable"; for both of the original words contain a complex sound in common, although it is spelled differently in the two words. It is spelled *ov* in *removable* and *euv* in *maneuverable*. They also contain the complex sound "able" in common, in the same position (namely, at the end), and this fact undoubtedly, helped to make that particular blend probable.

All the slips of the tongue that I have discussed are blends, and blends of a special sort: the speaker is wavering between two phrases, and is to choose only one. But there are many other kinds of slips of the tongue. The speaker mentioned in the opening paragraph, who said that the conversation "slagged slightly", produced a blend, but it was not a blend of two words between which he was trying to choose. It was not a matter of choosing between *lagged* and *slightly* but of saying first the one and then the other, and what the speaker did was to ANTICIPATE the second word while saying the first. Again, the speaker who said "obstretician" for "obstetrician" did not produce a blend at all, but a different kind of slip. And such a lapse as "put it on the sink of the edge" (for "put it on the edge of the sink"), where whole words are interchanged, is of a different kind still.

A complete study of linguistic lapses would classify these and all the other different kinds; for some of them, some laws are already known. The purpose of this article has not been to be exhaustive, but only to illustrate by a few examples what sort of contribution linguistics can make toward the detailed prediction of lapses. The linguistic approach has other uses too; for instance there is already evidence that certain people are more prone to one kind of slip of the tongue than to another. One person quite often produces blends but very seldom interchanges whole words, another person has the opposite tendency. The study of such tendencies is properly a collaborative job: the linguist furnishes the classification of slips of the tongue, and the psychoanalyst or other psychologist correlates the tendency to select this or that kind of slip with the personality type of the speaker. To date, collaboration between linguists and specialists in other biological and human sciences has not been at all common; but the time is more than ripe for it, as the present discussion may help to demonstrate.

ERRORS OF SPEECH AND THEIR IMPLICATION FOR UNDERSTANDING THE STRATEGY OF LANGUAGE USERS *

A. COHEN

Taking a cue from Lashley's (1951) observations on errors in executing the required articulatory or manual movements in speaking and typewriting, a study was made of errors occurring in spontaneous speech situations.

In line with Lashley the assumption underlying this study was that such lapses might give indications about the intricate processes involved in speaking and more specifically about the temporal ordering of the elements that are ultimately produced.

Lashley postulated a number of layers in the speaking process. We might render them as

(1) a plan, determining what is going to be said,
(2) a programme, controlling the temporal ordering in accordance with the rules of the language,
(3) the actual performance, in terms of movements of the articulating organs producing speech sounds.

In fact, the basic hypothesis in the present study was that "errors do not just happen, but are caused" (Morton 1964). It is only the output stage which is overt in the intricate speaking process, and any miscarriage to be observed here may well be revealing about hidden aspects of the processes involved in the generation of speech.

In the following, a survey will be given of the errors to be called 'spontaneous' since they occurred in situations outside the laboratory in everyday language usage (section 1).

To find corroboration for the results obtained from a heterogeneous collection, the need was felt to try and induce similar errors in a laboratory situation (section 2).

* Reprinted from *Zeitschrift für Phonetik* 21 (1/2): 177–81 (1966).

A NUMBER of additions including fig. 1 were made thanks to the work of Mr. S. G. Nooteboom of our laboratory who has followed up the work originally reported on in the preprint. Dutch readers are invited to turn to his report "Spontane fonologische versprekingen", Internal IPO-Report 93 (1967). In this report also a study of the influence of phonetic relationship between an error and its cause in terms of distinctive features may be found.

1. SPONTANEOUS ERRORS

The errors in this study were all observed in ordinary conversations or in informal discussions in the Dutch language. Only those errors were included in the material that laid themselves open to interpretation in terms of actually occurring speech segments in the immediate vicinity. These lapses constituted the large majority of all errors observed. They had the added advantage that they did not require any need to appeal to the speaker's introspection.

As a start a total of 600 errors were collected and subsequently divided into three main groups:

(1) anticipation, whenever the segment which is actually being produced clearly reflects the influence of a segment that should occur later in the utterance.

(2) perseveration, whenever a segment is produced which clearly reflects the influence of a segment that had already occurred earlier in the utterance.

(3) transposition, when two segments clearly manifest a mutual influence in the utterance.

The influence in these three groups of errors affects segments ranging in size from words to single phonemes. Three types of interference can then be distinguished: addition of one or more phonemes, e.g. *kwonsekwentie* (for *konsekwentie*); omission of one or more phonemes, e.g. ... *ertz er* ... (for ... *Hertz er* ...); substitution of one or more phonemes, e.g. *everylay life* (for *everyday life*).

Errors of speech

TABLE I

Classification of speech errors

Type of segment involved in speech errors

Groups	single vowel	single consonant	consonant cluster	syllable	word
1 Anticipations 469 78 %	150	164	121	34	—
2 Perseverations 90 15 %	22	39	25	4	—
3 Transpositions 41 7 %	9	21	2	5	4

As for the errors involving single consonants and consonant clusters it seems interesting to point out that about 70 % are to be found in prevocalic segments.

As for the span expressed in terms of the number of syllables between an error and its cause, counting one for adjoining syllables, a frequency distribution is given in Fig. 1.

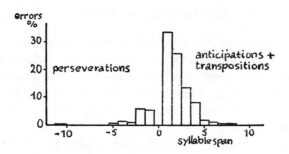

Fig. 1. Distribution of errors of perseveration (left) and anticipation and transposition (right) as a function of syllable span between error and cause. The total number is 600.

A number of salient points can be mentioned: (a) anticipatory errors greatly out-number those of the other two groups making up nearly 80 % of all the spontaneous errors observed. (b) Not only are perseveratory errors in the minority, about 15 %, but often a link with physical fatigue seemed to be indicated, a finding which would agree well with those based on a wider ranging enquiry by Meringer and Mayer (1895). (c) The average span between a cause and its error was 2.1 syllables for anticipation and perseveration (and 1.7 for transpositions) and the overall distributions of the spans of either group are much alike.

2. EXPERIMENTAL EVIDENCE

A further study was instigated which was based on the assumption that similar errors could be induced under favourable experimental conditions. Originally no notice was taken of errors accruing from reading scripts. Yet it appeared that though the two situations, spontaneous talking and reading aloud from prepared texts, seemed widely different, the errors that could be observed were of exactly the same nature. This unexpected finding was used as an encouragement to introduce written texts.

To create favourable experimental conditions, the following set-up was chosen: texts based on the original lapses were run on together without punctuation marks or capital letters and typed in a continuous single line on a paper ribbon. This was pre-sented to the subjects moving from right to left and visible over a length of about 12 cm, corresponding with about 11 syllables.

The subjects were instructed to read the texts with the best prosodic segmentation of sentences that they could achieve.

Of a total of 162 errors obtained in this way 59 % were anticipations ($n = 99$), 38 % perseverations ($n = 58$) and 3 % transpositions ($n = 5$).

3. DISCUSSION

The observation that the distance between an error and its cause normally exceeds the span of a single syllable and may extend up to seven syllables makes it necessary to distinguish between two mechanisms, those of programming and performance. The former must be assumed to operate in chunks consisting of a number of syllables at once, up to seven, whereas no such thing need be assumed about the performance.

Looking at the average span for spontaneous errors and for the experimental condition we see that there is a difference for anticipations. In the case of spontaneous speech the average is 2.1 syllables and in the experimental situation 1.6 syllables. This may be due to the fact that in free speech the potential programme may come in rather large chunks, whereas in the forced condition of the experiment, the subject is only partly aware of the actual words to be produced. No such clear discrepancy can be found for the average span in perseverations.

The finding that anticipatory errors, both in spontaneous speech and in the experimental condition, make up the larger part of all errors seems to indicate that in producing speech, the speaker's attention is directed to parts of the utterance yet to come.

The number of times when prevocalic segments are involved in all errors, viz. 70 %, may well be related to the higher amount of information inherent in that particular position of consonants in Dutch words (see e.g. van Katwijk 1966).

It is worth noting that of the various forms of interference in which consonants are involved omission plays a minor role, less that 5 % of all cases.

In fact, where clusters are involved, more often a single consonant was substituted by a cluster than v.v. These two observations may lead to the conclusion that difficult combinations tend to obtrude themselves to the speaker, who is inclined to overemphasize such difficulties rather than to slur over them.

A remarkable outcome in the reading experiment was that in a number of cases exact replicas of errors originally observed in spontaneous speech were made, sometimes even several times over by different subjects.

The difficulties confronting the subjects in the experimental condition may have caused the relatively high amount of perseverations (38 %) as compared with that found for spontaneous speech (15 %).

As for the transpositions, the total number obtained does not warrant much comment. Nevertheless it bears mentioning that in this group of errors relatively more often whole words were involved than in the other two groups.

4. CONCLUSION

Although the results so far do not allow a direct insight into the organisation of higher order mechanisms operative in speech, nevertheless a number of points may be made:

(a) In speaking we are constantly in danger of tumbling over words that come to mind more readily than they can be transmitted to the effector mechanism. We tend to take together a number of segments in single chunks which can vary from complete stock phrases (cliché's, proverbial expressions) to single phonemes (in awkward combinations).

It is the programming mechanism that should take care of the proper ordering as may appear from the errors produced in the experimental task, where the planning stage was absent.

(b) Very often errors went undetected by both the speaker himself and the average listener. Only in cases where the meaning was obviously deviant from the speaker's intentions could one be fairly sure of detection. (Such is normally the case with deliberate Spoonerisms.)

(c) The introduction of written texts to check hypotheses on speech habits, should not be taken for granted as being relevant in all cases but stands in need of justification.

(d) The study of errors as such can be a rewarding pursuit to gain a better understanding of the process of speech production and perception.

BIBLIOGRAPHY

Katwijk, A. F. V. van,
　1966　"On Perceptual Units in Speech", *IPO Annual Progress Report* 1: 51–55.
Meringer, R. and K. Mayer
　1895　*Versprechen und Verlesen* (Stuttgart), especially p. 52.
Morton, J.
　1964　"A Model for Continuous Language Behaviour", *Language and Speech* 7: 40–70, especially p. 41.
Lashley, K. S.
　1951　"The problem of Serial Order in Behavior", in: *Hixon Symposium on Cerebral Mechanisms in Behavior*, ed. by L. A. Jeferess (New York): 112–36.

WHERE THE TONGUE SLIPS, THERE SLIP I*

And the tongue is a fire, a world of iniquity: so is the tongue among our members, that it defileth the whole body, and setteth on fire the course of nature; and it is set on fire of hell. For every kind of beasts, and of birds, and of serpents, and of things in the sea, is tamed, and hath been tamed of ma kind: But the tongue can no man tame; it is an unruly evil, full of deadly poison. Therewith bless we God, even the Father; and therewith curse we men, which are made after the similitude of God. Out of the same mouth proceedeth blessing and cursing.

James 3 : 6-10.

0. THE PROBLEM AND THE APPROACH

At one point in his *Psychopathology of Everyday Life*, Sigmund Freud suggests that an understanding of the mechanisms involved in slips of the tongue may lead towards an elucidation of the "probable laws of formation of speech".[1] I propose here to take Freud's suggestion seriously. I am not aware that any linguist has yet done so, at least in the detailed way projected.[2]

There are two related aims. The linguistic tradition is richer now than it was in Freud's time. Thus, we may be in a position to offer a more searching interpretation of slips of the tongue, in some respects, than Freud did. Such an outcome would surely be of interest to our cousins in psychiatry. More important to us as linguists is that Freud's remarkable insights, properly supplemented and amplified, may tell us things about language that we have not known, and help us properly to evaluate the various incompatible theories and views of language design currently available.

We cannot hope to follow up the clues Freud has given us unless we are willing to do two things that are contrary to our usual professional custom.

---

*   Reprinted from *To Honor Roman Jakobson* (The Hague: Mouton, 1967).

[1]   All references to this are via a paperback reprint (Mentor Book MD67, sixth printing 1958, New York, The New American Library) of A. A. Brill's translation and adaptation of the fourth German edition; the first German edition appeared in 1901.

[2]   Many studies, of course, may not have come to my attention. I do know of Rulon S. Wells, "Predicting slips of the tongue", *Yale Scientific Magazine*, 26 (3) (December, 1951): 9ff. Wells deals exclusively with the relative frequency (and, hence, relative probability) of slips of different sorts, as conditioned by phonological habits. Insofar as the results of my observations agree with his, his are incorporated into the present paper, especially into § 1.

(1) There is a difference between the generation of speech (or, as Freud's translator puts it, the "formation of speech") and the structure of sentences. Our customary angle of approach in descriptive linguistics has been in terms of the latter. We have viewed sentences as stable wholes, and by comparing them have attempted to determine their content and organization. The structure of individual utterances thus revealed has been assumed to reflect, though perhaps only with great distortion, the abstract 'set of habits', or 'system', or 'internalized grammar' (terminologies, at least, differ) that constitutes the language. It is the language as a system or code or set of patterns ('langue'), rather than any particular utterance as a message ('parole'), that we have basically sought to characterize; observed sentences are simply a crucial part of the available evidence. But all of this, we have usually tacitly assumed, has little to do with the process by which a speaker builds an actual utterance.

However, it is also possible to think of a language as a system whose design is reflected not only by the utterances produced by its speakers but also by the process of production itself. To follow Freud's lead, we must be prepared to explore this possibility, even though it requires certain techniques of observation and interpretation at which none of us is particularly adept.

(2) The second and more radical requirement has to do with the difference between speech marred by blunders and what I shall simply call 'smooth speech'. Usual linguistic practice has ignored the problems connected with this difference by accepting, for further analytical examination, only 'normalized' text from which slips of the tongue and the like have been deleted (sometimes by the informant, often enough by the analyst). In the field, at work on an undescribed language, there is justification for this: one's aim is to discover and describe the specificities of a particular language, rather than those phenomena and mechanisms that recur, seemingly, in most or all languages or speech communities. Besides, the fruitful exegesis of specific slips of the tongue requires rather far-reaching control of the particular language (and culture) in which they occur: this degree of control lies beyond that achieved in the average term of field work.

But a transfer of the usual field procedure, and of the attitude it implies, to our deeper investigation of more familiar languages, or to our search for the basic and universal features of language design, is not justified. The commonest view of speech defects and lapses, among linguists and laymen alike, from Freud's day to our own, has been that smooth speech reflects the internalized system (the language, 'langue') more accurately, and that paralallies are pathologies external to the language, intrusions from some other realm or system, and annoyance to the users of a language because they disrupt communication ("the tongue is a fire") and a bother to linguists because one must somehow work around and past them to get at what really counts. This was the view of Meringer and Mayer, criticized by Freud;[3] it is, with consider-

---

[3] R. Meringer and K. Mayer, *Versprechen und Verlesen* (Stuttgart, 1895); Freud also refers to W. Wundt.

able elaboration, Chomsky's view today.[4] Freud does not altogether reject it – after all, he classes slips of the tongue among the PATHOLOGIES of everyday life–; nor should we, for there are specific instances in which a diagnosis of this sort is obviously correct. I once met a woman, a native speaker of English, whose speech contained brief silences where the rest of us have /s/. The etiology was known: she had learned to speak English as she heard it, but had a congenital hearing loss so that she HEARD silence where most of us hear /s/. The problem is, then: exactly what features of specific utterances (as historic events) are due to intrusive factors of this kind, and what features stem from the workings of the 'language' itself? The solution is not given us by divine inspiration nor by intuition. It must be sought through hard analytical work on specific examples.

An initial example will show us how lost we are, in confronting data of this sort, unless we modify our approach along the two lines described above. Here are two anecdotes. The first is true; the second is fictional but, I hope, realistic:

(1) A father, exasperated with his noisy children, said:

$$/^4\text{dòwnt} + {}^4\text{šél} + \text{sòw} + \text{lâwd}^1 \#/ \qquad\qquad\qquad \text{(E1)}$$
Don't shell so loud!

(2) A wife was sitting in the kitchen, removing fresh peas from their pods and dropping the pods into a metal pail, while her husband was trying to carry on a telephone conversation. He called to her:

$$/^4\text{dòwnt} + {}^4\text{šél} + \text{sòw} + \text{lâwd}^1 \#/ \qquad\qquad\qquad \text{(E1')}$$
Don't shell so loud!

Each of these episodes involves an English utterance. The phonological structure of the utterances is given,[5] and is the same for both. We wish to determine and to describe, in a systematic way, everything else about the two utterances that might be relevant.

For obvious reasons, a linguistic theory that merely sets E1 aside is of no use to us. In much the same way, we must reject any doctrine that purports to preclude altogether the use of semantic criteria. If such a constraint were taken seriously, then grammatical analysis would have to be based on a corpus of utterances in phonemic notation but free of glosses and annotations. In such a corpus, E1 and E1' would not be distinguished.

The purer sort of item-and-arrangement (IA) theory holds that any sentence consists of an integral number of minimal elements (morphemes) in a hierarchically nested set of constructions. IA procedures would treat E1 and E1' identically except for the element *shell* that appears (as a phonemic shape) in both. In E1', this element

---

[4] Or so I infer from Chomsky's publications. This point is discussed in greater detail in § 11 below.
[5] In the Trager-Smith phonemic notation, I am not convinced that the theory underlying this notation is correct in all detail, but regard the notation, at least, as vastly superior to any other so far proposed.

is just a particular morpheme, belonging to such-and-such a form class. What about the *shell* of E1? To treat this, also, merely as a particular morpheme (not the same one as that of E1′) ignores all the special characteristics of E1 in its setting. Alternatively, we might regard it as a composite form: say, an element *sh-* that recurs in *shout*, plus an element *−ell* that recurs in *yell*. But then, of course, *shout* must be this *sh-* plus *-out*, and *yell* must be *y-* plus *-ell*. If someone happens to say /šáwm/ instead of *shout* or *scream*, then the *-out* already dissected from *shout* is in turn revealed as composite, the *-ou-* recurring in /šáwm/. The ultimate end of this process of proliferation and subdivision is to recognize as many morpheme-occurrences in any utterance as there are phoneme-occurrences, or more. In particular, the *shell* of E1′ will turn out to be composite too (a particular *sh-*, plus a particular *-e-*, plus a particular *-ll*, or something of the kind); the distinction between E1 and E1′ again becomes blurred.

Item-and-process (IP) models allow us to interpret some forms in a sentence as produced from other forms by the application of a specifiable operation, the domain of application of which may be ordered *n*-ads of underlying forms where $n \geq 1$ (e.g., for $n = 1$, *boys* can be taken as underlying *boy* subjected to the operation 'pluralization'; the *-s* does not have to be a form at all). As within the IA framework, E1 and E1′ will be treated identically except for *shell*. But IP allows us to treat the *shell* of E1 in a more realistic way. We may regard it as built from the underlying ordered pair of forms (*shout*, *yell*) by the application of a certain operation. Let this operation be *B*: then we can say that $B(shout, yell) = shell$. Similarly, $B(yard, lawn) = yawn$; $B(corn, beans) = keans$; $B(yell, shout) = yout$. Other dyadic operations of the 'blending' sort would also have to be recognized, since the one we have illustrated would not act on (*pin down, get at*) to yield the attested phrase *pin at*, nor on (*Richard, William*) to yield Lewis Carroll's *Rilchiam*.[6] Our ultimate solution ought to incorporate the desirable features of this treatment, but should at the same time eliminate what seems to be a defect: that this approach neglects the possible relevance of the phonemic identity of (ordinary) *shell* and of *shell* blended from *shout* and *yell*.

1. BLENDING; PHONOLOGY AND PHONOLOGICAL CONSTRAINTS

Let us forget, for the present, our various more or less formalized models of language design, and try to discern what factors may actually have led the father in the first episode to say what he did say.

The second word of E1 is a *blend* of the two words *shout* and *yell*. There is nothing new about this term used in a purely descriptive or classificatory sense: but we intend to go beyond that and make it part of a diagnosis. In the situation in which the

---

[6] In his preface to *The Hunting of the Snark*, Carroll undertakes to explain the 'hard words' of the poem *Jabberwocky* as 'portmanteaus' (= our 'blends'), and gives *Rilchiam* as a further example. His exegesis is about as good as Freud's was a quarter of a century later; the invented blend *Rilchiam*, however, seems to be about as improbable as any conceivable blend of *Richard* and *William*.

speaker found himself, either of the two words *shout* and *yell* would have been appropriate. We may surmise that both words presented themselves to him as possibilities, but that their equal appropriateness precluded the rapid selection of one and rejection of the other, and that the pressure to keep speaking, rather than to delay in order to force a clear choice, led him to try to say both words at once.

Now the latter is impossible. A single individual's share of articulatory equipment is such that two words or phrases cannot be uttered simultaneously.[7] The attempt to do so can only result in the production of a string of sounds drawn partly from each of the two words or phrases. This actually uttered form is what we call a blend. A blend may occur as the result of conscious planning, in which case it may qualify as a witticism. Or it may be as much a surprise to the speaker who produces it as to anyone else; in this case it is a slip of the tongue, or lapse. Example E1 is known to have been a lapse, not a witticism.[8]

What we have so far said does not complete the explanation of E1, because *shell* is not the only possible blend of *shout* and *yell*. Other possibilities are /yáwt/, /yét/, /šáwl/, /šét/, and /yáwl/. We must do our best to account for the speaker's 'choice' of the particular blend *shell* rather than any of these alternatives. If our evidence in the case is not sufficiently detailed for us to be absolutely sure of the answer, then we must not speak with absolute sureness; but we can still profit from making the best guess we can.

Of the six possible blends of *shout* and *yell* that we have listed above, two, /šél/ and /yáwt/, are apparently somewhat more probable than the other four because of a feature of the phonetic habits of English. An English monosyllabic word seems to consist, in the first instance, of two immediate constituents: the consonantism (even if zero) at its beginning, and all that follows. Thus *shout* is /š-/ and /-áwt/, rather than /šáw-/ and /-t/ or /š ... t/ and /⟨áw⟩/. Similarly, *yell* is /y-/ and /-él/, not /yé-/ and /-l/ or /y ... l/ and ⟨é⟩/.

Part of the evidence for this view of phonetic IC structure is, true enough, just the predominant tendencies in slips of the tongue: for example, a metathesis like /stǽnd+sòwn/ for *sandstone* seems somewhat commoner than one like /grǽs+rìyk/ for *grease rack*.[9] But the argument is not circular: there is other evidence. In English verse, rhyming monosyllables differ only as to initial consonantism: *June, moon, spoon, croon*. Alliterative assonance appears in various proverbs and riddles, reversing the convention of rhyme to involve words with the same initial consonantism: '*Let us flee*', *said the fly*; '*let us fly*', *said the flea*; *so they flew through a flaw in the*

---

[7]   To this there is one exception, with which we shall deal in § 8.

[8]   For the sake of impersonality, I prefer to keep anonymous the source of the majority of the lapses cited in this paper. I assure the reader, however, that when I supply unusually detailed information about the attendant curcumstances, with no hedging, I speak with impeccable authority.

[9]   Mary Livingston pulled the second of these two years ago on a Jack Benny radio program. The references to statistics, here and later, are to an informal count I myself made, in a sample that was as large as practicable but probably not large enough to satisfy a professional statistician. Yet I did do SOME counting – the judgments are not entirely impressionistic.

flue. In the juvenile secrecy-system known as Pig Latin, monosyllables are broken between initial consonantism and remainder for coding: /áwt+šèy/ for *shout*: /él+ yèy/ for *yell*; /íg+pèy/ for *pig*; even, in some versions, /áwč+èy/ for *ouch*, showing zero initial consonantism treated as the first immediate constituent of the whole monosyllabic word.[10]

I propose that this IC structure of monosyllables is one of a multitude of features that, taken together, CONSTITUTE what we ordinarily call the phonological system of English.

The phonological system of a language imposes a variety of constraints on what speakers of the language may say, by way of either smooth speech or lapses. The most general of these constraints is the one already mentioned: that two words or phrases cannot be uttered simultaneously. This constraint is inherent in the phonological system of every language. Otherwise, languages are highly varied and few cross-language generalizations are possible. In English, *cone* /kówn/ might be metathesized to /nówk/, or *corn* /kórn/ to /nórk/, but hardly *corn* to */rnók/ or *song* /sóŋ/ to */ŋós/, since English words just do not begin with the consonant combination /rn-/ nor with the single consonant /ŋ-/.[11] The habits of other languages, and thus the constraints, are different: [rn]- occurs, for example, in Georgian, and [ŋ-] is very common.

However, phonological constraints are for the most part not absolute: they are made of rubber, not of steel. Thus it is not impossible for a blend of *shout* and *yell* to yield /yét/, /šáwl/, /šét/, or /yáwl/. Blending can yield a pronunciation with a phoneme (a simultaneous bundle of components) not present in either of the contributing forms: *bubbles* and *tough* yielding /bóvìlz/. Here the voicing of the /v/ is from the medial /b/ of *bubbles*, while its degree of aperture is from the final /f/ of *tough*. I have no doubt that blending can yield a pronunciation with constituent sounds that stand outside the 'normal' phonological system of the language, as, by way of an invented example, *sugar sack* yielding [čúgɨr+sæx] with the degree of aperture of the initial and final consonants interchanged. Observing instances of this sort is difficult: the hearer, we suppose, usually interprets the result as though it did not deviate, or else the speaker has gotten his speech organs so entangled that he backs up and starts over again. However, such deviant results are progressively rarer, hence progressively less probable. Since the actual blend in E1 was one of the two most probable, we may allow ourselves to limit further inquiry to the reasons

[10] See Morris Halle, "Phonology in generative grammar", *Word*, 18 (1962): 54–72, for a brief discussion of Pig Latin from another angle. Halle should note the obvious audible difference between /íyts+trêy/, from *treats*, and /íyt+strêy/, from *street*. It is a shame to see any scholar so thoroughly committed to a theoretical frame of reference that he can no longer register data that are embarrassing to that theory. Our masters, such as Jakobson, taught us better than that.

[11] Even here we have to do with relative probability, with no absolute barriers. One of my children, at one stage, regularly used the form /ŋówp/ for *comb*, metathesizing the manner, but not the position of articulation, of the initial and final consonants. Such instances are clear evidence for the objective reality of phonological components. Of course, a slip yielding an initial /ŋ/ would be much rarer in the speech of an adult speaker of English.

behind the 'choice' of *shell* rather than of the phonemically equally likely /yáwt/.

Since the blend *shell* begins with a piece drawn from *shout*, we might interpret the "choice" of *shell* rather than of /yáwt/ as signalling a slight imbalance between the speaker's tendency towards saying *shout* and his tendency towards saying *yell*, in favor of the former. Indeed, this is about as far as Freud's own diagnosis would carry us: he customarily assumes two tendencies, a stronger one that he calls the *disturbed tendency* and an interfering weaker one that he calls the *disturbing tendency*[12]. We cannot rule out this possibility, but we should not overlook an alternative or additional possibility: that the blend begins with the first part of *shout* and continues with the second part of *yell* just because this way of blending the two will yield the form *shell* rather than /yáwt/. The latter would be only a blend. The former is more than a blend: it is homophonous with an ordinary English word. Furthermore, this word is of apt, if marginal, connotations for the situation in which the blending occurred. The outer car is shaped like a shell and is sometimes (poetically) called a *shell*. And it is the ears that are offended by the shrillness of children. Also, there are very noisy objects shot very noisily from guns, named by the word *shell*.

I suspect that certain readers will prefer to take their departure at this point. In wishing them bon voyage, I must warn all readers that in our discussion of subsequent examples I shall allow imagination to roam just as widely as it has in the preceding paragraph. There is little point in trying to learn anything about language from Freud's approach unless we are willing to do this. But it should be noted that our exposition of the causes of E1 is not presented as *true*, only as *plausible*. A factual exposition of everything involved in any single lapse (as a historic event) is impossible, since there is no way in which all relevant factors could have been recorded. But if we examine many such events, we see now clearer evidence for certain kinds of contributory factors, now clearer evidence for other kinds. There can be useful convergence in such a sequential examination only if we allow ourselves maximum freedom of guessing for each individual instance.

2. EDITING

Describing his wife's unprecedented outdoor activity in trying to get the grounds around a new house to grow grass, a husband said:

> She's so anxious to get a yawn? — yard in.   (E2)

Here the symbol '?' represents sharp glottal cutoff by the speaker, and the dash represents a slight pause. In subsequent examples, we shall supplement either orthography or phonemic notation, as convenient, by these symbols. E2 thus differs from E1 in that it includes relevant features of articulation that are not phonemic; such features have been called 'paralinguistic'.[13]

---

[12] *Psychopathology of Everyday Life*, ch. 5, passim.
[13] For a brief introductory survey, see George L. Trager, "Paralanguage: a first approximation", *Studies in Linguistics*, 13 (1958), 1-12. For a fairly extended application, see Robert E. Pittenger, Charles F. Hockett, and John J. Danchy, *The First Five Minutes* (1960).

The speaker was conversing at the time in a casual way with people he did not know very well. *Yawn* is one of the two phonologically most likely blends of *yard* and *lawn*; the other is *lard*. As between *yard* and *lawn*, the latter really fits the overt context better: a yard (= British English *garden*) may have grass or not, but a grassless lawn is stretching things a bit. If E1 led us to suspect that the initial element of a blend points towards the more dominant of the two participating tendencies, then E2 should weaken our confidence in that notion. It seems more likely that the choice of the blend *yawn*, rather than *lard*, was due to the ordinary word of that shape: the blend was a comment on the immediate situation, indicative of some minor degree of boredom on the speaker's part, or, perhaps more likely, of a fear on his part that his interlocutors would be bored by what he was saying.

In addition to blending, this example shows us a second phenomenon of importance: overt correction or *editing*. The uttering of *yawn* was a lapse, not a witticism. The speaker heard the lapse as it occurred, and immediately — indeed, hastily — offered a correction. The intention was that *yawn* be erased, as though it had never been uttered, and *yard* substituted. There are many reasons why we can validly speak of intention here. Suppose the speaker had been writing a letter. He would then have corrected the error by erasing *yawn*, or by lining it out so that it could not be deciphered, or even by beginning over again on a clean sheet of paper: and then the recipient of the letter would not know what error had been made, and might not even know that one had occurred.

In speaking, however, erasure is a physical impossiblity, and its seeming social equivalent is only a polite convention that usually works only superficially. Nevertheless, all of us do try to cover up some of our lapses. In E2, the speaker was in such haste to cover up that the proffered replacement was the wrong one: *yard*, which does not literally make sense in the sentence, rather than *lawn*, which would have. Thus, we have two more things to account for if we can: the haste, and the choice of replacement.

The haste may have been due to the speaker's desire to hide the lapse before his interlocutors could interpret it, as we have above, as a somewhat derogatory comment on the conversational context. In order to entertain this theory, we must assume that the speaker himself registered (surely out of awareness) the possibility of this interpretation as he heard his lapse.

As to the choice of replacement, we may suspect that concern with the more superficial implications of the lapse — including some chagrin at having produced a lapse at all — lowered the threshold of any running censorship against double entendre of other sorts in the presence of a mixed audience of casual acquaintances. The sentence with *yawn* makes an obvious sexual allusion. If *yawn* is hastily replaced by *yard*, that allusion, far from being annulled, is reinforced. The sexual allusion may also have been in part responsible for the haste with which the correction was offered. If so, then there could hardly be a more appropriate train of events to which to apply the tired cliché 'out of the frying pan into the fire'.

Having noted the sexual allusion in the sentence as actually uttered, we must recognize that either unblended *lawn* or the alternative blend *lard* could also be twisted, with little difficulty, towards such an allusion. However, granting such potentialities – sexual allusions can be read into practically anything if we want to –, let us note that in general it requires some concatenation of signals pointing more or less in the same direction to render an interpretation realistic. Had the speaker's utterance been smooth, *She's so anxious to get a lawn in* (or with *yard* instead of *lawn*), the congruence with the overt topic of discussion would probably have masked any such overtones pretty effectively. Had *lard* been involved in the lapse, the effect might well have been in part that which we have described, except that the overtones of commentary on the immediate social situation would have been missing.

3. COUNTERBLENDS

Discussing the acquisition of something that would generally be regarded as a luxury, a speaker said:

We weren't sure we could avord? – affoid it.   (E3)
(/... əvórd ... əfóyd .../)

Avord was a lapse: a blend of *avoid* and *afford*. Either of the latter would have fit the sentence, though with directly opposite meanings, since if something cannot be avoided it is presumably done, while if something cannot be afforded it is presumably not done. However, the sentence specifies uncertainty, so that the one word would have been about as appropriate as the other. The speaker was clearly both boasting and apologizing. We might also guess that he was wondering whether he could afford to speak in this particular way to his audience, and also whether he could avoid doing so.

In any case, some of the immediate technical details are clear. The speaker heard his blending lapse, cut it off, and then offered a replacement (as in E2). But the replacement was neither of the original target words: instead, it was the other phonologically most likely blend of *avoid* and *afford*. The original blend, that is, was followed by a compensating COUNTERBLEND. We infer that the speaker's tendency to say *both* target words, each with its array of implications, was overpoweringly strong.

The role of phonological patterning in E3 deserves special mention. As the transcription shows, *afford* and *avoid* have highly similar phonemic shapes (for this speaker): they differ only in /f/ versus /v/ (that is, only as to voicelessness versus voicing at this point), and as to /r/ versus /y/ after the vowel. This similarity can be underscored by pointing out that, under conditions of a relatively small amount of ambient noise, either word could be misheard as the other. This degree of similarity in sound is much greater than that between *shout* and *yell*, or *lawn* and *yard*. When two words are not only this similar in sound but also akin in meaning, then we must assume that ANY occurrence of either may carry associative reverberations of the other.[14] The vocabulary of a language involves a vast and intricate tracery of such secondary associations among words: this is the stuff of which poetry and advertising are woven. A blend of *avoid* and *afford* is therefore an underscoring of an associative tie that is reasonably strong to begin with.

4. ASSIMILATIONS AND HAPLOLOGIES; READING ALOUD

A TV master of ceremonies introduced a commercial as follows:

> The question is, how can you tell one sil? – filter cigarette   (E4)
> from another these days?

Here *sil-* is only the beginning of a blend. If it had been completed, one would expect *silter*, from *filter* and *cigarette*. But the speaker quickly heard what he was doing and made a correction. The cover-up was extremely smooth, but I suspect that the lapse was nevertheless registered, at least out of awareness, by many viewers.

Presumably the announcer was reading his lines from a teleprompter. We must therefore consider what is involved in reading aloud. When a child is first learning to read, he examines each written word in succession and pronounces it before going on to the next. The result is a highly artificial kind of speech, in which the successive words are not tied together into groups by variations of stress, by intonation, and by junctures, as are the successive words of ordinary talking. A written text can be regarded as a set of instructions telling a reader what to say (aloud or silently as the case may be). But the instructions are incomplete. There are no special marks to tell him how to distribute stresses, and only skimpy indications of intonation. The adult who is effective at reading aloud makes an appropriate selection of stresses and intonations to fit the succession of words in their particular context. For him to do this, his eyes often have to scan ahead of the point which has been reached by his speech organs, since the proper stress and intonation for a given word often depends on what comes later. The eyes, and the 'mind's ear', as it were, lead the speech organs.

What has just been said is not a guess, but necessarily true. A single example will prove it. Suppose a written sentence begins

---

[14] See Charles F. Hockett, *A Course in Modern Linguistics* (1958), chs. 35 and 63, and the references cited; there is, of course, a vast literature on this subject, including stimulating contributions from Jakobson. I remember Jakobson discussing the POETIC function of language – in a properly broad sense of 'poetic': the specific denotations and connotations of a particular actual sentence, as over against the underlying patterns and regularities with which we are usually concerned. As a trivial example, consider *Peter Piper picked a peck of pickled peppers*. The recurrent /p/'s in this catch-phrase are not a 'morpheme' of any sort; yet a paraphrase or translation which ignores them (*Pierre le joueur de musette a cueilli une livre de poivrons marinés*) totally misses the point of the original. No theory of language that conceives of sentences as composed (at any level, shallow or 'deep') of an arrangement of an integral number of occurrences of elementary units, and nothing more, can possibly provide for such experimental realities as are afforded by even this trite tongue-twister.

After John had started the car ... (E5)

If the continuation is
... Mary jumped in. (E6)

then *car* will be read with primary stress and a following terminal contour (normally /|||/, conceivably /|/). But if the continuation is

... pulled up to the curb. (E7)

then the terminal contour will be placed after *started*. Thus the stress and intonation of E5 depends on what follows; therefore the reader must know what follows before he can properly deliver the initial part of the sentence. A written comma after *car* if the continuation is E6, after *started* if it is E7, would change the situation; but commas are often omitted.

Reading aloud is a complicated task, requiring precise but variable timing. Only the slightest disruption is needed to introduce an error – here definable quite simply as a deviation from the written text. Anyone who has read aloud (say, to children) can vouch for the high incidence of such errors.

A common type of error in this setting is wrong phrasing, due to a failure to scan ahead properly. Thus, one might read the printed sequence E5-E6 as:

^{2}Àfter Jôhn had ^{3}stárted^2|| ^{2}the câr^{3}Máry jûmped în^1 # (E8)

– which makes no sense. Or the error might be detected almost anywhere after the wrongly placed /|||/, and a correction made.

Again, a moment's inattention may lead the reader to supply words on his own, on the basis of what he has read so far, more or less deviant from those that are printed:

Those of your advisors who wished to throw us into the Garden (E9)
of Clinging Vines must twine? – must step within this circle
of light.

where the printed version lacks the first *must* and the *twine*. The reader's attention was caught by the phrase *Clinging Vines* as a name for something that two pages earlier had been called *Twining Vines*. This also shows us the source of the supplied word *twine*.

Again, a bit of what the eyes have scanned may be omitted from delivery:

(printed:) aroused her from her sleep (E10)
(read:) aroused her from sleep

(printed:) listened to Dorothy's story with attention (E11)
(read:) listened to Dory? – to Dorothy's story with attention

(printed:) looked at one another in wonder (E12)
(read:) looked at wonder? – at one another in wonder

In E10 there was no overt editing, since the reader recognized that there was no significant difference in meaning between the printed version and what he had actually said. E11 and E12, both with corrections, attest to a phenomenon that is apparently extremely common in such omissions: the part omitted and the next part begin phonemically in the same way. Thus *D(orothy's st)ory* or *Do(rothy's sto)ry*; (*one another in*) *wonder*. Presumably the eyes are just scanning the second occurrence of the recurrent phonemic shape (that is, of spellings that require that phonemic shape) as the speech organs are delivering the first occurrence. The result, of course, is what is ordinarily called HAPLOLOGY.

In a fourth type of lapse in reading aloud, the word that the eyes are scanning at a given moment is blended with the word that is scheduled for pronunciation at that moment:

> (printed:) added a sort of glue to his soapsuds, which made   (E13)
> his bubbles tough
> (read:) ... buvvles tough

Sturtevant's example[15] of a distant assimilation, THE ILLOPTICAL ILLUSION, may have arisen in the same way if it happened during reading (this we are not told).

In still a fifth type, one may suddenly wonder whether a word already scanned and read aloud was properly delivered, and in checking this (perhaps with the eyes, perhaps only in memory) the next word due for delivery may be blended with the one being checked:

> (printed:) they will soon crush you and devour your bodies   (E14)
> (read:) ... devour your bardies

Here |bárdiyz/ for |bádiyz| has an intrusive postvocalic |r| from *devour*. This is the other type of lapse that Sturtevant classes as a distant assimilation. A rough count in available lists of attested lapses suggests that this type may be the rarest, in either reading or free speaking; but possibly it is merely the hardest type to observe and record.

We can now return to E4 for further explication. The announcer's eyes, we assume, were scanning written *cigarette* as he came to the point of uttering *filter*, and the beginning of *cigarette* was routed through to his articulatory apparatus too quickly, so that he said *sil-* before he could readjust. The lapse was thus of the type illustrated above by E13. However, we must still ask why the disruption and the lapse should have occurred just as they did. Although we can only guess, it seems reasonable to suppose that *sil-*, homophonous with the beginning of *silly*, was an expression of the TV performer's private attitude towards the commercials in which he is obliged to participate. Out of the same mouth proceedeth blessing and cursing – occasionally at the same time.

---

[15]   Edgar H. Sturtevant, *An Introduction to Linguistic Science* (1947): 86.

We saw in our discussion of E3 that overt editing is not always 'successful': *affoid*, supplied to replace *avord*, was another lapse. One recalls an example of the same sort of persistence of error, on a larger time-scale, supplied (and perhaps invented) by Joan Riviere in her translation of Freud's *General Introduction to Psychoanalysis*:[16] A typographical error made a war-correspondent's account of an army general appear as *this battle-scared veteran*. The apology and 'correction' the next day changed it to *the bottle-scarred veteran*.

From E4 we learn something else about overt editing. The presence and exact timing of overt editing may play an essential part in transmitting additional information, particularly of the sort not consciously intended for transmission by the speaker. In a sense, the correction of a lapse can constitute a 'metalapse'. If our TV performer had ignored his slip, simply saying *one silter cigarette from another*, there would have been no discernible hint at *silly*. There is a good chance that few would have observed the error at all. For /s-/ and /f-/ are acoustically similar; the relatively low fidelity of the audio circuits in most TV receivers diminishes the difference even more; and the audience would have done the rest, since one hears largely what one expects to hear. Or if the performer had delayed his correction a bit longer, saying *one silter?* – *filter cigarette from another*, the slip, though more noticable, would hardly have suggested a hidden comment *silly*. These, however, would have been different events, not the one that actually occurred.

Reading aloud is superficially very different from extemporaneous monolog or free conversation. Yet the sorts of lapses that occur are very similar, if not identical. This suggests that ordinary speech may, at least at times, be more like reading aloud than we have thought: as though the speaker first constructed a 'text' somewhere inside himself and then read it off, sometimes inaccurately.

5. METATHESES

A common – one might also say popular – type of lapse is one known technically as the *distant metathesis*, colloquially as a *Spoonerism* (from the Rev. A. W. Spooner of Oxford, famous for such slips).[17] All distant metatheses belong together in this respect: that what is actually said differs from what is 'intended' by an interchange of two nonadjacent parts: *beery wenches* for *weary benches*, with the nonadjacent /w-/ and |b-| interchanged; *tons of soil* for *sons of toil*; *half-warmed fish* for *half-formed wish*. But the underlying mechanisms require us to distinguish two subtypes: the DOUBLE-BLEND metathesis and the SINGLE-BLEND metathesis.

I have no example of the first type for which the attendant circumstances were adequately recorded, so that our analysis must be confined to relatively obvious factors. Consider:

---

[16]   My copy is a paperback reprint (Permabooks M-5001, sixth printing, 1957) of Rivière's authorized translation of the revised German edition; the first German edition appeared in 1916.
[17]   Sturtevant, *Introduction*: 37.

(intended:) I feel so foolish (E15)
(spoken:) I fool so feelish

This is like E3 in that it involves a blend followed by a compensating counterblend. But it also differs essentially from E3. In E3, the first blend is of two words either of which would be suitable in the setting, and the following counterblend is another blend of the same two words. The sentence would not make sense with BOTH words, one after the other. In E15, on the other hand, the first blend is of the anticipatory kind illustrated in E13: a blend between a word due for pronunciation now and one due to be spoken a moment later; and the following compensating counterblend is of the type illustrated in E14: between a word due for pronunciation now and one already spoken a moment earlier. The blend *fool* is intended *feel* 'contaminated' by *foolish*; the blend *feelish* is intended *foolish* 'contaminated' by preceding *feel* (even though *feel* did not in fact, in the actually spoken form, precede). Both of the 'target' words involved actually belong: if the forms are remetathesized, without any deletion, the result is smooth and normal. There is also a key difference in the deliveries of E3 and E15. After the first blend of E3, the speaker cuts his articulation off sharply and pauses before continuing. There is no such interruption in E15. A proffered 'correction' might follow the whole metathesis: *I fool so feelish?* – (*I mean I*) *feel so foolish*.

Apart from any deep 'Freudian' motivations behind a lapse of this sort, one inevitably thinks of this: by following the original anticipatory blend by a compensating retrogressive blend, at least all the phonemic ingredients of the intended phrase have been uttered, even if in a distorted order. One reason to suspect the functioning of this factor is that in some instances we know that the second part of a distant metathesis is CONSCIOUSLY planned and produced by the speaker after he has heard himself 'accidentally' produce the first part. That is, the first blend is a lapse, the second a witticism. Here is an instance: the pause denoted by the dash was longer in this episode than in most earlier examples:

(intended:) according to Smith and Trager (E16)
(spoken:) according to Smayth? – and Trigger

During the pause, the speaker decided that it would be more fun to carry the lapse through as a metathesis than to make the obvious correction. Beyond this, it is clear that the production of distant metatheses is in our culture a sort of game: in a poorer version, *I can't be under the alfluence of incohol, I've only had tee martoonis*; more elegantly, in that the metathesized phrase is itself meaningful and apt, *Brittania waives the rules*; *Time wounds all heels*; *A willful group of little men*; a newspaper headline about a woman who foiled a purse-snatcher: *She conks to stupor*; name of a syndicated newspaper column: *The Sighs of Bridge*; a certain high-level diplomat described as wielding *a velvet hand in an iron glove*; name of a brand of sun-tan oil: *Tanfastic*; slogan: *Contraception is a sin, as any See can plainly fool*. Once one has heard both a common phrase and its metathesis, particularly if the latter is also obviously meaningful (like *beery wenches* for *weary benches*) and sharply different in connotation, one may have to take special care to avoid using the metathesized form rather than the original – or, indeed, when one wishes to quote the metathesized form, not to slip and use the original instead. Linguists speaking in public live in dread of improperly metathesizing STRESS AND PITCH.

A double-blend metathesis does not necessarily involve the distortion of any constituent words, since whole words may be interchanged. In addition to the examples of this in the preceding paragraph, we may cite:

We'll try to get it done without too much rubber pipe or lead hose.   (E17)

On the other hand, the form involved need not be longer than a single word: *Tanfastic*, cited above, or the case of a TV interviewer talking with a woman missionary, who glanced at his notes and said:

Then what mativoted? – what motivated you to go to Spain?   (E18)

When the woman hesitated, the interviewer continued, incidentally explaining his lapse to us: *Your husband had something to do with it, didn't he?*

A single-blend metathesis involves the confusion of two phrases which are only slightly different in meaning and which are composed of the same words in opposite orders – most often, probably, a phrase of the form *X and Y* and one of the form *Y and X*. Example E16, or something very much like it, might have come about as a single-blend metathesis. Anyone acquainted with the work of Trager and with that of Smith is familiar with two phrases: *Trager and Smith* and *Smith and Trager*. On the point of referring to these two collaborators, one might fail to choose cleanly between the two orderings of the names, and say *Smayth and Trigger* (or *Trith and Smayger*, or the like), not as one blend followed by another but as a single blend of the two whole phrases. We can often know that a metathesis must be of the double-blend type: example E15 must be, since the 'target' phrase is not one of a pair of the sort required for a single-blend metathesis. On the other hand, we can rarely be certain that a metathesis is of the single-blend type. We gave E16 as an example of the double-blend type, but that is far from certain. The pause after *Smayth*, and the completion of the metathesized phrase as a witticism, are not decisive either way: the speaker may have been headed towards a single-blend metathesis, which he decided, after the pause, to carry through with, or he may simply have produced a blend which he decided to follow by the appropriate counterblend.

Freud gives the example *the Freuer-Breudian method*, uttered by someone perhaps equally familiar with the phrases *Freud and Breuer* and *Breuer and Freud*. He infers that the person guilty of the lapse was probably not favorably impressed by psychoanalysis.

A metathesis, probably of the single-blend type, occurring as a lapse, initiated the following sequence, said as the speaker was heading his car east over the San Francisco Bay Bridge:

This is how we go to Berkland and Oakeley? – Erkland and   (E18)
Boakeley? – no, Boakland and Erkeley? – darn it! Oakland and Berkeley!

Note the progression. The original target is *Oakland and Berkeley*, or the reverse. In the first try, the entire first syllables are interchanged. In the second try, the initial consonants of the first try are interchanged. In the third try, the entire first syllables of the second try are interchanged. In the fourth try, the initial consonants of the third try are interchanged, resulting in the proper form. However, after the initial lapse, the speaker became dimly aware of playing the permutations for effect, so that the episode could be described as a half-witticism. Of course, some people, like St. James, have no sense of humor.

But E18 is our first example of another very important phenomenon: some of the words actually spoken are comments on the rest. There is a standard typographical convention to indicate that a word or phrase is being mentioned rather than used; we put it in single quotes:

The word 'eradicate' is a verb.

In such a sentence, the words outside the quotation marks are about the word enclosed by them. Since what we have in E18 is the reverse of this, let us use the opposite typographical device, enclosing the inserted comments between quotation marks that curve the opposite way:

This is how we go to Berkland and Oakeley? – Erkland and Boakeley? –   (E18′)
'no‛, Boakland and Erkeley? – 'darn‛ it! Oakland and Berkeley!

The words that we have enclosed in these reversed quotation marks (call them 'dequotation marks') are part of the apparatus of overt editing. Conversational speech is full of this, and writers of fiction imitate it accurately; here is an example from fiction, in which I have merely modified the typography to use our new convention:

"Do gangsters marry their molls? 'Or is it‛ frails?"

Dequotation, like quotation, occurs in 'smooth' speech as well as rough, and has found its way into logical and mathematical discourse – where its presence has unfortunately been hidden by the lack of any conventional punctuation. When a mathematician writes

$$x_1, x_2, \ldots$$

(or something else of this sort), the three dots are an ETCETERA SYMBOL: instructions to the reader to go on inventing similar items as long as he likes. Now, clearly, this etcetera symbol is a comment on what surrounds it, and, given our typographical convention, ought to be enclosed by dequotation marks:

$$x_1, x_2, '\ldots‛$$

This, given the conventional understandings shared by mathematicians, is now a GRAMMAR-GENERATING SENTENCE (in contrast to Chomsky's would-be 'sentence-generating grammars'). All mathematical discussion of infinite sets, and much of the mathematical treatment of finite sets, turns on the appropriate manipulation of such sentences; logicians have encountered various dilemmas and anomalies that might disappear if dequotation were regularly marked.

6. COMPLEX EXAMPLES

In the preceding sections we have seen how a wide variety of lapses, traditionally classed under a number of rubrics (assimilation, haplology, metathesis, etc.), can be handled in terms of two basic mechanisms: blending and editing. Here we shall examine two blunders too complicated to fall simply into any of the traditional classes, but still susceptible to analysis in terms of the same two basic mechanisms.

I'm going to buy a new broof? – broof keese today.   (E19)

Here the initial lapse is the first *broof*: a blend of intended *brief* and the preceding word *new* (/núw/, not /nyúw/, in this speaker's dialect). The speaker heard the lapse, cut off, and hesitated. Then he decided (more or less as in E16) not to correct, but to carry on what had begun, and to metathesize *brief case*. Of course, this decision was based on a faulty diagnosis of what he had already uttered, and the intent had to fail. The appropriate metathesis would be *brayf keese*. Instead of this, *broof keese* repeats the *broof* for which we have already accounted, and then adds *keese* as a parallel blend of intended *case* with the undistorted form of the preceding word. That is, just as *broof* was *brief* with the vowel of *new*, so *keese* was case with the vowel of *brief*.

This is not the whole story. The sequence /-uw- ... -iy-/ in *broof keese* is familiar from a very small set of commonplace nouns that have /-uw-/ in the singular and /-iy-/ in the plural: *tooth* : *teeth*; *goose* : *geese*. Also, *keese* sounds like *geese* except at the beginning, where the two differ only as to voicing. The speaker was acknowledging that in some respect – perhaps in his indulgence in rather silly word-play – he was making a goose of himself.

I drove down to the Brome Couty? – Broome Couty   (E20)
Airpoint? – (slower) Broome County Airport.

Here *Brome* was the wrong word: the speaker had known a man named *Brome* who took a job in the county named *Broome*, and his confusion of the two words had been persistent. In his instant concern with whether he had spoken the right name, he produced next what we may call an ANTIBLEND (ordinarily called a DISSIMILATION): instead of replacing something in the target word *county* by something in another relevant word (here the immediately preceding one), something that is actually present in both the target word and the interfering word – the postvocalic nasal continuant – is deleted, yielding *couty*. Such an antiblend is presumably due to overcompensation in trying to avoid a blend. After *couty* the speaker broke off and tried a correction, properly replacing *Brome* by *Broome* but repeating the distorted *couty*. Noting that the /n/ had again been left out of this word, he sticks it into the next. The replacement of the /or/ of *port* by /oy/, before the intrusive /n/, is obscure save that the prejunctural cluster /-rnt/ does not occur in this speaker's dialect, and that the resulting *point* is homophonous with an actual word – and just such factors may be those involved in all cases of what is traditionally classed as CONTAMINATION. Finally, with a longer pause and with more deliberate articulation, a complete correction is appended.

7. MALAPROPISMS, BRIGHT SAYINGS, AND TROUBLE WITH PERSONAL NAMES

There are a number of phenomena not usually classed as lapses that show a significant kinship thereto.

At a rather formal preliminary hearing, the Army officer in charge said:

> We should be reminisce in our duty if we did not investigate.   (E21)

Here *reminisce in our duty* is a blend of the cliché *remiss in our duty* and the word *reminisce*: the former predominates, as is shown by the grammatical inappropriateness of the context for the word *reminisce*. If this were spoken by someone thoroughly familiar with both the phrase and the word, we should class it either as a lapse or as a witticism. However, in this instance observers were able to infer from the speaker's other speech and behavior that neither the phrase nor the word was part of his everyday active vocabulary. This leads to the classification of the event as a MALAPROPISM rather than as an ordinary lapse: a malapropism is a ridiculous misuse of a word, in place of one it resembles in sound, especially when the speaker is seeking a more elevated or technical style than is his wont and the blunder destroys the intended effect. The incongruity is heightened if the speaker himself gives no sign of awareness of the blunder – and this speaker did not.

The key difference lies in the speaker's degree of familiarity with the vocabulary he is using. If we unintentionally blend familiar expressions, we produce an ordinary lapse; if we unintentionally blend unfamiliar expressions, we may produce the special kind of lapse that is also a malapropism.

There is a third possibility. We may, with conscious intent, use an expression in just the form in which we learned it, and yet turn out to be wrong (as measured in terms of prevalent usage). Perhaps the speaker of E21, in his previous history, was first exposed to *reminisce* and later to *remiss in one's duty*; and perhaps, in the very process of adding the latter to his vocabulary, he blended it with *reminisce*. If so, then any occasion appropriate for the phrase *remiss in one's duty* would elicit from this speaker, not that phrase, but rather the phrase *reminisce in one's duty* – not as a lapse of the moment but as the presumably appropriate form. We should still call the usage a malapropism, of course: it turns out that some malapropisms are lapses and some are not, while some lapses are malapropisms and some are not.

In the moment-to-moment generation of speech, a correct recall of an incorrectly learned expression is obviously a different mechanism from the blurred or blended recall and use of correctly learned expressions. Let us call this new mechanism IDIOLECTAL DIVERGENCE: the speaker is speaking in full accord with his own linguistic repertory, but on the particular point his idiolect differs from general usage. If blending is involved in idiolectal divergence (as perhaps it often is), it is a blending that occurred somewhere in the speaker's past history, not one occurring now.

We cannot always know which mechanism is responsible for a particular blunder, and perhaps in some cases both mechanisms play a part. Thus, a young woman who intended to express how hungry she was once said, in my presence: *I'm simply ravishing* (for *ravenous*). The confusion of the two words was a standing one, not an innovation of the moment. At the same time, even if she had only rarely had occasion to use either word, her familiarity with both was sufficient that we could properly draw inferences, from the blunder, as to her emotional state at the moment of speaking. Such inferences would not be valid in the case of pure idiolectal divergence, any more than we could accuse someone of obscenity if a word he used happened to sound like an obscene word in a language known to us but not to him.

Since anything that occurs in one person's speech can spread into more general usage, what begins as an idiolectal divergence due to noisy learning can cease to be a potential malapropism and become a new 'standard' expression, often in competition with the older one of which it is a distortion. American English *Here we go gathering nuts in May* probably stems in this way from British *Here we go gathering nuts and may*: the plant-name *may* is generally unfamiliar in the United States. *Cut-and-dried* methods are very different from *cut-and-try* methods; I learned the former first, but suspect that it is a distortion of the latter. One speaks of instances of something being *few and far between*; I once heard a politician, in a TV address, say *far and few between*, which may have been a lapse but may also be a competing 'standard' form with the sort of origin we have just described.

Malapropisms from idiolectal divergence show an unexpected kinship with two other phenomena: 'bright sayings' of children, and certain misapplications of personal names (or of place names, as in E20).

All parents know that what a child says must stem from the child's experience, and that that experience is limited in comparison with their own. When a remark from a child reveals a sharp idiolectal divergence, parents think it cute rather than ludicrous, and if (within their adult frame of reference) it is in some way particularly a propos they call it a 'bright saying'. The child is thus rewarded for linguistic experimentation; but typically the mentors of the child also try in some way to correct the divergence, so as to bring the child's linguistic habits more in line with those of adults. Yet some divergences may go uncorrected for years. The older the individual grows, the rarer become the circumstances in which it is culturally appropriate for anyone else to correct his speech. If that which during childhood would be merely a childish error, perhaps even a 'bright saying', survives to adulthood, it is then a malapropism that one's friends are too kind or too embarrassed to mention. Sometimes a malapropism stemming from idiolectal divergence is mistakenly interpreted as a slip of the tongue or a witticism, and a correction is offered; the sequel is usually agonizing.

Part of the new linguistic material to which one is exposed day after day throughout life in a complex society[18] consists of the names of new acquaintances. Sometimes the name one must learn is one never encountered before – say, when one meets for the first time a Chinese named *Eng*. But even when the name is itself familiar – say, *Smith* or *Bill* – an addition to one's LANGUAGE habits is required. In part, this typical situation can be compared to that which pertains when one first learns of a *frog* in a railroad track, having previously known only of a *frog* in a swamp or of a *frog* in one's throat. In either case, the phonemic shape is familiar (*frog*; *Bill*) while the semantics are such that former uses of the word are of little or no help in acquiring the new use. In another respect, this comparison breaks down, because of a unique property of arbitrariness about personal names: all the individual occurrences of frogs in railroad tracks, to which the word *frog* can apply, have obvious features in common not shared by anything to which the word does not apply; but there is no necessary uniquely shared feature about all the people one knows whose names are *Bill*, except, extrinsically, just the sharing of that name. When one learns a new ordinary word (or a new range of use of one already familiar), one has acquired a suitable label for any of an indefinitely large class of items or events. When one learns the name of a new acquaintance, one has acquired the proper label only for a single individual.[19]

In addition to this special property of personal names, it is a fact that the name of a person one has just met is, and for a while remains, a relatively rare item in one's vocabulary. This is why the forgetting or mixing-up of personal names is akin to malapropisms, rather than to lapses involving thoroughly familiar ordinary words and phrases.

8. PUNS

All the lapses we have chosen as examples involve, in one way or another, the mechanism of blending. But not every obvious blend is a lapse: some are produced 'on purpose' rather than as 'accidents'. Whether a PUN is a lapse or not depends on the

[18]   I do not believe we have any reports on the forgetting of personal names – or, indeed, on most of the kinds of phenomena we are here discussing – from small face-to-face communities in which everyone knows everyone else personally. Such information would be enormously valuable.
[19]   There is nothing new in this discussion of the difference between proper names and other kinds of words – what is said in the text has been known for a long time. This topic is another on which I owe a personal debt to Jakobson, without whose guidance I would not have known of the traditional treatment.

same thing. For the moment, let us set aside any consideration of the planning of speech in or out of awareness, and show the relationship between blending and punning.

A blend of words or phrases that have little phonemic similarity does not resemble a pun at all. Thus, in E1, *shell* in its context is reminiscent of *shout* and of *yell*, but no one would call it a pun.

A blend of words or phrases that are similar, but not identical, in phonemic shape is indistinguishable from an inexact pun. If, in the situation in which E3 was spoken, the speaker had merely said *We weren't sure we could avord it*, we should have an inexact pun. The judgment of inexactness is rendered because in order to make *afford* sound more like *avoid* than it normally does (or vice versa) the phonemic shape must be distorted. Here is another example:

> The Mexican weather forecast: Chili today and hot tamale. (E22)

The inexactness is obvious: although *chili* and *chilly* are phonemically identical for most speakers of English, *tamale* and *tomorrow* are only similar. It is easy to describe E22 as a blend, say of the phrases *chilly today and hot tomorrow* and *chili and tamales*.

An EXACT PUN is a stretch of speech of a determinate phonemic structure which is susceptible of two or more interpretations. In order for the pun to be noticeable, it is also necessary for at least two of the interpretations to be relevant in the context in which the pun occurs. Thus:

> A father called his cattle ranch 'Focus' because it was where (E23)
> $/^2$ðə + sânz + rêyz + ^{3}míyt^1 #/

The *double entendre* is at least similar to, perhaps the same as, the exact pun:

> The French missionaries moved westwards through the wilderness, (E24)
> converting the Indians, mainly to dust.

Theoretically, the difference is as follows. In the exact pun, two distinct words or phrases (*sons raise meat*, *sun's rays meet*) happen to be phonemically identical, whereas in the double entendre a single word or phrase (*converting*) has two relevant ranges of meaning, both brought to the hearer's attention by context. This distinction is not always easy to make, and may be spurious. In the examples, perhaps most speakers of English would agree that *meat* and *meet* are different words that 'just happen' to sound alike, and that *convert* 'change the state of' and *convert* 'render Christian' are the same word. But this agreement may stem from spelling habits.

If we insist that the essence of blending is that elements drawn from two phonemically different words or phrases must be present, then we cannot discern the mechanism of blending in exact puns. But it is more profitable to consider, as the essence of blending, the tendency to say more than one thing, with no participating tendency completely suppressed. When the words or phrases involved are quite dissimilar, the result is an unpunlike blend. When they are similar but not exactly the same, the result is an inexact pun. When they are phonemically identical, the result is an exact pun (or a double entendre, if there is any point in making the distinction), since, in this case, by exception, it is possible for the speaker to say two forms at the same time: neither expression requires any articulatory motions that conflict with those required for the other.

9. STUTTERING

A certain connection between slips of the tongue and STUTTERING (or STAMMERING) can be discerned in the following:

> You made so much noise you worke Cor? – wore? – w? –   (E25)
> woke Corky up.

The first slip here is an anticipatory blend: *worke* /wôrk/ was intended *woke* with the *-or-* of *Corky*, due to come next. The speaker noticed the lapse after he had gotten part way through *Corky*, and broke off. The first effort at a correction was itself wrong: instead of saying *woke*, the speaker began to repeat the wrong form he had already uttered. Again detecting the error, he again broke off. The next effort at a correction was broken off even more quickly. We cannot tell whether at this point the speaker was aimed properly at *woke* or was about to come out with another repetition of the blend. Perhaps the speaker could not tell either, and perhaps this was why he broke off again. The hesitation after the lone *w-* was a bit longer, as the speaker mar-shalled his attention to guarantee that on the next trial things would come out right. This is the point at which, in some instances of this sort of stammering, the speaker inserts a whistle, seemingly a device to 'untangle' the speech organs, but certainly also a conventional acknowledgment of the stammering and a would-be-humorous apology for it.

The most obvious affinity shown by this example is between stuttering and overt editing. After the first breaking-off, the speaker makes three successive tries at a re-placement for the incorrect phrase, and is successful only on the third. The resem-blance to stuttering would have been greater if the speaker had detected the initial error more quickly, and so had said *you worke? – wore? – w? – woke Corky up.* Or suppose he had detected that he was headed in the wrong direction – or that he had merely begun to fear that he was headed wrong – at the very beginning of the target word *woke*; he might then have said *you w? – w? – w? – woke Corky up.* In this version, all difference from stuttering has vanished.

A lapse is, in a sense, an indication of indecision: the speaker is operating under two (or more) conflicting tendencies and does not completely resolve them. Many a lapse is followed by a correction, but such overt editing can also involve lapses. No one's speech is completely free of lapses – the only way to avoid them altogether is to keep silent. Although many lapses are utterly trivial, nevertheless everyone would prefer to avoid certain lapses under certain conditions, and probably some people are permanently fearful of any lapse at all. Whenever, for whatever reason, a speaker feels some anxiety about a possible lapse, he will be led to focus attention more than normally on what he has just said and on what he is just about to say. These are ideal breeding grounds for stuttering. The stutter need not be preceded by an overt and obvious blend, as it is in E25: a word can be broken off virtually as it begins merely for fear that it will not come out right, and then indecision between one word and another, or between the right word and a threatening blend, can produce a series of attempted corrections, each in turn cut off, before the speaker gets back on the track – if, indeed, he does.

I propose the foregoing as a general diagnosis of the stuttering of ordinary people, but only as part of the diagnosis of the articulatory spasms of the pathological stutterer. Apart from possible gross neurophysiological factors, the latter differs from 'everyday' stuttering at least in that stuttering has itself become both a habit and a source of anxiety.

10. BLENDING AND ANALOGY

Jespersen[20] cites a report of a child who, stifled by the heat in a house in the tropics, said

It's three hot in here! (E26)

One of my own children (at age about 5), having often been told *Don't interrup(t)*, chose an appropriate occasion to say to me:

Daddy, you're înterring úp! (E27)

It does not matter whether we think of these as lapses, as 'bright sayings', or merely as childish errors: in any case, they are peculiar. The classical explanation is in terms not of blending but of ANALOGY. Thus, for the first we can sketch a frame of reference as follows:

I'd like two pieces	:	I'd like three pieces	::
We waited two minutes	:	We waited three minutes	::
Give me two hot ones	:	Give me three hot ones	::
...	:	...	::
It's too hot in here	:	X.	

All the listed sentences are supposed to be already familiar, as wholes, to the speaker; of course, lacking detailed records, we can only guess as to their actual identity. The dots represent any number of further pairs of familiar utterances. The members of each pair differ in sound only in that the second of the pair has /θrîy/ where the first has /tûw/; in meaning, they differ in that the second of the pair refers to something

[20] J. O. H. Jespersen, *Language* (1922: 122).

more or bigger than does the first. Solving for X is simple: this, it is supposed, is exactly what the child did when he uttered E26. For E27 a similar scheme can be guessed at; we have to suppose that ambient noise had masked out, for the child in question, the final /t/ of *interrupt* and the absence of any /+/ between the /r/ and the last vowel, but that is quite realistic:

Don't wake up the baby	:	You're waking up the baby	::
Don't burn up that paper	:	You're burning up that paper	::
Don't sit up	:	You're sitting up	::
...	:	...	::
Don't interrup(t)	:	X.	

A transformation, of course, is an analogy:

John shot the tiger	:	The tiger was shot by John	::
Bill read the book	:	The book was read by Bill	::
The butcher weighed the meat	:	The meat was weighed by the butcher	::
...	:	...	::
The meat weighed ten pounds	:	X.	

Thus the solution for X might be said, as a lapse or as a witticism.

In the context of nineteenth century historical linguistics, where matters such as blending and analogy were first discussed in detail, the concern was with the mechanisms by which a language changes in time. Analogy was proposed, on excellent empirical grounds, as one of the three basic mechanisms of linguistic change, the other two being borrowing and sound change[21]. It was recognized, however, that there are also some minor phenomena not clearly reducible to any of the major mechanisms, and yet felt in some obscure way to be more closely akin to analogy than to the other two. Blending was regularly listed as one of these subsidiary types, along with haplology, metathesis, progressive and regressive assimilation, contamination, and so on.

Now, the relation of blending to analogy is perfectly straightforward[22]. In many, perhaps most, speech situations, many different analogies are at work, each with its own degree of 'pressure'. Some of them are incompatible, in the sense that following one precludes accurately following another. If all incompatibilities are suppressed, the result is, at most, a lapse like E26 or E27. If two (or, in theory, perhaps more) incompatible analogies are followed – as best one can, considering the limitations of one speaker's quota of articulatory equipment – then the result is a blend. Hesitating between *sigh* : *sighed* :: *swim* : X and *sing* : *sang* :: *swim* : X, a child or a tired adult may come out with *swammed*, where both analogies are attested. All the examples of blends we have given in earlier sections illustrate the same point: the diagnosis given earlier are easily recast into terms of conflicting analogies.

[21]   Thus in all the standard basic works, from Paul through Bloomfield.
[22]   On this one point, my treatment in *A Course in Modern Linguistics* (1958: 443) goes beyond its predecessors: the kinship of blending to analogy is overtly recognized.

But this means that there is no longer any mystery about the relation of haplology, metathesis, and the like to analogy. In the preceding sections, we have shown how all the PHENOMENA classed under such labels can be accounted for in terms of two MECHANISMS: blending and editing. Given the relation of blending to analogy, which we have just reviewed, we can conclude that all the kinds of blunders and allied phenomena we have discussed in this paper can be explained in terms of just three fundamental mechanisms: analogy; blending (= unresolved conflict of analogies); and editing.

11. THE GENERATION OF SPEECH

Let us now turn to the consideration of all speech, smooth as well as blunderful.

Clearly the difference between smooth and blunderful speech is real, except that this simple pair of terms undercuts the facts. The difference is one of degree, not of kind, and there is more than one norm and more than one direction of possible deviation from each norm.

It is currently fashionable to assume that, underlying the actual more or less bumbling speech behavior of any human being, there is a subtle and complicated but determinate linguistic 'competence': a sentence-generating device whose design can only be roughly guessed at by any techniques so far available to us. This point of view makes linguistics very hard and very erudite, so that anyone who actually does discover facts about underlying 'competence' is entitled to considerable kudos.

Within this popular frame of reference, a theory of 'performance' – of the 'generation of speech' – must take more or less the following form. If a sentence is to be uttered aloud, or even thought silently to oneself, it must first be built by the internal 'competence' of the speaker, the functioning of which is by definition such that the sentence will be legal ('grammatical') in every respect. But this is not enough; the sentence as thus constructed must then be PERFORMED, either overtly so that others may hear it, or covertly so that it is perceived only by the speaker himself. It is in this second step that blunders may appear. That which is generated by the speaker's internal 'competence' is what the speaker 'intends to say', and is the only real concern of linguistics; blunders in actually performed speech are intrusions from elsewhere. Just if there are no such intrusions is what is performed an instance of 'smooth speech'.[23]

I believe this view is unmitigated nonsense, unsupported by any empirical evidence of any sort. In its place, I propose the following.

ALL speech, smooth as well as blunderful, can be and must be accounted for essentially in terms of the three mechanisms we have listed: analogy, blending, and editing. An individual's language, at a given moment, is a set of habits – that is, of analogies; where different analogies are in conflict, one may appear as a constraint on the working of another. Speech actualizes habits – and changes the habits as it does so. Speech

[23] This, or something very much like it, is the only interpretation I can make of what Chomsky says, particularly in his *Aspects of the Theory of Syntax* (1965), ch. 1.

reflects awareness of norms; but norms are themselves entirely a matter of analogy (that is, of habit), not some different kind of thing.

If, in a particular speech situation, only one analogy plays any part in determining what is said, then what is said is an exact repetition of something the speaker has heard or said before. The situation I face this morning is similar, as our culture categorizes things, to one yesterday morning, in which my satisfactory response was *Good morning*!; analogously, that is my response in the current situation. If the current situation is partly like various earlier situations, then various analogies may come into play, and what is said will often be new; even if, in historical fact, it is something that has been said before, it may be being newly composed now, by just the mechanisms we have discussed. It is the mechanisms of analogy, blending, and editing that account for our constant coinage of novel sentences. No more subtle or mysterious factor need be sought.

Anything that is actually said – unless it is just too long and complicated – may be registered as a unit, and may then recur by mere recitation from memory. This happens so often that we can never be sure, when we hear something novel to us, whether it is being coined at the moment or recited from memory. This is an important fact about language, but alters in no way our acceptance of analogy, blending and editing as the basic mechanisms of the generation of speech.

The act of speaking aloud is indeed, as the currently popular view holds, typically a two-stage process, but not in the strange sense proposed by that view. The 'inner' stage I shall call PRIMARY GENERATION. This goes on partly in and partly out of awareness. It is 'thinking in words': the virtually unbroken inner flow of 'heard' speech, from which we make certain selections to be spoken aloud (§ 4, end). On the psychiatrist's couch, one is supposed to read out this inner flow as accurately as one can, with no further editing or suppression. The inner flow is self-generating: it is carried along in trial-and-error fashion in response to changing external circumstances, the heard speech of others, and its own past history (especially its immediate past); it can be blunderful as well as smooth. Thus, I have observed 'slips of the tongue' in my own inner flow, often caught and edited out before they could be mapped into overt speech by tongue and lips. The mechanisms of this inner flow are not something weirdly different from those observable in overt speech. They are, in fact, exactly the same mechanisms, internalized from shared public experience. In SHORT perspective, that which goes on internally is causally prior to that which is spoken aloud. But in LONG perspective – that of the individual life-history – public events are causally prior to the private ones.

Editing in the internal flow is COVERT EDITING. The norms reflected in this editing must themselves be the result of internalization, since there is no other possible source; but they can function differently here precisely because some of the internal flow is not mapped into overt speech. We very often think of something, during a conversation, that we decide not to say: norms have not prevented our thinking of it – that is, have not prevented the internal flow from phrasing it, or beginning to – but lead us to decide to keep it to ourselves. In certain formal circumstances, covert editing is thorough, and overt speech is unusually smooth. Much more typically, what is actually said aloud includes various signs of OVERT EDITING, as discussed in preceding sections.

Beyond the design implied by the factors and mechanisms we have discussed, a language has no design. The search for an exact determinate formal system with which a language can be precisely characterized is a wild goose chase, because a language neither is nor reflects any such system. A language is not, as Saussure thought, a system "où tout se tient". Rather, the apt phrase is Sapir's "all grammars leak".

The mechanisms of the generation of speech are also the mechanisms of linguistic change, just as our predecessors of a century ago suspected, except that there are two factors in the latter which play only indirect parts in the former. What one person says aloud, another person may try to imitate; hence we have borrowing, including noisy borrowing (§ 7). And sound change, as a mass statistical phenomenon, plays no immediate role in controlling what one says, overtly or covertly, at a given moment.[24]

---

[24] See Charles F. Hockett, "Sound change", *Language*, 41 (1965): 185–204. However, honesty forces me to retract all the favorable remarks made about Chomsky and his proposals in connection with my discussion of the 'Fourth Breakthrough', which I now believe would more accurately be characterized as a 'breakdown'.

SLIPS OF THE TONGUE*

DONALD S. BOOMER

Laboratory of Psychology, National Institute of Mental Health, Bethesda, Maryland

JOHN D. M. LAVER

Department of Phonetics and Linguistics, University of Edinburgh

INTRODUCTION

Our usage of the term tongue-slip can be illustrated in a preliminary, informal way by reference to a characteristic example. Consider the following utterance, noted during a dinner-table conversation.

But those frunds... funds have been frozen.

Frunds, here, is a tongue-slip, a form involuntarily produced by the speaker instead of the intended *funds*. Such fleeting misarticulations are relatively common in ordinary spontaneous speech. They have been aptly characterised by one of our colleagues as an aspect of "the speech pathology of everyday life". This observation indirectly raises a theoretical issue which is an essential part of the context of the study to be reported here.

Abercrombie (1965) has drawn an important distinction between "conversation" and "spoken prose", a distinction which is almost never explicitly recognized in linguistics. The overwhelming bulk of man's daily use of spoken language comes under the heading of conversation. Spoken prose includes dramatic dialogue, monologues, prepared lectures, and – we would add – linguistic citation sentences. These forms, Abercrombie points out, are regularised, highly specialised abstractions from conversation and account for only a very small part of spoken language. Despite this unrepresentativeness, however, spoken prose continues unaccountably to be the exclusive subject matter of linguistics.

In order to justify this delimitation of its area of interest, linguistics has established an explicit distinction between 'well-formed' and 'deviant' utterances. Implicit in this distinction, and nearly unnoticed, has been a corollary equation of well-formed with 'normal' and deviant with 'abnormal'. Deviations are thus dismissed as linguistically

* Reprinted from the *British Journal of Disorders of Communication* 3(1) (1968).
This research was carried out during the academic year 1966–1967 at the University of Edinburgh, where the senior author was Honorary Lecturer in the Department of Phonetics at the kind invitation of Professor David Abercrombie.

irrelevant, since they represent trivial departures from the hypothetical norms which linguistics seeks to describe.

It is important to recognize that in speech 'normal' does not mean 'perfect'. The norm for spontaneous speech is demonstrably imperfect. Conversation is characterised by frequent pauses, hesitation sounds, false starts, misarticulations and corrections. In choosing to define away these characteristic irregularities, linguistics discards a potentially powerful check on the veridicality of competing models of speech performance.

Capsule demonstrations of the operation of a given linguistic model on carefully selected citation utterances are not compelling since any instance of spoken prose may be equally consonant with a number of internally consistent systems which have been expressly constructed to generate spoken prose. The study of natural, 'live' speech, however, with its characteristic irregularities preserved, can provide crucial theoretical leverage in that a careful analysis of the irregularities in context may reveal functional patterns which are consistent with one hypothetical model and contradictory of others. Neurophysiologists from Hughlings Jackson on have suggested that our understanding of complex mental processes may be facilitated by working into the system 'backwards' from its output rather than forward from its input. This research strategy is one of the foundations of the study to be reported here.

This paper, then, is addressed to only one aspect of the speech process: the control of sequencing of speech units, and even more narrowly, to the kinds of speech errors called tongue-slips which result from transient malfunctions of this system. To the degree that observed tongue-slips can be shown to be structured, and not simply the result of random malfunctioning of the speech producing process, then their obedience to the constraints of a descriptive and explanatory theory may provide the basis for deriving some of the relevant properties or characteristics of the sequencing system, of interest to linguistics, psychology and neurophysiology.

PREVIOUS WORK

Our search of the literature has turned up very few systematic studies of tongue-slips (Bawden 1900, Cohen 1966, Freud 1901, Fromkin 1966, Meringer 1908, Meringer and Mayer 1895, Oertel 1901, Simonini 1956, Sturtevant 1917, 1947, Wells 1951). In the light of the opening discussion this is perhaps not surprising. An additional explanation for this neglect may be afforded by the social-perceptual aspects of tongue-slips. In everyday circumstances we simply do not hear many of our own tongue-slips nor those made by others. They can be discerned in running speech only by adopting a specialised 'proofreader' mode of listening. In ordinary conversation it is as though we were bound by a shared, tacit, social agreement, both as listeners and as speakers, to keep the occurrence of tongue-slips out of conscious awareness, to look beyond them, as it were, to the regularised, idealised intended utterance. In this sense our everyday speech behaviour can be likened to the analytic behaviour of linguists, as discussed above. Thus it may be that the automatic perceptual screen which keeps tongue-slips out of social awareness has also operated to keep them out of scientific awareness, despite their frequent occurrence.

If this selective inattention toward tongue-slips which we posit helps to explain the limited amount of previous work, an additional explanation can be suggested for the general lack of penetration of the conclusions drawn from what work has been done. Most writers have been content with a superficial description of those tongue-slips they have observed, noting mainly a tendency for the contextual determination of the slip to be anticipatory in action, and borrowing chiefly from philology such descriptive categories as 'assimilation', 'dissimilation', 'analogy', etc. A possible reason for this superficiality is that tongue-slips have been assumed to constitute, for reasons outlined above, departures from 'normal' behaviour, and thus to lack the structure of normal behaviour. It is easy, though fallacious, to extend this assumption to support the belief that tongue-slips have practically no rigorous structure, and that a low-level description is adequately penetrating.

From the standpoint of psychology and of general phonetics such culturally conditioned labels as 'normal' and 'abnormal' are at odds with the fundamental scientific assumption that any aspect of human behaviour is potentially structured and thus subject to explanation.

Another possible influence here is the close and immediate psychoanalytic connotation of tongue-slip. Freud's careful observations and brilliant formulations concerning the unconscious motivations of tongue-slips have surrounded this term with an aura of psychopathology. It is our view, however, that the mechanics of slips can be studied linguistically without reference to their motivation. In the bulk of our examples a plausible origin for the intrusion can be found in the immediate environment of the slip. In many of Freud's examples, no such immediate environmental origin is apparent. Freud recognised this distinction in *Psychopathology of Everyday Life:* "The disturbance in speaking which is manifested in a slip of the tongue can ... be caused by the influence of another component of the same speech ... The disturbance could however be of a second kind ...; it could result from influences outside this word, sentence or context, and arise out of elements which are not intended to be uttered and of whose excitation we only learn precisely through the actual disturbance" (Freud 1901, trans. A. Tyson 1966, p. 56).

CORPUS

The speech material which was analysed for this study is a collection, made by the senior author over a period of several years, of more than a hundred tape-recorded brief excerpts of natural speech, each excerpt containing a slip and some context. These were taken from conference discussions, broadcasts, normal conversations, and from interviews with psychiatric patients whose speech was free from any pathological defects. Thirty-five different speakers are represented; all but one are native speakers of

English. The accents of most of the speakers can be characterised as General American; those of the remainder represent one or another of the varieties of British English.

The conclusions reached on the basis of this corpus were validated against an additional corpus of over a hundred orthographically-recorded slips personally heard in normal conversation by the authors.

DEFINITIONS

Before any further discussion of tongue-slips, it will be necessary to distinguish clearly between these events and other non-fluencies in the sequencing of speech such as stuttering and re-starts occasioned by in-process revisions of the speaker's linguistic intention.

A SLIP OF THE TONGUE (hereinafter SLIP), IS AN INVOLUNTARY DEVIATION IN PERFORMANCE FROM THE SPEAKER'S CURRENT PHONOLOGICAL, GRAMMATICAL OR LEXICAL INTENTION.
Slips involve units of varying size, from segments to sequences of segments, to whole syllables and words, on the phonological level; on the grammatical level units include morphemes and whole words, and, more rarely, higher-order constituent groups.

The deviation is almost always detected, not necessarily consciously, by the speaker, and corrected. In any given instance, the discrepancy between the aberrant utterance and the correction defines the slip. In a few instances in our corpus, where the deviation was uncorrected, we analysed the slip with reference to the inferred intention, or if the intention was unclear, we noted a number of alternative determinations and categorised the slip as not being unambiguously analysable by our procedure.

CLASSIFICATIONS

There are three general modes of slip: MISORDERING of units in the string, OMMISION of a unit, or REPLACEMENT of a unit. The units most often involved are segments, morphemes and words. Unit-mode categorisations allow descriptions of slips as SEGMENTAL REPLACEMENT (SR), MORPHEMIC OMISSION (MO), WORD MISORDERING (WM), etc., as summarized in the following table:

	Misordering	*Omission*	*Replacement*
Segment	SM	SO	SR
Morpheme	MM	MO	MR
Word	WM	WO	WR

Segmental slips are by far the most common, involving about sixty per cent of the examples. A detailed report including the higher-order classes of slips would take this article beyond its intended scope; hence this exposition of the analysis and results will be focused mainly on the segmental slips.

Within the class 'segmental slip', SR slips are the most common, and fall into three subcategories: (SIMPLE) SEGMENTAL REPLACEMENT (SR), where the slip has the same number of segments as the intended word; SEGMENTAL REPLACEMENT WITH AUGMENTATION (SR[A]), where the slip has more segments than the intended word; and SEGMENTAL REPLACEMENT WITH REDUCTION (SR[R]), where the slip has fewer segments than the intended word.

PROCEDURE

The exposition of the analytic procedure may be best understood by reference to Figure 1, a reproduction of the form which was employed in recording the analysis. The slip is the one which was quoted in the introduction.

In Figure 1, Line 1 is a transcription of the utterance in ordinary orthography, including the slip, but excluding other nonfluencies and any parenthetic remarks the speaker may have made about the slip.

Line 2 is a phonemic transcription of the utterance listed in Line 1. The capital letters above the transcription, S, T, O, identify, respectively, the slip, the target, and the origin. The TARGET word is the word at which the speaker was aiming when he made the slip. In the example cited, the word *frozen* has interfered with *funds* to produce *frunds*. *Frozen* is thus the origin, *funds* the target and *frunds* the slip. The short vertical arrow after *frunds* indicates the point at which the utterance was checked.

Line 3 is our reconstruction of the intended utterance, in phonemic transcription, omitting the slip and repetitions of any preceding function words which may accompany the correction.

1. Orthography: But those frunds funds have been frozen

                                                 S   ↓T   O

2. Utterance: /bət ðouz frʌndz fʌndz hav bin frouzn/

3. Intention: /bət ðouz   fʌndz hav bin frouzn/

4. Rhythm: W S   S   W   W   Ś   W |

                                        ←————————

5. Syllable structure	I^1	I^2	I^3	N	F^4	F^3	F^2	F^1
Origin	f	r	—	ou	—	—	—	—
Target	f	—	—	ʌ	—	n	d	z
Slip	f	r	—	ʌ	—	n	d	z
Source of segments in slip	T,O	O	—	T	—	T	T	T

6. Notes   SR(A) slip

(a) OI^2/r/ is substituted anticipatorily for TI^2 zero.

(b) O is in tonic syllable, T is in immediately preceding salient syllable.

(c) O and T share I^1 = /f/. O and T both in salient syllables.

Fig. 1. Illustrative Protocol for Analysis of Tongue Slips.

Line 4 contains the rhythmical and intonational information about the intended utterance, as far as it could be established from the actual utterance and the corrected utterance. *S* and *W* signify SALIENT (stressed) and WEAK syllables respectively in the unit of rhythm, the FOOT, a concept described by Abercrombie (1964). While this concept is applicable to the rhythm of both American and British English, one is less confident of the similarity of American and British intonation. We are only interested here, however, in two relatively uncontroversial aspects of intonation – the location of intonation unit boundaries, and the location of the most prominent syllable within units thus demarcated. We mark the former with vertical lines, the latter with an acute symbol (') over the syllable concerned. British readers can assume that the system uses Halliday's analysis of intonation (Halliday, 1963), marking TONE-GROUP boundaries and the location of the TONIC syllable in each tone-group. This terminology will be adopted throughout. American readers may transpose these features into the system described by Trager and Smith (1951). For TONE-GROUP, read PHONEMIC CLAUSE; for TONE-GROUP BOUNDARY, read TERMINAL JUNCTURE; for TONIC SYLLABLE, read PRIMARY STRESS. This equivalence obviously rests on our assumption that American and British forms of English do not differ importantly with regard to these particular features.

The sample utterance here, then, contains one tone-group or phonemic clause, with the boundary falling after *frozen*, and with the tonic or primary stress on the first syllable of *frózen*.

The horizontal arrow below Line 4 shows the span and direction of influence of the slip, from origin to target. A left-hand arrow, as is shown here, marks an ANTICIPATORY slip, in that the origin is in a word not yet uttered when the slip occurs. A right-hand arrow marks a PERSEVERATIVE slip, in which the origin is in a word already uttered.

Section 5 is an analysis of the segmental composition of the origin, target and slip syllables. The analytic framework is the canonical structure of the phonological syllable in English, in terms of which up to three initial consonant segments, (I), are possible, and up to four final consonant segments, (F), with the nuclear segment (N), located medially. Any English syllable can be portrayed in this framework with dashes (–) representing zeros in those positions not occupied by segments in that particular syllable.

The bottom line in Section 5 shows the provenance of each segment in the slip syllable. An entry T means that the segment also appears in the same position in the target syllable; an O that the segment also appears in the same position in the origin syllable; and T, O means that the slip segment appears in the same position in both the target and the origin syllables.

The tape-recorded examples were jointly analysed by the authors, using a tape-loop repeater. When we could not agree on a given feature, the opinion of one or more colleagues was solicited. It should be made clear that the present form of the analytic procedure grew out of the raw data rather than having been applied at the outset. Theoretical insights and procedural modifications growing out of the first analysis required a second and ultimately a third complete reanalysis of the entire corpus.

RESULTS

Analysis of the segmental slips in the terms outlined above revealed a number of significant patterns. These are presented below as a set of tongue-slip laws, with 'law' to be understood in a statistical rather than in an absolute sense.

A. Slips involve the tonic word, either as origin or as target, with tonic origins predominating.

B. The target and the origin of a tongue-slip are both located in the same tone-group.

C. Exceptions to Law B form another structured class of their own: where target and origin are located in different (usually adjacent), tone-groups, each will be in the tonic word in its own tone-group.

D. The origin syllable and the target syllable of a slip are metrically similar, in that both are salient, or both are weak, with salient-salient pairings predominating.

E. Segmental slips obey a structural law with regard to syllable-place; that is, initial segments in the origin syllable replace initial segments in the target syllable, nuclear replace nuclear, and final replace final.

F. Segmental slips obey phonologically orthodox sequence rules; that is, segmental slips do not result in sequences not permitted by normal phonology.[1]

A final generalisation will also be listed here although it is not strictly a law, but rather a failure to find obedience to a law. 'Similarity' has been previously proposed as a determinant of tongue-slips in such terms as "the coalescence of similars" (Bawden 1900). In a matrix tabulation of origin and target segments we could discern no general tendency for interactions to occur between segments sharing one or more articulatory features.[2] We conclude, accordingly, that articulatory similarity is not an important determinant.

It should be noted that Laws A and B considered together account for the prevalence of anticipatory slips over perseverative slips. Since (1) origins are predominantly tonic words, and (2) the tonic usually falls on the last lexical item in the tone-group, and (3) the target is usually in the same tone-group as the origin, then most slips are necessarily anticipatory. Thus the 'law' of anticipation reduces to an artefact.

As emphasized above, these are probability laws, not exceptionless statements. Not every slip obeys every law. On the other hand, no slip in our corpus violates all the laws. An overall confidence estimate in statistical terms is not feasible since the complex probabilities of the underlying events cannot be satisfactorily combined into a single statement. As a rough indication of the power of this set of laws and the

---

[1] Rulon Wells (1951) first expressed this conclusion in his "First Law" of tongue-slips, "A slip of the tongue is practically always a phonetically possible noise". By 'phonetically possible' he meant phonologically possible in the language concerned.

[2] There were two exceptions to this: (a) sequences of voiceless fricatives seemed to encourage mistakes of place of articulation, and (b) alveolar consonants showed a slight tendency to interact, The instability of alveolar consonants in English has been noted before, in other aspects of connected speech, such as assimilation, by A. C. Gimson (1960).

extent of their generalisability, however, their overall correctness as applied to the total corpus of segmental slips is over eighty per cent.

INTERPRETATION

1. At a phenomenal level, the segmental tongue slip has been shown to be considerably more structured than has previously been believed. The origin of the interfering sound can now be identified more precisely. In any segmental replacement slip there is a high probability that its origin will be found (a) in the tonic word in the tone-group in which it occurs, (b) in the salient syllable of the tonic word, if the slip occurs in a salient syllable; in a weak syllable if the slip is in a weak syllable, (c) at the same syllable place, i.e., initial, nuclear or final.

It is necessary, in a discussion of segmental slips, to distinguish between different aspects of articulation. While suprasegmental aspects relevant to higher-order articulatory units such as the syllable, the foot, and the tone-group are centrally involved in determining slips, the segmental aspects of articulation of vowels and consonants as such seem to be much less important.

2. More generally, these results provide an empirical basis for inferring some of the properties of the speech production system. The neurophysiological aspects of these interpretations are loosely descriptive, and nothing more rigorous is intended. We have not presumed to formulate a neurophysiological theory of speech sequencing, but merely to specify some functional properties of the neurophysiological system which seemed to be implied by the output characteristics we have observed.

A. The pivotal rôle of the tonic word in slips suggests that its phonological, syntactic and semantic prominence is matched by an analogous neurophysiological prominence, coded in the brain as a part of the articulatory programme. Note that the typical slip involves interference from the tonic word BEFORE it is uttered.

B. The fact that the span of interference in a slip is usually within one tone-group suggests that this unit is not simply a linguistic construct, but can plausibly be assumed to have behavioural properties, as well.[3] In our view, the tone-group is handled in the central nervous system as a unitary behavioural act, and the neural correlates of the separate elements are assembled and partially activated, or 'primed', before the performance of the utterance begins. This state of affairs whereby target and origin are simultaneously represented in an interim assembly maximizes the likelihood of interaction between them. This hypothesis also accounts for the observed fact that interactions across tone group boundaries are fairly rare.

When slips do transcend tone-group boundaries, it will be recalled from Law

---

[3] An initial formulation of the tone-group or phonemic clause as a unit with both linguistic and psychological properties was put forward by Boomer in a study of hesitation pauses (Boomer 1965). For related evidence on the perceptual side, see Dittmann and Llewellyn (1967).

C that the interaction is between the tonic words of the two tone-groups. In order to reconcile this fact with the above interpretation it is only necessary to add the not unreasonable assumption that the assembly of the next tone-group is already under way before the current one has been uttered and that the tonic syllable is the only element with sufficient neurophysiological prominence to break through the inhibitory forces holding the programme in check.[4]

C. We have seen that there is an obedience to structural and metric laws in the segmental slip; that is to say an initial segment in the target is likely to be interfered with by an initial segment in the origin, with the additional constraint that pairs of salient syllables or pairs of weak syllables are likely to interfere with one another as origin and target. This suggests that syllable structure and rhythm are also more than just linguistic constructs, and can be plausibly considered to be central aspects of the neural control programme in speech.

Lenneberg (1967) has drawn together a number of lines of evidence concerning rhythmic phenomena in the brain, proposing, as had Lashley, a fundamental neural "pacemaker" as a grid within which articulatory events are serially organized and integrated.

Suprasegmental features of structure and rhythm of units like the syllable are more relevant to the description of malfunctions in the sequencing control of speech than are narrowly segmental features of articulation. This suggests that a division of the speech chain into segments is a more artificial exercise than is a division into these higher-order units. Segments would seem to have reality in neural coding only as modifications, nuclear and marginal, of more basic units such as the syllable, the foot, and the tone-group. Or, to put the proposition more directly, segmental slips are the result of interaction, at the neural level, between higher-order units, even though the perceptual result of the slip may be apparently restricted to a change of segment-identity. That we perceive the result as involving segments, rather than as involving properties of syllables, for instance, may be attributable to a perceptual 'set' given to us, as listeners, by our alphabetic culture, and, as linguists, by a phonemic approach to phonological analysis.

ADDITIONAL HYPOTHESES

The tongue-slip laws presented above are supported by the main body of data, and are put forward with a reasonable degree of confidence. A number of less-supported ideas emerged in the course of the work, some of them deriving from only one or two

---

[4] Karl Lashley's disciplined speculations concerning the relation between speech and brain events have provided the neurological framework within which we have ordered our data. In speaking of 'spoonerisms', he wrote, "In these contaminations, it is as if the aggregate of words were in a state of partial excitation, held in check by the requirements of grammatical structure, but ready to activate the final common path, if the effectiveness of this check is in any way interfered with" (Lashley, 1951).

instances of a phenomenon. These will be presented more tentatively, as no more than promising leads.

1. ACCOMMODATORY ADJUSTMENTS. The following slip was made: ...*a fairly compus ... confusing pattern* /ə fɛrli kəmpjuz ... kənfjuziŋ patrn/. An optional accommodatory adjustment is involved, with an intended /n/ changing to /m/, as an accommodation to the following /p/ segment. This slip raises an interesting issue about the place in the speech process at which optional accommodation rules are applied. It suggests that they are applied to the performance string at some stage AFTER the speech process has been initiated. This follows from the reasonable assumption that segmental replacement, as a neural event, occurs late rather than early in the speech process, that is, after an initial 'correct' neural programme has been assembled. To place the event earlier is to require an additional assumption, that the misplaced segment, here the /p/ in *compus...*, was undetected by the one or more stages of internal neural monitoring that must be postulated. If, then, an error of execution at a late stage is assumed, optional accommodatory adjustments of this sort must come into play at least as late, or even later, during the neuromuscular stage, and furthermore, must be applied quite blindly and routinely. The bilabial accommodation in this instance was appropriate, if optional, even though the /p/ segment, to which the accommodation was made, was itself incorrect.

2. DETERMINANTS OF TONIC LOCATION. In another instance, a speaker, intending to say *how bad things were*, said instead *how things bad were*. The words *bad* and *things* were inadvertently transposed. The tonic, however, was not transposed. It was applied to the correct position, which was occupied by an incorrect word. There are a number of similar examples in the corpus, and they raise the interesting possibility that the physiological determinants of the location of the tonic within the tone-group, whatever they may be, are programmed independently of the other articulatory features of tone-groups.

3. ATYPICAL ORIGINS. In some of our slips, the presumed origin is not represented in the utterance. Consider the following examples:

(a) didn't bother me in the sleast ... slightest (SR(R))
(b) what I ... what she has given me to read ... to read (WR)
          /rɛd/   /rid/
(c) separite ... separating out the nucleuses (SR)

In (a) *slightest* was distorted, in fact nearly replaced, by *least*, which in this context is a synonym and a competing filler for the position. In (b) the ellipsis after *I* represents a hesitation. In context, it seems highly probable that the speaker had intended to say /rɛd/. The utterance is syntactically revised at this point, and the verb in the new intention now has an altered grammatical and phonological form /rid/. In its place, however, the original form is substituted.

In example (c), according to the report of the speaker (one of the authors), he had fleetingly considered, and rejected, the possibility of using the word *nuclei*, /njukliai/, instead of *nucleuses*. Here, interestingly, the rejected word distorts not its successful competitor, as in the first example but another word in the tone-group.

In these three examples (a), (b) and (c), the interactions that resulted in the slips can reasonably be assumed to have taken place in the earlier stages of formulation of the utterance, where syntactic and lexical decision are being made. These examples are structurally similar to those published by Freud, in that the origin of the intrusion is not a part of the ultimate utterance, and it may be that a better understanding of these ordinary lexical slips would also illuminate the mechanics of Freudian slips.

CONCLUSION

Tongue-slips have been shown to be transient malfunctions of the sequencing system of the speech production process which obey stringent linguistic constraints. Neuropsychological hypotheses have been offered which suggest that tongue slips may involve interactions at a number of different stages in the neural organisation of a speech act, from the earliest stages in the formulation of an utterance, when syntactic and lexical decisions are being made, to the final neuromuscular stages of executing the speech plan.[5] The data and interpretations are ordered to a speech unit, the tone-group or phonemic clause, which has both behavioural and formal linguistic properties.

The generalisations offered need to be tested and refined against larger corpora of slips in English. Beyond this, systematic studies of slips in other languages could conceivably expand the structure into a class of neurophysiologically based language universals.

Not least, we hope to have supported our original contention that the study of the characteristic irregularities of actual speech can yield data which are relevant to linguistics, psychology and neurophysiology.

BIBLIOGRAPHY

Abercrombie, D.
     1964   "Syllable quantity and enclitics in English", in: *In Honour of Daniel Jones*, D. Abercrombie, et al. (eds.) (London: Longmans).
     1965   "Conversation and spoken prose", in: *Studies in Phonetics and Linguistics* (London: Oxford University Press).
Bawden, H. H.
     1900   "A study of lapses", *Psychol. Rev. Monograph Suppl.* III, 4.
Boomer, D. S.
     1965   "Hesitation and grammatical encoding", *Lang. and Speech* 8: 148–58.
Cohen, A.
     1966   "Errors of speech and their implication for understanding the strategy of language users", 18th Int. Congress of Psychology, Moscow. Reprinted in this volume.

[5] An article which came to our attention after the manuscript of this article had been written is Hockett (1967), in which he makes some interesting comments on the relevance of tongue-slip data for models of performance, and for the distinction between the concepts of 'performance' and 'competence'.

Dittmann, A. T. and L. G. Llewellyn
  1967   "The phonemic clause as a unit of speech decoding", *J. Pers. Soc. Psychol.* 6: 341–49.
Freud, S.
  1901   *Zur Psychopathologie des Alltagsleben* [Psychopathology of everyday life] A. Tyson (trans.),
         J. Strachey (ed.) (London: E. Benn, 1966). Reprinted in this volume.
Fromkin, V. A.
  1966   "Some requirements for a model of performance", *University of California at Los Angeles
         Working Papers in Phonetics* 4: 19–39.
Gimson, A. C.
  1960   "The instability of English alveolar articulations", *Le Maitre Phonétique* 119.
Halliday, M. A. K.
  1963   "The tones of English" *Archivum Linguisticum* 15: 1–28.
Hockett, C. F.
  1967   "Where the tongue slips, there slip I", in: *To Honor Roman Jakobson*, Vol. II: 910–36
         (= *Janua Linguarum, Series Maior* XXXII) (The Hague: Mouton). Reprinted in this volume.
Lashley, K. S.
  1951   "Serial order in behaviour", in: *Cerebral Mechanisms in Behavior*, L. A. Jeffress (ed.)
         (New York: Wiley).
Lenneberg, E. H.
  1967   *Biological Foundations of Language* (New York: Wiley).
Meringer, R.
  1908   *Aus dem Leben der Sprache* (Berlin).
Meringer, R. and K. Mayer
  1895   *Versprechen und Verlesen, eine psychologischslinguistische Studie* (Vienna).
Oertel, H.
  1901   *Lectures on the Study of Language* (New York).
Simonini, R. C.(Jr.)
  1956   "Phonemic and analogic lapses in radio and television speech", *American Speech* 31: 252–63.
Sturtevant, E. H.
  1917   *Linguistic Change* (University of Chicago Press, 1961).
  1947   *An Introduction to Linguistic Science* (Yale University Press).
Trager, G. L. and H. L. Smith
  1951   "An outline of English structure", (= *Studies in Linguistics*: Occasional Paper 3) (Norman,
         Oklahoma).
Wells, R.
  1951   "Predicting slips of the tongue", *Yale Scientific Magazine* XXVI(3): 9–30. Reprinted in this
         volume.

THE DETECTION AND CORRECTION OF SLIPS OF THE TONGUE*

JOHN D. M. LAVER

Last year, Donald Boomer[1] and I published an article in which we tried to show that the speech-errors that are called slips of the tongue are transient malfunctions of neural control-programs in the speech-production process, and that they obey stringent linguistic constraints (Boomer and Laver 1968). That tongue-slips are so highly structured is in itself an interesting and important fact; but even more valuable is the fact than an examination of tongue-slips gives us a useful point of entry into speculation about the functional properties of the brain's control of speech.

In this article, I want to continue discussion of tongue-slips and cerebral functions, by exploring some of the implications which arise from the observation that slips of the tongue are usually detected and corrected by the speaker. In particular, I would like to offer some speculative comment on aspects of the neural function which allows this detection and correction to be achieved – the monitoring function.

The monitoring function is of course only one of the various functions in the brain's control of acts of speech performance, and I shall be obliged to say a little about the other functions and their relation to monitoring. Before I do so, however, I have to acknowledge that it is difficult to find a satisfactorily specific and adequate adjective to characterize such a functional model. The terms 'neurophysiological', 'neuro-psychological' and 'neurolinguistic' would each reflect some characteristic of the model. Because the current state of research restricts us largely to a consideration of functions rather than of mechanisms, perhaps the least satisfactory of the possible labels is 'neurophysiological'. 'Neuropsychological' would be more acceptable, and would be sympathetic to a view recently expressed by Chomsky (1968: 1), where he suggests that linguistics is itself a branch of a branch of psychology, namely cognitive

Reprinted from *Work in Progress* 3, Dept. of Phonetics and Linguistics, University of Edinburgh (1969).

* Most of the material of this article was originally presented in two conference papers: "Aspects of the Monitoring Function in Speech", to the December 1968 meeting of the British Society of Audiology, and "Speech and the Brain", to the March 1969 Colloquium of Academic Phoneticians of Great Britain.

[1] I owe much to Dr. Boomer, of the Laboratory of Psychology, National Institute of Mental Health, Bethesda, for early discussion of this area. Responsibility for the views expressed remains mine alone.

psychology. Personally, for the moment, I favour the most neutral term, 'neuro-linguistic'.

If I may use this label, the construction of a neurolinguistic model of speech production has attracted a growing attention from phoneticians and linguists, and from other disciplines concerned with language. To name but a few workers in this area, Boomer, Fant, Fromkin, Fry, Hockett, Kozhevnikov, Ladefoged, Lamb, Lane, Lenneberg, Lindblom, Miller, Öhman and Tatham have all recently published material on neural aspects of speech production. (An interest in neural aspects of speech reception is of much longer standing, and is not under immediate consideration here.) The relevance for phonetics and linguistics of a neurolinguistic model of the brain's control of speech should need no emphasis, and it is significant that neuro-linguistics is a field where the sub-disciplinary boundary between phonetics and linguistics, (which has probably always been of doubtful validity), is largely disappearing. In providing a satisfactory model of the psychological processes which allow the brain to generate speech, neurolinguistics will contribute importantly to the development of a more comprehensive and unified linguistic theory. To assert this is to take the position that linguistics should accept, together with its other criteria for comparative evaluation of linguistic theories, a criterion of psychological veridicality. If it can be shown that the brain uses a particular psychological process in generating speech, then the linguistic theory which allows for such a process, in its performance component, is a better theory, in terms of accounting comprehensively for language-behaviour, than one which does not.

However, the development of a sufficiently comprehensive neurolinguistic model of the brain's control of speech is a very long way ahead. One major difficulty is the scarcity of persuasive evidence. To all intents and purposes, the healthy adult brain is not itself accessible to neurolinguistic experiment. This restricts us to a (widely accepted) research strategy which makes use of the fact that functional properties of unobservable control-systems can be inferred from an examination of the output of those systems (Boomer and Laver 1968: 3). This strategy can be applied both to the efficient, error-free output, and, as I indicated at the beginning of the article, to the output when malfunctions occur in the control-systems. A third possible source of evidence is the output of the speech-process while the control-systems are being established and becoming skilled, – the acquisitional stage of young children's speech.

I should emphasize that error-free speech should not be equated with 'normal speech' (Boomer and Laver 1968: 2), nor should the malfunctions which occur in speech be considered necessarily the result of speech pathology. Spontaneous, normal speech is usually far from completely free of errors, and often contains ephemeral, nonpathological malfunctions such as slips of the tongue. Neither pathological malfunctions nor acquisitional speech will be discussed in this article, although they offer potentially valuable evidence for the construction of a neurolinguistic model of the normal adult brain.

Discussion in this article will be limited rather to slips of the tongue, and their detection and correction.

Detection is a logical prerequisite to correction, and detection and correction together are taken to be evidence of a monitoring function in the speech-producing process. In distinguishing between detection and correction as aspects of the monitoring function, I am trying to lay the foundation of a view that I shall return to as my principal conclusion at the end of the article; namely, that the activities of scrutiny and revision are not the monopoly of the monitoring function, but an integral characteristic of all the brain's processes for constructing and controlling speech-programs.

To show the similarity of underlying purpose in the monitoring and program-construction functions, it is necessary at this stage to say something about the different functions involved in the generation of any speech utterance. The outline I shall give is a very simplistic one, without commitment as to the actual mechanisms concerned; – it is simplistic because I am conscious of the ferocious complexity of the problem, and feel the need to approach the complexity with the help of what may well turn out to be merely convenient fictions.

There seem to be four chief functions (Laver 1968):

1. Ideation
2. Neurolinguistic program-planning
3. Myodynamic execution
4. Monitoring

1. IDEATION

I make the fundamental assumption that the speaker has an initial idea, which he intends to communicate. In using the term 'idea', I am not seeking to imply that a high degree of cognitive complexity is necessarily involved; the idea consists of the approximate semantic content of any verbal message that the speaker wishes to communicate.

2. NEUROLINGUISTIC PROGRAM-PLANNING

The next function is the construction of a neurolinguistic program for the expression of the idea – the organization of a neural program for the lexical, grammatical and phonological characteristics of the message the speaker intends to communicate. This presumably involves the selection from long-term storage of lexical items and grammatical arrangements, together with their associated phonology, by criteria of semantic appropriateness to expression of the initial idea. So the planning function, in this convenient model, needs access to the initial idea, to lexical and grammatical storage, and to the phonology.

A major area of difficulty here is that of the relation between the idea and the neurolinguistic program planned to communicate that idea. It is a difficult area to conceptualize, because it is only possible to discuss ideas in terms of their expository linguistic programs. Miller et al. (1960) quote a passage from William James's 'The Principles of Psychology' (1890), which I think captures the nature of this difficulty with great clarity:

And has the reader never asked himself what kind of a mental fact is his intention of saying a thing before he has said it? It is an entirely definite intention, distinct from all other intentions, an absolutely distinct state of consciousness, therefore; and yet how much of it consists of definite sensorial images, either of words or of things? Hardly anything! Linger, and the words and things come into the mind; the anticipatory intention, the divination is there no more. But as the words that replace it arrive, it welcomes them successively and calls them right if they agree with it, it rejects them and calls them wrong if they do not. It has therefore a nature of its own of the most positive sort, and yet what can we say about it without using words that belong to the later mental facts that replace it? The intention TO SAY SO AND SO is the only name it can receive. One may admit that a good third of our psychic life consists in these rapid premonitory schemes of thought not yet articulate.

Implied in this passage is the view that the planning function activates more items from storage than it finally selects for the neurolinguistic program. This is well supported by those slips of the tongue where the brain fails to complete its planning choice between competing alternatives before the speech-program reaches the utterance-stage. A lexical example would be:

didn't bother me in the sleast

with competition between *slightest* and *least* (Boomer and Laver 1968). A syntactic example would be:

He behaved as like a fool

with competition between *like a fool* and either or both *as if he were a fool* and *as though he were a fool*.

A number of conclusions derive from the suggestion that more items are activated than are selected for inclusion in the final program. Firstly, the planning function must be able to scrutinize the various alternatives that have been retrieved from storage, and come to a decision about the relative appropriateness of the competing items for expressing the initial idea. Secondly, to allow the planning function to come to a decision about appropriateness of items, the idea itself presumably has some kind of semantic indexing, which serves as a predisposition towards choosing one rather than another of the competing alternatives. That such a choice seems often to be made is one theoretical justification, following William James, for treating ideation as a separate function from neurolinguistic program-planning, in opposition to the possible view that an idea is itself necessarily an associative linguistic response to a stimulus of some sort.

To separate the ideation function from the planning function is not to imply that the latter may not influence the former. It seems intuitively reasonable to assume that the specific restrictions and associations characterizing particular items activated by the planning function may have the result of allowing the brain to reach a revised, and perhaps more precise, formulation of the original idea, which in turn may lead to a revision of parts of the neurolinguistic program.

The possibility of scrutiny and revision could thus be said to exist in both the ideation and the planning functions.

One of the conclusions that Donald Boomer and I reached in our article on slips of the tongue was that the brain pre-prepares stretches of speech, often of the extent of the tone-group (Halliday 1963), before the utterance of the whole stretch begins. Pre-preparation was first suggested by Lashley, in his classic article "Serial Order in Behavior" in 1951; he pointed out that a logical corollary is that the brain usually inhibits the stretch under preparation from being uttered until preparation is complete. A second implication is that the pre-prepared stretch has to be stored in short-term memory until its utterance, and a third implication would be that the planning function needs to make use of neural scanning of the pre-prepared stretch, in order to be able to decide when preparation is complete, and utterance can be allowed.

It is thus implicit in the concept of pre-preparation that the prepared stretch of speech is subjected to inhibition, short-term storage and scanning.

I make these points to emphasize that the planning function has many opportunities for revision of its programs, and for checking for program-errors which would lead to slips of the tongue.

I suspect that the Planner, (to abbreviate its label), does sometimes detect program-errors before the utterance-stage. I feel that I have had the experience of being aware that a slip of the tongue was imminent, and re-programming in time to maintain fluent speech. Hockett claims the same experience (1967: 936). It is interesting, though, that despite the multiple opportunities available to the Planner for checking for errors, some errors do get through to the utterance-stage. If an error does persist to the utterance-stage, then its detection and correction become the business of the monitoring function.

Before finally coming to a discussion of monitoring, I would like to make some brief comments about the myodynamic execution function, which so far I have been calling, rather loosely, the utterance-stage.

3. MYODYNAMIC EXECUTION

The neurolinguistic program constructed by the planning function is finally executed in the form of contractions of the muscles of the speech organs. It is important to emphasize that the myodynamic execution function is concerned exclusively with the contractions and movements of the muscles; all considerations of the neural control of those muscles are thus to be referred to the planning function and its various component sub-functions.

We know rather little at the moment about the detailed physiology of the vocal organs. Electromyography may eventually tell us a good deal, but the sheer complexity of the action of the different muscle systems used to manoeuvre the tongue, for example, is going to make progress rather slow. This is not to say that the electromyographic study of restricted numbers of muscles that is currently being carried out is not valuable, but rather that it seems likely to be a long time before a thoroughly well-founded and general theory of how such organs as the tongue move can be achieved.

However, when that time comes, one useful area of investigation may be the study of the degree of complexity and delicacy of adjustment of vocal musculature for different articulations; it seems logical to expect that the more complex and delicate the adjustments for a particular class of sounds, the greater the likelihood of members of that class being mutually involved in tongue-slips. One might expect, for example, that fricatives need more precise muscular control than plosives, and it certainly seems to be true that, in English, voiceless fricatives tend to interact in tongue slips more frequently than plosives and other consonant-categories. This is reflected in the maximal difficulty of tongue-twisters like *She sells sea-shells on the sea-shore*, and *The Leith police dismisseth us*.

4. MONITORING

I have used the term 'monitoring' to refer to the neural function of detecting and correcting errors in the neurolinguistic program. I would like to make it quite clear at this point that in discussing this type of monitoring, I am not thinking of the use of sensory feedback to control speech-movements directly. Lashley (1951: 188) characterizes this latter theory as assuming that "…. after a movement is initiated, it is continued until stopped by sensations of movement and position, which indicate that the limb has reached the desired position." He suggests that such a theory is not applicable to every type of complex muscular action, and that a series of movements is not necessarily a chain of sensory-motor reactions. He points out, for example, that the execution of very rapid, accurate movements such as whip-cracking is often completed in a shorter time than the reaction time for tactile or kinesthetic reports to be made on what happened.

Speech, also, often involves very fast, complex movements, as in the articulation of an alveolar tap. It seems reasonable to suggest, following Lashley, that speech-programs for such articulations can be pre-set for their muscular realization, relatively independently of any sensory controls. In this connection, Ladefoged (1967: 170) cites Craik (1947) as having shown that "complex, comparatively long, muscular movements may be 'triggered off as a whole' ". I think it follows, from these considerations, and from the fact that the planning function pre-prepares stretches of speech, that much of speech performance may well be achieved by synergisms – skilled, well-practised routines, which, once started, can be left to run to completion without sensory information making a primary contribution to their control.

While sensory information may not be primarily important in controlling such speech performance directly, the information is nevertheless still available to the brain for use in monitoring as defined in this article. To put it explicitly, monitoring in this sense refers to the reception and processing of sensory reports on myodynamic execution for the purpose of detecting and correcting errors in the neurolinguistic program.

I have been careful throughout this article to speak of 'program-errors', rather than 'myodynamic-errors', or 'utterance-errors', since in the model I have offered myodynamic execution, or utterance, consists of muscular actions, and any and every active muscular contraction is the result of a specific neural control program. When errors occur, they are thus to be attributed to incorrect programs.

It is important to consider by what criteria a program can be said to be 'incorrect', or to contain an 'error'.

One approach is to say that an incorrect program is one which in some detail does not correspond to the speaker's intention. This then transfers the problem to the nature of an 'intention', and this is conveniently thought of as the idea that the speaker is trying to communicate.

An incorrect program is therefore one which in some detail distorts the communication of the speaker's idea. It is striking that such considerations of program-errors lead us straight back into the heart of the language-process – the relation I discussed above between an idea and the linguistic program constructed to communicate that idea.

There are two different sorts of errors that distort accurate communication of a speaker's idea:

(a) errors which result in a form not found in the language, such as

didn't bother me in the sleast

and also

Those frunds, funds are frozen (Boomer and Laver 1968)

(b) errors which give linguistically permissible results, but which are semantically inappropriate for communicating the speaker's idea, such as

Our queer old dean

for

Our dear old Queen

(Lashley, op. cit.) and also

Take it out to the porch – er – verandah

In this last example, I'm suggesting that false-starts, (a revision of lexical choice, in this case) are errors which can be discussed in the same overall framework as other sorts of program-errors.

In the category of errors which give linguistically permissible results, it is often only the fact of correction that allows us, as observers, to know that an error has occurred.

In applying its detection apparatus to slips such as the above examples, the monitoring process can be seen as answering the question: 'Was the neurolinguistic program that was executed planned in all its details in such a way that it was capable of achieving communication of the intended idea?' To allow the posing and answering of this question, and the possibility of taking appropriate corrective action, the monitoring process needs four component sub-functions:

(1) PERIPHERAL RECEPTION

The sensory information in the peripheral reception component of monitoring includes auditory and tactile exteroceptive reports, and positional and kinesthetic proprioceptive reports. In normal speakers perhaps the most important of the peripheral report systems for monitoring purposes is the auditory system.

(2) DECODING

This sub-function gives the answer to two questions:
  (a) 'What was the neurolinguistic program that was executed?'
  (b) 'Was the program that was executed linguistically orthodox?'

There are two implications here: firstly, in decoding, it seems uneconomical to assume that the result arrived at would be expressed in terms different from the sort of neurolinguistic program used to produce speech – so that production and reception, in this special sense of reception, at least, seem likely to use the same neural units.

It is necessary to acknowledge here that the brain may well have additional information about the characteristics of the neurolinguistic program that was executed, from scanning its short-term memory of recent planning. If such neural scanning of short-term memory occurs, then I would still like to include the use of such information for the detection and correction of program-errors as part of the monitoring function, in this model. The definition of monitoring would have to be slightly enlarged, to include the reception and processing of reports from the internal scanning of short-term memory of recent programming, as well as of sensory reports upon myodynamic execution.

The second implication of decoding as a sub-function of monitoring is that, to assess the linguistic orthodoxy of the program that was executed, access is needed to lexical and grammatical storage, and to the rules of the phonology.

(3) EVALUATION

This sub-function scrutinizes the results of the decoding, to give the answers to two questions:
  (a) 'Is any disobedience to lexical, grammatical or phonological constraints likely to distort communication?'
  (b) 'Is the program that was executed, whether linguistically orthodox or not,

likely to be semantically successful in communicating the speaker's idea?' An implication of the second question is that access is needed to the idea, which is presumably being held in short-term memory. A major point which arises at this juncture is that the Monitor, in this model, is seen as having the same needs as the Planner, for access to the idea, to lexical and grammatical storage, and to the rules of the phonology.

(4) ACTION

This sub-function decides what to do about the results of the evaluation. There are two possibilities:

(a) 'Allow the myodynamic execution of the program to continue'

(b) 'Stop the myodynamic execution of the program; tell the Planner to revise the program, and restart the speech-process at a pre-error stage'.

Access is needed, for this sub-function, to the speaker's motivation in trying to communicate. Some slips are detected, and evaluated as likely to distort communication of the speaker's idea, but allowed to pass uncorrected, because the speaker is not highly enough motivated to take the trouble to correct the slip. Another possible explanation for the situation where a slip is detected, but not corrected, is where the speaker knows he made a slip, and knows the listener knows he made a slip, but the speaker believes that the general redundancy of the components of his message is sufficient to achieve satisfactorily accurate semantic communication.

When a slip is not corrected, and not commented on by the speaker, we have no means, as observers, of knowing whether the speaker detected the slip or not. There are thus two possible implications of failure to correct a slip: either the evaluation and action sub-functions of the Monitor decided to allow the myodynamic execution of the program to continue, or the Monitor failed to detect the slip.

This second possibility, of failure to detect a slip, is interesting. It is my impression that not many slips of the tongue are uncorrected, so it seems fair to assume that the Monitor maintains nearly constant surveillance, and is therefore an integral part of the speech-producing process. If it is possible for slips to get past the Monitor undetected, then this constitutes malfunction on the part of the Monitor. One explanation of the possibility of malfunction of monitoring is to posit attention as part of the Monitor's apparatus. It is useful to suggest that attention operates at all levels of the brain's control of speech, particularly in the Planner. Where slips are undetected, then perhaps attention is either momentarily elsewhere in the stream of speech, or is inefficient. Attention can be distracted, or its efficiency lowered, in a variety of ways, many of which are amenable to experimental manipulation. For example:

(a) when there are competing demands for attention

(b) under the influence of alcohol or drugs

(c) in the case of a marked degree of fatigue

(d) under the influence of psychological stress such as embarrassment, nervousness, anger, fear, et cetera.

This would certainly help to explain the informal observation that the incidence of uncorrected slips seems to be greater under these conditions, although the weakness in the argument remains – one can't argue that because the slips are uncorrected, they were therefore undetected.

Before coming on to some general conclusions, I should say that of course attention is not the same as awareness. It is often the case that a speaker makes a slip and corrects it, without either the speaker or the listener being aware that a slip has occurred. The conscious perception of speech in some sense regularizes and idealizes the actual data of speech (Boomer and Laver 1968). Conscious awareness is thus not a necessary part of the monitoring process.

To offer some general conclusions, a point I have been leading up to is that on the one hand the Planner and the Monitor need access to largely the same areas, namely to the idea, to lexical and grammatical storage, and to the rules of phonology; and that on the other hand the Planner and the Monitor are involved in much the same sort of decisions. Both the Planner and the Monitor have to assess semantic appropriateness of programs for communicating ideas, for example. Also, the decision to stop an utterance, in order to allow revision and re-start, is much the same sort of decision as the one to initiate an utterance. This implies that the Monitor's 'action' decisions, at least, are made, like many planning decisions, at a very central level.

Following on from this, I come to the most important general conclusion I want to offer – that planning and monitoring have so much in common, in terms of need for access, and level and type of decision, that it is economical to suggest that the two functions are merely different manifestations of a common major function.

Such a major function would be in the nature of a central control function, able to take decisions at the highest level, with access to the idea, to all types of long- and short-term storage concerned with speech-production, and to all levels of the process of generating a particular utterance.

To postulate a common central control function underlying both planning and monitoring is to assert that there is a very considerable overlap of purpose in planning and monitoring. Following this up, it becomes possible to unify one's approach to the error-free and malfunctioning aspects of normal speech. I want to suggest that the purpose of the Monitor, and a large part of the purpose of the Planner, is to edit the initial program, and by continual scrutiny, and, where necessary, revision, to allow the central control function to achieve fairly continuously successful linguistic communication.

If 'necessary revision' is a shared purpose of the Planner and the Monitor, then the revisionary activities of the two systems can be equated. The revisionary activity of the Planner leads to error-free speech, because revisions are carried out before the myodynamic execution of the program; and the revisionary activity of the Monitor is reflected in the correction, after the myodynamic execution of the program, of overt errors. The difference between error-free speech, and speech containing overt errors, in this view, would be a fairly trivial difference of the point in time at which the central control function's revisionary resources were applied – before or after myodynamic execution of the neurolinguistic program. This is substantially the same conclusion as that reached by Hockett, who first formalized the notion of editing, in this context, and who distinguishes between 'covert editing', and 'overt editing'. He writes: "Editing in the internal flow is *covert editing* ... In certain formal circumstances covert editing is thorough, and overt speech is unusually smooth. Much more typically, what is actually said aloud includes various signs of *overt editing*, ..." (Hockett 1967: 936). I would equate covert editing with editing carried out by the Planner, and overt editing with editing initiated by the Monitor.

This is really a re-statement of the view that I put forward at the beginning, that normal speech is not necessarily error-free speech, and, by extension, that errors are part and parcel of normal speech, and therefore worthy of study by linguists.

To conclude, I should emphasize that while speculations about cerebral functions are usually constrained by criteria of logic, not all such criteria may not apply in the real situation. Donald Boomer wrote to me recently, with a very salutary comment on this topic. He wrote: "Man's brain is an evolutionary outcome, and there is no reason to believe that the evolutionary process is subject to the logical canons of parsimony and elegance. On the contrary, in fact."

BIBLIOGRAPHY

Boomer, D. S.
   1965 "Hesitation and Grammatical Encoding", *Lang. and Speech* 8(3): 148–58.
Boomer, D. S. and J. D. M. Laver
   1968 "Slips of the Tongue", *Brit. J. Dis. Comm.* 3(1): 2–12. Reprinted in this volume.
Chomsky, N.
   1968 *Language and Mind* New York: Harcourt, Brace and World, Inc.
Craik, K. J. W.
   1947 "Theory of the Human Operator in Control Systems, *Brit. J. Psychol.* 38: 56–61.
Fant, G.
   1967 "Sound, Features, and Perception", in: *Proc. VIth Int. Congr. Phon. Sci.* (Prague, forth-
      coming).
Fromkin, V. A.
   1965 "Some Phonetic Specification of Linguistic Units: An Electromyographic Investigation",
      (= *Working Papers in Phonetics* 3) (University of California, Los Angeles).
   1968 "Speculations on Performance Models", *J. Ling.* 4(1): 47–68.
Fry, D. B.
   1964 "The Functions of the Syllable", *Zt. für Phon.* 17: 215–17.
   forthcoming "The Linguistic Evidence of Speech Errors", in: the *Vachek Festschrift*.
      Reprinted in this volume.
Halliday, M. A. K.
   1963 "The Tones of English", *Archivum Linguisticum* 15: 1–28.
Hockett, C. F.
   1967 "Where the Tongue Slips, there Slip I", in: *To Honor Roman Jakobson*, Vol. II (= *Janua
      Linguarum, Series Maior* XXXII): 910–936 (The Hague: Mouton). Reprinted in this volume.
James, W.
   1890 *The Principles of Psychology*, Vol. I (New York: Holt).
Kozhevnikov, V. A. and L. A. Chistovich
   1965 *Speech, Articulation and Perception*, U.S. Dept. of Commerce, Joint Publications Research
      Service, Washington, D.C.

Ladefoged, P.
1967 *Three Areas of Experimental Phonetics* (London: Oxford University Press).
Lamb, S. M.
  1966 "Linguistic Structure and the Production and Decoding of Discourse", in E. C. Carterette
    (ed.), *Brain Function*, Vol. III (Berkeley and Los Angeles: University of California Press).
Lane, H. n.d.
    "On the Necessity of Distinguishing Between Speaking and Listening", mimeo.
Lashley, K. S.
  1951 "Serial Order in Behavior", in: L. A. Jeffress (ed.), *Cerebral Mechanisms in Behavior*
    (New York: Wiley).
Laver, J.
  1968 "Phonetics and the Brain", *Work in Progress*, 2: 63–75 (Department of Phonetics and Lin-
    guistics, Edinburgh,University).
Lenneberg, E. H.
1967 *Biological Foundations of Language* (New York: Wiley).
Lindblom, B.
  1963 "On Vowel Reduction", (= *Report No. 29*, Speech Transmission Laboratory, Royal Insti-
    tute of Technology, Stockholm).
Miller, G. A., E. Galanter and K. H. Pribram
  1960 *Plans and the Structure of Behavior* (New York: Holt, Rinehart and Winston, Inc.).
Öhman, S.
  1968 "Peripheral Motor Commands in Labial Articulation", *QPSR* 4/1967: 30–63 (Speech
    Transmission Laboratory, Royal Institute of Technology, Stockholm).
Öhman, S., A. Persson and R. Leanderson
  1967 "Speech Production at the Neuromuscular Level", in: *Proc. VIth Congr. Phon. Sci.* (Prague,
    forthcoming).
Tatham, M. A. A.
  1969a "Classifying Allophones", *Occasional Papers* 3: 14–22 (University of Essex Language
    Centre).
  1969b The Control of Muscles in Speech, *Occasional Papers* 3: 23–40 (University of Essex Lan-
    guage Centre).
Tatham, M. A. A. and K. Morton
  1968a "Some Electromyography Data towards a Model of Speech Production", *Occasional Papers*
    1: 1–24 (University of Essex Language Centre).
  1968b "Further Electromyography Data towards a Model of Speech Production", *Occasional
    Papers* 1: 25–59 (University of Essex Language Centre).

THE TONGUE SLIPS INTO PATTERNS*

S. G. NOOTEBOOM

1. INTRODUCTION

The main concern of a professional linguist is with the grammatical sentences of a language. Now these grammatical sentences are very rare in actual speech, where numerous irregularities, such as false starts, additions, omissions, substitutions and interchangings of elements occur. In some way or other the linguist is able to abstract from all these deviations and to concentrate on the regularities which are believed to underlie the linguistic behaviour of the language user. The outcome of the linguist's enormous task should be a grammar which describes all (and only) the grammatical sentences of a language and which in some way is equivalent to the knowledge a native speaker possesses of his language.

But a grammar tells nothing about the way in which a speaker puts his knowledge of the language to use in actual speech. This article arises from the hope that the study of all these phenomena in actual speech which are discarded by the linguist as deviations might reveal something about the intricate processes involved in language use. The idea that regularities in linguistic irregularities might be useful for our insight into the mechanisms underlying the construction of utterances in actual speech is by no means a new one. In 1895 Meringer and Mayer published a collection of errors of speech and reading in German[1] which was extended by Meringer and published in 1908.[2] Meringer gave a classification of the speech errors on formal grounds. Seeing the many regularities in speech lapses he concluded: "Der Zufall ist beim Versprechen volkommen ausgeschlossen, das Versprechen ist geregelt". In the same period S. Freud had a quite different approach to speech lapses. He tried to give a psychoanalytical account of these phenomena and thoroughly disagreed with the mechanistic explanation given by Meringer.[3] The few later studies concerning speech errors followed mostly Meringer's line of thinking. E. Sturtevant considered speech errors to be

* Reprinted from Nomen, *Leyden Studies in Linguistics and Phonetics* (The Hague: Mouton, 1969).
[1] R. Meringer and K. Mayer, *Versprechen und Verlesen* (Stuttgart, 1895).
[2] K. Meringer and K. Meyer, *Aus dem Leben der Sprache* (Berlin, 1908).
[3] S. Freud, *Zur Psychopathologie des Alltagslebens* (= *Gesammelte Schriften von Sigmund Freud, Vierter Band*) (Wien, 1924). Reprinted in this volume.

important as a possible source of linguistic change.[4] K. S. Lashley, in his famous article "The problem of serial order in behaviour", pointed to performance errors as a possible means for studying the organization of linguistic behaviour.[5] The present study may be considered a following up of the work of A. Cohen, who reported upon his collection of speech errors on several occasions.[6] A more extensive bibliography on this subject was recently given by Donald S. Boomer and John D. Laver, who made an interesting study on phonemic slips of the tongue.[7] There is one recent study of lapses in speech following Freud's rather than Meringer's line of thinking, with the ominous title "Where the Tongue Slips, There Slip I", an essay by Charles F. Hockett, contributed to *To Honor Roman Jakobson*, 1967.[8] An example of his Freudian thinking is the following: A TV performer says:

The question is, how can you tell one sil – filter cigarette from another these days?

The blending of the first syllable of filter and the first syllable of cigarette to *sil*, might be, according to Hockett, influenced by the existing word silly and "so was an expression of the TV performer's private attitude towards the commercials in which he was obliged to participate".

In my opinion observations of this kind are neither verifiable nor reproducible and are therefore to be discarded in a systematic analysis of speech lapses. My own interpretation of this lapse would be that the prevocalic /s/ of cigarette (the origin element) is anticipated and has substituted the prevocalic /f/ of filter (the target element), which event may have been influenced by the phonetic similarity of /s/ and /f/ and by the similarity of their environment. Observations like this one lend themselves to a quantitative approach and may lead to the formulation of fundamental regularities in the occurrence of speech lapses. Hockett states further that there is no systematic difference between smooth speech and lapses and that the generation of both may be explained by three basic mechanisms, viz., analogy, blending and editing. Of these, "editing" accounts for the fact that speakers are aware of what they are saying and are able to correct errors in the inner speech or in the speech already produced. I think that the processes involved in the generation of speech are more intricate than simply these three mechanisms and that speech errors, as distinct from correct utterances, may in their own way give us some hints on these speech generation processes.

[4] E. H. Sturtevant, *An Introduction to Linguistic Science* (Yale University Press, 1947).
[5] K. S. Lashley, "The Problem of Serial Order in Behaviour", in: Sol Saporta, *Psycholinguistics* (New York, 1961).
[6] A. Cohen, "Versprekingen als Verklappers van het Proces van Spreken en Verstaan", *Forum der Letteren* 6 (1965); "Errors of Speech and their Implication for Understanding the Strategy of Language Users", in: *Models of Speech, International Congress of Psychology* (Moscow, 1966); "Errors of Speech and their Implication for Understanding the Strategy of Language Users", *IPO Annual Progress Report* I (1966). Reprinted in this volume.
[7] Donald S. Boomer and John D. M. Laver, "Slips of the Tongue", in: *Work in Progress*, Department of Phonetics, Edinburgh University (1967).
[8] Charles F. Hockett, "Where the Tongue Slips, There Slip I", in: *To Honor Roman Jakobson*, Vol. II (The Hague-Paris, 1967).

The material forming the basis of this study is a collection of spontaneous speech errors in spoken Dutch noted down in orthographical notation by Cohen during two years of careful listening and extended by myself during another year of collecting. For a first rough classification of these errors reference may be made to the four levels involved in the generation of a speech message that were earlier suggested by Cohen, viz., a language potential, a plan involving a selection from this potential, a programme, and the production of acoustic signals.[9] Errors in the language potential, being the result of poor acquisition, and errors in the production of acoustic signals resulting from slur in the movements of the articulators, will not be considered here. Errors in the plan mostly result in choosing the wrong word, for instance, somebody saying "I must come" instead of "I must go". Closer inspection of these errors will be given in Section 3.

I would like first to concentrate on errors in the programme which comprise most of the errors in the collection. In these errors two units in the same utterance interfere with one another, the result being an anomalous form. An example is provided by the above lapse cited from Hockett. The units interfering with one another may be vowels, consonants, consonant clusters, meaningless combinations of vowels and consonants, morphemes or words. In Section 2 first the phonemic speech errors will be considered and then the errors concerning larger units than consonant clusters. On some points of Section 2 reference will be made not only to the collection of spontaneous speech lapses, but also to errors that were induced by Cohen and myself under laboratory conditions by having subjects read aloud texts at a fast rate.

2. ERRORS IN THE PROGRAMME

A. *Phonemic speech errors*

If we use the syllable as a convenient reference unit, phonemic speech errors may be described as the substitution, addition or omission of an element of the syllable under the influence of another syllable in the same utterance. If the influencing syllable is in the part of the utterance that is still unspoken the errors are called anticipations. Examples are as follows:

> substitution: everything you hear → everyhing you hear
> addition: patriotic and liberal hearted → patriortic and liberal hearted
> omission: *broad building → boad building

If the influencing syllable has already been spoken the errors are said to be perseverations, examples being the following:

> substitution: what does that signify → what does that dignify

---

[9] A. Cohen, "Errors of Speech and their Implication for Understanding the Strategy of Language Users", *IPO Annual Progress Report* I (1966). Reprinted in this volume.

addition: I prefer to reserve → I prefer to preserve
omission: that sounds rather stilted → that sounds rather silted

And if two syllables act upon one another we call them transpositions:

substitution: to cut him short → to shut him court

Most of these examples were borrowed from Sturtevant (1947). The case marked with an asterisk is literally transposed from Dutch, because no English example was found. A classification of the phonemic speech errors in spontaneous Dutch is given in Table I.

TABLE I

Classification of Phonemic Speech Errors in Spontaneous Dutch

	Vowel	Consonant	Consonant Cluster
Anticipation (c. 75%)			
substitution	194	213	45
addition	–	123	2
omission	–	15	–
Perseveration (c. 20%)			
substitution	36	59	8
addition	–	45	1
omission	–	3	–
Transposition (c. 5%)			
substitution	11	22	2
addition	–	5	–
omission	–	3	–

A careful analysis of the collection of phonemic speech errors shows that these errors do not at all occur at random. The following remarks may be made:

(a) Anticipations far outnumber perseverations and transpositions.

This is shown by Table I. This predominance of anticipations gives us the impression that the speaker's attention is normally directed to the future. Preoccupation with what has already been spoken, resulting in perseverations seems to be a relatively rare event. Experimental evidence was given, however, that the percentage of perseverations increases considerably, when the speaker is forced to pronounce phrases that are intuitively felt as difficult. An experiment was carried out by having Subjects read aloud tongue twisters at a fast rate. When these tongue twisters were semantically acceptable sentences with an abundance of similar clusters, the percentage of perseverations increased from 20% in normal speech (Table I) to 40%. When these tongue twisters consisted of sequences of nonsense syllables with an abundance of similar clusters, the percentage of perseverations increased to 75%. The increase in difficulty was confirmed by an increase in percentage of errors relative to the total amount of spoken material over the three situations.[10]

[10]   S. G. Nooteboom, "Spontane fonologische versprekingen", *IPO Rapport* 93 (1966).

(b) The distance between origin and target does not generally exceed seven syllables.

This may follow from figure 1, which gives a frequency distribution of the phonemic errors in spontaneous speech as a function of the distance between the two elements involved in a speech error. Since we know that the short memory span of man may contain about seven units[11] at a time we might interpret our finding as an argument for the syllable to be a unit in the phonemic programming system. The very fact that we find speech errors with a span of one to seven syllables indicates that the processing of language material in the generation of utterances is not to be considered a Markoff system in which each element is only dependent on the preceding elements. This is in accordance with the evidence Chomsky has given of the impossibility of describing the grammatical sentences of a natural language by means of a Markoff chain.[12] We may conclude that some kind of parallel processing goes on in the construction of utterances.

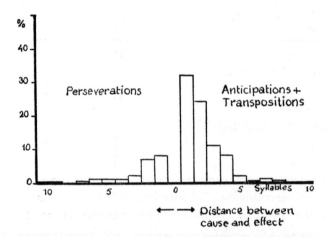

Fig. 1. Frequency distribution of spontaneous phonemic speech errors in Dutch as a function of the distance between origin and target. This distance has been measured in syllables.

The phonemic elements in the immediate memory may be assumed to be subject to decay,[13] that is to say that the longer the memory trace of such an element has been in existence, the greater the chance that it will be forgotten. If this is correct we may predict that the greater the distance between origin and target in an anticipation, the less chance there is that this anticipation will result in a transposition. This reasoning leads to the prediction that in our collection the mean distance between origin and

[11]   G. A. Miller, "The Magical Number Seven Plus or Minus Two: Some Limits on our Capacity for Processing Information", *Psychological Review* 63 (1962).

[12]   N. Chomsky, *Syntactic Structures* (The Hague, 1957).

[13]   J. Morton, "A Model for Continuous Language Behaviour", *Language and Speech* 7 (1964). Morton gave evidence that the decay theory of immediate memory has a similar explanatory value for certain categories of errors in fast reading aloud.

target for anticipations is greater than for transpositions. A simple count shows that the mean distance for anticipations is 2.2 syllables, and for transpositions 1.7 syllables. This might be an indication that there is some kind of relationship between anticipations and transpositions, which relationship may be explained by the decay theory of memory, although it is difficult to say anything definite about the significance of the numbers given.

(c) In the collection no errors are found in which a prevocalic consonant exerts influence on a postvocalic consonant or vice versa. If the origin element is prevocalic then the target element is also prevocalic and the same holds for postvocalic elements.[14]

This observation might be of use for our insight into syllable structure, for when the second consonantal element of a CVC form is immediately followed by an initial vowel of the next word, it might be conceivable, at least theoretically, that this consonantal element behaves as a prevocalic element in the organization of speech. This would be in accordance with the theoretical ideas of Kozhevnikov and Chistovich.[15] If that were so, one would expect to find a number of cases in which the final consonant of a word was substituted by a clearly prevocalic consonant and vice versa. Since this was never found we may perhaps conclude that, at least in Dutch, and at least for that part of the nervous system where phonemic speech errors are formed, final consonantal elements do not tend to become prevocalic when followed by a vowel.

(d) In significantly more cases than is to be expected in a random distribution the two elements involved in a substitution error are phonetically similar to one another.[16] This statement implies, for instance, that /p/ and /b/ are more likely to be substituted for one another than the phonemes /p/ and /z/. One might say that when /p/ becomes /b/ under the influence of a following /b/ only one distinctive feature is anticipated. However, if distinctive features behaved like more-or-less independent elements just as phonemes do, one would expect to find a number of cases of the anticipation of one distinctive feature, without resulting in the sameness of the two phonemes involved. Thus, for instance, /p/ becoming /b/ under the influence of a following /z/. If errors of this kind occur at all, they are very rare.

(e) In significantly more cases than is to be expected in a random distribution the two elements involved in a phonemic speech error have the same phonemic environment.[17] An example is provided by the lapse given by Hockett:

    sil filter cigarette

The fact that a sequence of similar but not identical syllables is difficult to pronounce is precisely the difficulty in pronouncing tongue twisters. The mechanism that is respon-

---

[14] S. G. Nooteboom, "Spontane fonologische versprekingen", *IPO Annual Progress Report* II (1967); "Some Regularities in Phonemic Speech Errors", *IPO Annual Progress Report* II (1967).
[15] V. A. Kozhevnikov and L. A. Chistovich, *Speech: Articulation and Perception* (Washington, 1966), Chapter IV.
[16] See note 14 above.
[17] See note 14 above.

sible for the ordering of the units in the programme apparently tends to break down when these units are similar to one another.

(f) In significantly more cases than is to be expected in a random distribution the elements involved in a speech error belong to stressed syllables.[18]

This observation seems to hold equally true for both elements involved in a speech error, thus for the origin as well as for the target element. I for one find this rather strange as it could be expected that the origin element belongs more often to a stressed syllable than the target element. This is actually what Boomer and Laver claim for their collection of English slips of the tongue. They state that "Slips involve the primary stressed word, either as origin or as target, with primary stressed origins predominating." These authors were in a better position to judge the question than I, because their collection consisted of tape-recordings, whereas the collection I used had been noted down in orthographic notation. But if, indeed, the origin element had more chance to belong to a stressed syllable than the target element, one would also expect that the origin element had more chance of belonging to an open-class word than the target element. That this is not the case may follow from Table II. Moreover in a tape-recorded collection of speech errors that Cohen induced under laboratory conditions by having subjects read aloud texts at a rapid rate, I was not able to find any evidence for the generality of the statement of Boomer and Laver.

(g) In significantly more cases than is to be expected in a random distribution the elements involved in a phonemic speech error belong to an open-class word rather than to a closed-class word.

TABLE II

	occurrence frequency of Relative	Subst.	Verb	Adj.	Adv.	Pron.	Numer.	Prep.	Conj.	Art. total
Subst.	18 %	66	50	73	12	7	2	–	–	210
Verb	23 %	115	27	4	27	3	–	–	1	177
Adj.	5 %	33	8	8	8	–	–	1	–	58
Adv.	11 %	29	22	5	20	–	–	–	–	76
Pron.	17 %	5	11	2	1	–	–	–	2	21
Numer.	0.2 %	4	3	–	–	1	1	–	–	9
Prep.	9 %	9	4	–	2	–	–	1	–	16
Conj.	3 %	2	–	–	–	–	–	1	–	3
Art.	14 %	–	–	–	–	–	–	–	–	–

In the rows is given the class of the word to which the origin belongs and in the columns the class of the word to which the target belongs. The relative frequencies of occurrence as indicated in the first column of the table are not very precise as they are based on a sample of only a few hundred words. Speech errors in which the origin and the target unit belong to the same word are not accounted for in this table.

[18] See note 14 above.

This may be concluded from Table II. A closer inspection of Table II shows that not only have open-class words more chance of attracting speech errors, but that substantives in particular seem to have more chance of attracting slips of the tongue than any other word class. This becomes even clearer, when we take into account the errors, where origin and target belong to the same word. The latter class of errors was not accounted for in Table II. These cases comprise 176 substantives, 19 verbs, 19 adjectives and 4 adverbs. One might argue that the findings could be a result of the selective listening of the observers, who collected the speech errors, in the same way as in proof-reading errors in informationally important words are more easily found than those in less important words.[19]

However, the same ratio was found for the tape-recorded errors mentioned earlier and here careful and repeated listening reduced the chance of faulty listening. Probably the fact that lapses have a statistical preference for substantives is a result of the preference for stressed syllables. Anyway, we come to the remarkable conclusion that speech errors occur most frequently in those fragments of the speech chain on which the attention of the speaker is focused.

A final remark which I would like to make with regard to phonemic speech errors is that these must be sharply distinguished from the phenomena of slurring, which Sturtevant failed to do, in putting speech errors of the kind described above under the heading of Assimilation together with phenomena as Latin *ad-peto* becoming *appeto*. Differences between these two kinds of phenomena are: First, contact assimilation and other phenomena of slurring tend to be more frequent in unstressed syllables. Speech errors, however, have a preference for stressed syllables. Secondly, as regressive assimilation is more frequent than progressive, there seems to be a tendency in contact assimilation to leave the prevocalic consonant unaffected. In phonemic speech errors, however, prevocalic consonants are certainly not less often affected than postvocalic consonants. Rather the reverse seems to be true. Thirdly, in speech errors prevocalic and postvocalic consonants seem to exert no influence on one another, whereas in contact assimilation this is just the normal situation. In general we may say that phonemic speech errors have a preference for syllables that are clearly and elaborately pronounced, while contact assimilation occurs more frequently in or between syllables which are not felt to be important by the speaker.

B. *Non-phonemic Errors in the Programme*

As may be seen from a comparison of Table I with Table III the errors within the programme involving larger units than phonemes or consonant clusters are far fewer in number than the phonemic speech errors. Although it is not at all certain that the ratio of phonemic to non-phonemic errors in the collection is an exact reflexion of the same ratio in daily speech, I am fairly confident that indeed the chance of occurrence

---

[19]   D. W. J. Corcoran, "An Acoustic Factor in Letter Cancellation", *Nature*, Vol. 210 (1966), p. 658; "Acoustic Factor in Proof Reading", *Nature*, Vol. 214 (1967), p. 851.

TABLE III

Classification of Speech Errors within the Programme Involving larger Units than Phonemes or Phoneme Clusters

	Meaningless combinations of phonemes	Affixes	Root morphemes	Whole words
Anticipation (c. 75 %)				
substitution	16	9	16	13
addition	6	6	–	–
Perseveration (c. 5 %)				
substitution	3	2	–	1
Transposition (c. 20 %)				
substitution	3	5	3	8

of these higher order errors is very small as compared to the chance of occurrence for phonemic errors. Nevertheless there are some interesting remarks to be made on these errors.

(1) *Meaningless Combinations of Phonemes*

This class of errors comprises VC combinations, CV combinations or more complex sequences of phonemes. An example in English may be:

*a book might → a bight might

Of the 28 errors of this kind in the collection, there are 19 cases concerning VC combinations against only 4 CV combinations and 5 more complex segments. If, indeed, this were interpreted as evidence that VC combinations are more likely to operate as one unit in speech errors than CV combination, the latter statement might be related to the fact that in Dutch the prevocalic consonant is distributionally freer than the postvocalic consonant, the latter being more intimately connected with the vowel.[20]

(2) *Affixes*

In errors concerning affixes the origin and the target have always both the same position with regard to the root morpheme, that is to say that both are suffixes or both are prefixes. The fact that prefixes and suffixes cannot replace each other is comparable to the one that in phonemic speech errors prevocalic and postvocalic consonants exert no influence on one another. An example concerning a prefix, might be:

inspiration in experiments → expiration in experiments.

[20]   A. van Katwijk, "On Perceptual Units in Speech", *IPO Annual Progress Report* I (1966).

(3) *Root Morphemes*
Examples in English might be:

> *a conceivable difference → a differable difference
> *he restates his story → he restories his story
> *that is cheaper than a new one → that is newer than a cheap one
>   he is taking a match → he is matching a take

These errors constitute an interesting class in that they show the various ways of word derivation as psychological processes separate from the actual forms to which they are applied. In examples such as the last the newly made substantive may be non-existent in the language, just as verbal forms such as *restories* or adjectivals like *differable* may be irregular. Of the 19 errors of this kind in the collection there are 12 cases in which the two words involved belong to the same word class and 7 in which they belong to different word classes.

(4) *Whole Words*
The errors involving whole words as units show the peculiar feature that the two words involved in all cases belong to the same word class.
    Examples might be:

> *the microphone of the president → the president of the president
> *on the table in the room → on the room in the table
> *to take place in time → to take time in place
> *Jack Brown → Brown Brown

In 12 of the 21 cases the two words involved were substantives, in 3 cases they were verbs, in 3 cases prepositions, in 2 cases adjectives and in one case proper names. So here again the substantives seem to have a privileged position. As Cohen observed earlier, the transpositions of whole words seem to have a preference for stock phrases.[21]

It is interesting to note that the class of errors involving meaningless combinations of phonemes is relatively small. This is the more apparent if it is borne in mind that a sequence of phonemes randomly taken from the speech chain has only a small chance of corresponding to a linguistic unit, so that, if errors concerning meaningless sequences of phonemes had the same chance of occurrence as errors concerning linguistic units such as affixes, root morphemes and words, the former would far outnumber the latter. That actually it is just the other way about may be taken as evidence for some kind of psychological reality of linguistic units.
    In connection with the phonemic speech errors, evidence was given that as a result of the decay of memory traces the chance that an anticipation results in a transposition

---

[21] "Errors of Speech and their Implication for Understanding the Strategy of Language Users", in: *Models of Speech, International Congress of Psychology* (Moscow, 1966).

decreases when the distance between origin and target increases. As we may assume that the memory traces corresponding to higher order units are less subject to decay than the memory traces corresponding to phonemic units, it is predictable that there are more transpositions in the class of errors concerning higher order units than in the class of errors concerning phonemic units. In the latter class, transpositions make out 5 % of the errors, whereas in the class of higher order units transpositions constitute 20 % of the errors. Thus our prediction is corroborated and this leads to the assumption that the memory traces of higher order units are indeed less subject to decay than those of phonemic elements. But if this assumption holds true one might also hypothesise that the mean distance between the two units is greater for higher order errors than it is for phonemic errors. This hypothesis is also corroborated. In fact, the mean distance between origin and target in phonemic errors is 2.1 syllables and in higher order errors 4.1 syllables. This seems to indicate that the immediate memory in speech production is not a fixed amount of speech forms, but differs for the various hierarchical levels of linguistic units.

3. ERRORS OF SELECTION

Errors of a wholly different kind are those that result from choosing the wrong word. For instance somebody wants to say *I am afraid that* but actually says *I am glad that*, and has to correct himself afterwards. As I have only just begun to concentrate on collecting this type of error such lapses are relatively few in number and therefore a quantitative approach will not make much sense. A preliminary survey of these selectional errors shows that at least 4 different categories may be distinguished.

(a) The chosen word is formally related to the intended word.

This category comprises cases in which a word is substituted for a formally similar word that is not necessarily semantically related to the intended word. Examples in English might be:

*prepare instead of prepay
*combination instead of contamination
*literature instead of temperature

As these examples show, the formal properties which the two words have in common may be concentrated at the beginning as well as at the end of the word. Until now I noted down 21 cases and in this small sample I cannot find any bias towards initial rather than towards final similarity or vice versa.

(b) The spoken form is not the form of an existing word but shares formal properties of two existing words.

This blending of word forms often results in forms built up from morphemes borrowed from different words. For instance, the blending of the words *propose* and *present* might lead to *prosent*. But sometimes even morphemes are blended together. So I noted down the nonsense form *krastisch* as a result of the mixing up of Dutch *krach-*

tig (strong) and Dutch *drastisch* (drastic). I also heard the blending of the two mono-syllabic names *Blom* and *Mol* to *Blol*. One more example: Dutch *zwak* and Dutch *flauw* both in the sense of faint, were contaminated to *flak*. In most cases I observed that the two words were synonyms.

(c) The wrongly chosen word is semantically related to the intended word.

This semantical relation may be of several kinds. The semantic opposite of the intended word was given in the following – translated – cases:

    *integrator instead of differentiator
    *gone instead of come
    *fall instead of rise

A very peculiar mistake was made by the man who said:

    the two contemporary, er ... sorry, adjacent buildings.

This mistake seems to involve a semantic switch from the space to the time dimension. Other switches of dimension may be found in the following cases:

    *during the apparatus, er ... behind the apparatus
    *the singular, sorry, the present time
    *I am pain, er ... cold

Quite inexplicable was the following uncorrected case:

    *near the viaduct instead of near the time table

(d) The wrongly chosen word is narrowly associated with one or more of the adjacent words.

    *2000 Hertz instead of 2000 guilders
    *12,000 Hertz instead of 12,000 guilders
    *a judgement was passed instead of a judgement was formed

These lapses seem to reveal that a word may be mistakenly selected as a result of the contextual probability induced by one or more of the adjacent words. With contextual probability I mean to say that it seems intuitively clear that the wrongly chosen words would have a great chance of being generated if the speakers were asked to guess the word on the basis of the adjacent words.

Although the collection of selectional errors is rather meagre, yet the evidence given above seems to warrant some preliminary conclusions. The very fact that a mistakenly selected word always or nearly always belongs to the same word class as the intended word, indicates that the grammatical structure of the phrase under construction imposes imperative restrictions on the selection of words. Furthermore, the contextual probability seems to exert influence on the selection of words. The fact that we find selectional mistakes in the semantic field as distinct from selectional mistakes in the formal field might be taken as an indication that the selection of a word meaning in the construction of an utterance must be distinguished as a separate process from the selection of a word form. The observation that a word may be wrongly replaced by a semantically-related word may lead to the conclusion that semantically-related meanings are easily activated by one another or by the same intentional determinant. Perhaps we might speak of semantic fields in a very real sense. It seems evident, however, that by the same token we may talk about formal fields since we see that word forms may be easily evoked by similar forms.

Finally, as we observe that two synonyms may be chosen at the same time, even to the extent that their forms are blended together into a nonsense-form, we may perhaps assume that in actual performance the meanings of two synonyms are often not distinguished from one another at all.

4. EPILOGUE

The above presentation of a tentative analysis of performance errors of speech has led to a few observational statements that are not yet integrated into an explicit theory of linguistic performance, and as far as I know, no such theory exists in a consolidated form. The distinction of four levels in linguistic performance as suggested by Cohen, viz. a language potential, a selection from this language potential, a programme, and the actual production of the speech signal, would presumably be a convenient starting point for a model of linguistic performance, but evidently such a model will have to be far more intricate. It will have to account, for instance, for the fact that prevocalic and postvocalic consonants cannot be substituted for one another, that phonemes in stressed syllables are more likely to get involved in speech errors than phonemes in unstressed syllables and that root morphemes may be interchanged but a root morpheme and an affix cannot take each other's places. It will have to explain that formally similar words are more likely to replace one another in selection than formally dissimilar words and that synonyms may be blended together to nonsense forms. A host of other as yet unexplained observations will have to be accounted for by such a theory. I really hope that the facts and observations given here may be of some use for the future construction of an explicit theory of language use.

THE LINGUISTIC EVIDENCE OF SPEECH ERRORS*

D. B. FRY

University College, London

At every moment of our clock time, our so-called 'real time', some millions of words are passing from speaker to listener over a considerable portion of the earth's surface. In only a negligibly small proportion of this vast number of words do errors occur, either on the speaker's side or on the listener's. It happens very infrequently that a speaker utters anything other than the sounds he intended to make or that a listener takes in anything other than the sequence the speaker meant him to receive. When errors do occur, they are usually corrected very rapidly; those made by the speaker are often corrected by the speaker himself or, if he fails to do this, by the listener in receiving the message; errors generated by the listener are almost always corrected later by the constraints of the message.

The almost incredibly high percentage of correct transmissions in speech generally is made possible only by the immense store of linguistic information that is continuously available to each individual speaker and listener. The majority of language-users are unaware of the existence of this knowledge and its application in correct transmissions passes unnoticed. When errors do occur, however, they cast valuable light on the processes which are normally going on and provide evidence of the linguistic information and the purely linguistic operations that communication by speech calls upon. This paper will be concerned only with errors in the generation of speech sequences and will examine examples of such errors in English in an attempt to show that they cannot be accounted for except by attributing to speakers a knowledge of a language system certainly similar to and even in many details coincident with that constructed by linguists. The examples given are all taken from direct observation of spontaneous speech; they have all actually occurred, even the seemingly most outlandish of them.

SPEECH PROGRAMMING

In common parlance we refer to all speech errors as 'slips of the tongue'. It happens rather rarely, however, that an error is actually a mistake in articulation. There are

* Reprinted from *Brno Studies in English* 8 (1969).

a number of stages between thinking of something to say and making the speech muscles work and errors can originate at all of these stages. We need first of all, therefore, some framework that will indicate the nature of the successive stages. What is in question is the programming of utterances, which is a specific function of some part of the speech centres in the brain. The programming entails calling upon large memory stores, which are also located in the cortex, but we shall not be much concerned here with those stores nor with the connections between them and the programming mechanisms.

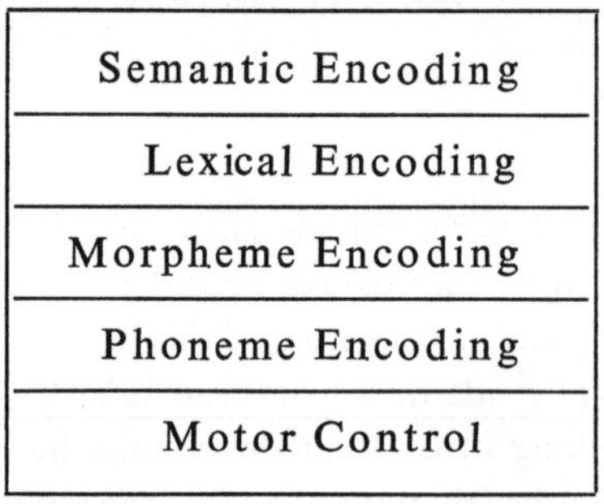

| Semantic Encoding |
| Lexical Encoding |
| Morpheme Encoding |
| Phoneme Encoding |
| Motor Control |

Fig. 1

The encoding process itself can be viewed somewhat in the manner suggested in Fig. 1. The first level, that of semantic encoding, is equivalent to what, in everyday terms, we call 'thinking what we want to say'. This is distinct from the selection of the words actually used in the message and is a necessary stage in the whole encoding operation. We can see a parallel and indeed an example of this activity in the case of a practised speaker who may write half-a-dozen words, one under the other, on a slip of paper and then talk for twenty minutes, using this as a guide and perhaps not even uttering the particular words noted. This is long-term semantic planning, but every speaker goes through a similar process on a short-term basis when he is encoding speech.

It will be made clear a little later that semantic encoding, like the encoding at all other levels, is a continuing process. The speaker does not complete the semantic encoding for any sequence before he embarks on the rest of the programming; operations at this level simply lead in time the corresponding operations at lower levels. We must, of course, accept the semantic encoding as an error-free process, since it does not make any sense to think of errors occurring at this level. In the very frequent case of the speaker's 'changing his mind' about what he wants to say, we are faced only with a particular time sequence in the semantic programme which differs from some other time sequence that would have resulted if there had been no change of plan.

At the next level, lexical encoding, the programme selects the words which the speaker intends to use in the actual message, but in their root form. This means that at this level polymorphemic words are specified in the programme only as to their roots, the necessary affixes being written into the programme at the next level, that of morphemic encoding. The lexical encoding level has access to the large store of word units; the morphemic encoding is connected to the circuits which store grammatical and syntactic rules and to the relatively small store of bound morphemes.

The task of the phoneme encoding level is to programme the sequence of phonemes in accordance with the morpheme string, selecting the items from the small store of phonemic units, and the motor control programme then instructs the muscles involved in respiration, phonation and articulation to carry out the actions demanded by the phoneme sequence. In doing so it draws upon the memory store of patterns of habitual movement in such a way as to specify very accurately the timing and sequence of muscle actions.

Whenever speech is being generated, these five programmes are running continuously in the speaker's brain. The first important feature to be noted is that if we take any point in the programme on one level and look for the corresponding point in the programme below, a time-lag will be apparent. Let us imagine that the legends in the different levels of Fig. 1 represent the form of the programme that is being implemented. We take a given instant in clock-time and examine the progress of each programme up to that moment. The state of affairs will in principle be that indicated by Fig. 2. At the selected instant, the semantic programme is well-advanced,

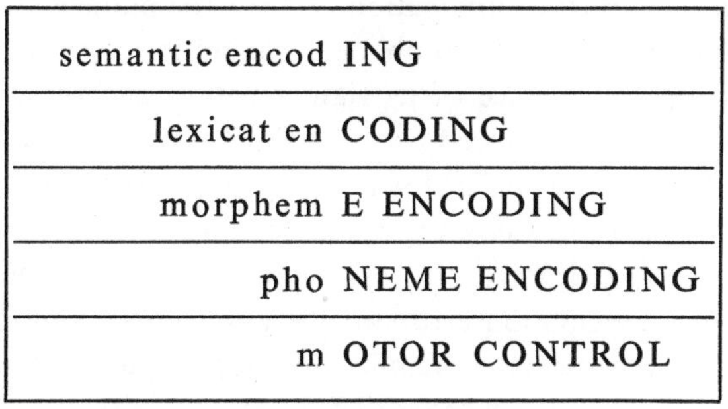

semantic encod ING
lexicat en CODING
morphem E ENCODING
pho NEME ENCODING
m OTOR CONTROL

Past: Future
Fig. 2

the lexical encoding is lagging behind it by a certain amount, and at each level below, the time-lag is progressive. The time difference between levels is variable, though it does not of course change in such a way as to cause any level to lead the one above. We might think of the five programmes as being each on a moving belt with its own drive; as the generation of a message proceeds, the programme on one belt may move up on or lag further behind the one above. It is this variable time relation between programmes which appears to lie behind a considerable proportion of the errors in speech.

In the following sections we shall try to classify a number of examples of speech errors, showing how they may be due to changing time relations between levels, and how they may be accounted for by errors occurring in the phonemic, the morphemic or the lexical encoding programmes.

PHONEME ERRORS

Although the time-lag between programmes is variable, it is probable that in normal error-free working the range of variation is not very great and it is quite likely that any individual speaker has a preferred set of time-relations which he likes to keep to, within certain limits. When for some reason the time-relations change rather abruptly, perhaps because the time-lag has become uncomfortably large, then errors may occur which are triggered off by the new relation between one programme and another. If this happens, for example, between the phoneme programme and the morpheme and lexical encoding, there may be ANTICIPATION ERRORS at the phoneme level, that is to say that a phoneme will appear in the phoneme string in advance of its proper position in the sequence. This seems to have happened in examples like: [ə weðəz nou ju:s wiðaut wo:tə] for *a leather's no use without water*, [grotl strein] for *glottal strain*, [ðə depjutri redʒistra:] for *the deputy registrar*. Anticipation errors in the phoneme encoding affect vowels as well as consonants. as in [wi not i:nli ni:d tə nou] for *we not only need to know*, [daitekeʃn kraitiəriən] for *detection criterion* and [teibl nipkinz] for *table napkins*.

A very common form of the anticipation error at the phoneme level is the spoonerism. Here the serial position of two phonemes is reversed; anticipation inserts one phoneme in the string in advance of its right position and the error is then compensated for by putting the displaced phoneme in the gap left in the sequence. Thus we get examples like: [ə gei əv deilz] for *a day of gales*, [lə:n tə ripli:d] for *learn to lip-read*, [ə tilvə si:spu:n] for *a silver teaspoon* [ə reəli wə:d hə:k] for *a rarely heard work*. Spoonerisms are traditionally reversals of the initial phonemes of words or at least syllables, but anticipation errors in the phoneme programme can also produce more unusual reversals, as in [fəmilə tə miljə] for *familiar to Miller*, and can affect vowel phonemes, as in [kə:v ðə ta:ki] for *carve the turkey*.

One further type of anticipation error is that which leads to the dropping out of some considerable portion of the complete sequence. Such mistakes are invariably noticed by the speaker and are corrected by going back and uttering the expanded form of the sequence. Naturally they may and generally do affect the programmes at higher levels and these effects will be referred to in later sections. One example of such an error is: [ətʃi:vl] for *achievement level*; an extreme case heard from one speaker was the utterance of the syllable [biɔ], which was a contraction of the phrase *bent on ruining*; and a further example which has implications at the morpheme level to be discussed below was: [əsŋtl jo:self] for *observe subtlety yourself*.

The reverse of the anticipation error is the type which appears to be due to persistence, what we might term PERSEVERATION ERRORS. Here the part of the programme which has already been implemented at a given level is not cleared and there is an iteration of a short sequence or item before the continuation of the programme begins to operate. If anticipation errors at the phoneme level are due to the fact that the phoneme encoding has lagged too far behind the morpheme encoding and there has consequently been a rather abrupt moving up of the phoneme programme on the morpheme programme, then perseveration errors may conceivably be the result of the opposite operation, that is to say the time-lag between phoneme and morpheme encoding has become uncomfortably small and there is a rather sudden increase in the lag. In fact, perseveration errors at the phoneme level do not seem to be as common as anticipation errors, but they do occur fairly often at the morpheme level. The following are some examples of the effect in the phoneme programme : [kiŋstən ənd hampstən] for *Kingston and Hampton*, [ətribjuːtidit] for *attributed*, [reprizenti-teiʃn] for *representation*, [simbələlədʒi] for *symbology*.

It is worth pointing out in passing that the occurrence of such phonemic errors makes it impossible to accept the hypothesis which has sometimes been advanced that language-users do not operate with phonemes and that we must regard the syllable or the word as the smallest functional unit for speakers and listeners. If this were true, then all the errors just given could not have occurred at all. To account for a spoonerism such as [ən isteip əv skiːm] for *an escape of steam*, we should be compelled to say that the speaker had, on the spur of the moment, coined a word-final syllable new to the language in [steip] and had followed this up by selecting the word *scheme* from the word store in the face of all the constraints of semantic planning and sequential probability. To call such an explanation far-fetched would be an understatement.

Over thirty years ago, Twaddell in his monograph "On Defining the Phoneme" referred to a "mythological view of the linguistic process according to which a speaker reaches into his store of phonemes, selects the proper number of each, arranges them tastefully and then produces an utterance". All the evidence points to the fact that this is what the speaker does, if we discard the ironical adjective 'tastefully', and far from being mythological, this view is the only one which allows us to account for many of the things which actually happen in speech, particularly the kind of errors in speech generation which have been cited above.

MORPHEME AND WORD ERRORS

We will now turn to errors in morpheme and word encoding and see whether the same types of error tend to occur. The reason for considering the two levels in conjunction with each other is that the first question to be answered is clearly whether we need to postulate separate programmes for morphemes and words, or whether we cannot think of the processing as being carried out with a word programme only, polymorphemic words being selected as single items from the store. It will in fact be evident from the errors that occur that there are two separate programmes and that there is a certain freedom between the word and morpheme encoding.

The morpheme programme appears to be in general rather resistant to error; it shows markedly fewer errors than either phoneme or word encoding. The principal reason for regarding it as a separate programme is indeed that examples are fairly frequent in which word errors do not upset the morphemic structure of the sequence. Nonetheless there are some morpheme errors, like the following anticipation errors: [ðis iz naisli wenzlideil] for *this is nice Wensleydale*, [testəriŋ hə ri:fleksiz] for *testing her reflexes*, and these perseveration errors: [nou mi:nz əv letiŋ dð famli nouiŋ] for *no means of letting the family know* and [əz tenəz ənd beisiz əv ko:siz] for *tenors and basses of course*.

One further type of error occurs at the morpheme and word levels which we might term a selection error. In cases of this kind, the wrong morpheme or word inserted into the string is not obviously linked with another item which is about to occur or has occurred in the same or a neighbouring sequence. This probably means only that it is difficult to see the connection or that the link is with some alternative programme which is not implemented in actual speech. Whatever the basis for the error, the result is the selection of the wrong item from the store. The following are some examples of this kind of error in morpheme encoding: [fansi hiz θo:tiŋ] for *Fancy his thinking* might represent a confusion of this construction with *Fancy, he thought* … [didnt, ʃi bikeim] for *Didn't she become*, perhaps confounded with *She became, didn't she,* …; [ai fəget hu:m sədʒestid] for *I forget who suggested*; [intrədʌkt] for *introduce*; [kəmpleksibiliti] for *complexity*.

These last examples already indicate that word and morpheme encoding have some degree of independence from each other, for no English speaker will find ready-made in his word store the forms *thoughting, introduct* or *complexibility*. These must be *ad hoc* creations of the current programme and they must be formed by combining a root word with bound morphemes in an unorthodox way. Examples are much more frequent however in which an error in lexical encoding fails to disturb the proper arrangement of bound morphemes. For instance, [wi:v lʌvd tə lə:n mauntənz] for *We've learned to love mountains* is a reversal equivalent to a spoonerism on the word level. If there were no morpheme programme and words had to be selected in their entirety from a word store, then the error form of this sequence would have to be: [wi:v lʌv tə lə:nd mauntənz]. Yet this kind of double error practically never seems to occur. The following are examples of a similar kind: [θri: digri: sʌbdʒikts] when the speaker intended to say *three-subject degrees* (here he would be incapable of saying [θri: digri:z sʌbdʒikt]): (vəkeiʃnəli obviəs) for *obviously vocational* (but not [vəkeiʃnl obviəsli], which would require a different context).

The example given earlier in which a sequence was telescoped also illustrates the same point. The speaker meant to say: *observe subtlety yourself* and this was contracted to [əsʌtl jo:self]. In this anticipation error the root [sʌtl] is moved up so that it appears in the sequence at the verb position, but we notice that it is not the whole word which is transposed; the noun-forming suffix [-ti] is discarded altogether and the root combines with [ə-] to form a pseudo-verb with the correct ending.

Another example in which the semantic level is also involved is provided by the case in which the speaker said: [ʌnfoːtʃnitli its egenst wilz dizaiə]. What he intended to say was: *unfortunately it's against Leigh's will*. There is an anticipation error in the lexical encoding so that the word *will* is moved up and functions as the proper name, but notice that the morpheme [-z] showing possession is correctly placed. Now the semantic programme has to be completed, the word *will* has already occurred and the speaker, looking for a substitute, finds the word *desire*, a very reasonable choice in the context. It seems that errors of this nature cannot be accounted for except by assuming that word and morpheme encoding, though interconnected, are in some sense separate processes.

The lexical errors given above are all anticipation errors. If the hypothesis suggested earlier is well-founded, this will mean that the word encoding gets too far behind the semantic encoding and the lag has to be abruptly reduced. This is on the whole much more likely to happen than the reverse; we should not expect lexical encoding to tend to get too far ahead in time compared with semantic encoding, since the semantic programme provides the only basis for word selection. This suggests a further contrast between the word and the morpheme levels which we might express by saying that the coupling between the semantic and lexical programmes is tighter than that between the lexical and morpheme programmes. Lexical encoding is a matter of word selection and is wholly dependent on the semantic programme, morpheme encoding is only partly dependent on the lexical programme and is in part dictated by the selection of sentence form and syntactic rules.

In addition to word errors which call for some adjustment on the morpheme level, it is possible to find both anticipation and perseveration errors confined to the word level, such as: [ʃal ai bai ə kliːn ʃət] for *Shall I wear a clean shirt (or shall I buy a new one?)*, [ðə prəfesə əv ði iːvniŋ standəd] for *the editor of the Evening Standard* (referred to him as a professor) and [bel paeze wið biskits oː tʃiːz] for *Bel Paese, with biscuits or bread?*, and also selection errors such as: [juːl hav tə speʃəlaiz ðe rikwaiəmənts] for *you'll have to specify the requirements* and [ðeiə not iːzili əksesəbl] for *they're not easily assessable*.

The complete process of speech generation is so complex as to be at present beyond our comprehension and so of course the errors in speech depend on a far more intricate mechanism than we can describe in the present state of our knowledge. It is doubtful whether this mechanism could ever be indicated by any diagram or verbal explanation. The purpose of this paper has been simply to show that errors of different kinds are made in the generation of speech and that they are all of such a nature as to indicate that speakers are operating with a linguistic system essentially similar to that arrived at by linguistic analysis.

SPOONERISMS: THE STRUCTURE OF ERRORS IN
THE SERIAL ORDER OF SPEECH*

DONALD G. MacKAY

University of California, Los Angeles

INTRODUCTION

SPOONERISMS are defined as involuntary reversals in the serial order of speech as in (1) and (2) from Goldstein (1968).

overinflated state → overinstated flate[1]	(1)
pus pocket → pos pucket	(2)

Curiously enough the Spoonerism is named after a man who rarely made Spoonerisms as dictionaries define them. A recent study indicates that Spooner's Spoonerisms were rather carefully planned – high level humor rather than unintentional error (Robbins 1966). This of course means that Spooner's original reversals (e.g. [3] and [4]) probably tell us little about the normal mechanisms of speech production.

You've missed my history lectures → You've hissed my mystery lectures	(3)
Pardon me, madam, this pew is occupied. May I show you to a seat?	
→ Mardon me, padam, this pie is occupewed. May I sew you to a sheet?	(4)

But involuntary reversals do occur and, since Lashley's famous paper in 1951, attention has been focused on the challenge of Spoonerisms to theories of the serial order of behavior. Involuntary Spoonerisms are crucial facts to be explained in theories of serial behavior in the same sense that illusions are crucial for theories of perception (Teuber 1960).

In the present study we analyzed a large collection of Spoonerisms in the hope of gaining some insight into mechanisms that might underlie the serial ordering of behaviour. Our approach was similar to that recommended by John Hughlings Jackson: to infer the properties of a complex and unobservable system from its transitory malfunctions, working backwards from its output rather than forwards from its input.

* Reprinted from *Neuropsychologia* 8 (1970): 323–350.
This work was supported in part by an MIT intramural fellowship, UCLA Grant 2428, and USPHS Grant 16668-01. The author thanks H. Schulze for his help in translating Meringer.
[1] The arrow in these formulae is synonymous with "was spoken as".

Insofar as the malfunctions in the real system are not the result of random disturbances, results of such an approach could be of interest to linguists, psychologists, speech
pathologists, and neurophysiologists.

More specific questions that motivated the study were these: What factors contribute to Spoonerisms? For example, do repeated phonemes frequently precede reversed
phonemes as suggested in a recent theory of serial order in speech (Wickelgren
1965, 1966a, 1969)? Are reversed phonemes usually similar in articulatory form? Do
reversed phonemes obey a syllable-place law (i.e. originate in identical syllabic positions)? Do reversed phonemes usually occur in the initial syllable of words? Are
reversed phonemes usually close together or widely separated? How are phonemes intervening between reversed phonemes correctly produced? What mechanisms underlie
the occurrence of Spoonerisms, and specifically, how do Spoonerisms bear on the
general problem of serial order in behaviour and perception?

DATA

Numerous collections of Spoonerisms have already been published (Meringer and Mayer
1895; Bawden 1900; Meringer 1908; Goldstein 1968). But strict criteria should be adopted for
evaluating any given collection of errors:

Extensiveness
How many examples are available? As Bawden (1900) points out, conclusions from errors
in speech only become possible when the errors are collected in large numbers. Inductive
generalizations from a small number of cases are out of the question.

Context
The entire sentential context in which an error occurs should be reported.

Validity
Care must be taken to ensure that a speech error is really a speech error and not an educational deficiency. Similarly, the possibility that an error was intentional or planned must be
ruled out (e.g. by asking the individual what caused his error).

Accuracy
The help of the indvidual who made the error should also be elecited to ensure the error is
accurately recorded.

Documentation
The name of the individual making the error should be provided with his age, state of fatigue,
etc., as well as his introspections concerning the cause of his error.

Non-selective report
The possibility of selective recording or reporting of errors should be ruled out.

By these criteria, Meringer's corpus is far superior to all other collections. His two books
include an estimated 4400 errors in natural speech (124 of which were involuntary Spoonerisms). For every error he heard, Meringer noted the date of birth and name of the speaker,
most of whom were professors at the University of Vienna, and whenever the speaker's

educational background was slightly less extensive than this, Meringer reported this deficit. [ ]
He also recorded the time of day the error occurred, the state of fatigue of the speaker, his
estimated rate of speech at the time of the error, and the speaker's intuitions concerning
the cause of his error. Moreover, the errors occured in conversational speech rather than in
prepared speeches, thereby further reducing the possibility that the speakers had planned or
fabricated the errors. Meringer also reported the exact linguistic context in which each error
occurred, recording verbatim what the speaker had just said and what he was about to say,
and when relevant, what the speaker had just heard said or saw written!

Finally, the possibility that Meringer was selective in his recording, hearing, or reporting
of errors seems unlikely. First, even though slips of the tongue might occur too frequently to
permit noting every one of them (Bawden 1900), Meringer at least attempted to be completely thorough. As an interesting comment on Meringer's success in this regard, Sturtevant
(1947) reports that Meringer was so exhaustive in his collection of errors and interrogation
of speakers, that as a result he became very unpopular among his acquaintances at the University of Vienna. Second, Meringer was careful to note the possibility of misrecording an
error when the conditions for either hearing the error, or interrogating the speaker were less
than optimal. And third, Meringer himself was less interested in confirming any theories of
his own than in classifying speech errors, much like a Linnean zoologist would classify a new
species of insect he discovered. Finally, Meringer called special attention to errors falling
outside of pre-established classifications, so that the possibility of observer selectivity or
distortion in collecting the errors seems remote.

We therefore based our analyses almost exclusively on Meringer's data, using other sources
(e.g. Bawden 1900) as a supplement to Meringer's corpus.

NULL HYPOTHESES

For each factor we examined we determined a Null Hypothesis (the assumption that
the factor played only a chance role in the occurrence of Spoonerisms). These Null
Hypotheses were based on the frequency of the factor under consideration in speech
not containing Spoonerisms. Of course we wanted the natural speech to be as representative of Meringer's speakers as possible. But since Meringer only published the
errors of his speakers, we corrected the errors in sentences containing semantic and
syntactic anomalies (as in [5]) to provide a corpus of natural speech.

$$\text{Es macht den Eindruck} \rightarrow \text{Es hat den Eindruck} \tag{5}$$

Because of the difficulty in constructing null hypotheses for semantic factors, we
were limited to the analysis of phonetic factors. Thus the possibility of a semantic
factor in errors such as (6) was noted,

$$\text{Freimaurer} \rightarrow \text{Fraumeirer} \tag{6}$$

but was overlooked in our analyses.

(a) *Repeated phoneme hypothesis*

Chain association models of speech production predict that repeated phonemes
should frequently precede the reversed phonemes in Spoonerisms [6]. For example,

abracadabra might be produced as *abradacabra* in this model, all other factors being equal (see Fig. 1).

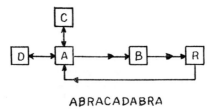

ABRACADABRA

Fig. 1. The Chain Association Hypothesis (after Wickelgren 1969). Wickelgren's context sensitive chain association differs from this model in that allophones are represented and not phonemes. But the principle of serial order is unidirectional associative bonds as represented here.

As a test of this prediction we analyzed the frequency with which identical phonemes preceded the reversed phonemes in Meringer's corpus. Two analyses were carried out. In the first analysis, #, the space between words, was counted as a phoneme, as demanded by Wickelgren's theory. Thus examples such as (7–11) would fit Wickelgren's model with this analysis (repeated phonemes underlined).

damit # bin → damin # bit   (7)

Cavalerie → Calaverie   (8)

Kolonial → Konolial   (9)

nichtnutzig → nuchtnitzig   (10)

Mond # und # Sonne → Sond # und # Monne   (11)

A second analysis was carried out not using # as a phoneme. Then the chance probability of phoneme repetition prior to reversed consonants was calculated on the assumption that any pair of phonemes in natural speech can be reversed. Here as well, phoneme repetition was analyzed with and without counting # as a phoneme. In order to facilitate the construction of the null hypothesis, only Spoonerisms within a word or between adjacent words were analyzed. Thus the null hypothesis was:

$$F(R) = \frac{1 \sum\limits_{x=1}^{z} NR_x(100)}{2 \sum\limits_{x=1}^{z} [(nP_2) - iP_2]} \quad \text{(in per cent)}$$

where $F(R)$ is the possible frequency of reversals (within or between adjacent words in the corpus of natural speech) with identical phonemes preceding the reversed phonemes; where $_nP_2$ is the number of possible permutations of two phonemes in the n

phonemes of the words, and $_iP_2$ is the number of possible permutations of identical phonemes, and NR_x is the number of possible reversals preceded or followed by identical phonemes for word pair X, and Z is the total number of word pairs in the corpus of natural speech.

The resulting data are shown in Table 1. When $\neq$ was counted as a phoneme, the

TABLE 1

Reversals involving repeated phonemes, proactively

	Proactive repetition	Chance
$\neq$ Counted as phoneme	38	8
$\neq$ Not counted as phoneme	24	4

Chance is calculated from natural speech.

null hypothesis predicted that 8 per cent of reversals would be preceded by repeated phonemes, whereas in reality 38 per cent of them were. This difference was significant at the 0.001 level (Chi Square Test). Similarly when $\neq$ was not counted as a phoneme, identical phonemes preceded the reversed phonemes more frequently than would be expected by chance (see Table 1). On the surface these data appear to support Wickelgren's chain association theory of speech production. However, our data contradict another prediction of the chain association model. The model predicts that repeated phonemes should precede reversed phonemes more frequently than follow them (since associative bonds are unidirectional). In fact, however, repeated phonemes followed the reversed phonemes at least as frequently as they preceded them. Examples of such Retroactive Spoonerisms (where repeated phonemes follow the reversed phonemes) are shown in (12–14) (repeated phonemes underlined). Note that (15) exemplifies a Proactive and Retroactive Spoonerism since a repeated phoneme also precedes the reversed phonemes.

$$\text{Wasserflasche} \rightarrow \text{Flasserwasche} \tag{12}$$

$$\text{Mond und Sonne} \rightarrow \text{Sond und Monne} \tag{13}$$

$$\text{Wachsen die Haar} \rightarrow \text{Hachsen die Waar} \tag{14}$$

$$\text{Tiefstufe} \rightarrow \text{Tufstiefe} \tag{15}$$

A comparison of the frequency of Proactive and Retroactive Spoonerisms is shown in Table 2. As can be seen there, Retroactive Spoonerisms were slightly more frequent than Proactive ones when $\neq$ was counted as a phoneme. This finding does not support the chain association prediction, especially since this analysis would bias the outcome in favor of Proactive Spoonerisms if the initial phoneme of words plays a special role in Spoonerisms. For this reason a second analysis was carried out excluding $\neq$ as a phoneme. The results of this analysis are also shown in Table 2 where it can be seen that Retroactive reversals were much more common than Proactive ones. This difference was significant at the 0.05 level, by Chi Square test, a finding that directly contradicts the chain association prediction. Apparently the repeated phoneme effect operates both forwards and backwards in the serial order of speech.

Finally we combined the frequencies with which identical phonemes preceded or followed the reversed phonemes in our corpus. The resulting data are shown in Table 3. Seventy-eight per cent of the Spoonerisms were preceded or followed by repeated phonemes, whereas the chance expectation was only 14 per cent. This difference was significant at the 0.001 level.[2]

TABLE 2

Reversals involving repeated phonemes, retroactively and proactively
(see text for explanation)

		Phoneme repetition	
		Proactive	Retroactive
# Counted as a phoneme	Data	48	52
	Chance	49	51
# Not counted as a phoneme	Data	38	62
	Chance	50	50

Chance is calculated from natural speech.

A similar analysis was carried out where # space was not counted as a phoneme. The results are shown in Table 2. Again, the transposed phonemes were surrounded by identical phonemes much more frequently than would be expected by chance.

TABLE 3

Reversals involving repeated phonemes (in per cent)

		Repeated phonemes: Proactive or Retroactive	No repeated phonemes
# Counted as a phoneme	Data	78	22
	Chance	14	86
# Not counted as a phoneme	Data	47	53
	Chance	9	91

Chance is calculated from natural speech (from Meringer).

(b) *Proximity hypothesis*

One theory of Spoonerisms (Mackay 1969) predicts that reversed phonemes will occur more closely together than would be expected by chance. This Proximity Hypothesis was separately tested for within word Spoonerisms (e.g. [16–17]) and between-word Spoonerisms (e.g. [18–19]).

[2] Since two-tailed tests were used in all statistical tests in this study, this information will not be repeated.

Helena $\rightarrow$ Henela   (16)

Karabacek $\rightarrow$ Barakacek   (17)

Senile Demenz $\rightarrow$ Denile Semenz   (18)

Knoten in die Nase $\rightarrow$ Knaten in die Nose   (19)

1. *Within-word Spoonerisms* – Proximity was analyzed in several ways. Since all of the analyses gave similar results, only the syllable analysis is presented here. Since reversed phonemes almost invariably occurred in different syllables, we let 0 represent reversed phonemes in immediately adjacent syllables, separation 1, one intervening syllable, and so on. The average separation of reversed phonemes is shown in Fig. 2 where it can be seen that reversed phonemes occurred in adjacent syllables more frequently than in non-adjacent syllables.

However this finding is somewhat meaningless until we know the chance proximity of phoneme reversal in these words, since reversals in anything but immediately adjacent syllables would be logically impossible if these words never exceeded two syllables in length. The null hypothesis was based on the assumption that any pair of phonemes can be reversed at any point in these words. Thus the chance probability of reversals with separation j (in syllables) is:

$$P(Rj) = \frac{\sum\limits_{i=0}^{n} Sij}{\sum\limits_{j=0}^{n-2} \sum\limits_{i=1}^{n} Sij}$$

where $Sij = F(li)[i-(j+1)]$ (20)

if $i \geqq j+2$,

and otherwise $Sij = 0$

where $P(R)$ is the probability of reversals with separation j, $F(li)$ is the frequency of words i syllables long, and n is the length of the longest word (in syllables). Thus by chance the expected proximity of reversed phonemes is:

$$F(Rj) = P(Rj) \times 100 \quad \text{(in per cent)}$$ (21)

for each of the j degrees of separation.

These expected frequencies are plotted in Fig. 2, where it can be seen that Spoonerisms occurred in adjacent syllables with greater than chance probability, and in more distant syllables with less than chance probability. Thus reversed phonemes occurred closer together than would be expected by chance. For some reason, reversed phonemes 'like to be' close together.

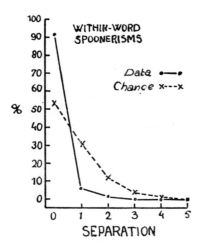

Fig. 2. The proximity (in syllables) of reversed phonemes of within-word Spoonerisms. Chance is calculated as the possible frequency of reversal in words containing the within-word Spoonerisms, assuming that reversals occur at random.

2. *Between-word reversals* – The null hypothesis for determining the chance proximity of between-word reversals had to be based on the number of syllables per sentence rather than per word. The average sentence length in the corpus of natural speech was 10 syllables (based on those cases where Meringer gave the entire sentential context). Thus the chance proximity of between-word reversals is:

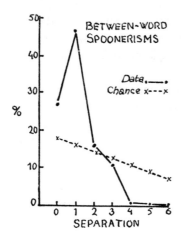

Fig. 3. The proximity (in syllables) of the reversed phonemes of between-word Spoonerisms in sentences. Chance is calculated as the possible frequency of reversals in sentences of that length, assuming that reversals occur at random.

$$F(Rj) = \frac{\sum\limits_{j=0}^{10} Sj(100)}{10-j} \tag{22}$$

where $Sj = F(li)[i-(j+1)]$ as before, and j is the separation in syllables.

The data are shown in Fig. 3 where it can be seen that reversals with separation 0 and 1 occurred more frequently than would be expected by chance, but wider separations were less frequent than chance expectation. Thus the reversed phonemes in both WITHIN WORD AND BETWEEN WORD reversals were more closely together than would be expected by chance.

Finally vowels and consonant reversals were compared for proximity. The data are shown in Table 4 (averaged for within and between word reversals). As can be seen, these reversed consonants tended to occur more closely together than reversed vowels.

TABLE 4

Proximity of reversed consonants and vowels (in phonemes)

		Separation of reversed phonemes	
		Within-word reversals	Between-word reversals
German	Consonants	1.1	3.3
	Vowels	2.4	5.3
English	Consonants	2.0	4.0
	Vowels	2.2	5.7

(c) *Phonetic similarity hypothesis*

One theory of Spoonerisms (outlined in the discussion) predicts similarity in the phonetic form of reversed phonemes. One piece of evidence for this Phonetic Similarity Hypothesis is the fact that consonants and vowels were never interchanged with one another. Consonants were always interchanged with other consonants and vowels with other vowels.

More detailed support for the Similarity Hypothesis was obtained by comparing the similarity of single consonant reversals. Similarity was measured in terms of the number of shared distinctive features. The standard ICL distinctive feature system (as modified by Wickelgren 1966b) was used in this analysis since it was based on articulatory rather than acoustic criteria, which seemed less relevant to errors in articulation. For each distinctive feature system j, the similarity S of reversed consonant pair i was calculated as:

$$Si = \sum_{j=1}^{4} \sum_{i=1}^{81} I_{ij} \tag{23}$$

where 81 was the number of single consonant reversals, I was 1 when the reversed consonants took identical values on a distinctive feature dimension, and 0 when non-identical. Thus S varied from 1 (when the reversed consonants were identical in all but one distinctive feature) to 4 (when the reversed consonants were completely different). Thus the overall similarity (in per cent) was:

$$F(Sj) = \sum_{i=1}^{81} \frac{S_{ij}(100)}{81} \tag{24}$$

where $F(Sj) =$ is the frequency of Spoonerisms of similarity j.

The data are shown in Fig. 4 and indicate that most reversed consonants differed in only one distinctive feature (56 per cent) and very few differed in all 4 distinctive features. For some reason reversed consonants 'like to be similar'.

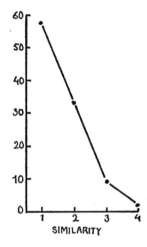

Fig. 4. Frequency of Spoonerisms as a function of similarity of the reversed phonemes (i.e. the number of different distinctive features).

The next question was whether reversed phonemes differ in some distinctive features more than others. The similarity on each distinctive feature dimension was separately analyzed using a modification of formula 19, namely

$$S = \sum_{i=1}^{81} Ti$$

Chance similarity was then calculated on the assumption that consonants are reversed at random, dependent only on their frequency of occurrence in natural speech. Thus the probability of occurrence in natural speech of each of n values on a distinctive feature dimension j is:

$$Pj(n) = \sum_{i=1}^{24} \frac{Fi(n)}{N} \tag{25}$$

where $Fi(n)$ is the frequency that phoneme i takes feature n of distinctive feature dimension j, 24 is the number of different consonants, and N is the total sample size.

Now the probability that any two consonants taken at random from a sample of natural speech will take the same value n for feature j is $Pj(S_n)$ where

$$Pj(Sn) = [P_j(n)]^2 \qquad (26)$$

Thus any pair of consonants will have the same value on feature dimensions with frequency $F_j(S)$, where

$$Fj(S) = \sum_{n=0}^{k-1} Pn(Sj)(100) \qquad (27)$$

where n is the value on the distinctive feature dimension, and k is the number of values on the dimension.

Thus the expected frequency of a different value for a distinctive feature is simply

$$F(D) = 100 - F(S) \qquad (28)$$

The data for each of the four distinctive feature dimensions are discussed separately below.

1. *Openness, Voicing and Nasality* – Consonants fall into three main classes along the openness dimension (Wickelgren 1965, 1966a, 1969), stops representing openness 0; fricatives openness 1; with semivowels, laterals and aspirants representing openness 2. About 65 per cent of the reversed consonants had the same openness value (see Table 5), whereas only 35 per cent would be expected by chance. This difference was statistically significant at the 0.05 level (Chi-Square test). Further analyses showed that this trend held for all three degrees of openness: stops were usually interchanged with

TABLE 5

The similarity of reversed consonants: a comparison of four distinctive features, nosality, openness, voicing and place of articulation

Feature		Similarity(%)	
		Same	Different
Place of Articulation	Data	10	90
	Chance	26	74
Openness	Data	65	35
	Chance	36	64
Voicing	Data	75	25
	Chance	52	48
Nasality	Data	93	7
	Chance	65	35

Chance was calculated on the assumption that reversed consonants will take distinctive feature values in proportion to the frequency of that value in natural speech.

other stops, fricatives with other fricatives, and semivowels with other semivowels (see Table 6). Thus the feature Openness conformed to the Similarity Hypothesis.

The same was true of Voicing and Nasality. Reversed consonants tended to have the same Voicing and Nasality more frequently than would be expected by chance (see Table 5). Thus Openness, Voicing and Nasality all fit the Similarity Hypothesis.

TABLE 6

The similarity of reserved consonants on the openness dimension

		Same	Different
Stops	Data	78	22
	Chance	57	43
Fricatives	Data	38	62
	Chance	19	81
Semivowels, Laterals,	Data	60	40
Aspirants	Chance	24	76

2. *Place of articulation* – Five places of articulation were examined, the extremes being 0, a point of articulation at the lips, and 4 a point of articulation at the back of the mouth. The data are shown in Table 5 where it can be seen that place of articulation of reversed consonants differed more frequently than would be expected by chance. This difference was significant at the 0.05 level (Chi Square test). Thus place of articulation did not fit the Similarity Hypothesis.

A further analysis showed that front and back consonants were more frequently interchanged with each other than with consonants having other places of articulation. The data are shown in Table 7 where it can be seen that front and back consonants were interchanged with much greater than chance expectation. For some reason front and back consonants 'like to be interchanged'.

TABLE 7

The similarity of reversed consonants along the place of articulation dimension

		Place of articulation of second consonant		
		0	4	other
Place of articulation	Data	10	54	36
at first consonant	Chance	18	12	70
	Data	62	15	23
	Chance	18	12	70

Finally the fact that reversed phonemes were usually similar (except for place of articulation) suggests that single features may be transposed in Spoonerisms. But in no case in our data was feature reversal the only possible explanation of an error.

Hockett (1967) presents an example (29) that suggests the possibility of feature reversal (of manner but not place of articultation). Fromkin presents

comb → ngowp   (29)

clear blue sky → plear glue sky   (30)

a better example (30) where "the place of articulation of two phonemes may have been interchanged, but not the voicing." However these examples are extremely rare, and other explanations are possible. For example these examples might represent partial fusions of phonemes in natural speech, a frequently occurring event in studies of delayed auditory feedback. But the possibility of phoneme reversals is not eliminated even if feature reversal were demonstrable. The relevance of distinctive features no more disproves the Phonetic Unit Hypothesis for speech production than the relevance of distinctive features to speech perception disproves the importance of phonemes in speech perception.

Finally, none of Meringer's Spoonerisms violated Wells' (1906) First Law of Lapses: "A slip of the tongue is practically always a' [phonologically] possible noise." No reversal resulted in a sequence of phonemes that were inadmissable in German (e.g. initial *lk*).

(d) *Syllabic Similarity Hypothesis*

The Syllabic Similarity Hypothesis is based on Boomer and Laver's (1968) fifth Law of Lapses: Phonemes in initial syllabic position replace those in initial position, nuclear replace nuclear, and final replace final. The Syllabic Similarity Hypothesis was tested using Haugen's (1956) syllabic position rules where vowels occur in three syllabic positions: initial as in *ist*; final as in *wo*; and mid-position as in *mit*. Consonants occur in four possible syllabic positions: initial position, next to initial, next to final, and final positions. For example in the monosyllabic word *stand*, *s* occurs in initial position, *t* in next to initial, *n* in next to final, and *d* in final position. But of course for *tan* by itself, *t* occurs in initial position and *n* in final position. Our question was whether reversed phonemes usually originated in identical syllabic position (determined from Breul (1906).

The data for consonant reversals are shown in Table 8, where it can be seen that reversed consonants occurred in the same syllabic positions 98 per cent of the time. In only one case did the syllabic position of reversed phonemes differ and this instance ([31] below) might readily be viewed as a higher order Spoonerism of the sort Lashley described in typing (compare [32]). However, Lashley's suggested "doubling mechanism" is not the only possible explanation of these higher-order Spoonerisms (see discussion).

Plural → Prular (from Meringer 1908)   (31)

These → Thses (typing error from Lashley 1951)   (32)

TABLE 8

The similarity of syllabic positions of reversed phonemes

		Same syllabic position	Different syllabic position
Consonants	Data	98	2
	Chance	30	70
Vowels	Data	81	19
	Chance	40	60

Also shown in Table 8, about 81 per cent of the reversed vowels originated in the same syllabic position. The data for both vowels and consonants exceeded chance expectation significantly (0.01 level, Chi Square test). Thus our data supported the Syllabic Similarity Hypothesis. Reversals in our corpus tended to have the same syllabic position. Several explanations of this Syllabic Similarity Phenomenon are possible. One is that the manner of producing a phoneme varies with its syllabic position; perhaps in the way Stëtson (1951) suggested, initial phonemes performing a syllable-releasing role, and final phonemes, a syllabic-arresting role. This interpretation would allow the tentative generalization that reversed phonemes are similar in Form of Articulation, which includes voicing, openness, nasality, and syllabic position. But reversed phonemes usually differ in Place of Articulation so that motor mechanisms underlying Form and Place of articulation must differ.

(e) *The Syllabic Structure Hypothesis*

Our next question was whether the nature of Spoonerisms can tell us anything about syllabic structure. Are reversals more likely in some syllabic positions than in others? The frequency of consonant reversals is shown in Table 9 as a function of syllabic

TABLE 9

Consonant reversals as a function of syllabic position

		Consonant position			
		Syllable initial	Next to initial	Next to final	Final
Within-word reversals	Data	96	0	0	4
	Chance	50	8	8	34
Between-word reversals	Data	81	3	3	13
	Chance	50	8	8	34

Chance is calculated on the assumption that reversals occur at random.

position. As can be seen there, about 96 per cent of the within-word reversals and 81 per cent of the between-word reversals originated in initial syllabic position.

The null hypothesis was that reversals in various syllabic position occur by chance and so reflect the frequency of these syllabic positions in natural speech. Thus, by chance, consonant reversals in position *i* should occur with frequency,

$$F(Pi) = \frac{n_i(100)}{N} \tag{33}$$

where n_i is the number of consonants in position i, and N is the total number of consonants.

Reversals in initial syllabic position occurred significantly more often than would be expected by chance for both within and between-word reversals (0.01 level, Chi-Square test). This of course implies that syllable final reversals occurred significantly less frequently than would be expected by chance.

Why are final consonants so rarely reversed and initial consonants so frequently reversed? One possible explanation can be based on Hockett's (1967) Syllable Structure Hypothesis. The basic assumption of this hypothesis is that consonant clusters form subgroups within the syllable, and the vowel is grouped with the final consonant or consonant cluster. Now it would be reasonable to assume that transpositions will break up the members of a subgroup less often than not. This means that under the Syllable Structure Hypothesis, syllable initial reversals should be more frequent than syllable final reversals, since final consonants form a subgroup with the vowels. Thus our data support the Syllable Structure Hypothesis. Vowel reversals should be quite rare for the same reason. Interestingly enough vowel reversals occurred about as infrequently as final consonant reversals, which further supports the Syllable Structure Hypothesis.

Furthermore, exchanges of consonant clusters (e.g. [34–35]) were quite frequent, as were exchanges of single consonants and consonant clusters (e.g. [36–38]).

Dropf krücken → Knopf drücken (34)

kriegt er Schläg → schliegt er Kräg (35)

vergass ganz → verganz gass (36)

kräht kein Hahn → häht kein Krahn (37)

Paprikaschnitzl → Schniprikapatzl (38)

However, reversals rarely broke up consonant clusters (as in [39]),

Gut und Blut → But und Glut (39)

which again suggests that consonant clusters form a group. Thus our data support Hockett's (1967) model of syllable structure.

We also examined the syllabic position of vowel reversals, using the same null hypothesis as for consonants. The data (shown in Table 10) did not exceed chance expectation, but this may have been due to our small sample size.

(f) Word factors

Does the structure of words play a role in Spoonerisms? Specifically, is the initial

TABLE 10

Vowel reversals as a function of syllabic position

	Vowel position		
	Initial vowel	Mid vowel	Final vowel
Within-word reversals	0	61	39
Between-word reversals	0	67	33
Chance	18	54	28

Chance is calculated on the assumption that vowels are reversed at random.

phoneme in words more likely to be transposed than non-initial phonemes? One of the problems in answering this question is the fact that word-initial phonemes are also syllable initial. We therefore had to determine whether syllable-initial reversals at the beginning of words were more frequent than syllable-initial reversals not at the beginning of words. The data are shown in Table 11 for both within and between-word Spoonerisms. In both cases the null hypothesis was:

$$F(R) = \frac{\sum N_j}{N}(100) \quad \text{(in per cent)} \tag{40}$$

where $F(R)$ is the frequency of reversal of the initial phoneme in a word, assuming that syllable initial phonemes are reversed at random; N_j is the number of words in the corpus of length j (in syllables), and N is the total number of syllables in all of the words in the corpus.

TABLE 11

The frequency of consonant reversals at the beginning of words

		Syllable initial		Not Syllable initial
		Word initial	Not word initial	
Within-word reversals	Data	33	63	4
	Chance	15	35	50
Between-word reversals	Data	73	8	19
	Chance	28	22	50

As can be seen in Table 11, a word initial effect was found. For both within and between-word Spoonerisms, reversals at the beginning of words occurred more often than would be expected by chance (0.01 level, Chi-Square test).

Moreover, this word-initial effect was more pronounced for between-word than for within-word reversals. About 33 per cent of the syllable-initial reversals occurred in word-initial position in within-word Spoonerisms, and about 73 per cent in between-word Spoonerisms. This difference was statistically reliable, indicating a stronger effect in between than within word Spoonerisms.

Thus the initial phoneme of words stands out in the occurrence of Spoonerisms, just as it stands out in the recall of words (cf. the tip-of-the-tongue phenomenon, Brown and McNeil 1966).

What underlies the word-initial effect? One hypothesis is that the first phoneme of a word is grouped separately, so that the frequency of word initial reversals could be explained on the same grounds as the frequency of syllable initial reversals.

But the question now arises as to why initial phonemes of words are special. One rather interesting guess is found in the Relational Memory Hypothesis. In the Relational Memory Theory, phonemes of words are stored in an abstract, relational form, like a melody that can be played in any key. However, in such a system the first note would have to be separately stored (e.g. as c in absolute memory) if the melody is to be produced correctly.

(g) *Cross-language comparisons*

Our next question was whether the factors conditioning Spoonerisms are universal or common to all speakers regardless of language. As a preliminary test of this Linguistic Universal Hypothesis we compared Meringer's Spoonerisms with a corpus of Spoonerisms in English. Our question was simply whether factors such as stress and phoneme repetition play the same role in English Spoonerisms as in German ones.

The English corpus was published in 1900 by H. H. Bawden, apparently without knowledge of Meringer's work. Bawden was perhaps less careful than Meringer and in any case less explicit about his methods of data collection. Thus although exclusive reliance on Bawden's corpus seemed inadvisable, his data allowed an initial test of the Language Universal Hypothesis.

1. *Phoneme repetition* – An analysis of proactive and retroactive phoneme repetition was carried out on the English corpus in the same way as before. The data are shown in Table 12.

TABLE 12

A comparison of the repeated phoneme effect in German and English with # counted as phoneme

	Repeated phonemes before or after reversal	No repeated phonemes
German	78	22
English	72	28

About 72 per cent of Bawden's 55 Spoonerisms involved repeated phonemes before or after the reversed phonemes, a figure very close to the 78 per cent for Spoonerisms in German. Apparently the repeated phoneme effect in Spoonerisms spans any differences between German and English as languages.

Further research on Spoonerisms in other languages is needed to test the generality of the repeated phoneme effect. However, the fragmentary data we now have on Spoonerisms in Latin, French, Greek, and Croatian, support the hypothesis that the phoneme repetition effect is language independent (see [41–44] below; repeated phonemes underlined); suggesting that this aspect of Spoonerisms may reflect a universal underlying mechanism common to all speakers.

tegmine fagi → fagmine tegi (Latin from Virgil; in: Meringer 1908)   (41)

cini stvoriti → cinit stvori (Croatian from Valjavec 1862)   (42)

Pithios → Phitios (Greek from Sturtevant 1947)   (43)

tous les trois → trous les tois (French from Grammont; in: Meringer and
Mayer 1895)   (44)

2. *Proactive and retroactive Spoonerisms* – The frequency of proactive Spoonerisms (where the phonemes preceding the reversed phonemes are identical) in Bawden's corpus is shown in Table 13 with space (#) counted as a phoneme. As can be seen

TABLE 13

*The frequency of proactive and retroactive reversals in German and English (in per cent) with #
counted as a phoneme*

	Proactive	Retroactive
German	48	52
English	47	53

there, proactive Spoonerisms were as frequent as retroactive ones, corroborating Meringer's data. Again it should be noted that this finding contradicts chain association theories of Spoonerisms (Wickelgren 1965, 1966a, 1969).

DISCUSSION

Recently, Wickelgren outlined a set of chain association theories for explaining the serial order of speech and behavior in general; i.e. context-free chain association; multiple-trace chain association; and context-sensitive chain association theories. He then proceeded to rule out all but one of these theories, contending that the nature of errors in speech (including Spoonerisms) supports context-sensitive chain association. However, careful examination of this theory proves it unable (without serious revision) to handle the following aspects of Spoonerisms: the retroactive repeated phoneme effect; the stress pre-entry phenomenon (discussed below); the effects of syllabic position on Spoonerisms; the phonetic similarity of the reversed phonemes; and the fact that phonemes intervening between reversed phonemes are produced without error.

Moreover context-sensitive chain association fares just as badly with other types of errors in speech such as masking (e.g. [45, 46], repeated phonemes underlined).

$$\text{Schreibebrief} \rightarrow \text{Scheibebrief} \tag{45}$$

$$\text{Finsternis} \rightarrow \text{Finternis} \tag{46}$$

Thus our data called for a new approach to the problem of serial order in behavior. But first it seemed appropriate to outline the problems with which a model of Spoonerisms is faced.

1. *Preprogramming*

Several sources of evidence suggest that acts stretching some distance ahead of the ongoing output must be preprimed or partially activated before they are executed. In this regard, natural speech may resemble reading: we seem to construct phrases somewhere inside ourselves and then read them off, sometimes inaccurately (Hockett 1967). That is, an entire phrase may be simultaneously displayed in a buffer system similar to that proposed by Broadbent (1958), and then read off or scanned in a unidirectional fashion not altogether unlike reading.

2. *Prior entry*

A second problem for a model of Spoonerisms is explanation of how a later phoneme "explodes before its time" (William James 1890). This problem is handled in detail in MacKay (1969), and concerns the nature of stress or motor intensity in speech production. The basic assumption there was that the speech motor units are preprimed in proportion to their degree of stress, stressed elements taking a higher level of subthreshold activation than unstressed ones. Priming results whenever the internal text is displayed in the buffer system, and final activation depends on scanning by a broadband scanning device such as that shown in Fig. 5. Of course, triggering the motor units would require a period of temporal summation. But the duration of temporal summation would depend on the subthreshold activation of the units, so that less time would be needed to trigger the motor units that are stressed than those that are unstressed. Parenthetically this means that stressed units will have longer duration than unstressed ones, which is in fact the case (see Heffner 1964). Now this model predicts prior-entry of a later phoneme when

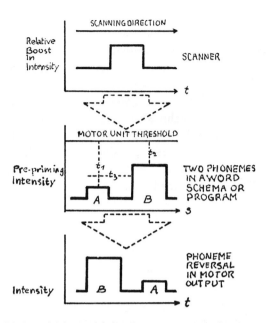

Fig. 5. An oversimplified model for explaining the stress preentry phonemenon. The model consists of three basic components: speech motor units (not shown), word engrams displayed in a buffer system where stressed segments prime the motor units to a greater extent than unstressed segments; and a scanning mechanism of the type assumed in visual systems (Sperling [1963]; see also Aaronson [1967]; Neisser [1963] and Steinberg [1966]). The scanning mechanism is assumed to sweep over the motor engrams in unidirectional fashion at a voluntarily controlled rate, thereby serially boosting the level of excitation of the motor units to threshold. Since the segments of the motor program are in proper serial order, the speech motor units will be activated in correct serial order if scanning is sufficiently slow. However, at rapid rates of scanning (i.e. when t_3 is short), excitation of a stressed segment of the motor program for a word may reach motor threshold sooner than a preceding unstressed segment, resulting in stress-dependent transpositions in the serial order of speech output. The form of the scanning mechanism was arbitrarily chosen, pending further research. Note that t stands for the temporal dimension, s for the spatial dimension, t_1 and t_2 for the hypothetical summation times for the two phonemes and t_3 for their temporal separation for a given rate of scanning.

$$S > 0 \tag{47}$$

where

$$S = t_i - (t_2 + t_3)$$

and t_1 and t_z are the durations of temporal summation for the first and the second phonemes (in the buffer prior to reversal), and t_3 is the time between onset of scanning these phonemes.

Now this model makes several predictions for Spoonerisms. First, the probability of phoneme reversal will be high when t_3 is short. One of the factors determining t_3 is the separation of the phonemes in the buffer. Now in this model separations of phonemes in the buffer and in the output are isometric. Thus the fact that reversed phonemes are usually close together in the output supports this model. Another factor determining t_3 is the rate of scanning which in this model determines the rate of speech. Most investigators (including Lashley 1951) agree that Spoonerisms occur most frequently during attempts to speak rapidly, thereby supporting this model. However, direct experimental data on the rate of speech question would be desirable.

The model also predicts that Spoonerisms will usually occur when t_2 is small – that is, when the second phoneme is highly stressed, which accounts for the Stress Pre-Entry Effect. Finally, it should be noted that the spatial or display aspect of the buffer system is irrelevant to the mathematical expression of this model (formula [47]) and is only a simple way of formulating the problem. The validity of this model does not depend on a spatial display within the brain.

3. *The Segmentation Problem*

What are the units in speech production? The phrase is probably one of the units, since errors rarely transcend phrase boundaries (Boomer and Laver 1968). In the present study the reversed phonemes always originated in the same phrase, which further suggests that the buffer system displays no more than one phrase at a time. The syllable must be another unit since reversed phonemes tend to maintain the same syllabic position. However, syllables cannot be the "most basic" unit in speech production as Kozhevnikov and Chistovich (1966) and others have suggested. The fact that in Spoonerisms a unit smaller than the syllable crosses syllable boundaries, suggests the existence of smaller units. The question now arises as to whether phonemes are a unit in this hierarchy, a hotly debated question in present-day linguistics. Perhaps Lashley has advanced the best evidence for believing the phoneme to be a unit in speech production, namely, the fact that everyone (including children) can voluntarily reverse phonemes with considerable ease. Everyone can speak in ig-Pay atin-Lay. The next logical unit in the hierarchy would be the distinctive feature, but even these units should be viewed as highly abstract, and quite removed from the final motor acts. However, assuming both phonemic (and distinctive feature) units raises two additional problems.

The Coarticulation Problem

The essence of the Coarticulation Problem is that even though we 'perceive' phonemes in connected speech which can be recognized as the same in various contexts, they are not the same. Phoneticians have been unable to discover invariance in the acoustic signal, in the vocal tract configuration or in the low level neuromuscular activity for the same phoneme in different phonetic contexts (MacNeilage and Sholes 1964; Liberman et al. 1967; Harris 1963; Fromkin 1966). Moreover (Kozhevnikov and Chistovich 1966) recent evidence suggests that both earlier and later contexts play a role in coarticulation (MacNeilage and De Clerk 1967). This suggests that phonemes are modified to fit both prior and subsequent contexts.

The Prior Position Phenomenon

The fact that movement patterns depend on their position of origin constitutes the Prior Position Problem. Specifically if one pattern of movement causes some part of the body to move from A to B, a radically different movement pattern Y may be required to move the same body part to the same position B from a different prior position C. For example one direction of muscular action is needed to produce the *i* following *ng* in *singing* but the opposite direction of movement for producing *i* following *t* in *sitting*. Thus the muscular pattern for producing *i* is context dependent.

One solution to the Coarticulation and Prior Position Problems is to assume that the basic units in speech production are context sensitive allophones. But this solution, advanced in detail by Wickelgren (1965, 1966a, 1969) runs into other difficulties. A simpler solution is that phonemes are modified to fit the context in which they occur. That is, for each adjacent phoneme pair *ab*, *a* is modified proactively to fit *b* and *b* is modified retroactively to fit *a*. This 'contextual integration' assumption corresponds to the digital to analog conversion widely assumed for all motor systems (Ruch 1965; Miller er al. 1960). And as we will see, this assumption proves valuable in explaining other aspects of Spoonerisms.

4. *The Similarity Problem*

Another set of problems for an adequate model of the Spoonerism is the phonetic similarity of reversed phonemes. The fact that reversed phonemes 'like to be similar' suggests an interaction between them. One Interaction Hypothesis suggested in MacKay (1969) is that "Contradictory aspects of similar motor programs interact in mutually inhibitory fashion. That is when different motor commands involving the same muscles are simultaneously activated, these commands interact in mutually inhibitory fashion." Note that a similar assumption is prevalent in studies of perceptual systems (Hubel and Wiesel 1962, Ratliff 1961). This assumption seemed logical for a number of reasons. First, reciprocal inhibition is essentially an either-or device which is exactly the sort of mechanism that would keep phonemes distinct (see Fig. 6).

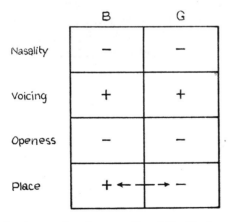

Fig. 6. The distinctive features for phonemes B and G with the reciprocal inhibition assumption indicated with a broken line.

That is, reciprocal interaction between features, would ensure that a phoneme half way between a *p* and an *m* (for example) would never be produced. Second, the principle of reciprocal inhibition seems to characterize many other motor systems besides speech (see Bullock 1965).

Moreover, this same reciprocal inhibition assumption has proven essential in explaining completely different types of errors such as the omission of speech sounds (see MacKay 1969). Finally, the reciprocal inhibition assumption proves useful in explaining several remaining problems confronting a model of Spoonerisms.

5. *The Intervening Phoneme Problem*

The fact that phonemes intervening between reversed phonemes can be correctly produced presents a major problem for the chain association models of Spoonerisms described by Wickelgren (1965, 1966a, 1969). But the Intervening Phoneme Problem disappears in a model where only the reversed phonemes interact and not the intervening phonemes.

6. *The Fusion Problem*

The fusion problem is somewhat specific to scanning models of Spoonerisms: pre-activation of a later act during the ongoing production of an act should result in fusion of the two. Of course short range fusion does occur and so would favor a scanning model. For example, the nasalization of *n* in *stanley* carries over into the *l*, and the lips are rounded during the *k* in *kween* (i.e. *queen*) in anticipation of the *w* (Heffner 1964). But fusions of phonemes in different syllables rarely, if ever, occur. The question that now arises is how a scanning mechanism can explain the transposition of more widely separated phonemes, but the fusion of these same phonemes is prevented. Again the answer may lie in a reciprocal inhibitory mechanism that prevents the simultaneous execution of different commands for the same muscles. A scanning model predicts short-range fusions whenever a muscle is not otherwise in use: that is, an articulator will perseverate or anticipate a position unless otherwise engaged, according to this model. Further research is needed to test this view of short-range fusions.

7. *The Post-Entry Problem*

The next problem facing a model of Spoonerisms is how the earlier phoneme gets to be produced later. If some inhibitory mechanism blocks an earlier phoneme, some excitatory mechanism must release this inhibition and cause the subsequent production of this phoneme. Exactly such a property is built into reciprocal inhibitory mechanisms. After one of the components of a reciprocal inhibitory system is activated, the other component becomes hyperexcited and this rebound in excitability is sometimes sufficient to influence behavior (Von Holst and Von St. Paul 1963). Thus rebound after-discharge due to inhibitory interaction between similar phonemes may cause post-entry of the earlier phoneme in Spoonerisms.

8. *Positional specification*

A major question for scanning models is how pre-entry and post-entry occur in appropriate places. This problem is solved with the contextual-integration assumption. Consider the reversal in (48).

Kutschkasten → Kustkatschen   (48)

This is rather a special example, since the phonemes *sch* and *s* do not simply exchange places with each other. Rather they maintain their position relative to the repeated *t*: the *sch* follows *t* before and after reversal, and the *s* precedes *t* before and after reversal.

Why do these phonemes maintain their position relative to a repeated phoneme rather than simply exchanging places? One answer is that the form and position of phonemes in the final output is relationally determined as suggested in the Contextual-Integration Hypothesis discussed earlier. Thus in (48) the *s* must be proactively integrated with *t* and the *sch* must be retroactively integrated with *t* before being produced. Thus pre-entry of *sch* occurs exactly before *t*, and post-entry of *s* occurs exactly after *t*, rather than exchanging places.

9. *The repeated phoneme effect*

The final problem for a model of Spoonerisms is the repeated phoneme effect. Now under the contextual integration assumption the repeated phoneme before or after the reversed phonemes acts as a sort of pivot: in retroactive Spoonerisms the reversed phonemes are both retroactively integrated with the same (pivot) phoneme; and in proactive Spoonerisms the reversed phonemes are both proactively integrated with the same (pivot) phoneme. The problem is that when the pivot is repeated, phonemes may maintain their position relative to the wrong pivot.

SERIAL ORDER IN PERCEPTION. As Lashley pointed out in 1951, motor and perceptual processes have too much in common to depend on wholly different mechanisms. This being the case, analogies between motor errors and illusions in sense perception might provide fruitful hypotheses for further research. Consider the following problem in the serial order of visual perception. When two visual stimuli of similar form are presented in succession, a dim one first, and a very intense one second, the second will seem to occur before the first for certain spatio-temporal relations between the two stimuli – a phenomenon known as Phi Reversal (Korte 1915).

Overlooking for now the concomitant apparent movement in Phi Reversal (Graham 1966), Spoonerisms and Phi Reversal seem to obey analogous principles. Consider first the relation of Phi Reversal to differences in intensity of the reversed stimuli:

$$P(R) = K_1 d \tag{49}$$

where $P(R)$ is the probability of reversal and $d = i_2 - i_1$ where i_1 and i_2 are the intensities of the first and second stimuli respectively, and K_1 is a proportionality constant.

Now consider motor intensity in speech as analogous to input intensity in perceptual systems. By analogy the probability of Spoonerisms $P(S)$ should be

$$P(S) = K_2 d_2 \tag{50}$$

where $d_2 = S_2 - S_1$ and S_1 and S_2 are the intensities of the first and second phonemes that become reversed in a word. Unpublished data confirm this prediction. The first phoneme (prior to reversal) is usually unstressed, and the second stressed or intense.

Next consider the form of the reversed stimuli. Several investigators have shown that Phi phenomena depend on similarity in the form of the successive stimuli (Linke 1918; Kenkel 1913). By analogy we would expect the reversed phonemes in Spoonerisms to be similar, as indeed we have found.

Moreover similarity for certain aspects of the form of the stimuli is more important than for others in Phi Reversal. For example, color of the two stimuli can be varied greatly without effecting Phi reversal (Korte 1915), but quite the opposite is true for stimulus size and duration: By analogy we would expect similarity of some features of phonemes to be more important than others in Spoonerisms, which seems to be the case. Of course this analogy does not explain why the Place of Articulation of reversed phonemes usually differs, but the Form of Articulation usually remains the same in Spoonerisms.

Next consider the perception of forms interposed between stimuli involved in Phi phenomena. Kolers (1963) showed that Phi phenomena failed to interfere with the perception of such intervening forms. By analogy we would expect no interference with the production of phonemes intervening between transposed phonemes in Spoonerisms, and indeed this appears to be the case, even with a large number of intervening phonemes as in (51)

> Wenn er geritten ist auf der Rosinante
> → Wenn er gerissen ist auf der Rotinante (51)

Finally, the proximal or phenomenal rather than distal or retinal separation is relevant to the occurrence of Phi phenomena (Rock and Ebenholz 1962). Similarly, the phenomenal separation of words may be more relevant to Spoonerisms than the distal separation. For example, *liar* in sentence (52) is phenomenally closer to *boy* than *man*, despite its distal or surface proximity.

> The boy who saw the man is a liar. (52)

The question of phenomenal vs. distal proximity in speech errors deserves further investigation.

However, it is apparent that several aspects of the problem of serial order in perception and speech are similar at least in principle. In fact, our model of Spoonerisms is formally identical to Korte's (1915) model of the Phi Reversal. That is, in Phi Reversal,

$$P(R) = \frac{It}{s} \times K_8 \tag{53}$$

Here K_8 is some constant, I is the intensity of the stimuli, t is the time between onset of the two stimuli, and s is the distance between them.

Now Korte showed that:

$$I = dK_9 \tag{54}$$

where

$$d = i_2 - i_1 \tag{55}$$

so that when these expressions are translated into time measures in a proximal (central) scanning system, we find

$$s = t_3 \tag{56}$$

$$t = t_3, \tag{57}$$

and

$$d = t_2 + t_3 - t_1 \tag{58}$$

so that (53) becomes

$$P(R) = \frac{dt}{s} = [K_9(t_2 + t_3 - t_1)]K_8$$

$$= [t_2 + t_3 - t_1]K_{10} \tag{59}$$

which is identical to formula 47 for Spoonerisms. However, the limitations of analogies should be emphasized. No matter how fine the grain of similarity, analogies are merely descriptive. Explanation of either Spoonerisms or Phi Reversals remains as much a mystery now as before the analogy. Nevertheless, analogies allow the hope that a model for one of the analogous phenomena will also explain the other: i.e. that a completely adequate explanation of Spoonerisms would serve as a model for research into perceptual reversals.

QUESTIONS FOR FURTHER RESEARCH

The questions raised by the present research are perhaps as numerous as those answered. For example, where does contextual integration of phonemes occur – before the buffer display or after? If the buffer system is as Lashley (1951) suggested, a flexible system where the order of elements can be voluntarily adjusted, a model of speech production would be simplified if the buffer display preceded and fed into the contextual integration level. One reason for this is the ease with which we can switch the order of phonemes around, as in ig-Pay atin-Lay where *pay* involves a different modification of *p* than *pig*. Another reason why the buffer display should come first is that contextual integration requires specification of the order of phonemes which the buffer gives. Thus the buffer provides information needed by the Contextual Integration Level.

A second question concerns the nature of the scanning device. What is its bandwidth, i.e. how many elements does it normally cover at any point in time? What is its shape? Is it symmetrical as shown in Fig. 5, or is it skewed?

Another set of questions relates to the buffer system. How much is specified in the buffer system? In the present model, for example, duration of phonemes is left unspecified, but phonemes, syllables and stress are marked. In what form are the units in the buffer specified? Are articulatory goals or targets represented in the buffer rather than phonemes? Is stress independent of the elements that are stressed? How are syllables coded – in abstract form independent of the phonetic elements comprising them? That is, at some level in the system, the syllables of words might be represented abstractly as, for example, $C_1 V_1 C_2$, with a set of rules such as $C_1 \rightarrow t$, $V_1 \rightarrow a$, and $C_2 \rightarrow n$. This being the case, a new factor may play a role on the occurrence of Spoonerisms. The search for $C_1 \rightarrow t$ could turn up a highly similar and partially activated phoneme (e.g. *d*) due to occur later in a preprogramed sequence such as *tandem*. This similar phoneme could be erroneously selected giving *dantem*. Moreover, a similar factor could be involved at the syntactic level. For example, abstract syntactic forms may be ordered in concatenative fashion, e.g. D + N with a set of rules such as D → *the*, and N → *Boy*. Thus, when similar nouns appear together in the context of a sequence, e.g. $N_1 \rightarrow$ *Spiel*, $N_2 \rightarrow$ *Seele*, then errors in the serial order of words as in (60) would be expected.

die Seele des Spiels → die Spiele des Seels (from Meringer and Mayer 1895) (60)

It should be emphasized that this higher-level explanation of Spoonerisms in no way contradicts the lower-level mechanisms proposed earlier. Several different types of mechanisms may converge to produce Spoonerisms.

The final question for further research is whether the mechanisms for serial order are similar in all motor systems? For example, do errors in the serial order of typing obey the same laws as Spoonerisms? (see MacNeilage 1964).

SUMMARY AND CONCLUSION

Analysis of 179 Spoonerisms in German and English revealed the following facts:

1. Repeated phonemes usually occurred before and after the reversed phonemes.

2. Reversals before repeated phonemes were as common as reversals after repeated phonemes, contradicting chain association theories.

3. The syllabic position of reversed phonemes was almost invariably identical, indicating that syllables must be a unit in speech production.

4. Consonants in the initial position of syllables were more frequently reversed than would be expected by chance. This supported Hockett's Syllable Structure Hypothesis.

5. Significantly more reversals involved the initial phoneme of words than would be expected by chance, indicating a lexical factor in Spoonerisms.

6. Distinctive features of reversed phonemes were usually similar except for place of articulation which differed more frequently than would be expected by chance. This suggested the possibility of two distinct types of mechanism in speech production: one for Form of Articulation, including voicing, nasality, and openness, and another for Place of Articulation.

7. Consonants were more frequently transposed than vowels.

8. Reversed phonemes occurred closer together in words and sentences than could be expected by chance.

9. Effects of the above factors on Spoonerisms in German and English were shown to be quantitatively similar. These factors were also noted in Spoonerisms in Latin, Croatian, Greek and French, suggesting that phoneme reversals may result from universal underlying mechanisms common to all speakers.

10. No support was found for chain association explanations of Spoonerisms. Even the most sophisticated chain association theory was incompatible with most of the above facts.

11. Analogies between Spoonerisms and temporal reversals in sensory perception were explored.

12. At least four basic assumptions seemed necessary for adequate explanations of Spoonerisms.

ASSUMPTION 1. $P(R) = (t_2 + t_3 - t_1)K$, where $P(R)$ is the probability of reversal, t_1 and t_2 are the hypothetical summation times for producing the first and second phonemes, and t_3 is the temporal separation of the two phonemes in a central scanning system.

ASSUMPTION 2. Both phonemes and syllables are units in a whole hierarchy of units in the speech production system.

ASSUMPTION 3. Adjacent phonemes are reciprocally integrated in programming speech output. That is, for any phoneme pair, AB, A is modified proactively to fit B, and B is modified retroactively to fit A.

ASSUMPTION 4. Contradictory aspects of similar programs in the speech production process interact in mutually inhibitory fashion.

Thus four different levels are assumed to interact on the manner shown in Fig. 7. A buffer level displays phonetic units, abstractly represented in correct serial order, with the possibility of multiple representation of the same phoneme (C_1, C_2, etc.). The buffer level feeds into an individual phoneme level, partially activating a set of singly represented phonemic units through a set of correspondence rules such as $C_1 \to B$ and $C_2 \to D$. When C_1 and C_2 are similar, Spoonerisms could result from an exchange of correspondence rules so that $C_1 \to D$ and $C_2 \to B$, for example. The units at the Individual Phoneme level are unordered, and are activated in correct serial order through scanning of the buffer system.

Words displayed in the buffer system also partially activate a set of programs or rules for modifying phonemes to fit the phonetic context in which they occur. The rules are of the form $A \to A'$ before D. Thus when D is repeated, integration with D_2 may occur rather than with D_1, resulting in a Spoonerism.

The final level is the motor unit level that codes the contextual variants of phonemes (i.e. A'). Reciprocal inhibition is assumed to occur at this level, so that prior entry of one unit may result in postentry of the other unit of a mutually inhibitory pair.

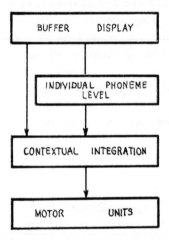

Fig. 7. An oversimplified model of speech production at the phonetic level (stress parameters not shown). Words are selected by higher-order semantic and syntactic criteria and displayed in the buffer system shown above. When this buffer system contains a word the corresponding phonemic units at the Individual Phoneme Level become partially activated, along with a set of programs for modifying these phonemes at the Contextual Integration Level. These levels in turn feed into the motor unit level, where reciprocal inhibition is assumed to occur. These motor units code the contextual variants of phonemes. But final activation of these units depends on serial scanning of the buffer system (see Fig. 5).

BIBLIOGRAPHY

Aaronson, D.
    1967 "Temporal Factors in Perception and Short-Term Memory", *Psychol. Bull.* 75: 130–155.
Bawden, H. H.
    1900 "A study of Lapses", *Psychol. Monogr.* 3: 1–121.
Boomer, D. S. and J. D. Laver
    1968 "Slips of the Tongue", *Br. J. Disorders Communication* 3: 1–12. Reprinted in this volume.

Breul, K. (ed).
   1906   *German and English Dictionary* (Boston: Heath).
Broadbent, D. E.
   1958   *Perception and Communication* (Oxford: Pergamom Press).
Brown, R. and D. McNeil
   1966   "The Tip of the Tongue Phenomenon", *J. Verb. Learn. Verb. Behav.* 5: 325–337.
Bullock, T. H.
   1965   "Mechanisms of Integration", in: *Structure and Function in the Nervous System of Inverte-brates*, T. H. Bullock and G. A. Horrige (eds.) (London: Freeman).
Fromkin, V. A.
   1966   "Neuromuscular Specification of Linguistic Units", *Language and Speech* 1: 1170–1199.
Goldstein, M.
   1968   "Some Slips of the Tongue", *Psychol. Rep.* 22: 1009–1013.
Graham, C. H. (ed.)
   1966   *Vision and Visual Perception* (New York: Wiley).
Harris, K. S.
   1963   "Behavior of the Tongue in the Production of Some Alveolar Consonants", *J. Acoust. Soc. Am.* 35: 784.
Haugen, E.
   1956   "The Syllable in Linguistic Description", in: *For Roman Jakobson* (The Hague-Paris: Mouton): 213–221.
Heffner, R. M. S.
   1964   *General Phonetics* (Madison: University of Wisconsin Press).
Hockett, C. F.
   1967   "Where the Tongue Slips, there Slip I", in: *To Honor Roman Jakobson* (The Hague: Mouton). Reprinted in this volume.
Hubel, D. H. and T. N. Wiesel
   1962   "Receptive Fields, Binocular Interaction and Functional Architecture of the Cat's Visual Cortex", *J. Psychol.* 160: 106–154.
James, W.
   1890   *The Principles of Psychology* (New York: Holt).
Kenkel, F.
   1913   "Optische Täuschungen", *Z. Psychol.* 67: 358–449.
Kolers, P. A.
   1963   "Some Differences between Real and Apparent Visual Movement", *Vision Res.* 3: 191–206.
Korte, A.
   1915   "Kinematoskopische Untersuchungen", *Z. Psychol.* 72: 123–296.
Kozhevnikov, V. A., and L. A. Chistovich
   1966   *Speech: Articulation and Perception* (Washington, D.C.: U.S. Government Printing Office).
Lashley, K. S.
   1951   "The Problem of Serial Order in Behavior", in: *Cerebral Mechanisms in Behavior: The Hixon Symposium*, L. A. Jefferess (ed.) (New York: Wiley).
Liberman, A. M., F. S. Cooper, D. P. Shankweiler, and M. Studdert-Kennedy
   1967   "Perception of the Speech Mode", *Psychol. Rev.* 74: 431–461.
Linke, P.
   1918   *Grundfragen der Wahrnehmungslehre*: 269–360 (München: Reinhart).
Mackay, D. G.
   1969   "Forward and Backward Masking in Motor Systems", *Kybernetik* 2: 57–64.
MacNeilage, P. F.
   1964   "Typing Errors as Clues to Serial Ordering Mechanisms in Language Behavior", *Language and Speech*: 144–159.
   1968   Personal Communication.
MacNeilage, P. F. and J. L. De Clerk
   1967   "On the Motor Control of Coarticulation in CVC Monosyllables", paper presented at the 1967 Conference on Speech Communication and Processing (MIT).

MacNeilage, P. F. and G. N. Sholes
  1964 "An Electromyographic Study of the Tongue During Vowel Production", *J. Speech Hear. Res.* 7:209–232.
Meringer, R.
  1908 *Aus dem Leben der Sprache*: *Versprechen, Kindersprache, Nachahmungstrieb* (Berlin: Behr's Verlag).
Meringer, R. and K. Mayer
  1895 *Versprechen und Verlesen*: *Eine Psychologisch-Linguistische Studie* (Stuttgart: Göschensche Verlagsbuchhandlung).
Miller, G. A., E. Galanter, and K. H. Pribram
  1960 *Plans and the Structure of Behavior* (New York: Holt, Rinehart and Winston).
Neisser, U.
  1963 "Decision-Time Without Reaction-Time: Experiments in Visual Scanning", *Am. J. Psychol.* 76: 376–385.
Öhman, S. E. G., R. Leanderson and A. Pearson
  1966 "EMG Studies of Facial Muscle Activity in Speech III", Speech Transmission Laboratory Quarterly Progress and Status Report, Royal Institute of Technology (Stockholm, Sweden).
Ratiliff, F.
  1961 "Inhibitory Interaction and the Detection and Enhancement of Contours", in: *Sensory Communication*, W. A. Rosenblith (ed.) : 183–203 (New York: Wiley).
Robbins, R. H.
  1966 "The Warden's Wordplay: Toward a Redefinition of the Spoonerism", *Dalhousie Rev.* 46: 457–465.
Rock, I. and S. Ebenholz
  1962 "Stroboscopic Movement Based on Change of Phenomenal Rather than Retinal Location", *Am. J. Psychol.* 75: 193–207.
Ruch, T. C.
  1965 "The Cerebral Cortex: Is Structure and Motor Functions", in: *Neurophysiology*[2], T. C. Ruch et al. (eds.) (Philadelphia: Saunders).
Sperling, G.
  1963 "A Model for Visual Memory Tasks", *Human Factors* 5: 19–31.
Sternberg, S.
  1966 "High Speed Scanning in Human Memory", *Science* 153: 652–654.
Stëtson, R. H.
  1951 *Motor Phonetics*: *A Study of Speech Movements in Action* (Amsterdam: North Holland).
Sturtevant, E. H.
  1947 *Linguistic Science* (New Haven: Yale University Press.)
Teuber, H. L.
  1960 Ch. 65 in: *Handbook of Psychology III. Neuro-Physiology*, Field et al. (ed). (New York): 1596–1668.
Valjavec, M.
  1862 *Stari pici hravtski* (Zengger).
Van Holst, E. and U. Von St. Paul
  1963 "On the Functional Organization of Drives", *Animal Behav.* 11: 1–20.
Wells, F. L.
  1906 *Linguistic Lapses* (New York: Science Press).
Wickelgren, W. A.
  1965 "Short-Term Memory for Repeated and Non-Repeated Items", *Q. Jl. Exp. Psychol.* 17: 14–25.
  1966a "Associative Intrusions in Short-Term Recall", *J. Exp. Psychol.* 72: 853–858.
  1966b "Distinctive Features and Errors in Short-Term Memory for English Consonants", *J. Acoust. Soc. Amer.* 39: 388–398.
  1969 "Context-Sensitive Coding, Associative Memory, and Serial Order in (Speech) Behavior", *Psychol. Rev.* 76: 1–15.

MERINGER'S CORPUS REVISITED

M. CELCE-MURCIA *

The most complete collection to date – and very likely the first extensive investigation of speech errors – was carried out by Rudolf Meringer, a linguist at the University of Vienna, who published *Versprechen und Verlesen*[1] (VUV) in 1895 and *Aus dem Leben der Sprache* (LDS) in 1908; both books are full of examples of speech, reading, hearing, and writing errors.

In his Forward to VUV, Meringer explains that he was interested in finding an explanation for "dissimilation" in Indo-European languages. He admits that his data are not conclusive and he decided that speech errors would have to be collected for many different modern Indo-European languages for his hypotheses to be proven or disproven. Aside from the historical problem that he wanted to investigate, Meringer was also interested in certain synchronic questions of psychological and linguistic interest. In fact he stressed that linguists and psychologists should work together on common problems.

Meringer recognized that speaking and writing were productive and motor-oriented activities whereas listening and reading were interpretive and sensory-oriented activities. He also noted that speech errors did not occur randomly, but rather in formally predictable ways. He was emphatic in his belief that speech errors were non-pathological and to be expected. In his concluding remarks he mentions that the ultimate source and goal of all language experience is to be found in the central and not the peripheral nervous system.

One type of error that Meringer classified were contaminations or blends (e.g. *Jakuba* from *Jakob* plus *Hekuba*). Such errors will not be considered in this paper because of their basically semantic or lexical nature. However, it should be stated in

* I wish to thank Donald G. Mackay of the UCLA Psychology Department for bringing Meringer's work on speech errors to my attention. He was the first to acquaint me with this area of psycholinguistics. I am also grateful to him for permitting me to borrow the two rare Meringer books. Victoria Fromkin of the UCLA Department of Linguistics was also instrumental in stimulating my interest in speech errors as important data for linguistic theory. I am also very grateful for the background in German phonology I received from Theo Venneman, UCLA Department of Linguistics.
[1] Also listed as an author of *Versprechen und Verlesen*, is Karl Mayer, a neuro-psychiatrist at the University of Innsbruck. Meringer, however, was the principle investigator.

passing that blends like other speech errors never seem to produce a phonologically unacceptable sequence in the language.

Another category of errors discussed by Meringer was 'spoonerisms' – reversals or switchings of words, morphemes, syllables, sound segments, and sound features. Feature switches such as those exemplified by *O, Du Saukramer* for *O, Du Grausamer*, in which a voiced /g/ is uttered as a voiceless /k/ bothered Meringer. He had no way of explaining the change of voicing and he tried to develop ad hoc arguments to account for such errors.

Meringer said that none of his errors were examples of metathesis (e.g. Indo-European **pōtmen → ptōmen*) but on the morpheme level he does cite examples of such processes (e.g. *Wertlaut* for *Lautwert*). Evidence from English indicates that such errors are at least possible on the phonological level. (See other papers in this volume.)

The kinds of switching errors Meringer found are given in Table 1 below. The examples from Meringer's corpus are organized somewhat more precisely than is found in his writings.

Since this paper is concerned primarily with phonological problems, only sub-morphemic sound segments (clusters, single sounds, features) will be considered. Also, only non-adjacent phenomena will be discussed since examples involving adjacent segments or sequences are not found in Meringer's data. Thus the focus is on the last four types of errors in Table 1.

TABLE 1[a]

Type of sequence or segment switched	non-adjacent	adjacent
word	*Die Milo von Venus* (for *Die Venus von Milo*)	—
free (or root) morpheme	*... auf einer Worte drei, vier Seiten* (for *auf einer Seite drei, vier Worten*)	*Wertlaut* (for *Lautwert*)
bound (or affixal) morpheme	*Gebrecherverhirne* (for *Verbrechergehirne*)	—
sound clusters	*Postkustkatschen* for *Postkutschkasten*	—
single segments	*preblomatisch* for *problematisch*	—
single segments with clusters	*Taps und Schnabak* for *Schnaps und Tabak*	—
features or feature values	Note that many of the so-called examples of 2 single sounds switching can be explained as feature values switching (e.g. *Nomat* for *Monat*)	—

[a] " – " means: I did not find any examples in Meringer's data.

Two other common types of errors are 'anticipations' and 'perseverations', called "Anticipationen" and "Postpositionen" respectively by Meringer. An anticipation is where something is anticipated and completely blocks the element it replaces – no switching occurs – (e.g. *Strang und Drang* for *Sturm und Drang*). Perseverations occur where some element that has already occurred perseveres to replace some other element (c.f. *Konkret und Kontrakt* for *Konkret und Abstrakt*). Table 2 gives examples of both error types from Meringer's data.

TABLE 2

Segment or sequence involved	Anticipations	Perseverations
Sequence cluster replaces sequence/cluster	*Haben Sie Bruck auf der Brust?* for *Haben Sie Druck auf der Brust?*	*... ein furchtbar glattes Glas* for *ein furchtbar glattes Gras*
sequence cluster replaces/is replaced by single segment	*ungehallt verhallen...* for *ungehört verhallen*	*... bei den Jägern und so weitern* for *bei den Jägern und so weiter*
segment replaces segment	*Lokuskapital* for *Lotuskapital*	*Stoss eines Erdbobens* for *Stoss eines Erdbebens*
feature value replaces feature value	*Bündinger* for *Büdinger*	*... Fälle gesämmelt* for *... Fälle gesammelt*

Another type of error found less frequently in Meringer (and a type he infelicitously referred to as "Dissimilationen") is what MacKay (1969) calls "maskings". As MacKay has pointed out there are both "forward" and "backward" maskings in the data: In forward masking a sound or feature blocks out a later occurrence of an identical sound or feature (e.g. *Friedich* for *Friedrich* where the second /r/ has been blocked.) In backward maskings the opposite occurs: a sound or feature gets blocked out by a later identical sound or feature (e.g. *unsere Faschen sind zu klein* for *unsere Flaschen sind zu klein*).

Meringer's other classes of errors were not significant in terms of the phonological phenomena investigated here. These kinds of speech errors have particular relevance to linguistic theory. Since they are errors in PERFORMANCE one may question their importance as evidence in a theory of linguistic COMPETENCE. There are those linguists who make a sharp dichotomy between these two aspects of language.

... the performance of the speaker or hearer is a complex matter that involves many factors. One factor involved in the speaker-hearer's performance is the knowledge of the grammar that determines an intrinsic connection of sound and meaning for each sentence. We refer to this knowledge – for the most part, obviously, unconscious knowledge – as the speaker-hearer's "competence". Competence, in this sense, is not to be confused with performance. Performance, that is, what the speaker-hearer actually does, is based not only on his knowledge of the language, but on many other factors as well – factors such as memory restriction, inattention, distraction, nonlonguistic knowledge and beliefs, and so on. We may, if we like, think of the study of competence as the study of potential performance of an idealized speaker-hearer who is unaffected by such grammatically irrelevant factors (Chomsky and Halle 1968: 3).

Some supporters of the strong 'competence/performance' distinction insist that a full model of the speaker's competence must be available before any model of performance can even be considered. In this respect, Langacker's remarks (1967) are of interest:

... the linguist does not aim ... to give a step-by-step account of verbal behaviour. In other words, he attempts to describe linguistic competence rather than linguistic performance.

It is not that linguistic performance is devoid of interest ... the reason for this concern with linguistic competence is, quite simply, that a description of linguistic competence is logically prior to a description of linguistic performance. Any adequate account of linguistic performance ... presupposes an adequate account of the abstract linguistic system, but the opposite is not true (36–37).

Fromkin (1968), however, states that the interrelationship between competence and performance must be of concern to linguists. She maintains further that certain aspects of performance are no more random and unpredictable than is competence. This of course does not imply that a model of performance can predict what one will say or the errors which may occur in linguistic behavior, but rather that there are strict constraints on both production and perception, two major aspects of linguistic performance.

Bever and Langendoen (1969) also argue against a strict 'competence/performance' dichotomy with reference to historical changes which have occurred in English syntax; rule simplification and rule changes are not sufficient principles. To look for causes they claim that one must look at the interactions between the competence and performance systems of language. They introduce the notion "perceptual strategy" and argue that performance can constrain competence as well as vice versa.

One aim of this paper is to show that by an examination of speech errors, i.e. performance data, one can arrive at a greater understanding of the competence grammar which underlies linguistic behavior.

It has been shown that an adequate theory of phonology must view phonemic segments as a combination of distinctive features. That is, segments are not indissoluble wholes. It is therefore of interest to see whether such independent features play a role in actual linguistic behavior. If one finds that certain errors do indeed involve features rather than whole segments this provides stronger evidence for the existence of features.

MacKay (1969) while recognizing that features probably play some role in speech errors considers them less important than larger units.

... the fact that reversed phonemes were usually similar (except for place of articulation) suggests that single features may be transposed in Spoonerisms. But in no case in our data was feature reversal the only possible explanation of an error ... these examples are extremely rare, and other explanations are possible. For example, these examples might represent partial fusions of phonemes in natural speech, a frequently occurring event in studies of delayed auditory feedback (MacKay 1969: 12).

Fromkin (1971) states that many speech errors can only be explained by "postulating that certain properties or features constitute independent elements in the production of speech". This observation plus the research on speech perception which has shown that features as well as segments are perceived and confused, leads Fromkin to conclude that features do have a place in performance models as well as competence models.

The evidence from Meringer's corpus suggests that MacKay places too little importance on features and that Fromkin's conclusions are probably correct.

The following sections present a number of Meringer's examples grouped according to specific features. Where relevant there will be a discussion of a particular set of errors. Each error is numbered and documented as to where it is found in Meringer's data.

A. *Umlaut*

Error	Intended Utterance	Possible Explanation
(1) zükunftig (LDS: 20)	zukünftig	Either the vowel segments were transposed or umlaut was misapplied.
(2) schmäl und langer (LDS: 19)	schmal und länger	Same as (1).
(3) ... in den anderen Vortragen (LDS: 109)	in den anderen Vorträgen	Umlaut failed to apply or an unumlauted /a/ persevered.
(4) ...kann mann um so langer laufen (LDS: 109)	kann mann um so länger laufen	Same as (3).
(5) Gotter (LDS: 109)	Götter	Umlaut failed to apply.
(6) Das ist auch ein glanzender Einfall (LDS: 109)	Das ist auch ein glänzender Einfall	Umlaut failed to apply or an unumlauted /a/ is anticipated, or perseveres.
(7) Soweit die in den Klostern reichen (LDS: 109)	Soweit die in den Klöstern reichen (LDS: 109)	Umlaut fails to apply or the unumlauted vowel /o/ perseveres.
(8) Gerüchseindrücke (VUV: 35)	Geruchseindrücke	Anticipation of umlaut or of a whole vowel segment.
(9) Sie haben längere Öhren (LDS: 109)	Sie haben längere Ohren	Umlaut perseveres.
(10) Wir müssten Böck'schönen (VUCV: 50)	Wir müssten Böck' schonen	Either umlaut alone or whole umlauted /ö/ segment perseveres.
(11) Ich habe selbst ein Menge solcher Fälle gesämmelt (VUV: 49)	Ich habe selbst eine Menge solcher Fälle gesammelt	Same as above, except /ä/ instead of /ö/.
(12) ...die ich selbst für eine Judin halte (LDS: 109)	...die ich selbst für eine Jüdin halte	Masking of umlaut or failure of umlaut to apply.

In interpreting the above errors, I am following Vennemann (1968) who demonstrated that phonological rules alone were sufficient to account for umlaut in German. Most of the above errors, as MacKay has suggested, do seem to allow a dual interpretation of umlaut as either a separate feature or an inseparable feature of certain vowel segments. However, example (5) and examples (9) and (12) attest to the independence of 'umlaut' as a potentially independent feature in speech production. Therefore, a phonological grammar that analyzes umlaut as a feature should be more highly valued than a grammar of German which does not.

B. *Ablauting Verbs, Irregular Verbs, and Related Matters*

Error	Intended Utterance	Possible Explanation
(1) wenn es heisste (LDS: 110)	wenn es hiess	Ablaut was omitted (i.e. verb was regularized).
(2) hat sich eine Weil' besinnt (LDS: 111)	...eine Weil' besonnen	Same as (1).
(3) von da an hat's gehissen... (LDS: 110)	von da an hat's geheissen...	Ablaut applied but wrong verb class was selected.

(4) dass einer da gesitzen ist (LDS: 110)	dass einer da gesessen ist	Ablaut applied only inflectionally; infinitive form perseveres.
(5) das ist nur mehr hinein-geziehen (LDS: 111)	das ist nur mehr hinein-gezogen	Same as (4).
(6) Er hat davon gesprachen (LDS: 111)	Er hat davon gesprochen	Ablaut applied but with the preterite form intruding on the past participle form (i.e. the wrong grammatical info.)
(7) Da weissen Sie es! (LDS: 111)	Da wissen Sie es!	Irregular verb: singular person form of root replaces infinitive.
(8) Ich wiss Keinen (LDS: 111)	Ich weiss Keinen	Irregular verb; infinitive form perseveres over first pers. sing.
(9) Ich dürf wirklich nicht?	Ich darf wirklich nicht?	Same as (8).
(10) gedenkt	gedacht	Irregular verb gets regularized.
(11) S: Niemand spricht ö und ä. L: Verzeihen Sie, ich sprich …ich spreche es! (LDS: 110)	correction in data	The vowel raising rule that should apply only to 2nd and 3rd person singular applies incorrectly to 1st person.

Although less coherent a set of examples than the Umlaut section above, these speech errors seem to indicate that ablaut is a partially independent yet highly complicated feature that may be omitted altogether (1, 2) applied along with certain incorrect information (3, 6), or applied only partially (4, 5). Here also Vennemann's account of ablaut as a basically phonological or morphophonological process – rather than as a syntactic process – in German is indirectly supported by examples such as (1) and (2), which can be most easily explained as the omission of one morphophonemic rule. Vennemann's treatment of certain vowel-raising environments as a process similar to but separate from umlaut also gets some support from example (11); (11), however, could be a case of perseverance (or duplication). The psychological validity of exception features such as [+irregular] is supported by (10); and the confusion that can be caused by unpredictable irregular values of person and number is illustrated in errors (7), (8) and (9).

C. *Questions of Vowel Length and Vowel Structure*

Error	*Intended Utterance*	*Possible Explanation*
(1) Lebenstrieb in siech (VUV: 51)	Lebenstrieb in sich	Could be either vowel length alone or a whole segment persevering.
(2) Sie verzahlen (VUV: 22)	Sie zerfallen	A long vowel secondarily replaces an equivalent short vowel as consonants shift.
(3) vauler Bauch	voller Bauch	In this anticipation, a diphthong replaces a short vowel(i.e. vowels seem to act as units regardless of length or shape).

The first two examples (1, 2) offer very tentative support for the notion that vowel length is distinctive and marked in German. The third example (3) indicates that at some level, all vowels (be they long, short, or diphthongal) function very similarly with respect to word and morpheme structures in German.

D. *Voicing*

Error	Intended Utterance	Possible Explanation
(1) Diese Muse ist in Pier getauft (VUV: 42)	Diese Muse ist in Bier getauft.	Devoicing of /b.
(2) O, Du Saukramer! (VUV: 21)	O, du Grausamer!	Switch of /s/ and /gr/ plus devoicing of /g/.

These examples indicate that the unmarked or 'minus' value of voice which occurs in positions of neutralization (i.e. stops and spirants in final position) may also intrude on 'plus' values of voice elsewhere – as an independent error (1) or in combination with another error (2). The general tendency seems to be to make an error that goes from marked to unmarked, not vice versa.

E. *Other Potential 'Marked – Unmarked' Examples*

Error	Intended Utterance	Possible Explanation
(1) alabister-Bachse (VUV: 18)	alabaster-Büchse	In addition to the switch of /a/ and /ü/ the highly marked /ü/ goes to unmarked /i/.
(2) Verschleppt durch die Schippe (LDS: 64)	verschleppt durch die Schiffe	Either /p/ simply perseveres or a more highly marked /f/ goes to a less highly marked /p/.

In these examples, (1) convincingly and (2) less convincingly support the notion that more highly marked forms tend to become less highly marked forms when speech errors occur – all other factors being equal.

F. *Affricates*

Error	Intended Utterance	Possible Explanation
(1) Gipft tropfen (VUV: 40)	Gift tropfen	Affricate anticipated replacing homorganic fricative, or merely feature of affrication is anticipated.
(2) Meine Erpfahrungen zu Pferd (VUV: 39)	Meine Erfahrungen zu Pferd	same as (1).
(3) Zwölf sind fertsig, vier sind nicht zu haben (VUV: 40)	Zwölf sind fertig, vier sind nicht zu haben.	Either the affricate perseveres replacing the homorganic stop, or other factors such as semantic association of number obtain (e.g. *fertsig* is close to *40* in So. dialects).

The converse of what happened in Sections D and E seems to be illustrated by the above examples (i.e. optimally marked segments [or features] are being anticipated or they persevere because the speech mechanism puts out a special effort to actualize correctly the preceding or following optimally marked segment). Indeed, this type of speech error where a segment becomes more highly marked only seems to occur when a feature as highly marked as affrication (or a segment as highly marked as an affricate) is involved.

G. *Nasal, Stop Consonant Sequences*

Error	Intended Utterance	Possible Explanation
(1) ein Stünkl stinkende Leber (LDS: 32)	ein Stückl stinkende Leber	Nasal segment is anticipated in a homorganic environment.
(2) mit eingelenkter Lanze (LDS: 29)	mit eingelegter Lanze	Same as (1).
(3) Bündinger	Büdinger	Nasal segment is anticipated in a nonhormoganic environment then adjusted to conform to new environment.
(4) Wie oft habe ich meiner Muttn, eine suppm gemacht! (LDS: 29)	Wie oft habe ich meiner Mutter eine Suppm gemacht!	Syllabic nasal is anticipated replacing a syllabic resonant; position is nonhomorganic and nasal segment adapts to new environment.

In example (2) I am not certain whether there is also a change in /g/ to /k/ involved in this error; my feeling is that before *ter* there would be no contrast between *leng* and *lenk* in German. If I am correct, Meringer's differences in spelling are irrelevant here.

These examples are extremely interesting. Although (1) and (2) can be described as [ŋ] anticipation, a parallel explanation will not suffice for (3) and (4) where one must posit the anticipation of a homorganically neutral nasal segment /N/ which then adapts to the new environment in which it occurs; differences in place of articulation of the adjacent stop consonant cause differences in the phonetic realization of /N/. This therefore suggests that for the sake of consistency, (1) and (2) should also be called cases of /N/ anticipation and that Vennemann's analysis of German [ŋ] as /Ng/ at the systematic phonemic level is explanatorily adequate as well as descriptively correct.

H. *Some Miscellaneous Examples*

Error	Intended Utterance
(1) Nachbittag bin ich... (LDS: 29)	Nachmittag bin ich
(2) Er hat einen Erzfehler (LDS: 97)	Er hat einen Herzfehler
(3) die Exen, die Elfen (LDS: 28)	die Hexen, die Elfen
(4) Unterhaut-Misglied, Unterhaut-Mitglied, Unterhaus-Mitglied! (LDS: 23)	correction in data

Error (1) could be explained as anticipation of the segment /b/ or as some sort of dissimilation of /m/ to /b/; the former interpretation seems more consistent with the data already examined, but since there are very few examples involving syllable-initial nasals and stops (homorganic or otherwise) the question remains open. In both errors (2) and (3) it looks as if an /h/ is being masked by something; since it is a phonetic fact of German that stressed word-initial syllables of the shape VC's are spoken with an initial glottal stop [ʔ], it is perhaps also possible to analyze (2) and (3) as instances of [ʔ] perseveration and anticipation respectively. If this is correct, then perhaps the glottal stop plays a more significant role in German Phonology (i.e. and morpheme structure) than has hitherto been thought. The last error (4) is of interest in that an apparent case of phoneme reversal gets progressively corrected in two steps, which may support an analysis of spoonerisms or reversals as complex cases involving simultaneous errors of anticipation and perseveration.

This study of Meringer's corpus of speech errors has, I believe, demonstrated that certain highly systematic data of performance are well worth the linguist's attention. It is difficult to imagine how one can describe a speaker's competence adequately, without considering the actual data of performance. Not only are features 'revealed' in such data, but evidence in support of a theory of 'markedness' is provided. One is reminded of some advice offered more than a hundred years ago by Hughlings Jackson who suggested that certain properties of a complex and unobservable system can be inferred from its transitory malfunctions.

Interesting contributions may be made with respect to language universals as well as specific language differences if speech errors in a variety of non-Germanic languages are collected in sufficient quantity and variety and with sufficient accuracy. Meringer, for example, reports (LDS: 20) that in Prague one hears speakers of Czech making errors such as *Poltar* for *Portal*, a type of error Meringer intuitively feels a speaker of German is unlikely to utter. Perhaps an explanation of this can be found in a difference in syllable structure between the two languages. German may, on the abstract level, syllabify *portal* as *port-al* and Czech as *por-tal*. This explanation is of course highly speculative; more cross-linguistic errors must be collected to arrive at non-trivial hypotheses.

As a final note – for anyone who may still doubt that speech errors are uncontrollable, omnipresent (and perhaps slightly perverse), I cite an error Meringer heard a university student make (VUV: 111). The student in question who had just noticed another student make a speech error, said instead of the intended *Er hat sich versprochen* 'he just made a speech error', *Er hat sich versprechen*.

BIBLIOGRAPHY

Bever, T. and D. T. Langendoen
1969 "The Interaction of Speech Perception and Grammatical Structure in the Evolution of Language", paper presented at the UCLA Conference on Historical Linguistics.

204   M. CELCE-MURCIA

Chomsky, N. and M. Halle
   1968   *The Sound Pattern of English* (New York: Harper and Row).
Fromkin, V. A.
   1968   "Speculations on Performance Models", *J. of Ling.* 4: 47–68.
   1971   "Tips of the Slung – or – to Err is Human", uncorrected version of a paper to appear in
           UCLA Working Papers in Phonetics.
Langacker, R. W.
           Language and its Structure (New York: Harper and Row).
MacKay, D. G.
   1969   "Forward and Backward Masking in Motor Systems", *Kybernetic* 2: 57–64.
   1969   "Spoonerisms: The Structure of Errors in the Serial Order of Speech", *Neuropsychologia*:
           1–26. Reprinted in this volume.
Meringer, R.
   1908   *Aus dem Leben der Sprache* (Berlin: B. Behr's Verlag).
Meringer, R. und K. Mayer
   1895   *Versprechen und Verlesen* (Stuttgart: G. J. Goschen'sche Verlagshandlung).
Vennemann, T.
   1968   *German Phonology*, UCLA Ph. D. dissertation in Germanic linguistics.

A THEORY OF SPEECH ERRORS*

ARCHIBALD A. HILL

I have long been interested in speech errors, and have long wished that I could collect an extensive corpus, together with any information the speaker could give of the cause. There have always been difficulties in the way of collecting such a corpus, one of which is that helpful observers have a way of reporting as genuinely observed errors, utterances which are no more than bits of folklore, like the anecdote of the drunk who is supposed to have said that he was a 'thick quinker'. Another difficulty is that unless one is resolute enough to stop any conversation, note down the error, and question the speaker, errors will slip away without recording. And not least is the fact that we all have a sort of internal editing mechanism which enables us to correct a speaker's error without noticing that an error has occurred. But though I have not been successful in a systematic collection of errors, I think I have a fairly representative, though short, list of them, enough to illustrate the various types. I must also say that my interest in them has been recently stimulated by an article written by D. B. Fry which is the first attempt, in modern terms, at a comprehensive classification of errors and explanation of how they occur. Fry's article is important and enlightening, and should be consulted in entirety by anyone interested in the subject. Nonetheless, it is possible to disagree with some of Fry's conclusions, and in what follows I shall try to present an alternative classification of the types of error, and consequently an alternative view of how they come about. Fry sets up three types, phoneme, morpheme, and word errors. In his classification he is following tradition, as in Sturtevant's *Introduction to Linguistic Science*. I can illustrate the three types briefly by quotation – *gay of dales* for *day of gales* is an error in phonemes. *Didn't she* BECAME (instead of *become*) is the wrong morpheme, and an utterance in which *Leigh's will* became *Will's desire* is a confusion in words.

In place of this classification I would propose another, also threefold, but on a different basis. The three types that I would propose are errors in word-search, as when I recently said *flock of goldsmiths* in place of *flock of goldfinches*; blends of any

* Reprinted from *Studies Offered to Einar Haugen,* ed. by E. S. Firchow et al. (The Hague: Mouton, 1972).

type, such as *sagic* for *sad* and *tragic*; and errors in articulation. The last can be represented by one reported by Sturtevant, *Posties* for *Post Toasties*.

Before I can take up each of these types in detail, however, I must present a hypothesis about the speech-producing process, the evidence for which is the errors themselves. If, of course, a different explanation of speech errors than the one I shall present is eventually shown to be preferable, then a different hypothesis of the nature of speech-production will necessarily follow. I believe that there is an internal 'message center' in which sentences are assembled, and that an assembled message comes into existence a short but appreciable amount of time ahead of articulation. The internal message also lingers in existence for an appreciable period after articulation is complete, and finally, an internal message can be assembled and completed without ever being articulated at all.[1] In this case what occurs is internal language, which may be loosely organized and random as in day-dreaming, or tightly organized as in logical thought. As well as the message center in which sentences are constructed, something (presumably the nervous center) searches for and presents words and sentence-nuclei to the message center. This word-search and presentation can continue through all stages of the production of sentences. These processes are very deeply habituated and so far out of consciousness that the speaker often cannot recover them.

Though to do so is to present a type of error out of the chronological order in which errors occur, it is simplest to begin with errors in articulation, confining the presentation to haplologies. These can be explained as simple telescoping, without interference from any extraneous linguistic material. A typical example is *Posties* for *Post Toasties* mentioned above. Though it is a figurative way of explaining it, the articulatory needle jumped the groove to an exactly corresponding spot in the next groove. The mechanism is the same as an eye-skip in copying, and as in copying, suggests the existence of a text, here the internal message, which the articulatory operation was following with a small time-lag. The persistence of the internal message after articulation, is suggested by the fact that we can so easily correct an erroneous utterance with the proper one, by giving a more exact copy of the internal message – the process which we rationalize by saying 'what we meant to say'. It is also true that the processes of multiple blending which are described below, also show the persistence of the internal message, though it is more common for such errors to show anticipation. Haplologies are so regularly recurrent that they can, as is well known, become established speech forms, as is ironically shown by the adjective *haplogical*, itself an example of the process, since it is from the form **haplological*. The importance of these forms, let me repeat, is that they show the separate and earlier existence of the internal message, which articulation is following.

If we now revert to errors presented in the chronological order of formation, I can

[1] Writing in *Studia Linguistica* a year ago, I said that I could not verify Hockett's statement that he had caught slips of the tongue in his own internal language. Since that time I have caught myself producing *befate befall us* for *fate befall us* in internal language (cf. Hockett 1968: 98).

discuss the type-form *flock of goldsmiths*. The essential confusion was the presentation of *goldsmith* in place of *goldfinch* to the message center. The word *goldsmith* was an erroneous response to a stimulus, in this instance a memory image of a flight of birds seen a decade and a half previously. The memory image, in turn, was a response to a very different flight of birds physically present in the environment. I believe that it was *goldsmith* and *goldfinch*, the singular forms not the plurals, which were confused, since the singular forms are alike in number of syllables, where the plural forms are not. Again I can describe the process only figuratively. It is as if the 'searcher' 'saw' a sort of ticket, labelled with something like 'two-syllable compound of *gold*, referring to an animate and human entity', and the searcher pulled the word indicated by this ticket, instead of going on to the better one, 'two-syllable compound of *gold*, referring to an animate but non-human entity'. The reader will recognize that in describing the mechanism of word-search in this way, I am following the description of Roger Brown in his experiments on the " 'tip-of-the-tongue' phenomenon", in which subjects were asked to give information about words which they knew (or had known) but had not been able to recall (Carroll 1969).

I have called the third type of errors blends and said that they were of several kinds. The two main divisions of blends are those which involve a jumble of two items only, and the multiple blends which involve mixing of more than two. Each division contains more than one type of error. Thus simple blends can occur as jumbles of two sentences, or of two smaller constructions. An example of a short sentence-blend is my own recent utterance, given in response to the statement that a boy was lame. What I said was *Poor bad*! a quite obvious blend of the two sentences *Poor boy*! and *Too bad*! In order to understand what happened it is necessary to suppose that both sentences had been presented to the message center, and that the articulatory operation switched from one to the other. What I should regard as a more complex sentence blend is one reported by Fry, *Didn't she* BECAME ... It seems to me likely that this is a blend of two sentences, *Didn't she become* ... and *She became* ... I do not regard this error as proof that the lexical items, like *become*, are presented to the message center in their root forms, to have the proper affixes added in a later stage of processing, as Fry maintains.

A simple blend of words is *sagic* mentioned above. On the occasion on which I heard it, the speaker corrected herself by giving both full forms, *sad and tragic*, and then went on to say that it was too bad that *sagic* was not a proper form, since it "seemed so expressive". It is to be noted that in all these blends there is an element of phonetic similarity. In *Poor bad*! the initial /b-/ occurs in both *bad* and *boy*; in *Didn't she became* ... most of the blended sentences are phonetically alike, and in *sagic* there is the shared /-æ-/ and at least the closure of the following consonant. I shall return to these shared sounds in blends when I take up the more complex examples. Here, however, it is worth pointing out that one type of blend is seldom mentioned – the occurrence or the segmental elements of a word with the stress pattern which belongs to a different form. One such error from my own speech was *forest fires* with the stress of an adjective and following noun-head, instead of with the stress of a noun compound. I suspect that the utterance was a blend of *forest fires* with some such other phrase as *terrible fires*. A clearer example, since it contains a semantic link between the blended forms, was reported to me by a friend, who pronounced *proof read* with the stress pattern of *read proof*.

The simple blends we have been describing involve only the intrusion of a single form at some point in formation of the internal message, with mixture of the proper and the intrusive form at the point of intrusion. The more complex type of error is that in which blending occurs at two points – the point of original intrusion and point elsewhere in the internal message where the material displaced in the primary blend also intrudes, giving a transposition of elements. A typical example is quoted by Sturtevant – *Here's your* CAT *and* HOAT, for *Here's your* HAT *and* COAT. A blend of some sort occurred at *hat*, displacing the initial /h-/, which then replaced the already articulated /k-/ of *coat*, resulting in a transposition. This type, of course, is that which has been given the name of spoonerism. I believe, however, that it makes little differ-ence whether what is transposed in this fashion are sounds, sequences of sounds, word-elements, or complete words, but it is convenient to begin with transposition of sounds. A preliminary observation is that transposition of vowels is curiously rare. I known of only three genuine examples, one heard and two reported. The observed example was ODD HACK *procedure*, for AD HOC (/æd hák/) *procedure*. One reported example was *your* FEET *is* SAILED, for your *fate* is *sealed*, and the second was Fry's CURVE *the* TARKEY, for CARVE *the* TURKEY. I believe the rarity of these examples is connected with the fact that errors most frequently involve the initial sounds of words, so that a transposition of postconsonantal vocalic elements is not to be expected as often as either initial consonant, or initial vowel, transpositions. Thus the *odd hack* utterance is more to be expected than either of the reported errors, since in *odd hack* one of the vowels is initial. The frequency of transposition of initial material is one of the several reasons for regarding the essential factor of most errors as blending of words and word elements. In these vocalic transpositions, I can guess at least at two of the intrusive forms which have resulted in blending. In the form which I heard, *odd* was probably a blend of *odd* and *ad*, entailing a further blend of *hoc* and *hack*, so that one suspects that the speaker's message center con-tained both AD HOC *procedure* and something like *odd hack*(*ing*) *procedure*. In CURVE *the* TARKEY I would guess that *curve*, as an appropriate description of the turkey's shape, might have been the trigger.

When we go on to the more typical consonantal transpositions, I can return to an example which I have described elsewhere, but which can now be fitted into a more complete description. The example is *snovelling show* for *shovelling snow*. The two primary blended elements are *shovelling* and an intrusive sentence fragment presented to the message center as a response to a physical stimulus, *sniffling*. The secondary blending-element was the form *snow*, from a point later in the internal message. *Snow* acted as a sort of reinforcement for the impulse which gave the intrusive /sn-/ of the error *snovelling*, and *snow* then further acted as the recipient for the displaced /š-/ from *shovelling*. The confusion arises, I believe, because the two forms *shovelling* and *sniffling* were present in the message center, one as part of an already perfected sentence, and the other as the response to an intrusive stimulus. But confusion in the message center is not enough to explain the error without reference to articulation. Not only is there a general similarity between *shovelling* and *sniffling* in syllabic structure and recurrent sounds, but the initial sounds of each, /š-/ and /s-/, differ in only one feature, a distinction which offers articulatory difficulty, as the tongue-twister *She sells seashells* proves. The *snovelling show* utterance is one where the background is unusually complete, since I, as speaker, know the intrusive sentence fragment which presented itself as a response to a physical stimulus. Usually spoonerisms and other errors are recorded without any information about the outside stimulus. The Sturtevant example, CAT *and* HOAT is not complete enough to be explainable. If the outside stimulus were something which called up the response *cat*, we would have an example exactly like *snovelling show*.

A transposition involving word-elements, the second type, was produced by a member of my family who described an aquaintance as a *lift-weighter* instead of a *weight-lifter*. The mistake was quite unconscious, and was momentarily defended as the right way of saying it. The trigger was not given, but it seems reasonable to suppose that there was blending with the word *waiter*, producing a form which was superficially similar to the pattern of noun and agent-noun in *wine-waiter*.

A startling example of the third type, the displacement of complete words, is a sentence reported by a friend. The proper sentence was *his bubble would be pricked*, but the erroneous sentence transposed the noun and participle, producing a new and grammatical, if unfortunate, sentence. An interesting feature of the erroneous sentence was that the /-t/ ending of *pricked* was replaced by the /-d/ which is appropriate to the new participle, *bubbled*. Though on the surface this utterance seems like a causeless transposition and no more. I believe that it also was a multiple blend, and that the intrusive form was the strongly tabooed noun which was actually uttered. The secondary blending-form was the orginal participle which was replaced by the original noun.

That the types of error we have been describing are indeed blends of words is suggested by a fact which was long ago noticed by H. H. Bawden, in his exhaustive, older study of lapses of all sorts. This is that spoonerisms tend to produce recognizable words. Indeed, in my experience every genuine spoonerism produces at least one English word. This characteristic of the genuine forms can, I believe, be used to reject some apparent spoonerisms which are the result of conscious word-play rather than error, such as my own *University* BUTTLE SHUSS, for *University shuttle bus*. Another characteristic of genuine spoonerisms can also be used to reject spurious examples. In all examples which I believe to be genuine, sounds are transposed from no more than two words or constructions. Sturtevant's example *Here's your* CAT *and* HOAT is normal. A hypothetical *Here's your* CAT, GLOAT, *and* HOVES for *Here's your*

HAT, COAT *and* GLOVES would be quite suspicious. A third and more important characteristic can be used to reject further spurious spoonerisms, even one which is ascribed
to the good Dean himself – *It is* BEERY *work preaching to empty* WENCHES, for *It is*
WEARY *work preaching to empty* BENCHES. The trouble is that the span between the
transposed sounds is suspiciously long – something over twenty sounds even with
all due allowance for different phonetic analyses. One advantage that a really extensive
corpus of genuine spoonerisms would offer as a basis of study would be that we could
determine the length of transposition-span with accuracy, and this in turn would tell
us much about the length of lag between perfected message and articulation.

Many of the errors we have been describing were caused by the intrusion of an
extraneous response to a physical stimulus, but the intrusion is by no means always
thus explainable. A commonly observed fact is that spoonerisms and simple blends
often produce tabooed forms, even under conditions where it is unlikely that the
speaker was aware of the tabooed word or words. This was the case with the *bubble
would be pricked* utterance, which occurred in a serious and polite discussion of
church affairs. In other instances, what is produced is an apparently causeless word,
which is merely fairly highly charged emotionally, or even merely commoner than the
proper form. An example of a fairly highly charged word is in the error *University
of* VIRGINITY for *University of Virginia,* heard in a public address. The production
of a common word was in an error heard recently on television – *will establish*MENT –
*establish*MENT – *establish minimum requirements* ... In this winter of our discontent,
establishment is certainly a common word. These apparently causeless errors tell us
something important about internal language activity. It is that the stimulus to language activity need not be physical, either immediate, or displaced. The stimulus
often is, as with these forms, language activity itself. That is, a form like *Virginia*
stimulates the similar form *virginity*, and the sequence *establish min* ... stimulates
establishment. Nor does the stimulus always have to be dependent upon phonetic
similarity. One of Fry's examples, quoted above, was *against* WILL'S DESIRE, for
against LEIGH'S WILL. Though phonetic similarity between *will*, noun, and *Will*,
name, led to the replacement of *Leigh* by *Will*, the replacement of *will* by *desire*
depended upon semantic similarity only. The statement that there is a group of
errors which results from responses to stimuli which are themselves linguistic seems
to me very important for the light it throws on internal language activity. It is a
commonplace that we all carry on a continuous flow of internal images, but I would
strongly maintain that the fact that there is evidence that internal language activity
can be the stimulus for further language activity makes it possible to understand thinking and day-dreaming in language. That is, a flow from image to word is not ruled out,
but the reverse flow, from word to image, is strongly suggested.

We can now return to some of the individual types of error for a consideration of
what each can show us about internal processes. The first type to take up is the error
in word-search, for which the example was *goldsmith* instead of *goldfinch*. I believe
that this mistaken form was not the result of a blend of a fragment and a partially

completed sentence, but the starting point of a sentence, what I can call a sentence-nucleus. As the starting point of a sentence, it was what the Prague School would call the THEME – what was to be talked about, in contrast to what was to be said about it. Often the theme of the sentence is also the peak of information, as in this instance, where the final sentence was *Do you remember that flock of goldfinches that we used to see*? The results of word-search, as with *goldsmith* can, therefore, be considered from two points of view. One is as a response to a stimulus of whatever sort, and the second is as a sentence nucleus and theme. As a response to a stimulus, let me repeat, the nucleus form may be responding to something present, something distant, or something linguistic and not present in the real world at all. It is this ability to respond to an incredibly wide range of stimuli that makes it possible for us to talk about all sorts of things – cabbages, kings, and even chimaeras. As men we do far more than respond with *ouch*! to a pounded finger.

If we consider these first responses as the nuclei of sentences, on the other hand, then it seems to me that they are examples of the most primitive stratum of language activity. They are names, the symbols for concrete objects and classes of objects, or of objects and classes of objects treated as if concrete. They are the sort of things that children first learn, and that have been the subject of recent experiments on apes. They have been shown to be possible for nonhuman species, though with gesture-names rather than words (Gardner and Gardner 1969; Bronowski and Bellugi 1970; and Bryan 1970). It is obvious that not all names are thus concrete, but at least it seems to follow that concrete names are now shown to be in some sense earlier and more fundamental, since use of them is shared with other species.[2] There is then, some evidence at last that concrete names precede abstract ones.

I believe the sentence-nucleus occurs in essentially the shape it would have as a citation form. There is, as we have said, some evidence that the word *goldsmith* occurred in the singular form, which could more easily be confused with *goldfinch* than could the plural form. The plural ending, then, would occur only as the original nucleus is fitted into a larger construction, in this instance a noun phrase, *flock of goldsmiths*. But though occurring as a citation form, the nucleus must also act as the carrier for the intonation pattern of the final sentence. It is, I believe, essentially the intonation pattern which distinguishes the sentence type, and consequently to select the intonation pattern is to select the type of sentence to be spoken – statement, echo question, exclamation. Neither the sentence type, nor the intonation pattern, can be selected as pure abstractions. Something has to act as the carrier, and this carrier is then the sentence nucleus.

An apparent difficulty is that very often the carrier of intonation is something quite vague, as when we say *Look, here's your what-you-may-call-it*! In fact, the carrier

---

[2]   Derek Bickerton, "Prolegomena to a Linguistic Theory of Metaphor", *Foundations of Language* 5 (1969): 43, states flatly that there is no evidence that concrete signs preceded abstract ones in the development of language. Bickerton's statement is no longer tenable in the light of the Gardner experiments.

may be nothing more than the hesitation vowel. I think this kind of utterance can be explained by Fry's hypothesis of overlap in programming, that is that the stage of sentence perfecting begins before the stage of word-search is complete. The sentence pattern can then be completed, leaving the nucleus, and therefore the peak of information, unidentified except by the context.

Once the sentence-nucleus has been presented to the message center, words and morphemes are assembled in the familiar patterns of the language. We have already seen that there is evidence that it is words, morphemes, and constructions – the meaningful elements of language – which are the operational units in this process, since errors show that these meaningful elements are the operational units in blending also. A question arises, however. I believe that with the *bubble would be pricked* utterance, the participial ending was added to the new verb-base as a part of sentence-perfection. Was it presented as a morphophoneme, that is as some representative of the variants of the ending, /-d/, /-t/, and /-ɨd/? And if it was a representative of this class of sounds, in what shape was it? At least it would have had to be in some shape, since I do not believe that it can have been completely bodiless. It would seem necessary to say that what was presented to the message center was a morpheme carried by a sound, a sound capable of being modified as needed to accomodate itself to the new form to which it was to be attached. Any other conclusion would necessitate the assumption that what was added was a verb ending carried by nothing, or by a curious blend of the three shapes of the ending given above. (Hill 1962).

When the question of what shape words and morphemes have when they are presented to the message center is considered in relation to blends and spoonerisms in general, there is a further conclusion. Granted that a spoonerism is a mixture of words, it is still true that what finally results is a mixture of sounds. That is, the sounds are manipulable units, and when a blend forces them out of position in one word, they are bodily transported to another. They must, therefore, have existed as an internal reality in the word from which they were forced out, else they could not have been thus reshuffled. I would contend, therefore, that sounds exist as internal realities, abstractable from words, much as the conscious mind makes realities of words by abstracting them from sentences. In fact, speech errors are one of the two most important evidences for internal reality of sounds, rather than of morphophonemes. The other type of evidence is from rhyme, in languages which employ it. Thus in all dialects that I know, *Britain* and *kitten* are perfect rhymes. Yet it can be maintained that the second syllable of *Britain* contains a morphophoneme different from that in *kitten*, since *Britain* shows an /æ/ when the ending *-ic* is added. If the fundamental structural reality in phonology is the morphophoneme, then the rhyme should be bad, or we should assume that the word *kitten* also contains the morphophoneme /æ/, and that it would appear if the *-ic* ending were someday added.

In addition to giving support to a belief in the internal reality of sounds, speech errors give support to the belief that phonotactic rules are also real. One of Fry's examples is GROTTAL *strain*, for *glottal strain*. If we can assume that the intrusive /r/

is at least in part due to the /r/ of *strain*, one wonders why there was not a complete spoonerism, giving GR*ottal* *STL*ain*. The answer is that /stl-/ is not an English group. It is therefore likely that its production was inhibited, forcing the articulatory operation back into the correct sequence. In my experience of spoonerisms, however, the arrival of an impossible group frequently results in blockage. Whether the result is blockage or return to a normal sequence, it would seem that spoonerisms follow normal phonotactic rules and habits. The inhibition against such a group as /*stl-/ is thus an internal reality, just as sounds are.

Another one of the facts about spoonerisms and blends which leads to conclusions about internal activity is the fact that spoonerisms occur predominantly at word boundaries. Their correlation with boundaries suggests not only that boundaries are real in the internal message center, even though they may not be audible realities in the articulated sentence, but more importantly, the correlation with initial boundaries suggests that internal operations, both those of sentence-perfecting and the stimuli for articulation, proceed in a linear fashion. There is, however, a final conclusion more important than any so far mentioned, which springs from the sum total of the picture resulting from a consideration of speech errors. Except for possible nonlinguistic stimuli of often unrecoverable identity, which result in the operation of word-search, all stages in the production of sentences involve the use of language, even though often in fragmentary form. Whatever may be said about thinking in systems of symbols other than those of language, it seems therefore unnecessary to assume as many scholars have always done, that the starting point of utterance is a fully articulated message in semantic entities of some other (and unrecoverable) shape than linguistic units. Such a preexistent message which is encoded into language, is an entity not necessary for a coherent picture of sentence formation, and it is therefore one which we would do well to follow Occam in discarding until such time as further evidence demands it.

BIBLIOGRAPHY

Bawden, H. Heath
    1900   "A Study of Lapses", *Psychological Review*, Monograph supplement III (4).
Bronowski, J. and Ursula Bellugi
    1970   "Language, Name, and Concept", *Science* 168: 168–170.
Bryan, Alan L.
    1970   "Reply", *Current Anthropology* II: 166–167.
Carroll, John
    1969   "Language and Psychology", in: *Linguistics Today*, ed. by Archibald A. Hill (New York: Basic Books): 158–159.
Fry, D. B.
    1969   "The Linguistic Evidence of Speech Errors", in: *Charisteria Josepho Vachek sexegenario oblata*", ed. by Jan Firbas and Josef Hladky (= *Brno Studies in English* 8): 69–74. Reprinted in this volume.
Gardner, R. Allen and Beatrice Gardner
    1969   "Teaching Sign Language to a Chimpanzee", *Science* 164: 664–672.

Hill, Archibald, A.
    1962   " A Postulate for Linguistics in the Sixties", *Language* 38: 345–351.
    1970   "The hypothesis of Deep Structure", *Studia Linguistica* 24: 6–8.
Hockett, Charles F.
    1968   *The State of the Art* (The Hague: Mouton).
Sturtevant, Edgar H.
    1947   *An Introduction to Linguistic Science* (Yale): 90–95 and 110–117.

THE NON-ANOMALOUS NATURE OF ANOMALOUS UTTERANCES*

VICTORIA A. FROMKIN

1. In current linguistic and psychological literature a sizable number of articles have appeared dealing with 'slips of the tongue' and errors in speech (see Bibliography). This interest is not, however, of recent origin. Historically, speech errors have been a source of humor as well as of serious study. In the sixteenth century, Rabelais utilized such errors to display his pungent wit; and in the *Compleat gentleman* (1622), Henry Peacham refers to a "melancholy Gentleman" who says "Sir, I must goe dye a beggar" instead of the intended "I must goe buy a dagger".[1] 'Spoonerisms' were uttered before and after the long happy life of the Reverend William A. Spooner, who is credited as the originator of a particular kind of 'lapse'. In fact, if one assumes that the origin of man and the origin of language and speech were simultaneous, then a further assumption follows – that 'spoonerisms' began with Adam.

Speech-error data have been studied as a source of historical linguistic change (Sturtevant 1917, 1947; Jesperson 1922; MacKay 1970d); as a means for understanding the actual mechanisms of the speech production process (Lashley 1951; Boomer & Laver 1968; MacKay 1969, 1970a; Hockett 1967; Fromkin 1968; Nooteboom 1969); and to gain insight into psychological repressions (Freud 1924). Speech errors have also been investigated in attempts to show the 'reality' of phonological units and rules, and the relationship between linguistic 'competence' and 'performance' (Fromkin 1968; Green 1969). Freud, in his *Psychopathology of everyday life*, questioned "whether the mechanisms of this (speech) disturbance cannot also suggest the probable laws of the formation of speech" ([1924] 1938:71). It is to that general question that this paper is directed.

* Reprinted from *Language* 47(1): 27–52 (1971)
This research was supported in part by United States Public Health Services (NIH) grant NB-04595, and in part by Office of Naval Research contract NR-049-226.

[1] Robbins (1966) suggests that the earliest literary example is found in Rabelais, in the following: "Il n'y a point d'enchantement. Chascun de vous l'a veu. Je y suis *maistre passé*. A brum, a brum, je suis *prestre Macé*." The contrived error of transposing the *m* and *p* in *maistre passé* (past master) creates *prestre Macé* ('priest Macé'), "a monk whose name was synonymous with simple or foolish." In the same article, Robbins (457–458) cites a 'near-spoonerism' found in the *Lives* of celebrities by John Aubrey (1626–1697), who, discussing a flirtation between Sir Walter Raleigh and a young girl, has the wench's protest "Sweet Sir Walter" changed into "swisser Swatter".

DATA

2. Every book and article which refers to speech errors is replete with examples. The most extensive collection, an estimated 8,800 errors, appears in Meringer & Mayer (1895) and in Meringer (1908). A rigorous statistical analysis of these errors is contained in a number of articles by MacKay (1969, 1970a, b, d). This corpus of German errors is augmented by errors in spoken Dutch noted by Cohen (1966), by more than a hundred errors in English tape-recorded by Boomer & Laver, and by other errors cited in various articles listed in the Bibliography.

In this paper, while taking into consideration the extensive published data, I will primarily make use of a collection of speech errors collected by myself over the past three years. More than six hundred errors were collected by myself, or by colleagues and friends who reported in detail errors which they either made or heard others produce.[2] For each error which I myself noted, I recorded the name of the speaker and the date, and where possible (particularly in the case of blends) the speaker was questioned as to what he had been thinking of saying. This is scanty information indeed when compared with the data recorded by Meringer for each error in speech which he heard. In true Teutonic style, he also included the birthdate of the speaker, the educational background, the time of day, the state of health and tiredness, the rate of speech etc. Sturtevant reports that Meringer thus became the most unpopular man at the University of Vienna; and since "no correlations between any of the above factors and the nature of the error were found" (MacKay 1970d), my own data-collecting omitted such information, in order to protect my personal reputation while maintaining the scientific accuracy of the data. It is important to note, however, that my method of data-collecting has a built-in fault, since many errors occur when it is just not feasible to note them, and unquestionably many errors made are not 'heard' at all. The data-collection method used by Boomer & Laver, in which they analysed tapes of conference discussions, psychiatric interviews etc. for the errors which they contained, is free of this fault. Fortunately, however, there were no sharp discrepancies between the kinds of errors recorded by them and by myself. There are certain kinds of errors included in my corpus which did not seem to occur among the hundred or so errors recorded by them; but I only included such errors when heard and attested by other listeners, or when the speaker himself caught the error and corrected it. I felt this precaution necessary to mitigate my own 'desire' to hear certain kinds of errors.

The aim of this paper, then, is not to treat the errors in the corpus as a random sample of all errors made, but to attempt an explanation for the errors which were recorded.

---

[2]   Most of the examples cited in the text will be from my own data. In the citation of examples, the arrow is to be interpreted as 'spoken as'. The pronunciation of the utterance will be given in phonetic symbols, within square brackets, only when the orthography may create an ambiguous interpretation or obscure the actual speech errors. A dash represents a pause by the speaker; a series of dots (...) indicates that no errors occurred in the intended words.

DISCRETENESS OF PERFORMANCE UNITS

3. Sturtevant defines a 'lapse' or a 'speech error' as "an unintentional linguistic innovation" (1947:38). Boomer & Laver's definition echoes Sturtevant's: "A slip of the tongue ... is an involuntary deviation in performance from the speaker's current phonological, grammatical or lexical intention" (4). Because such 'unintentional' or 'involuntary' errors may result in utterances which provoke laughter, speakers and writers have also used them intentionally. Such conscious 'creations' will not be considered here, although one finds that these 'intentional errors' usually follow the same 'rules' as do non-intentional errors.[3]

Meringer was mainly interested in classifying the kinds of errors which occurred in spontaneous speech; and since his time, one finds in the literature different classification schemes and varying terminology. In Boomer & Laver's classification scheme, speech errors show a "MISORDERING of units in the string, OMISSION of a unit, or REPLACEMENT of a unit" (5). According to them, the units so misordered, omitted, or replaced may be segments, morphemes, or words. Nooteboom (1969) classifies segmental errors as "phonemic speech errors" and "non-phonemic errors", including in the latter classification "meaningless combination of phonemes", morphemes (including affixes and root morphemes), and whole words. Nooteboom dismisses the possibility that "distinctive features" behave "more or less (like) independent elements just as phonemes do", but Hockett implies the independence of such features (915).

Further classification is not the concern of this paper. The interest is rather in how particular errors shed light on the underlying units of linguistic performance, and on the production of speech. What is apparent, in the analyses and conclusions of all linguists and psychologists dealing with errors in speech, is that, despite the semi-continuous nature of the speech signal, there are discrete units at some level of PERFORMANCE which can be substituted, omitted, transposed, or added. It should be stated here that, were we to find no evidence in actual speech production or percep-

---

[3] Lewis Carroll, in his preface to *The hunting of the snark* (1876), discusses his 'portmanteau' words: "... let me take this opportunity of answering a question that has often been asked me, how to pronounce 'slithy toves'. The 'i' in 'slithy' is long, as in 'writhe'; and 'toves' is pronounced so as to rhyme with 'groves'. Again, the first 'o' in 'borogoves' is pronounced like the 'o' in 'borrow'. I have heard people try to give it the sound of the 'o' in 'worry'. Such is Human Perversity ... Humpty-Dumpty's theory, of two meanings packed into one word like a portmanteau, seems to me the right explanation for all. For instance, take the two words 'fuming' and 'furious'. Make up your mind that you will say both words but leave it unsettled which you will say first. Now open your mouth and speak. If your thoughts incline ever so little towards 'fuming' you will say 'fuming-furious'; if they turn, by even a hair's breath, towards 'furious', you will say 'furious-fuming'; but if you have that rarest of gifts, a prefectly balanced mind, you will say 'frumious'."
  I have quoted extensively from Lewis Carroll, not only because it is always a delight to read or reread any of his comments, but because in this passage he states that his 'portmanteaus' or 'blends' are possible in natural speech and proposes a hypothesis as to how they occur. As we shall see below, however, these 'complete' blends are seldom found in just this way in 'normal' speech. That is, a blend of [fjurijəs] and [fjumiŋ] is more apt to occur as [fjumijəs] or [fjuriŋ], particularly because the first syllables are identical.

tion for such discrete units, this would be insufficient cause to eliminate discrete units in phonology or syntax. The fact that it is impossible to describe the grammars of languages without such units is itself grounds for postulating them in a theory of grammar. But when one finds it similarly impossible to explain speech production (which must include errors made) without discrete performance units, this is further substantiation of the psychological reality of such discrete units. In other words, behavioral data of the kind described here may not be necessary to validate hypotheses about linguistic competence, but they certainly are sufficient for such verification.

3.1. THE REALITY OF THE SEGMENT OR PHONE. By far the largest percentage of speech errors of all kinds show substitution, transposition (metathesis), omission, or addition of segments of the size of a phone. These occur both within words and across word boundaries, the latter case being most frequent in our corpus. Most of these segmental errors are errors of anticipation, which is in keeping with the conclusions reached in the literature. Simple anticipations result in a substitution of one sound in anticipation of a sound which occurs later in the utterance, with no other substitutions occurring. The following examples illustrate such errors:

(1) (a) John dropped his cup of coffee → ... cuff... coffee
    (b) also share → alsho share [ɔlšo šer]
    (c) such observation → sub – such ...
    (d) delayed auditory feedback → ... audif – auditory ...
    (e) week long race → reek long race
    (f) M-U values [ɛm juw væljuwz] → [ɛm vjuw] values
    (g) the third and surviving brother → the sird and – the bird – the third ...

Examples (1a–e) illustrate the substitution of one segment for another. In (1f), however, anticipating the [v], a segment is added where there is no segment in the intended word. And in (1g) the error is compounded: first the *s* is anticipated, and then, in an attempt to correct the error, a later *b* is anticipated.

Perseverance errors are also not uncommon, as exemplified in the following:

(2) (a) I'm not allowing any proliferation of nodes → ... proliperation
    (b) John gave the boy → ... gave the goy
    (c) Spanish speaking people → ... speaping people
    (d) irreplaceable → irrepraceable
    (e) Chomsky and Halle → Chomsky and Challe

It should be noted that one cannot unambiguously classify the error in (2c), since it could be considered an error of either perseverance or anticipation. As shown by MacKay (1970d), the probability that errors occur when there are repeated phonemes is much greater than chance, and in this case the alliterative structure of the utterance seems to add to the substitution which occurs. As will be seen, this is true of many of the errors to be discussed.

Classic Spoonerisms reveal a more complex error, in that there is a transposition or metathesis of two segments. One possible interpretation is that such errors involve an anticipation plus a perseverance, but it seems more likely that what occurs is a simple (or not so simple) switch in the linear ordering of the sounds intended. Such errors, attributed to Spooner, made him famous, as in his purported admonition to an undergraduate student: "You have hissed all my mystery lectures. I saw you fight a liar in the back quad; in fact, you have tasted a whole worm" (Robbins).

Whether or not the notorious Reverend or his students sat up nights inventing such errors, attested errors reveal the same kind of metathesis, as is shown in these examples:

(3) (a) keep a tape → teep a cape
   (b) the zipper is narrow → the nipper is zarrow
   (c) should serve → [svd šǝrv]
   (d) for far more → for mar fore
   (e) with this ring I do wed → ... wing ... red
   (f) I'm going to die young but I'll die less young → ... yes lung
   (g) in the past few weeks → ... fast pew [pjuw] weeks.

In a number of cases, where the speaker catches his error, we cannot be sure whether a mere anticipation and substitution is involved, or whether a transposition is caught before completed, as in the following examples:

(4) (a) Kathy can type → tathy – Kathy can type
   (b) correct class of → collect – correct ...
   (c) shown in the present slide → shown in the pleasant – I mean present slide
   (d) greater pressure → [greyšr̩] – greater pressure
   (e) delayed auditory feedback → delayed audif – auditory feedback

All the above examples reflect errors involving consonants. Vowels are also anticipated, metathesized, etc., as shown below:

(5) (a) ad hoc [æd hak] → odd hack [ad hæk]
   (b) Wang's bibliography → Wing's babliography
   (c) turn the corner → torn the kerner [tɔrn] ... [kǝrŋr]
   (d) feet moving → [fuwt mijving]
   (e) fish and tackle → fash and tickle [fæš] ... [tɪkl̩]
   (f) the new Sony → the no suny [now suwnij]
   (g) place the stress → [plɛs] the [strejs]
   (h) dissertation topic [dɪsr̩tejšn̩ tapɪk] → [dɪsrtašn tejpɪk]
   (i) available for exploitation → avoilable for ...
   (j) prevailing temperature → [prejvijliŋ] ...
   (k) the waterfall [wɔtr̩fǝll] isn't working → ... isn't [wɔkɪŋ]

3.2. Clusters as sequences of discrete phones or segments. The above examples show errors of transposition, substitution, omission, and deletion of individual segments, which may be either vowels or consonants. The error may be either of anticipation (i.e., the interfering segment follows the error), of perseveration (i.e., the interfering segment precedes the error), or of transposition (i.e., the order of sound segments is changed). Further justification for assuming that individual segments are units in speech performance is suggested by the fact that, in many errors where the intended utterance included consonant clusters, only one segment of the cluster is involved:

(6) (a) fish grotto → frish gotto
    (b) fresh clear water → flesh queer water
    (c) split pea soup → plit spea soup
    (d) brake fluid → blake fruid
    (e) no strings attached → no strings attrached
    (f) at the Broadway stores the prices are → ... spores the prices are
    (g) in a split second → ... slit second
    (h) that's a sticky point → ... spicky point
    (i) a car with a stick shift → ... [št'k sɨft][4]

As seen in (6a), the intended *fish grotto* has been pronounced *frish grotto* [frɪš gaDo] (the [D] represents a voiced flap), the addition of an [r] in the first word producing an initial cluster instead of the intended single segment. The substitution of the single [g] for the intended cluster [gr] may be explained by postulating that the cluster [gr] can be 'broken down' into individual segments, [g] followed by [r]. This being so, the individual segments can themselves be transposed. Similarly, the error cited in (6b) can be explained as an anticipation of the [l] in *clear*, causing the replacement of the intended [fr] in *fresh* by [fl]. The substitution of [kw] in [kwir], for the intended [klir], may again be explained by an anticipation of the [w] in *water*. It is of course true that (6b) may be simply an error in word substitution, since *flesh* is a word, as is *queer*. Such an explanation will not, however, explain a number of the other examples given; i.e., [frɪš] is not a word, nor is [gaDo], [plɪt], [spij], [blejk], [fruwɪd], [ətrætšt], [spɪkij] etc. If we are seeking an explanation for such errors, it seems highly likely that we have here again single segmental errors, the difference being that the segments involved occur in consonant clusters.

The omission of elements or segments in clusters also justifies the conclusion that clusters are not unitary units of performance, as in these examples:

(7) (a) two hundred drugs → two hundred [dʌgz].
    (b) property that excludes [ɛkskluwdz] → property that [ekskudz]

---

[4]   For the speaker who made this error, [š] followed by a consonant is not an unusual sequence. In fact, this might represent a word substitution, since [št'k] as a word exists in his dialect as well as *shmuck* [šmʌk], *shtunk* [štvŋk], *shmo* [šmow] etc.

Errors involving final clusters show that they are also sequences of individual segments, as in the following examples:

(8) (a) tab stops → tap [stabz]
    (b) weeks and months → [wɪŋks] and …
    (c) great risk → great rist [rɪst]
    (d) french fried potatoes → frend fried potatoes
    (e) there's a pest in every class → … pet …
    (f) art of the fugue → arg of the [feuwt]

That some errors reveal the transposition of whole clusters is NOT evidence for
the fact that such clusters are indissoluble units. Such errors do, of course, occur
very often, as in these examples:

(9) (a) at the bottom of the pay scale → at the bottom of the [skej peyl]
    (b) little island in Brittany → brittle island in litany
    (c) sweater drying → dreater swying [drɛDr̩ swajɪŋ]
    (d) throat cutting → coat thrutting

Such movement of whole clusters is but further evidence that the 'syllable' is not
a single indissoluble unit in speech production, but is itself composed of a sequence
of segments. This is attested by the fact that a CV or a VC sequence which is part of a
syllable can be involved in speech errors:

(10) (a) pussy cat → cassy put
     (b) foolish argument → farlish …
     (c) a heap of junk → a hunk of jeep
     (d) stress and pitch → piss and stretch
     (e) lost and found → [fawst] and [lɔnd]

Example (10a) shows the monosyllable [kæt] as a sequence of three segments
[k+æ+t], with the first two segments transposed with the first two segments of
[p+v+s+ɪj]. In (10d), the transposition which occurs can easily be explained as

$$[\text{stre}s\text{…}\text{pɪ}t\text{š}]$$

Another explanation is that the word *piss* is substituted for *stress* (the reasons for
such a substitution I leave to Freud), and *stretch* for *pitch*; or instead, that the speaker
started to say *pitch and stress* and the error is one of final consonant substitutions.
There are, however, numerous examples which show errors involving CV or VC
sequences which cannot be so explained.

3.3. AFFRICATES. The assumption that clusters on a performance level should be
interpreted as sequences of consonants raises the question of affricates. It is interesting
to note that while [str], [pl], [kr], [bl], [fr] etc., as well as final clusters, reveal the

splitting of clusters into segments, not a single example in my own data, or the English examples cited by others, shows a splitting of [tš] or [dž] into sequences of stop plus fricative:

(11) (a) pinch hit → pinch hitch, but not *[pint hiš]
     (b) pretty chilly → chitty pilly [tšɪtij pɪlij]
     (c) entire chapter → enchire [əntšajr] ...
     (d) further surgery → furger [fərdžr̩] surgery
     (e) Ray Jackendoff → Jay Rackendoff
     (f) last cigarette Tim had in June → ... Jim had in tune
     (g) in St. Louis John said → in St. Jouis John said

We do not find cases like "St. [duəs]", or "St. [žuis]". One may assume that the old phonemic controversy, as to whether such affricates should be considered one segment or two, is solved for linguistic performance, and that affricates should be considered single segments in the production of speech, for speakers of English.

3.4. COMPLEX VOWELS. One finds a similar situation with diphthongs. If [ey] or [uw] or [æw] are interpreted as a succession of V+y, or V+w, one could expect the non-glide section of the diphthong to be subject to substitution without a change of the particular glide. In other words, one would anticipate that *feet moving* might be articulated as [fʊyt mɪwving]. The examples in 12 show that where vowel+glide or [r] is involved, the error always includes the entire diphthong, or the vowel with its 'r-quality':

(12) (a) first and goal to go → first and girl to go
     (b) took part in the first → took pirt [pərt] in the farst
     (c) dissertation topic → [dɪsr̩tašn̩ tejpɪk]
     (d) we're going to have to fight very hard → we're going to have to fart very [fayd]
     (e) feet moving → [fuwt mijving]
     (f) available for exploitation → avoilable for ...
     (g) soup is served → serp is [suwvd]

These examples are, of course, taken only from English, and the conclusions regarding affricates and complex vowel nuclei have meaning only for English.

It is a fact that one never finds an error which results in a 'non-permissible' sequence of, for example, front vowel plus back glide (e.g. [ɪw], [ɛw]), or of back vowel plus front glide (e.g. [ʋj]); but this may have an alternative explanation, which is discussed below. One example above, (5i) available [əvejləbl̩] → *avoilable* [əvɔjləbl̩], could be interpreted as a switch only in the non-glide portion of the vowel nucleus, as could all examples of errors which involve only tense front vowels or tense back vowels. The errors involving both front and back diphthongs, along with those involving a vowel followed by *r*, cannot be explained in this way, and seem to suggest that the complex vowels are single units, or that errors which 'violate' phonological constraints are 'corrected' after the substitution occurs. (See below for discussion on this point.)

3.5. THE STATUS OF [ŋ] IN ENGLISH. Sapir (1925) and Chomsky & Halle (1968) present arguments for deriving [ŋ] from an underlying sequence of /ng/. Their phonological analysis is justified in itself. It is of interest, however, that behavioral data, found in speech errors, indicate that, at one level of performance, [ŋ] may derive from the sequence of [n+g] – or, because of the constraints which change [n] to [ŋ] before a velar, the sequence of [ŋ+g]:

(13) (a) sing for the man [sɪŋ ... mæn] → [sɪg ... mæŋ]
    (b) Chuck Young [tšʌk jʌŋ] → [tšʌŋk jʌg]
    (c) shilling [šɪlɪŋ] → shingle [šɪŋgl̩]
    (d) cut the string → [kʌnt] the [strɪg]

A possible explanation for the [g]'s in the actual utterances is to postulate that, prior to the execution of the articulatory commands, the following transposition of segments has occurred:

    (a) [sɪŋg ... mæn] → sɪØg ... mæŋ]
    (b) [tšʌk jʌŋg] → [tšʌŋk jʌØg]
    (c) [šɪlɪŋg] → [šɪŋgəl]
    (d) [kʌt] ... [strɪŋg] → [kʌnt] ... [strɪØg]

If this highly speculative hypothesis can be demonstrated by other experimental data, the postulated phonological rule for English, $g \rightarrow \emptyset / n - \#$, may be validated, in that when the nasal is deleted, the [g] emerges.

The data can, however, be given an alternative explanation. Example (13a) may show persistence of the velar articulation from [sɪŋ], producing [mæŋ], and a simple loss of the nasality of the final velar in *sing*. In (13b), since in English a vowel is nasalized preceding a nasal consonant, we may have an example of a transposition of oral vowel with nasal vowel, and a concomitant non-nasalization of the final nasal:

$$[tšʌk j\tilde{ʌ}ŋ] \rightarrow [tš\tilde{ʌ}k jʌg]$$

Example (13c) may be similarly disposed of, but (13d) cannot be so easily explained. The only explanation, other than that which postulates an underlying abstract /strɪng/, is to suggest that only the nasality of the vowel is anticipated – which, as we shall see below, is certainly possible. The examples are given, however, since they permit speculation as to the reality of the *g* in utterances containing [ŋ].

3.6. THE REALITY OF PHONETIC FEATURES. Research on the perception of speech has shown that units smaller than the segment, i.e. properties or features of speech sounds, are 'perceived' and confused (Miller & Nicely 1955; Wickelgren 1965a, b, 1966).

Thirty-two cases in the present corpus can be explained by postulating that certain properties or features also constitute independent elements in the production of speech. The fact that one finds no errors in which consonants and vowels are involved (i.e., vowels do not switch with consonants, etc.) may be explained by suggesting that true vowels ([+vocalic, -consonantal]) constitute one class of segments in a performance model, as opposed to another class composed of true consonants, glides, and liquids ([+consonantal) or [-vocalic]), but that the segments which are members of these two non-intersecting sets cannot be further analysed into independent features.

As we shall see below, there are other explanations for why consonants and vowels do not 'interfere' with each other (e.g., are not transposed, anticipated, etc.) The data, however, suggest that while a HIERARCHY probably exists, other features are independently involved in speech errors:

(14) (a) spell mother → smell [bʌðɹ]
   (b) pity the new teacher → mity the due teacher – I mean – nity the poor teacher
      – no – pity the new teacher
   (c) bang the nail → mang the mail
   (d) Did you hear what Malcolm said → did you hear what balcolm – Malcolm said?
   (e) Cedars of Lebanon → Cedars of Lemadon

These examples show a change in the value of the feature [nasality], acting in many cases independent of other features. In (14a–b), the [–nasal] of [p] becomes [+nasal] (i.e. [p] → [m]). If the [m] of *mother* remained [+nasal], this example could be dismissed as merely an anticipation of the segment [m]. However, since [m] → [b], or since the value of the nasality feature in the [m] of *mother* switches from [+nasal] to [-nasal], all other features remaining the same, a better explanation for the error is that what occurred was a single feature switch. Otherwise, no explanation is provided for the [m] → [b] substitution.

Example (14b) illustrates the same phenomenon. [p], which is [-nasal], becomes [m], which is [+nasal], other features remaining intact; and [n] is changed from [+nasal] to [d], which is [-nasal].

Example (14c) shows a switch of two features. [b], which is [−nasal, +anterior, −coronal], switches to [+nasal]; and [n] switches from [+coronal] to [−coronal]. Even if one wished to explain the [m] of *mail* as a perseveration of the [m] which has occurred in [mæŋ], the substitution [b] → [m] would be left unexplained. The anticipation of the lowered velum which accompanies the following [n] is a possible explanation.

Example (14d) represents a simple substitution, in the first segment of *Malcolm*, from [+nasal] to [−nasal].

The following examples represent a change of value for the feature [voiced]:

(15) (a) What does the course consist of → what does the gorse consist of
    (b) referendum → reverendum
    (c) clear blue sky → glear plue sky
    (d) reveal → refeel
    (e) define → devine
    (f) big and fat → pig and vat

In these examples, only the value of the feature [voice] is changed, all other features remaining intact.

Other errors which appear to involve properties or features of whole sounds, rather than whole segments, are as follows:

(16) (a) pedestrian → tebestrian ([p] → [t] and [d] → [b])
    (b) scatterbrain [skæDr̩brejn] → [spæDr̩grejn]
    (c) spaghetti → skabetti
    (d) Death Valley [dɛθ vælij] → [fɛθ ðælij]

In (16a), only the value of the feature [coronal] – i.e., only the PLACE of articulation – is changed. It is of course possible to argue that this is rather to be interpreted as segmental transposition, with [p] → [t] in anticipation of the subsequent [t]. But what of [d] → [b]? If we explain [p] → [t] as a switch of labial ([−coronal]) to alveolar ([+coronal]), then [d] → [b] is seen as the result of a change from alveolar ([+coronal]) to labial ([−coronal]).

Similar cases are seen in (16b–c). Again, one can suggest a segment transposition, particularly since the voicing feature of the [g] is neutralized after an [s]. But then how does one explain the [g] → [b] switch? If a mere segment transposition was involved, we would expect [sgəpɛtij] in (16c).

A more complex error is seen in (16d): the switch from [d] → [f] seems to be an anticipation of the subsequent [v]. The coronality of the [d] seems to influence the switch from [v] to [d], with the [+voice] and [+continuant] features remaining.

It is certainly true that errors which involve a substitution of features are rare, compared to errors involving larger units. They nevertheless require some explanation, and one can only conclude that some features appear to be independently extractable as performance units. Many segmental errors may also be examples of such feature errors; but since they can also be accounted for as errors of larger units, we are unable to conclude that individual features are independently involved in all cases. However, the following examples show that feature errors may be obscured in this way:

(17) (a) extracted → extrapted ([k] → [p], or [+back, −ant] → [−back, +ant])
    (b) goofing off → gooping off ([f] → [p], or [+cont] → [−cont])
    (c) call the girl → gall the curl ([k] → [g], or [−voice] → [+voice])
    (d) documentation → documendation ([t] → [d], or [−voice] → [+voice])

In fact, most of the segmental errors can be so interpreted. In the transposition of *brake fluid* to *brake fruid*, one might suggest that what is involved is a transposition of the feature [lateral] or [anterior] rather than transposition of the two segments. If segmental errors are analysed as feature errors, we will find that many distinctive features other than those cited above do indeed represent a reality, in speech performance.

This suggestion is supported by the findings of Nooteboom: "In significantly more cases than is to be expected in a random distribution the two elements involved in a substitution error are phonetically similar to one another" (1969:121). MacKay found that "most pairs of reversed consonants differed in only one distinctive feature (56 percent) and very few (2 percent) differed in all four distinctive features" (1969).[5] This is in contradiction to the conclusion of Boomer & Laver "that articulatory similarity is not an important determinant" in speech errors, although they do note two exceptions: "sequences of voiceless fricatives seemed to encourage mistakes of place of articulation, and (b) alveolar consonants showed a slight tendency to interact" (p. 8, and fn.). But they were examining errors to see if any particular features were involved more often than any others. Their data were not analysed for the degree of similarity of the segments involved. It is interesting to note that an analysis of jargon aphasia errors also shows that most errors involve no more than a confusion of one distinctive feature (Green). Whether or not further analysis of substitution errors confirms or contradicts the MacKay-Nooteboom conclusions regarding the 'similarity' of substituted segments, the only conclusion one can draw from the examples of feature switching given above is that at least some of the proposed distinctive features are independent behavioral units.

But an examination of the errors, whether analysed as errors of whole segments or of independent features, definitely shows a hierarchy and interdependence of certain features. Thus, while there are errors showing just addition or subtraction of nasality, one does not find a 'nasality' switch which results in a voiceless nasal. At least for English, nasality and voicing seem to be interdependent features. This again prevents the occurrence of an 'inadmissible' sound in English.

The claim that certain features are independent units, which must be postulated as such in a model of performance, seems to contradict the earlier hypothesis that segments (or feature complexes) are 'real' performance units. Actually, there is no contradiction. Features cannot exist except as properties of larger segments (just as segments, as we shall see, exist as parts of larger units). In other words, in the generation of speech, there is a hierarchy of different-sized units. A linear ordering of the segments (discussed below) occurs, and this linear ordering may be disrupted. Since the discrete segments are specified by actual physiological properties (or neural commands), some of these properties or features may also get disordered, i.e. 'attached' to other segments. But the claim that all distinctive features (as proposed by

---

[5] Wickelgren's features were used by MacKay.

Chomsky & Halle) are identical with phonetic properties that can in principle be independently controlled in speech is not borne out by the data of speech errors. Unless "controllable in speech" is defined in some new strange and abstract way, it would appear that whatever the needs for certain separate phonological features may be, in actual speech performance only certain of these phonological features have their counterpart as phonetic features.[6] Thus, while the two features [consonantal] and [vocalic] very nicely divide segments into four separate classes, needed for phonology, the idea that such features have any independent phonetic reality seems highly improbable. To suggest that a substitution of a [p] for a [k] involves the PHONETIC substitution of [−anterior] for [+anterior], [−high] for [+high], [−back] for [+ back], etc., is saying no more, on an articulatory level, than stating that there is a change from a velar articulation to a bilabial articulation. The motor commands to the muscles, specifying a bilabial or velar articulation, specify the part of the tongue to be raised, where it is to be raised, etc. In other words, on a phonetic level a complex of the features [−anterior, +high, +back] is indissolubly a velar place of articulation, and one does not expect to find (and indeed, one doesn't find) a simple switch of the feature [+coronal], for example, without other phonetic effects. In the example *pedestrian* → *tebestrian*, the error can be specified as a switch in the feature of coronality, but it is obvious that this feature is not 'independently controlled'. What I am suggesting is that segments as feature complexes do exist; that some of these features or properties can be independently controlled, such as nasality, voicing, place of articulation (if considered as a single multi-valued feature) etc.; but that some properties are highly dependent on the existence of other properties of the segment. It is thus that [delayed release] does not seem to be independent of affricates, and one can only suppose that, on the neuro-physiological level, there is some command for a stop closure combined with delayed release, which command cannot be split into two segments. That is, the command for the initial and final consonants of *church* at one level of the generation of speech is a command for just such an affricate. On the other hand, when one says *did you* as [dɪdžuw], in rapid speech the affrication occurs by a different process, i.e. by automatic and mechanical movements of the vocal organs. However, the results at the level of muscle movements are identical.

3.7 THE REALITY OF THE SYLLABIC UNIT. While it seems plausible to assume, as was done above, that units smaller than syllables (segments and features) have independent status as behavioral units, this does not negate the possibility that syllable-size units are also units of speech performance. In fact, all the evidence from tongue slips supports such a view. Nooteboom (1969:119) suggests that since "the distance be-

[6] Chomsky & Halle are of course concerned with the grammatically determined aspects of the signal. The occurrence or lack of occurrence of speech errors involving phonetic features are being discussed in this article as they relate to a model of linguistic performance rather than competence. However, when Chomsky & Halle talk about "the set of phonetic properties that can in principle be controlled in speech" (295), it is difficult to find the clear separation between competence and performance.

tween origin and target (or the substituted segments) does not generally exceed seven syllables, (and) since we know that the short memory span of man may contain about seven units ... we might interpret our findings as an argument for the syllable to be a unit in the phonemic programming system". Nooteboom (1969), MacKay (1969, 1970a), and Fromkin (1968) all support the statement that "segmental slips obey a structural law with regard to syllable-place; that is, initial segments in the origin syllable replace initial segments in the target syllable, nuclear replace nuclear, and final replace final" (Boomer & Laver 1968:7). Furthermore, Nooteboom points out that "when the second consonantal element of a CVC form is immediately followed by an initial vowel of the next word ... final consonantal elements do not tend to become prevocalic" (1969). In other words, in a string CVC#VC ... CV#CVC, one never finds in errors a substitution of the final consonant of the first word for the initial consonant of the final words. My own English data support the analysis of Nooteboom's Dutch data, and seem to contradict the position taken by Kozhevnikov & Chistovich (1965), where the suggestion is made that in the production of Russian utterances a CVC#VC sequence is reorganized into articulatory programs for each CV sequence. This does not seem to be the case in English or Dutch. The evidence for the syllable suggested by Nooteboom can, of course, also be used as evidence for the reality of the unit 'word', which will be discussed below.

MacKay (1969) found that the "syllabic position of reversed consonants was almost invariably identical". The only examples in my data which do not support this finding are two examples of metathesis occurring within words of two sequential segments:

(18) (a) whisper → whipser
     (b) ask → aks

It has been suggested (Peter Ladefoged, personal communication) that we should note the rarity of such examples, and the fact that all such errors seem to involve the sibilant *s*. In a number of perception tests, the hiss (such as occurs with [s]) is often 'misplaced'; i.e., it is difficult for subjects to judge where the noise occurs in an utterance. This perceptual difficulty seems to be reflected in production errors of the above kind.

All other examples of errors occurring within the same word show sequential ordering of segments within syllables, as in these examples (a hyphen represents a syllable division):

(19) (a) harp-si-chord → carp-si-hord
     (b) ma-ga-zine → ma-za-gine
     (c) phi-lo-so-phy → phi-so-lo-phy
     (d) e-le-phant → e-phe-lant
     (e) a-ni-mal → a-mi-nal
     (f) spe-ci-fy → spe-fi-cy

(g) Ra-be-lais → Ra-le-bais
(h) pan-cakes → can-pakes
(i) neural mo-de-ling → neural mo-le-ding

Because of the co-articulation effects of segments within a syllable, it is impossible to omit the syllable as a unit of articulation, even if one were to ignore the evidence of the fixed order in the reversal, anticipation, or perseveration of segments (Fromkin 1968).

There are of course many errors which involve the substitution, omission, re-placement, addition etc. of one or more whole syllables, which further substantiates the claim that syllabic units are real performance units:

(20) (a) Morton and Broadbent point → Morton and Broadpoint
  (b) revealed the generalization → reeled the generalization
  (c) tremendously → tremenly
  (d) which I analyse as the following → which I analyse as the follow
  (e) butterfly and caterpillar → butterpillar and catterfly
  (f) opacity and specificity → opacity and specifity
  (g) we want to reveal all the facts → we want to feel all ...

In many of the above, several factors are at work. Some of these examples are what are commonly called 'blends', as are the following:

(21) (a) Did you bring your clarinola (a blend of *clarinet* plus *viola*)
  (b) switch and changed → swinged [swindžd]
  (c) importance of [ədžɔjsn̩t] rules (a blend of *adjacent* plus *adjoining*)
  (d) my data consists [monlij] – [mejstlij] (a blend of *mainly* plus *mostly*)

THE REALITY OF PHONOLOGICAL AND MORPHOPHONEMIC CONSTRAINTS

4. The speech of jargon aphasics, as well as errors made by non-pathological speakers, reveal that 'normal' slips of the tongue and aphasic jargon utterances are constrained by the linguistic system. One does not find 'phonemes' (or more correctly, 'phones') which are not found in regular utterances. For example, an English speaker does not substitute a rounded front vowel in anticipation of a rounded back vowel, nor a lateral click for a lateral liquid. Furthermore, only permitted segmental sequences occur. Wells (1951) stated this as his "First law" of tongue slips: "A slip of the tongue is practically always a phonetically possible noise." It is obvious that Wells meant a 'phonetically possible noise' in a particular language. As I have stated in an earlier article (Fromkin 1968): "The segments constituting each syllable must have sequential ordering, so that only initial consonants, vowels, and final consonants may interchange, IF AND ONLY IF THE TRANSPOSITIONS ARE IN KEEPING WITH THE PHONOLOGICAL RULES OF THE LANGUAGE" (64). This 'First Rule' appears to explain a 'Spoonerism' attributed to Spooner:

sphinx in moonlight → minx in spoonlight.

What is of interest here is the transformation of the [sf] in *sphinx* to [sp] when the cluster is transposed with the [m]. While [sf] does occur in words like *sphincter*, *sphere*, and *sphinx*, such words (and the dozen or other 'technical' words listed in Webster's Third) are 'exceptions' to the regular morpheme-structure rule in English which permits only voiceless stop obstruents after an initial *s*. [sfuwn-light] would thus not be a permitted sequence, and consequently [f] → [p].

All the examples already cited include only permitted English sequences. Further examples will support the 'reality' of such constraints:

(22) (a) play the victor → flay the pictor
     (b) tab stops → tap [stabz]
     (c) plant the seeds [sijdz] → plan the seats [sijts]
     (d) bloody students [blʌdij stuwdənts] → [blʌdənt stuwdijz]

There are two ways of interpreting the error shown in (22a). One might suggest that it is simply the manner of articulation (stop vs. fricative) which is switched. If such an interpretation is given, one must also add that, when the [v] is changed to a stop, the place of articulation changes from labio-dental to bilabial. Another possible explanation is that the two segments switch ($p \leftrightarrow v$), and that since [vl] is not a permitted sequence in English, the [v] is devoiced. This suggests that these phonological constraints, when learned, become behavioral constraints which occur AFTER the segmental transpositions occur.

A similar example is shown by (22b), in which the final consonant (or just the voicing feature) of the first word is transposed with the penultimate consonant of the second word (or the final stem consonant, prior to the plural morpheme addition). Again, the intended [ps] is changed not to [bs] but to [bz], in keeping with the phonological (and morphological) constraints of English.

Examples (22b–d) represent another phenomenon. In these errors, the original syntactic structure of the phrases remains intact, in that the intended plural nouns occuring as the last words of the phrases remain as words with plural endings, despite the errors which occur; but the phonetic realization of the plural morpheme changes, as well as the preceding segments. Thus [stabz] and [sijts] can be explained simply as due to phonological or phonetic constraints, since [bs] and [tz] never occur as final clusters; but the error in (22d) is more complex. [js] can occur in English as in *Reese* [rijs], *mice* [majs], *feast* [fijst], *face* [fejs] etc. But [ij+s] cannot occur when the final sibilant represents the plural morpheme. One can then suggest that the phonetic representation of the plural morpheme is specified prior to the automatic phonetic specifications which serve as the units for articulatory commands. If this were not the case, one could not understand the change of the [s] to [z] in [stuwdijz].

Further examples of the reality of morphophonemic rules are evidenced in errors which include the alternation of the non-specific determiner *a/an*:

(23) (a) a current argument [ə kʌrn̩t argjumənt] → an arrent curgument [ən arn̩t kʌrgjumənt]
   (b) an eating marathon → a meeting arathon
   (c) a history of an ideology → an istory of a hideology
   (d) an ice cream cone → a kice ream cone

The changes *a → an* and *an → a* indicate that, in the generation of speech, the segmental errors or transpositions must take place PRIOR to the actual neural muscular commands, since there are possible sound sequences of [ə] plus vowel, as in *America is* [əɪz].

Such errors show the separation of morphophonemic rules and phonological rules. In other words, it is not a phonological rule which changes the *a* to *an*, since there is no general restriction on vowel sequences like those of *America is, Rosa and I*. Thus the ordering of events must be as follows: (1) segmental errors, (2) morphophonemic adjustments, (3) P-rules.

The reality of the P-rules is attested by many of the errors cited above, e.g. (8a) [tæb staps] → [tæp stabz]. The transposition of the /b/ and /p/ must have occurred prior to the rule which constrains final clusters to be voiced or voiceless. In (8b), [wijks ən mʌnθs] → [wɪŋks ...] can only be explained by the following sequence: /wĩks/ → /wĩnks/ → [wiŋks]. The tense /ĩ/ is not diphthongized because it occurs before a nasal, and the /n/ is made homorganic with the following velar stop by a general rule.

STRESS

5. MacKay, Boomer & Laver, and Nooteboom (1969) all investigate the influence of stress on errors in speech. Boomer & Laver conclude that "The origin syllable and the target syllable of a slip are metrically similar, in that both are salient (stressed) or both are weak (unstressed), with salient-salient pairings predominating" (7). Nooteboom agrees with this conclusion, stating that "In significantly more cases than is to be expected in a random distribution the elements involved in a speech error belong to stressed syllables" (1969). He disagrees, however, with Boomer & Laver's finding that "Slips involve the tonic (primary stressed) word, either as origin or as target, with tonic origins predominating." But from Nooteboom's own data, the disagreement seems to be the result of a misinterpretation of the difference between primary stress (tonic word) and salient stress. Differences between English and Dutch may also be relevant. MacKay finds that transpositions occurring within words appear in syllables with different stress, while in between-word reversals his findings corroborate those of Boomer & Laver.

What seems to be of greater interest is that, when vowels or syllables or parts of syllables or whole words are substituted or transposed, there is no change in the stress pattern or contour of the sentence. Boomer & Laver cite an example in which a speaker, instead of saying *how bád things were*, said *how thíngs bad were*. It is evident that there was no transposition of the stress, despite the transposition of the words. The following examples show the same phenomenon (an acute accent ['] represents primary stress, as does '1' above the vowel; a grave accent [`] represents non-primary stress – secondary or tertiary; a '2' above the vowel represents secondary stress, and a '3' tertiary stress).

(24) (a)   ³hammer and ¹sickle → ³sickle and ¹hammer

     (b)   ³peoples ¹park → [³parklz ¹pijp]

     (c)   ²verge of a ³nervous ¹breakdown → ²nerve of a ³vergeous ¹breakdown

     (d)   he's been ²around a ³long ¹time → he's been ²long ³around ¹time

     (e)   a ²computer in our ³own ¹laboratory → a ²laboratory in our ³own ¹computer

     (f)   ²examine the ³eyes of the ¹horse → ²examine the ³horse of the ¹eyes

     (g)   ³broke the ²crystal on my ¹watch → ³broke the ²whistle on my ¹crotch

     (h)   in the ²theory of ¹phonology → in the ²phonology of ¹theory

Examples (24e) and (24h) show that, while the word position of primary stress in the phrase is not transposed, the stressed syllable of the word in isolation is the syllable which receives the sentence stress. That is, if the primary stress is to be placed on *laboratory*, it is placed on the first syllable; and if it is to be placed on *computer*, it is placed on the second syllable.

Thus it seems that two aspects of stress must be accounted for: first, the word stress moves with the word itself (i.e. the syllable of the word which receives main stress in isolation also receives the primary stress when the word is moved); second, the stress contour of the phrase is fixed by the syntactic structure of the phrase itself, and must be generated independently of the word order in the utterance.

One may then suggest that the word stress is stored as part of the articulatory specifications of the stored unit 'word', but that the sentence or phrase stress and over-all intonation contour is generated separately, as part of what Boomer & Laver call the "tone-group". I would therefore agree with them that "The pivotal role of the tonic word in slips suggests that its phonological, syntactic and semantic prominence is matched by an analogous neuro-physiological prominence, coded in the brain as a part of the articulatory programme" (8), and further that "the tone group is handled in the central nervous system as a unitary behavioral act, and the neural correlates of the separate elements are assembled and partially activated, or 'primed' before the performance of the utterance begins" (9). However, in the construction of a model of linguistic performance, it is necessary to specify the nature, i.e. the syntactic structure, of this tone group, for the 'priming' of the 'tonic' syllable depends on the syntactic structure of the utterance.

The suggestion that the stress placement on words is fixed in the lexicon does not mean that one cannot, or should not, attempt to generalize stress assignment rules in the phonology of English. In fact there may be some evidence from speech errors that not only in a grammar of competence, but also in the actual stored lexicon, words (or perhaps formatives) are stored in a more abstract form than by their actual articulatory specifications. There are speech errors which display a movement of stress, and in certain cases a change in the vowel qualities depending on where the stress is placed:

(25) (a) This can viewed altérnately – altérnatively – no – álternately

    (b) símilarly → [similǽrəlij]

    (c) homogéneous → [homàdžəníjəs]

    (d) in favor of [həmádžə – homodžíjniəs]

    (e) syllabíf – syllábification [sɪləbíf – sɪlǽbəfəkejšn̩]

    (f) opácity and specifícity → opácity and spécifity

One may speculate (perhaps wildly) that in the generation of speech a word is selected, stress is assigned, and then the articulatory program is assembled to produce the sounds, reducing unstressed vowels etc. By this hypothesis, the changes [ər] → [ǽr] in (25b), [o] → [a] and [ij] → [ə] in (25c), are 'explained' by the suggestion that the words are stored as stems plus endings, and with their unreduced vowel qualities. While such a suggestion cannot be entirely ruled out, alternative explanations can be provided for all the examples in (25) above, which, from the performance viewpoint, seem more intuitively satisfying. In (25b), for example, the speaker might have begun to say *similarity*, or in Carroll's terms have had *similarly* and *similarity* in mind at the same time, just as he clearly had both *alternately* and *alternatively* in mind in (25a). It should be clear, without laboring the point, that all the above examples of errors involving stress can be similarly explained. Before one can seriously put forth the hypothesis that the stress of words is generated by phonological rules, and not stored as part of the specification of the word (in one's performance lexicon), a crucial experiment must be found.

THE REALITY OF SYNTACTIC WORD CLASSES AND SYNTACTIC PHRASES

6. Nooteboom (1969:130) found that "a mistakenly selected word always or nearly always belongs to the same word class as the intended word [indicating] that the grammatical structure of the phrase under construction imposes imperative restrictions on the selection of words." In my own corpus of errors, a similar conclusion can be drawn. When words are switched, nouns transpose with nouns, verbs with verbs, etc.:

(26) (a) a computer in our own laboratory → a laboratory in our own computer
    (b) that no English manufacturer could name these projects – products
    (c) naturalness of rules → nationalness of rules
    (d) bottom of page five → bottle of page five
    (e) I have some additional proposals to hand out → hang out
    (f) book of sixes → book of twos
    (g) chamber music → chamber maid
    (h) a speaker doesn't go through all the worlds – rules he has in his head
    (i) while the present – pressure indicates
    (j) How come if you're a Scorpio you don't read – wear oriental spice?

The fact that in many cases the substituted word has some phonetic (or phonological) similarity to the target word was also noted by Nooteboom. This suggests that our stored lexicon is ordered in some dictionary-like fashion, and any crossword puzzle addict can confirm this fact. But there must be a complicated addressing system in the computer-like brain mechanism, since each listing must be specified under semantic features, phonological features, number of syllables, syntactic features etc. Thus, in (26h), the phonetic similarity of [wərldz] and [rulz] is based on two identical segments – which, however, do not have the same sequenced ordering in the words. Of course, this may be a chance error.

The reality of the word as a unit is evidenced by the above. Furthermore, speech errors show that derivationally complex items may be stored as combinations of separate formatives, i.e. stems and affixes. Example (26c), above, *natural+ness* → *national+ness*, attests this, as do the following examples:

(27) (a) infinitive clauses → infinity clauses
    (b) grouping → groupment
    (c) intervening node → intervenient – intervening node
    (d) and so in conclusion → and so in concludement

Example (27d) suggests again that *conclusion* may be stored as *conclude+ion* with rules for $d →$ [ž]. It is, however, possible and highly probable that we have here a blend of *concluding* and *conclusion*.

Hockett's analysis would relegate such affix substitutions to what he calls "analogy". Unfortunately, this label does not explain how the process takes place. One possible explanation is there are rules of word formation, plus a vocabulary of stems and a vocabulary of affixes which, as the above examples show, can be manipulated to create neologisms which do not occur in the language, such as *groupment*. MacKay's finding (unpublished) that affixes are involved with a probability greater than chance, among syllable errors, would support the hypothesis that affixes do form a separate sub-set of the lexicon.

The constancy of the syntactic structure, and the reality of performance units larger than words, morphemes, stems, etc., is seen in the following:

(28) (a) I wouldn't buy macadamia nuts for the kids → I wouldn't buy kids for the macadamia nuts

   (b) A fall in pitch occurs at the end of the sentence → an end of the sentence occurs at the fall in pitch

   (c) He's a far better man than anyone here → he's a farther man than anyone better here

The displacement of *better* in (28c) also results in an adjectival ending added to the adverb *far*, maintaining a correct and intended syntactic structure.

In structures such as $_{NP}[_{ADJ}[macadamia]_N[nuts]]$ (or, this may be a compound noun), $_N[_N[fall]_{PP}[in\ pitch]]$, and $_N[_N[end\ _{PP}[_{PREP}[of]_{NP}[_{DET}[the]_N[sentence]]]$, syntactic phrases can interchange as entire units; similar word classes can also interchange. Furthermore, when (as in 28c) an intended adverb+adjective+noun is involved in an error, a shift of the adjective to another place in the sentence seems simultaneously to change the remaining adverb *far* to an adjective, thus maintaining the over-all structure. Such facts seem to point to the reality of syntactic phrases and of syntactic features of words.

SEMANTIC FEATURES

7. Blends occur in which non-existent words are produced as the result of composites of two words with similar semantic features. These are indeed common errors, not only invented by Lewis Carroll, but occurring naturally. In the examples given in (29) the speaker was questioned as to what he had in mind, or as to what he thought the reason for the blend was. The subject's answers are given in parentheses:

(29) (a) My data consists [mownlij] – [mejstlij] ... (mainly/mostly)

   (b) I swindged [swɪndžd] ... (switch/changed)

   (c) It's a lot of [ba] – [brʌðl] (bother/trouble)

   (d) She's a real [swɪp] chick (swinging/hip)

   (e) it's a [spajrətɪv] (spirant/fricative)

   (f) a tennis [æθlər] (player/athlete)

Such errors seem to support Carroll's assumptions. A speaker has in mind some meaning which he wishes to convey. In selecting words, it appears that he is matching semantic features. Where there are a number of alternative possibilities, rather than making an immediate selection, he brings them both into a buffer storage compartment, with their phonological specifications. Either a selection occurs at this point, or the words are blended, resulting in the above kind of errors.

The literature and my own data attest the fact that, besides the phonological similarity in substituted words, errors often involve semantic features in common, or substitution of antonyms, i.e. words having the same features with opposite values:

(30) (a) I really like to – hate to get up in the morning

(b) It's at the bottom – I mean – top of the stack of books
(c) This room is too damn hot – cold
(d) the oral – written part of the exam

Nooteboom presents a number of examples which seem "to involve a semantic switch from the space to the time dimension" (1967:14) as in the following:

(31) (a) the two contemporary, er – sorry, adjacent buildings
     (b) during the apparatus, er – behind the apparatus
     (c) the singular, sorry, the present time

Evidence from aphasia studies also show that substituted words often fall into the same semantic class, as in cases where patients will read *tree* for *flower*, *night* for *dark*, *spoon* for *fork*, *liberty* for *democracy* etc. (Marshall & Newcombe 1966; Luria & Vinogradova 1959; Jakobson 1966). Such errors provide important evidence as to the storage of vocabulary and the generation of speech.

IMPLICATIONS OF SPEECH ERRORS FOR A MODEL OF LINGUISTIC PERFORMANCE

8.1. THE LEXICON. When one learns a language, he learns among other things a vocabulary. Judging both from errors of speech and from speakers' ability to form new words by adding derivational affixes to stems (e.g. *He's a real computerish type*) and by inflecting newly coined words in keeping with the rules of the language (e.g. 22d, [stuwdijz]), it seems plausible to assume that the stored lexicon consists of stems and affixes, as well as idioms, compounds, whole words etc. Given the higher than chance probability that prefixes and suffixes are involved in syllable errors (McKay, unpublished), one can further assume that, even if words are stored with their affixes, the stem and affix have a separate status. Thus it is not unlikely that *grouping* is stored as *group+ing*, which permits a substitution of *ment* for the affix *ing*. The fact that one does not find stems substituting for or transposing with affixes further justifies their separate status.

Since phonological or phonetic specifications, semantic features, and syntactic word-class features all play a role in the speech errors that occur, it is obvious that vocabulary items must be stored with such features indicated. But we cannot simply assume that there is one dictionary-like storage starting with all words beginning with A and ending with all words beginning with Z, with other features given. Semantic errors show that words are selected to convey certain meanings as specified by their semantic features. And for literate speakers the listing must also specify the orthography, to account for the ability of people to play 'geography', a game in which one must name a country, river, city, etc. beginning with the same LETTER with which the previous word ended: thus, *Passaic* ends with the letter *c*, pronounced [k], and the next player can offer *Charleston*, which begins with *c*, pronounced [tš]. The relationship between orthography and sound must be accounted for. Crossword puzzles, doublecrostics, and the 'tip of the tongue' phenomenon (Brown & McNeil 1966) also attest this fact. For example, it is often the case that in trying to remember someone's name, forgotten at the moment, a speaker will say, "I know it begins with a C." The name may be *Cohen*, which begins with a C pronounced [k]. And of course a game like 'geography' is further evidence for the storage of words in semantic classes.

One may then suggest that the vocabulary is stored in a thesaurus-like lattice structure. It is possible to conceive of this network as a listing of all the stems and affixes in some fixed phonological order, each one with all of its feature specifications, and each one with a particular address. The separate semantic section of this lexicon may then be divided into semantic classes, with semantic features under which are listed, not the particular vocabulary item, but the addresses of those items which satisfy the features indicated. One might suggest also that the listings under the semantic headings are grouped under syntactic headings such as [+noun], [+verb] etc., to account for the proper grammatical selection in the generation of utterances.

Since the 'tip of the tongue' phenomenon suggests that speakers recall the number of syllables – the metrical beat of the word – a further division under the full phonological listing is suggested. In other words, it is not impossible to assume that all monosyllables beginning with the same phonological segment constitute one block, followed by disyllables, etc.

The error cited in (30a) might then occur in the following way: the speaker wishes to say (at least on a conscious level – we leave the unconscious motivations to be explained by others) *I really hate to get up in the morning*. At the point in the generation of the utterance prior to the selection of the words, in the 'slot' representing *hate*, the features [+verb, −desire ...] occur, and an address for a word is sought from the semantic class which includes [±desire]. But either because of unconscious wishes or due to a random error, the address for a verb with the feature [+desire] rather than one specified as [−desire] is selected, and the item at that address called forth with its accompanying phonological features turns out as [lajk] rather than [hejt].

The complexity of the stored lexicon is enormous, and it is obvious that there are too many lacunae in our knowledge to suggest anything more than the kinds of subparts or components it must contain. I have suggested an 'indirect-addressing' system above with nothing to justify this except a vague appeal to storage simplicity. It seems plausible to assume, however, that any model of a lexicon must include the following sub-parts:

(a) A complete list of formatives with all features specified, i.e. phonological, orthographic, syntactic, and semantic.

(b) A subdivision of the phonological listings according to number of syllables. This is necessitated by the fact that speakers can remember the number of syllables of a word without remembering the phonological shape of the syllables. It is also suggested by the fact that one can get a subject to produce a list of one-, two-, or three-syllable words.

(c) A reverse dictionary sub-component, to account for the ability of speakers to produce a list of words all ending in a particular sound or letter.

(d) A sub-component of phonologically grouped final syllables, to account for the ability of speakers to form rhymes.

(e) Formatives grouped according to syntactic categories, to account for the errors noted above, and the ability of speakers to list nouns, or verbs, or adverbs on command, as well as the more important ability to form grammatical sentences.

(f) Formatives grouped according to hierarchical sets of semantic classes.

(g) Words listed alphabetically by orthographic spelling.

Furthermore, it seems plausible to assume that all these components must be intricately linked in a complicated network.

This highly speculative, oversimplified model of the lexicon is suggested as a first approximation to what must be a most complicated storage mechanism. What seems certain, however, is that any model of the lexicon must account for the observed types of errors, which require the specification of various kinds of properties which we have called phonological, syntactic, and semantic features; no lexicon consisting of a single listing of items can explain what occurs.

8.2. THE GENERATION OF UTTERANCES. It seems quite evident from all the examples of speech errors cited above that, in the production of speech, it is not true that 'anything goes', or that speech performance obeys no rules, or that the errors are totally random and unexplainable (see discussion of this in Fromkin 1968). While we may not be able to explain as yet the exact mechanisms involved in speech errors, the errors made are not only highly constrained, but provide information about speech performance which non-deviant speech obscures. In other words, if we had no record of errors in which consonant clusters are split into segments, we would not be able to justify the assumption that clusters in performance are strings of individual discrete segments.

Any model of speech performance must therefore account for the kinds of errors which do occur. Such a model must account for the following:

(a) that features, segments, syllables constitute units in the production of a speech utterance;

(b) that segments are ordered within a syllable, and that only segments similarly ordered are involved in the same error;

(c) that "root morphemes may be interchanged but root morphemes and an affix cannot take each other's places" (Nooteboom 1967:16), or that words of the same syntactic or morphological class usually interchange with each other;

(d) that intonation contours (including the placement of primary stress) remain fixed, and are generated separately from the individual word stresses;

(e) that morphological constraints and phonetic or phonological constraints must occur at different times in the production of an utterance;

(f) that non-permissible phones or phonetic sequences do not occur;

(g) that errors may be semantic in nature, as in the case of blends or word-substitutions involving similar semantic features; and

(h) that the similarity of the phonological form of words appears to play a role in word substitutions.

To account for such phenomena we may suggest the following (over-simplified) order in the actual generation of an utterance:

STAGE 1. A 'meaning' to be conveyed is generated.

STAGE 2. The 'idea' or 'meaning' is structured syntactically, with semantic features associated with parts of the syntactic structure. For example, if a speaker wishes to convey the fact that 'a ball' rather than 'a bat' was thrown by a boy, the utterance *A ball was thrown* or alternately *He threw a báll* is structured at this stage. If he uses the second structure, part of the features specified for the final nouns must include [+emphasis] together with the features selected for 'ball', i.e. [−animate, −human, +count, +round, +used in games etc.] This suggests that the STRUCTURE itself is put into buffer storage prior to actual articulation of the utterance; this would account for the switching of noun for noun, verb for verb etc., when such transpositions occur.

STAGE 3. The output of Stage 2 is thus a syntactic structure with semantic and syntactic features specified for the word slots. In order to explain the fact that "the tone group is handled in the central nervous system as a unitary behavioural act" (Boomer & Laver 1968:9), one can suggest that the intonation contour, with the placement of primary stress, occurs at this stage. Since a transposition of words in the utterance will cause a transfer of primary stress to the main stressed syllable of the word in a given position, one can posit that only the position of the primary stress is indicated at this stage, and not the particular syllable. That is, the generation of the sentence intonation contour must occur prior to the selection of the words themselves.

STAGE 4. We now have in the buffer a syntactic phrase with semantic features indicated, and with sentence stress assigned. A lexicon look-up now occurs; the semantic class sub-section of the lexicon is first consulted, with features being matched, and the direction is obtained to go to a certain address in the over-all vocabulary. The item in the specified address is then selected, this word being specified as to its phonological segments, which are identified and ordered into syllabic units. At this stage in the process, errors resulting in a choice of a 'wrong' word may occur. Such errors may involve the matching of values of semantic features, resulting in a wrong address being specified. Or the correct address may be specified, but a different address substituted which is 'in the vicinity' of the intended address. Thus, if the intended word is *like* and the produced word is *hate*, the error occurs in the selection of the wrong address in the semantic component of the lexicon. But if the intended word is *pressure* and the produced word is *present*, the correct address is obtained, but the wrong address selected, given that *pressure* and *present* have addresses in the same section of the vocabulary. This would be due to the phonological similarity of their first three segments. This process thus results in a string of phonological segments, each segment specified by certain features or properties and also specified as to

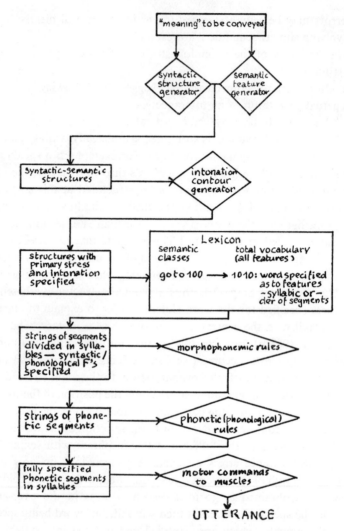

Fig. 1. Utterance generator.

syllabic order, with the syntactic bracketing remaining intact. But it is at this stage, when the string of phonological segments is put into the buffer, that a mis-ordering of segments may occur. In other words, as the segments are 'sent' into the short-term memory buffer, segment 1 of syllable 1 may be substituted for segment 1 of syllable 4. I am not concerned at this stage with an explanation of why and how this occurs, but with the fact that it can occur at this stage without disturbing the syllabic ordering. It is also here that whole syllables or parts of syllables may get transposed or mis-placed. These errors must occur before Stage 5, which is where the morphophonemic rules or constraints take over.

STAGE 5. The morphophonemic constraints of the language at this stage change, if necessary, or perhaps 'spell out', the phonological shapes of morphemes. The segmental errors must occur before this stage to account for the alternations of *a/an* and *s/z* of the plural.

We have now reached the stage where automatic phonetic and phonological rules take over, converting the sequences of segments into actual neuro-motor commands to the muscles in the articulation of the utterance.

The above stages may be diagrammed as shown in Figure 1. It must be emphasized that the various 'black-boxes' are highly schematic, and what actually occurs in them is outside the concern of this paper. Rather, the attempt is to show a possible ordering of events in the production of an utterance which can account for non-deviant utterances, as well as for utterances containing errors in speech.

BIBLIOGRAPHY

Applegate, R. B.
  1968 "Segmental analysis of articulatory errors under delayed auditory feedback", (= *POLA reports* 8) (Berkeley: University of California).
Boomer, D. S. and J. D. M. Laver
Bowden, H. H.
  1899 *A Study of Lapses, Psychological Review*, Monograph Supplement 3, (4).
  1968 "Slips of the tongue", *British Journal of Disorders of Communication* 3: 1–12. Reprinted in this volume.
Broadbent, D. E.
  1966 "The well ordered mind", *American Educational Research Journal* 3: 281–295.
Brown, R. and D. McNeil
  1966 "The tip of the tongue phenomenon", *Journal of Verbal Learning and Verbal Behavior* 5: 325–337.
Carroll, Lewis
  1876 *The hunting of the snark* (London: Macmillan).
Chomsky, N. and M. Halle
  1968 *The sound pattern of English* (New York: Harper & Row).
Cohen, A.
  1966 "Errors of speech and their implication for understanding the strategy of language users" (Instituut voor Perceptie Onderzoek, *Annual progress report* 1, Eindhoven) (To appear in: *Models of speech, Proceedings of the International Congress of Psychologists, Moscow*). Reprinted in this volume.
Freud, Sigmund
  1924 *Zur Psychopathologie des Alltaglebens*, 10th ed. (Leipzig: Internationaler Psychoanalytischer Verlag (English version in: *Basic writings of Sigmund Freud*, ed. by A. A. Brill, New York: Modern Library, 1938).
Fromkin, V. A.
  1968 "Speculations on performance models", *Journ. of Ling.* 4: 47–68.
Green, E.
  1969 "Phonological and grammatical aspects of jargon in an aphasic patient: a case study", *Lang. and Speech* 12: 80–103.
Hockett, C. F.
  1967 "Where the tongue slips, there slip I", in: *To honor Roman Jakobson*, 2: 910–936. (= *Janua linguarum, series maior* 32) (The Hague: Mouton). Reprinted in this volume.
Jakobson, R.
  1964 "Towards a linguistic typology of aphasic impairments", *Disorders of Language*, *CIBA Foundation Symposium* London: 21–46.
  1966 "Linguistic types of aphasia", in: *Brain function*, ed. by E. C. Carterette: 67–91 (Berkeley & Los Angeles: University of California Press).

Jespersen, O.
    1922   *Language: its nature, development, and origin* (London: Allen and Unwin).
Kozhevnikov, V. A. and L. A. Chistovich
    1965   *Speech: articulation and perception* (revised)(*Joint Publications Research Service* 30, 543)
           (Washington: U.S. Department of Commerce).
Lashley, K. S.
    1951   "The problem of serial order in behavior", in: *Cerebral mechanisms in behavior*, ed. by
           L. A. Jeffress: 112–136 (New York: Wiley).
Laver, J.
    1969   "The detection and correction of slips of the tongue", *Work in progress* 3, Dept. of Phonetics
           and Linguistics, Edinburgh University: 1–13. Reprinted in this volume.
Luria, A. R. and O. S. Vinogradova
    1959   "An objective investigation of the dynamics of semantic systems", *Brit. Journ. of Psych.* 50:
           89–105.
MacKay, D. G.
    1969   "Forward and backward masking in motor systems", *Kybernetik* 6: 57–64.
    1970a "Spoonerisms: the structure of errors in the serial order of speech", *Neuropsychologia* 8:
           323–350. Reprinted in this volume.
    1970b "Context dependent stuttering", to appear in Kybernetik.
    1970c "Spoonerisms of children", to appear in Neuropsychologia.
    1970d "Sound change and errors in speech", unpublished.
Marshall, J. C. and F. Newcombe
    1966   "Syntactic and semantic errors in paralexia", *Neuropsychologia* 4: 169–176.
Meringer, R.
    1908   *Aus dem Leben der Sprache* (Berlin).
Meringer, R. and K. Mayer
    1895   *Versprechen und Verlesen, eine psychologisch linguistische Studie* (Vienna).
Miller, G. A.
    1962   "Decision units in the perception of speech", *IRE Transactions on Information Theory*,
           IT-8: 81–83.
Miller G. A. and P. E. Nicely
    1955   "An analysis of perceptual confusions among some English consonants", *Journal of the
           Acoustical Society of America* 27: 338–352.
Nooteboom, S. G.
    1967   "Some regularities in phonemic speech errors", (Instituut voor Perceptie Onderzoek, *Annual
           progress report* 2) (Eindhoven).
    1969   "The tongue slips into patterns", in: Nomen: *Leyden studies in linguistics and phonetics*,
           ed. by A. G. Sciarone et al.: 114–132 (The Hague: Mouton). Reprinted in this volume.
Robbins, Rossell Hope.
    1966   "The warden's wordplay: toward a redefinition of the spoonerism", *Dalhousie Review* 46:
           457–465.
Sapir, Edward
    1925   "Sound patterns in language", *Lg.* 1: 37–51.
Sturtevant, E. H.
    1917   *Linguistic change* (Chicago: University of Chicago Press).
    1947   *An introduction to linguistic science* (New Haven: Yale University Press).
Wells, R.
    1951   "Predicting slips of the tongue", *Yale Scientific Magazine*, December: 9–12.
           Reprinted in this volume.
Wickelgren, W. A.
    1965a "Acoustic similarity and intrusion errors in short-term memory", *Journal of Experimental
           Psychology* 70: 102–108.
    1965b "Distinctive features and errors in short-term memory for English vowels", *Journal of the
           Acoustical Society of America* 38: 583–588.
    1966   "Distinctive features and errors in short-term memory for English consonants", *Journal of
           the Acoustical Society of America* 39: 388–398.

APPENDIX

The errors listed in this Appendix are selected from a corpus of over four thousand spontaneous slips of the tongue. They have been selected to show the wide variety of such slips which occur in normal speech.

The classification is in some ways arbitrary, since some of the errors fall into a number of classes. A.3. *the hiring of minority faculty → the firing of – uh – the hiring of* ... could have been listed as a word substitution. Similarly, many of the 'segmental errors' may be errors involving a single 'feature' reversal or substitution. This is also true of the other classes.

Phonetic transcriptions are 'broad' transcriptions and are provided only where there may be questions as to the actual pronunciation. Contexts are given where they may be helpful in revealing the causes for the errors.

The column on the left of the arrow lists the intended or 'target' utterances; the actual utterances containing the errors are given on the right of the arrow. A series of dots (...) means that the intended words were produced. Dashes (–) represent a pause by the speaker. 'Initial' and 'final' means syllable initial and final although in most cases the syllables are the initial and final syllables of words.

A. Anticipation of Initial Consonants

1. a Canadian from Toronto	→	1. ... Tanadian ...
2. Paris is the most beautiful city	→	2. Baris ...
3. the hiring of minority faculty	→	3. the firing of – uh – the hiring of ...
4. a reading list	→	4. a leading list
5. tonal phonology	→	5. fonal phonology
6. factive verbs	→	6. vactive verbs
7. it's a real mystery	→	7. ... a meal mystery
8. we'll put your trash cans back	→	8. ... trash bans back
9. the first thing	→	9. the thirst thing
10. paddle tennis	→	10. taddle tennis
11. some funny kind	→	11. some kunny kind

12. role of simplicity   → 12. soul of simplicity
13. roman numeral   → 13. noman numeral
14. pinch hit   → 14. hinch hit
15. made its views known   → 15. made its news – views ...
16. Kathy can type   → 16. tathy can type
17. M-U [ɛm juw] values   → 17. M-view values
18. about to fall out of the balcony → 18. ... about to ball – fall ...
19. you can anticipate, persevere or → 19. ... panticipate ...
    transpose sounds
20. take my bike   → 20. bake my bike
21. telepathic fox   → 21. telefathic fox
22. morphemic alternation   → 22. morphenic alternation
23. particle shift   → 23. farticle shift
24. it was such a good course because → 24. ... a good force ...
    we had informants
25. left after one inning with a tender → 25. ... one inding ...
    elbow

B. Perseveration of Initial Consonants

1. cortical   → 1. corkical
2. that kid was escorting us   → 2. ... escorking ...
3. black boxes   → 3. black bloxes
4. I can't cook worth a damn   → 4. ... cook worth a cam [kæm]
5. Michael Halliday   → 5. Michael Malliday
6. Filmore's case grammar   → 6. Filmore's face grammar
7. moving is no picnic when you're   → 7. ... when you're perking
   working
8. she can see it   → 8. she can she it
9. how the leaflet's written   → 9. leaflet's litten
10. the purpose of one-ninety-nines   → 10. ... of pun ninety-nines
11. he's not a revolutionist he's a liberal → 11. ... he's a riberal
12. a phonological rule   → 12. a phonological fool
13. would the chair entertain a motion → 13. ... enterchain a motion
14. Sure, life can be a game   → 14. ... be a lame – a game
15. pulled a tantrum   → 15. ... a pantrum
16. Prator's written him a long letter → 16. ... a wrong letter
17. I don't know Twi like you know Twi → 17. ... like you low Twi
18. it depends on the formant frequencies → 18. ... the dormant frequencies
19. gave the boy   → 19. gave the goy
20. take P.S.A. to San Francisco   → 20. ... to Pan – to San ...
21. Liverpool lullabye   → 21. liverpool lullapie

22. somebody will proceed to show   → 22. ... to sow
23. I've been away   → 23. ... been abay [əbej]
24. at the beginning of the turn   → 24. ... of the burn
25. Bach distinguishes three different types → 25. ... three different bipes

C. Consonant Reversals

1. left hemisphere   → 1. heft lemisphere
2. with this ring I thee wed   → 2. ... wing ... red
3. keep a tape   → 3. ... [tijp] a cape
4. Hockett or Lamb   → 4. locket or ham
5. Lakoffs and Zimmers   → 5. zakoffs and limmers
6. you better stop for gas   → 6. you getter stop for bass
7. Roman Jakobson   → 7. Yoman Rakobson
8. well made   → 8. mell wade
9. lawfully joined together   → 9. jawfully loined ...
10. Katz and Fodor   → 10. fats and kodor
11. copy of my paper   → 11. poppy of my caper
12. he taught courses   → 12. ... caught torses
13. a two pen set   → 13. ... sen pet
14. boggy marsh   → 14. moggy barsh
15. guinea pig hair   → 15. ... hig pair
16. New York   → 16. Yew Nork
17. I have baked a cake   → 17. ... caked a bake
18. my money is running out   → 18. ...runny is moning ...
                                     [rʌnij] ... [mʌniŋ]
19. the sign thing   → 19. the thine [θajn] sing
20. if the cap fits   → 20. if the fap kits
21. heap of rubbish   → 21. reap of hubbish
22. cold hard cash   → 22. hold card cash
23. rope tow   → 23. tope row
24. wind mill   → 24. [mɪnd] will
25. wine racks   → 25. rhine wacks

D. Final Consonants (Perseverance, Anticipation, and Reversal)

1. on the top shelf   → 1. ... [taf] shelp
2. in the argot lexicon   → 2. ... argon lexicot
3. with a brush   → 3. ... wish a brush
4. cup of coffee   → 4. cuff of coffee
5. of such observations   → 5. of sub observations
6. tag along   → 6. tag alog [əlɔg]

7. if George Jackson were trying to escape	→ 7. ... Jackson... ekscape
8. ace, king, queen	→ 8. ace, king, quing
9. mental capacity	→ 9. mental capality
10. write it or type it	→ 10. ripe it or type it
11. pass out	→ 11. pat ous [æws]
12. mirror image	→ 12. mirrage immor [mirədʒɪmər]
13. have you given your paper a title	→ 13. ... paper a [taytr̩]
14. gone to seed	→ 14. god to seen
15. hash or grass	→ 15. hass [hæs] or grash
16. steak or chops	→ 16. steak or [tʃaks]
17. roses in June	→ 17. roses in jews [dʒuz]
18. thick slab	→ 18. thick slack
19. Jack's pen [pẽn]	→ 19. Jack's peck [pɛk]
20. it's the red book	→ 20. ... red [bʊd]

E. Consonant Deletion, Addition, Movement

1. in order for the cell to form	→ 1. ... the stell to form
2. it's the optimal number	→ 2. ... moptimal number
3. significantly	→ 3. significlantly
4. a whole box of flowers	→ 4. a whole blox of flowers
5. the blood saturates	→ 5. ... satutrates
6. enjoying it	→ 6. enjoyding it
7. try to understand	→ 7. try to understrand
8. a gift for Christmas	→ 8. a grift....
9. kitchen sink	→ 9. kinchen sink
10. I'm making all sorts of errors	→ 10. ... all sports of errors
11. steel feet	→ 11. steel fleet
12. leather seats	→ 12. leather sleats
13. involving underlying vee's	→ 13. ... underlying vivs [vijvz]
14. think through	→ 14. thrink through
15. a fellowship which also pays tuition	→ 15. ... also plays tuition
16. if it's any consolation	→ 16. ... any consultation
17. stretch your legs	→ 17. retch your legs
18. below the glottis	→ 18. below the gottis
19. because he brought in the city police	→ 19. ... he bought in...
20. chrysanthemum plants	→ 20. ... pants
21. disturbances	→ 21. disturbaces
22. with response options	→ 22. with [rijsans] options
23. tumbled	→ 23. tubbled
24. posed nude	→ 24. poed [powd] nude

25. squib	→ 25. quib
26. split brain	→ 26. split bain
27. speech error	→ 27. peach error
28. steep price to pay	→ 28. steep pry to pace
29. she prefers Magnins to Ohrbachs	→ 29. ... agnins to mohrbachs
30. a copy of the bibliography	→ 30. a copley of the bibiography
31. the pastor placed his hand	→ 31. the plaster paced...
32. dinner at eight	→ 32. inner at date
33. Ed and Bessy	→ 33. bed and essy
34. bacon and eggs	→ 34. acon [ejkn̩] and begs
35. pinch hit	→ 35. pitch hint
36. the feature back plus labial	→ 36. ... black puss [pʌs]...
37. ballet	→ 37. albey [ælbej]
38. conjunction reduction	→ 38. cojunction redunction
39. I'll paint in the studio	→ 39. ... spaint in the tudio
40. very clear cut	→ 40. very [kijr] clut [klʌt]

F. Consonant Clusters (as units)

1. pedal steel guitar	→ 1. stedal peel guitar
2. the heater switch	→ 2. the sweeter hitch
3. to make a long story short	→ 3. ... a long shory stort
4. drop a bomb	→ 4. bop a dromb [dram]
5. I can see through the wall	→ 5. ... three sue the wall
6. space food	→ 6. face spood
7. spoon feeding	→ 7. foon speeding
8. a low front rounded vowel	→ 8. a low runt frounded vowel
9. thinly sliced	→ 9. slinly thiced [θajst]
10. stereo tape deck	→ 10. tereo stape deck
11. damage claim	→ 11. clamage dame
12. throat cutting	→ 12. coat thrutting
13. finger spell	→ 13. spinger fell
14. it's a blue jay	→ 14. its a jew blay
15. black and brown	→ 15. brack and blown [blæwn]
16. squeaky floor	→ 16. fleaky squoor
17. new steeds and swifter	→ 17. new swedes and stifter
18. when you get old your spine shrinks	→ 18. ... your shrine spinks
19. three toed sloth	→ 19. slow winged toad – uh – slee throwed toth
20. throat slitter	→ 20. sloat thritter
21. western Mexico	→ 21. weksern mestico
22. the feature flat and plain	→ 22. ... plat and flain

23. skip one stage   → 23. stip one skage
24. trees are pretty   → 24. prees are tritty
25. the official dressing taster   → 25. ... dresting taser [tejsər]
26. taxes have trippled   → 26. traxes have tippled
27. if Bill Bright comes   → 27. if Brill bite....
28. does your tummy still hurt   → 28. ... stummy til hurt
29. tongue tip trill   → 29. tongue trip till
30. instead of spacefood   → 30. inspead of...
31. parking space   → 31. sparking space
32. start smoking   → 32. smart smoking
33. the zoo keepers could be creative → 33. ... creepers could be...
34. the road is dry   → 34. the droad is dry
35. discontinuous constituent   → 35. disconstinuous...
36. M: ... prefixes   → 36. ... according to Vicksy
    D: according to Vicky
37. fatal flaws   → 37. flatal flaws
38. city school   → 38. skitty school
39. second slide   → 39. slecond slide
40. Cassius Clay   → 40. Classius Clay
41. to buy a floating point package → 41. to bly a....
42. I can knit but I can't crochet → 42. I can krit but....
43. that's previously determined by your → 43. .... by your prast state
    past state
44. still waters do run deep   → 44. ... do run steep
45. steady state vowels   → 45. steady state stowels

G. Division of Consonant Clusters

 1. strive for perfection   → 1. sprive for perfection
 2. my whole childhood was spent in → 2. ... was spelt in Welsh
    Welsh...
 3. English speakers   → 3. English speapers
 4. Stendahl is an author who   → 4. tendahl is....
 5. speech production   → 5. peach seduction
 6. stick in the mud   → 6. smuck in the tid
 7. retroflexed   → 7. retrofrexed
 8. the gutters are flooded   → 8. the glutters are fudded
 9. the bride of Frankenstein   → 9. the blide of....
10. from pounds to franks   → 10. from prounds to fanks
11. draperies cleaned   → 11. craperies cleaned
12. in my Spanish class   → 12. in my Splanish class
13. brisket and potatoes   → 13. ... protatoes

14. the quartet's playing Mozart on Friday → 14. ... praying Mozart...

15. stick around and try to see → 15. sick around and tie to tree — I mean — trick around and sigh to tea — oh you know what I mean

16. there's a pest in every class → 16. ... a pess in every clatt
17. french fried potatoes → 17. friend fried potatoes
18. fish grotto → 18. frish gotto
19. steak and potatoes → 19. speak and tomatoes
20. slumber party → 20. lumber sparty
21. deep structure → 21. steep dructure
22. split pea soup → 22. plit spea soup
23. brake fluid → 23. blake fruid
24. excludes → 24. exkudes
25. splicing block → 25. spicing block
26. irreplaceable → 26. irrepraceable
27. I'm gonna chew the fat with Slim → 27. ... chew the fla [flæ] — the fat with...

28. fresh clear water → 28. flesh queer water
29. equally complex → 29. equally compex
30. no strings attached → 30. no strings attrached
31. in the present slide → 31. in the pleasant slide
32. steak knives → 32. snake knives
33. strange reasons → 33. strain regions
34. the third and surviving brother → 34. the sird [sərd] and — the bird and — the third...

35. two hundred drugs → 35. two hundred dugs
36. long and strong → 36. trong and slong
37. how much time you want to spend → 37. ... time you want to stend
38. look up my brother → 38. look up my blother
39. slick looking chick → 39. sick looking — uh — slick looking chick

40. streak of bad luck → 40. steek [stijk] of brad luck

H. Affricates

1. key chain → 1. chee cane
2. an ex top-notch tennis player → 2. an ex [tatʃ nap]...
3. national stature → 3. natural — national...
4. Rafferty is a jackass → 4. Jafferty is a jackass
5. further surgery → 5. furger surgery

6. the protestant prince   → 6. … princh
7. ocean perch   → 7. ochen [otʃən] perch
8. prince charming   → 8. chints [tʃɪnts] charming
9. do a one step switch   → 9. … stetch − step switch
10. in St. Louis John said   → 10. in St. [dʒuwəs] John…
11. pretty chilly   → 11. chitty prilly
12. cream cheese   → 12. cheam creese
13. Ray Jackendoff   → 13. Jay Rackendoff
14. Leon Jacobson is going to get his   → 14. … his press chest
    chest pressed
15. Angela Davis   → 15. Andela Javis
16. last cigarette Tim had in June → 16. … Jim had in tune
17. entire chapter   → 17. enchire chapter
18. the 1967 version of his dissertation → 18. … virgin of his dissertation
19. Daniel, go tell Janet   → 19. Janiel, go tell Janet
20. John's work   → 20. Juan's [wanz] jerk

I. Velar Nasals

1. the rank [ræ̃ŋk] order of the subjects → 1. the rand [rænd] orker…
2. the red tide will stink [stɪ̃ŋk] up the → 2. … will [stɪn] up the [sijk]
   sea
3. I'll wring her neck   → 3. … [rɪ̃ŋk] her [nɛg]
   [rɪ̃ŋ]   [nɛk]
4. the bank will pay 5.6 %   → 4. … ban [bæn] will [pejk]…
   [bæ̃ŋk]
5. sink [sɪ̃nk] a ship   → 5. [sɪ̃mp] a [ʃɪk]
6. bringing up Bantu   → 6. [brɪgɪ̃ŋ] up….
7. proposals to hand out   → 7. … to hang [hæ̃ŋ] out
   [hæ̃nd]
8. swing and sway   → 8. swin and swayg
   [swɪ̃ŋ]   [swej]   [swɪ̃n]   [swejg]
9. sing for the man   → 9. [sɪg] for the [mæ̃ŋ]
   [sɪ̃ŋ]   [mæ̃n]
10. cut the string [strɪ̃ŋ]   → 10. cunt [kʌnt] the [strɪg]
11. springtime for Hitler   → 11. [sprɪg]time for [hɪ̃ntlər]
    [sprɪ̃ŋ tajm]
12. morphemes in the verb   → 12. … [vʌrg strɪ̃n]
    string [strɪ̃ŋ]
13. Chuck Young [tʃʌk jʌ̃ŋ]   → 13. chunk yug [tʃʌ̃ŋk jʌg]
14. clinging vine [klɪ̃ŋgɪ̃ŋ vãjn] → 14. [klɪ̃nɪ̃ŋ] vine
15. shilling [ʃɪlɪ̃ŋ]   → 15. shingle [ʃɪ̃ŋgəl]

J. Vowels (reversals, additions, deletions, substitutions)

1. feet moving	→ 1. fuwt meeving
2. prevailing [prijvejliŋ]	→ 2. [prejvijliŋ]
3. the new [nuw] Sony [sownij]	→ 3. ... no [now] [suwnij]
4. jokes about Jacobson	→ 4. jakes about jocobson
5. sonorant, strident	→ 5. sonorant, strodent
6. David, feed the pooch	→ 6. ... food the peach
7. ad hoc	→ 7. odd hack
8. fill the pool	→ 8. fool the pill
9. bed bugs	→ 9. bud begs
10. dots from dashes	→ 10. dats [dæts] from [daʃəz]
11. Bev and Bill	→ 11. Biv and Bell
12. annotated bibliography	→ 12. annototed....
13. right Veda [rajt vijdə]	→ 13. [rijt vajdə]
14. I beat the shit out of him	→ 14. ... bit the sheet....
15. a pipe smoker	→ 15. a pope smiker
16. look after	→ 16. lack [ʊftər]
17. Sir Stafford Cripps	→ 17. Sir Stifford Craps
18. Wang's bibliography	→ 18. wing's babliography
19. brain research	→ 19. [brijn rejsərtʃ]
20. Sacco and Vanzetti	→ 20. [sǽkij] and [vænzɛ́ Dow]
21. dissertation topic	→ 21. [dɪsərtaʃn̩ tejpək]
22. place the stress	→ 22. [plɛs] the [strejs]
23. the strong alternation condition	→ 23. alternition condation
24. moonlight sonata	→ 24. [manlajt sənuwtə]
25. clip peak	→ 25. cleap pick
26. foreground items	→ 26. foregrind items
	[fɔrgrajnd ajDəmz]
27. group three	→ 27. greep three
28. But Nixon in China is an historical event	→ 28. .... an hysterical − historical...
29. the committee will have to meet more often	→ 29. the commeetee [kəmijtij] will have to [mijt]...
30. as the wage price freeze	→ 30. ... [wajdʒ prajs]...
31. you picked out such a nice book	→ 31. you][pʊkt ... [bʊk]
32. the place which advertised Brittainy crepes	→ 32. ... which idvertised...
33. several cars reported	→ 33. ... [kɔrz ripɔrtid]
34. available for exploitation	→ 34. avoilable...
35. set him an exam	→ 35. sat him an exam
36. competing rules	→ 36. computing [kəmpjuwtiŋ][ruwlz]

37. living with Jean   → 37. leaving with Jean
38. beef noodle soup   → 38. beef needle soup
39. the data is derived   → 39. [dejtə] is [dərejvd]
40. environment before voice   → 40. ... before [vajs]

K. Vowel + r

1. famous alternations as permit   → 1. fermous...
2. the Kansas City Chiefs remained the   → 2. ...Kansas City [tʃərfs] — chiefs,
   first team   that is, remained the [fərst]
3. cards sorted   → 3. cords sorted
4. took part in the first   → 4. took [pərt] in the [fərst]
5. support the movement [səpɔrt]   → 5. [səpuwt] the [muwvmɪnt]
6. foolish argument   → 6. farlish argument
7. from Filmore and Gruber   → 7. ... [fɪlmər]... [gruwbər]
8. integer   → 8. interger
9. but the point on the timing   → 9. ... the [pərnt]...
10. turn the corner   → 10. torn the kerner
11. in Mort's class as in Marty's   → 11. in Mart's ... as in Morty's
12. first and goal to go   → 12. first and girl to go
13. the waterfall isn't working   → 13. ... waterfall isn't walking
14. that's the generic term for a two-   → 14. ... generic tomb ... a two...
    wheeled vehicle
15. barred i [bard aj]   → 15. ... [bayd ar]
16. fight very hard   → 16. fart very hide
17. soup is served   → 17. serp is souved
18. rhubarb pie party   → 18. ... par [pajtij]
19. the shot didn't hurt much   → 19. the shirt didn't hot much
20. our backyard is full of toads   → 20. ... backyoad is full of tards

L. Single Features

1. what Malcolm said   → 1. what balcolm said
2. spell mother   → 2. smell bother
3. money falling out of the picture   → 3. bunny malling out ...
4. pity the new teacher   → 4. mity the due teacher – I mean –
                                               nity the poor teacher – uh – ...
5. Cedars of Lebanon   → 5. ... lemadon
6. bang the nail   → 6. mang the mail
7. Bohr's atom   → 7. mohr's batom [mɔrz bæDəm]
8. I'm married almost 15 years   → 8. I'm barried – married ...
9. all these magnificent sights   → 9. ... bagnificent ...

10. a bank of America in Montebello → 10. mank of aberica in bontemello
11. the party will go on all night → 11. the marty will go on all tight
12. phonetic data → 12. pholetic data
13. the morning light → 13. ... morning night
14. capacity → 14. camacity
15. Dick Carter is a musician → 15. Nick Carter is a musician
16. a mystery fan → 16. a bystery man
17. Terry and Julia → 17. Derry and Chulia [tʃulja]
18. what does the course consist of → 18. ... gorse consist of
19. defined → 19. devined
20. seeing is not believing → 20. zeeing ...
21. Bob McCord → 21. Bob McGord
22. referendum → 22. reverendum
23. vocal cords → 23. vocal gourds
24. taxi cab → 24. capsy tag
25. a real pussy cat → 25. ... bussy [busij] ...
26. big and fat → 26. pig and vat
27. clear blue sky → 27. glear plue sky
28. reveal → 28. refeel
29. documentation → 29. documendation
30. call the girl → 30. gall the curl
31. Arthur Abramson → 31. [arðər] – Arthur ...
32. sit all day → 32. zit all day
33. paradigms → 33. paratimes
34. seek verification → 34. zeek ferification
35. if you consider a spider exercising volition → 35. ... volision [volɪʒən]
36. the relative clause has served to [sʌrvd] to → 36. ... has surfed [sʌrft] to
37. pedestrian → 37. tebestrian
38. Zwicky has gotten skinny → 38. ... skwinny
39. shoulder seams → 39. soldier seams
40. San Bernardino → 40. ... Bermardino
41. meditation garden → 41. medication darden
42. flipping his lid → 42. flipping his lib
43. scatterbrain → 43. spattergrain
44. spontaneous sound change → 44. ...shound [ʃæwnd] ...
45. goofing off → 45. gooping off
46. conditions → 46. [kʌndʒɪʃənz]
47. extracted → 47. extrapted
48. lemon meringue pie → 48. leaden meringue by
49. student welfare → 49. student welpare

50. nasal infix   → 50. navel infix
51. hit the roof   → 51. hit the roop
52. Daily Bruin [bruwn̩]   → 52. Daily Broom
53. head coach   → 53. hedge coach
54. is there any cheese darling   → 54. … cheese [dʒaliŋ]
55. chair a session   → 55. chair a shession [ʃɛʃən]

M. Within word errors

 1. courtesy   → 1. coursety
 2. Kimura   → 2. Mikura
 3. revelation   → 3. relevation
 4. fixed [fɪkst]   → 4. sixed [sɪkst]
 5. Harrisian [hæˈrɪsijɨn]   → 5. hasserian [hæˈsérijɨn]
 6. sahara [səhǽrə]   → 6. saraha [sərǽhə]
 7. Rabelais   → 7. ralebais
 8. philosophy   → 8. phisolophy
 9. reverse [rijvərs]   → 9. [rijzərv] reserve
10. relevance   → 10. revelance
11. protoplasm   → 11. plotoprasm
12. university   → 12. uvinersity
13. paraphasias   → 13. farapasias
14. felony   → 14. fenoly
15. psycho-dynamics   → 15. dymanics
16. whisper   → 16. whipser
17. I'n not sure I can ask this   → 17. … aks this
18. medal [mɛdəl]   → 18. [mɛ́ləd]
19. catterpillar   → 19. patterkiller
20. terminus   → 20. ternimus
21. pancakes   → 21. canpakes
22. harpsichord   → 22. karpsihord
23. neural modeling   → 23. … moleding [málədiŋ]
24. peculiarity   → 24. peculiality
25. fish   → 25. shiff

N. ʃ-Clusters

 1. book return (slot/chute)   → 1. … shlute
 2. short lady   → 2. short shlady
 3. shut his mouth   → 3. shmut his mouth
 4. sling shot   → 4. shling shot
 5. pot shot   → 5. shpat shot

6. (shot/slug) of whiskey   → 6. shlug of whiskey
7. pantry shelves   → 7. shpantry shelves
8. shallow structure   → 8. shallow shtructure

O. Stress

1. the tòwn fárm   → 1. the tówn fàrm
2. símilarly   → 2. [sɪmɨlǽrɨlij]
3. propósed/sáid   → 3. proposaid [prəpòwsɛ́d]
4. I'm páying for it   → 4. I'm pay fóring it
5. supíne   → 5. súpine
6. so that we can progréss   → 6. so that we can prógress – progréss
7. polisyllábic   → 7. [palísəbək]
8. próphesy   → 8. [prəfásij]
9. artículatory   → 9. [artɪkjuwlǽtərij]
10. he said 5000 marines were covered   → 10. ... by lànding néts – by lánding
    up by lánding nèts   nèts, that is
11. the Jèrry Wèst Nìght gáme   → 11. the Jèrry Wèst níght gàme –
                                          (then corrected)
12. by averaging the sìx scóres   → 12. ... the síx – the sìx scóres
13. it depends on your óutlòok   → 13. ... on your lóok òut – on your
                                          lòok óut – I mean – on your
                                          óutlòok
14. he lives in the bìg whìte hóuse   → 14. in the bìg whíte hòuse – the whìte
                                          hóuse I mean
15. you can buy the cóle slàw   → 15. ... the còle sláw – cóle slàw

P. Word Reversals

(Note: in the following examples the intended intonation of the phrase or sentence is unchanged. The first few examples are marked to illustrate this: a grave accent is placed over stressed syllables; an acute accent is placed over the syllable receiving the primary or main stress.)

1. the còst of the clèaning of the cárpet → 1. the clèaning of the còst of the
                                                cárpet
2. Sèymour slìced the salàmi with a knífe → 2. Sèymour slìced the knífe with a
                                                salámi
3. in her páper dòll bòx   → 3. in her dóll pàper bòx
4. the ... organization takes plàce in the   → 4. ... takes plànt in the pláce
   plánt
5. threw the clock through the window → 5. threw the window through the
                                                clock

6. a fifty-pound bag of dog food → 6. a fifty pound dog of bag food
7. a fine first half → 7. a first fine half
8. a ... card I just sent to him → 8. ... I just sent him to
9. a plus nasal segment → 9. a plus segment nasal
10. my father's other remark → 10. my other father's remark
11. a half-eaten bag of candy → 11. a half bag of eaten candy
12. I didn't get a cover with my copy → 12. ... a copy with my cover
13. a tank of gas → 13. a gas of tank
14. what grammar will a child learn → 14. what child will a grammar learn
15. the unique feature of factor analysis → 15. the unique factor of feature analysis
16. gold mine → 16. mine gold
17. used the key to open the door → 17. ... the door to open the key
18. the quake caused extensive damage in the valley → 18. ... extensive valley in the damage
19. a small body of compositions written for these instruments → 19. ... body of instruments ... for these compositions
20. Hey, Mike have you heard the joke about ... → 20. Hey, joke, have you heard the Mike about
21. the worst for both schools → 21. the both for worst schools
22. I would like to remind you all → 22. ... to all remind you
23. he's been around a long time → 23. he's been a long around time
24. all planned out → 24. planned all out
25. how much do you want for this → 25. ... want this for
26. Hockett's 'State of the Art' → 26. ... art of the state
27. the problem of subject raising → 27. the subject of problem raising
28. a lighter for every purse → 28. a purse for every lighter
29. dòes Jàck smóke? → 29. dòes smòke jáck?
30. the way we can characterize the situation would be by ... → 30. ... would by be
31. he's at U.S.C. [jù ès síj] → 31. ... at U.C.S. [jù sì és]
32. a good many years → 32. a many good years
33. a job for his wife → 33. a wife for his job
34. wine is being served at dinner → 34. dinner is being served at wine
35. you got as far as typing page one → 35. ... as far as page typing one

Q. Haplologies and other Telescopic Errors

1. shrimp and egg souffle → 1. shrig souffle
2. I have a spot in my heart for him → 2. I have a spart for him
3. extinguish your cigarettes and fasten your seat belts → 3. extinguish your seat belts

4. Herb Alpert said	→	4. Halpert said
5. a rule that's called tone movement	→	5. ... called tonement
6. subtle and cultural differences	→	6. suteral differences
7. mud puddle	→	7. muddle
8. production and perception of speech	→	8. prodeption of speech
9. Nixon witness	→	9. nitness
10. rubber overshoes	→	10. ruvershoes
11. very difficult to separate out	→	11. ... to separout
12. where are the new counselling forms	→	12. ... the newselling forms
13. near record	→	13. necord
14. it's a pretty idiotic idea	→	14. it's a prettiotic idea [prɪtijati̇k]
15. in the metrapolitan area	→	15. ... metralitan area
16. it's too detailed	→	16. it's too dailed
17. revealed	→	17. reeled
18. a parking permit	→	18. a parking pit
19. relexicalizable	→	19. relexalizable
20. lateralization	→	20. laterization
21. lexicalization	→	21. lecalization
22. increasingly	→	22. increasely
23. repetitively	→	23. repetively
24. rigorous	→	24. rigous
25. late afternoon classes	→	25. laternoon classes [lejtərnuwn]
26. abandoning	→	26. abanding
27. Morton and Broadbent point out	→	27. Morton and Broadpoint out
28. tremendously	→	28. tremenly
29. aspectual	→	29. aspectal
30. jettisoning	→	30. jettisung
31. infantry men	→	31. intrymen
32. Ray's examples	→	32. Ray's exams
33. get his ideas across	→	33. get his eyes across
34. velar nasal	→	34. vesal [vijzəl]
35. copulating	→	35. copuling

R. Derivational Affixes

1. grouping	→	1. groupment
2. an intervening node	→	2. an intervenient node
3. infinitive clauses	→	3. infinity clauses
4. they sit there motionless	→	4. ... motionly
5. often	→	5. oftenly
6. in a minute	→	6. mining [mɪniŋ]
7. sequentially	→	7. sequencingly

8. the performative verb	→ 8.	the performing verb
9. acoustic theory	→ 9.	acoustal theory
10. clearly	→ 10.	cleary
11. Biology 2	→ 11.	Biological 2
12. counter indicator	→ 12.	counter indicant
13. flashing light	→ 13.	flasher light
14. executive committee	→ 14.	executor committee
15. explanations	→ 15.	explanatings
16. perceptual monitoring	→ 16.	perceptic – perceptual …
17. attention	→ 17.	intention
18. persistent rules	→ 18.	consistent – persistent …
19. my teeth have improved	→ 19.	… reproved
20. maybe it's not meaningless	→ 20.	… meaningful
21. desirable	→ 21.	resirable
22. I think he's a distinguished looking man	→ 22.	… a distinguishable
23. *John shaves John* is not ambiguous	→ 23.	… is not ambigual
24. strictly logically speaking	→ 24.	… speakingly
25. she's twelve going on thirteen	→ 25.	… going on thirty
26. journal of the Acoustical Society	→ 26.	journical …
27. He's pointed out as being undependable	→ 27.	… independable
28. which you could have partly or completely	→ 28.	… partly or impartly – completely …
29. there's a good likelihood	→ 29.	… likeliness
30. bloody students	→ 30.	bloodent studies [stuwdijz]
31. I analyze as the following	→ 31.	as the follow
32. five uninterrupted days	→ 32.	five interrupted …
33. to hand it in	→ 33.	to handle it in
34. horizontal	→ 34.	horizontical
35. the democrats	→ 35.	the democratics
36. instead of	→ 36.	insteady of
37. they can't quite make it	→ 37.	… quitely …
38. peculiarity	→ 38.	peculiaracy
39. specializing in	→ 39.	specialating in
40. introduction	→ 40.	introducting

S. Independence of Grammatical Morphemes and Morphophonemic Rules

1. a floor full of holes	→ 1.	a hole full of floors
2. there aren't as many days [dej+z] in the week	→ 2.	… weeks [wijk+s] in the day
3. both kids [kɪd+z] are sick	→ 3.	… sicks [sɪk+s] are kid

4. Dick was Sylvia's [sɪlvijə+z] husband → 4. Sylvia was Dick's [dɪk+s] husband

5. seven runs in one inning → 5. seven innings in one run

6. the students should acknowledge the department → 6. the departments should ... the student

7. can you pick up the things [θɪŋ+z] → 7. can you thing up the picks [pɪk+s]

8. I carved a pumpkin [karv+d] → 8. I pumped [pʌmp+t] a carven

9. I cooked [kʊk+t] a roast → 9. I roasted [rowst+ɪd] a cook

10. the Coach likes to have his team rested [rɛst+ɪd] → 10. ... his rest teamed [tijm+d]

11. I turned in a change of address → 11. I changed in a turn of ...

12. a language learner needs → 12. a language needer learns

13. where are the chicken livers → 13. ... the living chickens

14. going to get them cleaned [klijn+d] → 14. ... to get them teethed [tijθ+t]

15. I wanted to get the fire started [start+ɪd] → 15. ... to get the star fired [fajr+d]

16. George's lab [dʒɔrdʒ+ɪz] → 16. lab's [læb+z] George

17. she's just beginning to form two word sentences (sɛntins+ɪz] → 17. ... to form two sentence words [wʌrd+z]

18. the guy's name → 18. the name's guy

19. Ralph's [rælf+s] and my → 19. Ralph and my's [maj+z]

20. wage hikes [hajk+s] → 20. hike wages [wejdʒ+ɪz]

21. ministers in the church [mɪnɪstər+z] → 21. churches [tʃʌrtʃ+ɪz]

22. bunnies [bʌnij+z] don't eat steak → 22. steaks [stejk+s] don't eat bunnies

23. she has one uncle and two aunts [ænt+s] → 23. ... one aunt and two uncles [ʌŋkəl+z]

24. top of the head thoughts [θɔt+s] → 24. top of the thought heads [hɛd+z]

25. words that rhyme → 25. rhymes that word

26. oxen's yoke → 26. oxen yokes

27. a weekend for maniacs [mejnijæk+s] → 27. a maniac for weekends [wijkɛnd+z]

28. take the steaks [stejk+s] out of the freezer → 28. ... the freezes [frijz+ɪz] out of the steaker

29. the tulip bulbs [bʌlb+z] → 29. the bulb tulips [tulɪp+s]

30. I put one parenthesis over the six → 30. ... one parenthesi [pərɛnθəsij] ...

T. *a/an*

1. don't take this as a rejection on my part → 1. ... as an erection on my part

2. a system of computer programs → 2. an istem – a system ...

3. at the end of a sentence → 3. at the end of an S – a sentence

4. an eating marathon → 4. a meeting arathon

5. an ice cream cone	→	5. a [kajs rijm] cone
6. a history of an ideology	→	6. an istory of a hideology
7. at an early period	→	7. at a pearly period
8. an oscillatory mode and a differential mode	→	8. a doscillatory mode ...
9. an interesting fact about clinical work	→	9. a clinical fact about ...
10. it's an expensive hotel	→	10. it's a pensive – an expensive hotel
11. he's an unusual teacher	→	11. he's a usual – an unusual ...
12. there's a small restaurant on the island	→	12. there's an island on the small restaurant
13. an occurrence	→	13. *a occurrence
14. an anniversary celebration	→	14. *a anniversary celebration
15. an impossible character	→	15. *a impossible ...

U. Blends

1. instantaneous/momentary	→	1. momentaneous
2. N-ary/binary	→	2. benary
3. to determine what/which	→	3. watch
4. omnipotent/omniscient	→	4. omnipicent
5. splinters/blisters	→	5. splisters
6. what she/Fromkin said	→	6. ... shromkin
7. you don't even/ever have to	→	7. ... [ijvər]
8. mainly/mostly	→	8. maistly [mejstlij]
9. the resolution says/states	→	9. stais [stɛz]
10. striving/trying	→	10. strying
11. public/popular	→	11. poplic
12. salary/scale	→	12. scalary
13. minor/trivial point	→	13. minal [majnəl]
14. pain pills/killers	→	14. pain kills
15. insufficient/inferior	→	15. insufferior
16. edited/annotated	→	16. editated
17. slick/slippery	→	17. slickery
18. population/pollution	→	18. populution
19. spank/paddle	→	19. spaddle
20. person/people	→	20. perple
21. grizzly/ghastly	→	21. grastly
22. liquids/linguals	→	22. liquals
23. draft/breeze	→	23. dreeze
24. avoid/evade	→	24. evoid [ijvojd]
25. tummy/stomach	→	25. stummy
26. removing wow and flutter	→	26. ... [flæw]

27. Irvine's quite near/close	→ 27. ... clear
28. dealer/salesman	→ 28. dealsman
29. terrible/horrible	→ 29. herrible
30. which means/meant that	→ 30. ... meanst [mɛnst]
31. grab/reach	→ 31. [grijtʃ]
32. a drink first/a drink before I play	→ 32. a drink befirst
33. the final/finished copy	→ 33. the [fɪnəl] copy
34. specifically/precisely	→ 34. specisely [spəsayslij]
35. velars/dentals	→ 35. dentars
36. three pulls of the muscles/muscular (?)	→ 36. ... of the [mʌskəlz]
37. opacity and specificity	→ 37. specifity
38. He's a real music buff (movie buff?)	→ 38. ... [mjuvək] ...
39. importance of adjacent/adjoining rules	→ 39. ... adjoicent ...
40. clarinet/viola	→ 40. clarinola
41. best/most	→ 41. boast
42. switch/changed	→ 42. swinged [swɪndʒd]
43. corollary/parallel	→ 43. corallel
44. Joe Emonds	→ 44. Jemonds [dʒɛmənz]
45. quite a few/bit	→ 45. ... [bju]
46. boiled/wild rice	→ 46. biled rice
47. transposed/transcribed	→ 47. transpised
48. everybody/everyone	→ 48. everybun
49. headaches/migraines	→ 49. hegraines [hɛ́grejnz]
50. the competition is a little stiffer/ tougher	→ 50. ... stougher ...
51. this applies mainly/only to under- graduates	→ 51. ... monely [mównlij]
52. Ross/Chomsky	→ 52. Romsky
53. feature shifting/switching	→ 53. swifting
54. moment/minute	→ 54. momute [mowmɨt]
55. I can't even get the jargon correct/right	→ 55. ... corright [kərájt]
56. survey/review	→ 56. surview
57. related/directed to	→ 57. relected
58. coins/change	→ 58. canes
59. hanging/dangling	→ 59. hangling
60. George Lakoff's class	→ 60. Jakoff's class
61. smart/clever	→ 61. smever
62. recognize/reflect	→ 62. recoflect
63. complicate (simplify?)	→ 63. complify
64. acid/marijuana	→ 64. marácid
65. right up my alley (intrusion of knowledge?)	→ 65. ... alledge [ǽlidʒ]

V. Word Substitution

1. she's marked with a big scarlet A	→	1. ... scarlet R
2. white Anglo-saxon Protestant	→	2. ... prostitute
3. we're playing the art of the fugue	→	3. ... arg of the flute
4. the Razamouvsky Number 3 (it is Opus 59)	→	4. ... Number 59
5. pay by check	→	5. pay by rent
6. a book with a most magnificent dialogue	→	6. .... magnificent dialect
7. he got hot under the collar	→	7. ... under the belt
8. a fairly immediate thing	→	8. ... instamatic thing
9. I thought Westerns were where people ride horses instead of cars	→	9. ... instead of cows
10. three, five and eight are the worst years for wine	→	10. ... worst years for beer – I mean wine
11. the native values	→	11. the native vowels
12. I'm glad that Wilson Riles was elected	→	12. ... that Woodrow Wilson ...
13. blond hair	→	13. blond eyes
14. take him to the lab last	→	14. ... the lab first – I mean last
15. he's not that happy in Illinois. (was to say: he's considering Hawaii)	→	15. ... happy in Hawaii
16. a routine proposal	→	16. ... routine promotion
17. he's here tonight	→	17. he's there – here ...
18. to work with George	→	18. ... with Steve – George
19. a branch falling on the roof	→	19. falling on the tree
20. The Mafia moved into Boston	→	20. ... into Italy – I mean Boston
21. I urgently request you to release the hostages unharmed	→	21. ... the hostages unarmed – unharmed
22. my dissertation is too long	→	22. ... is too short – long
23. Don't forget to return Aspects	→	23. ... to return Structures – uh – Aspects
24. the conquest of Peru (speaker had been at Purdue)	→	24. the conquest of Purdue
25. a phrase structure generation of derived nominals	→	25. a phrase structure generalization
26. Q: when are you going to have the ale? A: with the dinner	→	26. A: with the beer
27. in our academic ivory tower	→	27. ... academic ivy league
28. There's a small Japanese restaurant	→	28. ... Chinese – I mean ...
29. the A over A constraint	→	29. the A over B constraint
30. there are a lot of questions	→	30. ... of answers – I mean questions

31. he's a low grader   → 31. he's a high –low grader
32. When were you last on the east coast   → 32. ... on the west – east ...
33. you'll have to call later   → 33. ... call earlier – later
34. before the place opens   → 34. ... the place closes
35. if I write any smaller   → 35. ... any slower – smaller
36. everything under the sun   → 36. ... under the world – ...
37. I couldn't get if off my back   → 37. ... off my foot
38. bridge of the nose   → 38. bridge of the neck
39. rewrite your dissertation to your   → 39. ... to your heart's dissent
    heart's content
40. in many cases   → 40. in many times
41. this must be excluded   → 41. ... be included
42. the four deaf children   → 42. ... blind – deaf ...
43. bang my finger with a hammer   → 43. ... my thumb ... hanger
44. the feature back   → 44. the feature round
45. I know his father-in-law   → 45. ... his brother-in – ...
46. Lewis Carrol, Jonothan Swift, and   → 46. ... and Tom Paine
    Mark Twain
47. *Jack* is the subject of the sentence   → 47. ... is the president of ...
48. I should stand on my head (was   → 48. ... stand on my nose
    discussing Yoga cure for sinus
    infection)
49. I've been continuously impressed by her → 49. ... distressed – impressed ..
50. don't burn your fingers   → 50. ... your toes
51. some semantic facts   → 51. ... syntactic facts
52. Kivadi, a language about which we   → 52. ... know very much
    know very little
53. I don't sleep very well in a single bed → 53. ... speak very well ...
54. when my gums bled   → 54. ... tongues bled
55. I would have come   → 55. ... have gone – come
56. my boss's wife   → 56. my boss's husband
57. it might be evidence for   → 57. ... emphasis for
58. chamber music   → 58. chamber maid
59. I've never heard of classes on Good   → 59. ... classes on April 9th
    Friday. (Good Friday fell on April 9)
60. deep phrase structure   → 60. deep freeze structure
61. look at the lady with the dachshund   → 61. ... with the Volkswagon
62. blue sky and yellow sun   → 62. blue sky and blond hair
63. we are in basic agreement   → 63. ... in basic reality
64. if someone steals my protoMiwok,   → 64. ... automatic suffixes
    you ... are automatic suspects
65. I'm not going to claim   → 65. ... to complain

W. Pronoun, Preposition, Article

1. Laurie's boyfriend has longer hair than she does → 1. ... than he does
2. I told him (Peter) you were not coming in today → 2. ... told her – him ...
3. I think your honor has really put your finger on it → 3. ... put the finger ...
4. It looks as if → 4. I look as if ...
5. Father in Heaven, thank You for this food → 5. ... thank us ...
6. the problem I ran into → 6. ... I ran up to
7. they fear that we might go → 7. ... that me might go
8. there are places in the text where one finds → 8. ... which one finds
9. bring sketches with you when you go → 9. ... with him ...
10. if you use the further distal form for that → 10. ... from that
11. it doesn't sound as good to me → 11. ... to you – to me
12. let's assume there's only one language box and it's in the left hemisphere → 12. ... and it's on the left ...
13. are you going to be in town on June 22nd → 13. ... to be on town ....
14. I'm picking them up → 14. ... picking her – them up
15. when will you be home → 15. what will you be – I mean – when ...
16. how in the hell can you say that → 16. who in the hell can you ....
17. there are (some) beautiful houses on the hill → 17. there are a beautiful houses
18. the city has a personality of its own → 18. ... of his own
19. a student who is in my quiz section → 19. ... student what is ....
20. the key is under the mat → 20. ... over – under the mat
21. the day when I was born → 21. ... where I was born
22. whatever his name is → 22. whoever his name is
23. the sentences which are ambiguous → 23. sentences who are ambiguous
24. when I gave it to him → 24. ... to he – him ...
25. we → 25. we and I

X. Multi-word Errors

1. the trouble with markedness theory → 1. the markedness theory with trouble

2. when you apply the P-rule to the underlying string → 2. when you apply the underlying string to the P-rule

3. if you'll stick around you'll meet him → 3. if you'll meet him you'll stick around

4. a difference in the syntactic behavior of gerunds → 4. a difference in gerunds of the syntactic be – in the ...

5. I'd like to speak to you about this matter → 5. I'd like to speak to this matter about you

6. a model of performance → 6. performance of a model

7. what we want to do is train a cat to move its tongue → 7. ... is train its tongue to move – the cat to ....

8. I have to smoke a cigarette with my coffee → 8. I have to smoke my coffee with a cigarette

9. When Angela was in the Philosophy Department → 9. when the Philosophy Department was in Angela

10. It was on page a hundred and eight → 10. it was on a hundred and page eight

11. how in the hell do you get there? → 11. how do you get in the hell there?

12. it's a matter of days → 12. it's days of a matter

13. in the sentence 'many arrows didn't hit the target' → 13. in many arrows, the sentence – uh – the sentence ...

14. when the pigs swept through UCLA → 14. when UCLA swept through the pi – UCLA

15. I'm going to talk about three main points → 15. I'm going to mainly point about – talk about ...

Y. Ungrammatical utterances (various causes)

1. Turkish and German just don't have it; neither does Swedish → 1. ... so does Swedish

2. Do you know where the Grand Ballroom is, by any chance → 2. where is the Grand Ballroom, by any chance?

3. This is an oversimplification/ or This is highly oversimplified → 3. This is a highly oversimplification

4. You're in a better position → 4. ... in a more better ...

5. That's what we're going to be doing today → 5. ... going to be do today

6. As Chomsky and Halle point out → 6. ... pointing out

7. You are going, aren't you → 7. ..., isn't it

8. He has spent most of the time on his synthesizer → 8. ... spent the most of time ...

9. one might want to have → 9. ... want have

10. At Berkeley High there are special programs (or) (?) ... there's a special program → 10. ... there's a special programs

11. it's a startling proposal → 11. ... a startlingly ...

12. it's a crazy notion → 12. ... a crazy notions – notion

13. what you're doing is, in fact, wrong → 13. what you're doing is a fact wrong

14. when a person grows old → 14. ... a person grow old

15. Theo comes up with → 15. Theo come up with

16. how jealous he is → 16. ... he am

17. some conclusions and (some) recommendations → 17. ... and a recommendations

18. Are our people happy about his teaching → 18. Is our people ...

19. if the syllable breaks come at the morpheme junctures → 19. ... breaks comes ...

20. where it occurs and where it doesn't occur → 20. ... it doesn't occurs

21. she prided herself → 21. she prouded herself

22. this is something that we should discuss/ (or) ... about which ... → 22. ... that we should discuss about

23. the earliest acquired → 23. the most earliest ...

24. knowing what she wanted → 24. knewing what she wanted

25. I didn't go in yesterday → 25. I didn't go in tomorrow

26. if he swam in the pool naked → 26. ... swimmed – swam in ...

27. he has read it → 27. he has [rijd] it

28. the last I knew → 28. ... I knowed

29. now you can relax (or)/be relaxed → 29. ... you can relaxed

30. I learned how to write it → 30. ... how to wrote it

31. you ought to get some input → 31. ... ought to got ...

32. I didn't know he could do it → 32. ... could did it

33. the doctor said you should have been dead twenty years ago → 33. ... should be dead ...

34. they forgot to wake me → 34. ... to woke me

35. the last I knew about that → 35. ... I know ...

36. she was so drunk → 36. ... so drank

37. if you did it yesterday → 37. ... do it ...

38. I've begun to change → 38. ... began ...

39. he had to have it → 39. he haved to have it

40. all the dogs in the neighborhood bury their bones → 40. dogs ... bury its bones ...

41. the subject lies in a prone position → 41. the subject lie in a ...

42. I can hear her → 42. I can her hear

43. What I'm working on, then → 43. what I'm working, then, on
44. how old are you? → 44. how old you are?
45. people tend to make up words → 45. people tend up to make words
46. the girl who I taught last year → 46. the girl who taught I ...
47. are you going to the Renaissance Fair this year? → 47. are going you to the ....
48. she didn't come home til 2 a.m. → 48. she not come home ...
49. what time is it? → 49. which time is it?
50. she'll wash herself in the pool → 50. she'll wash themself ...
51. most people don't know → 51. most people doesn't know
52. that just came out → 52. that was just come out
53. the director of the institute is applying/applied (?) → 53. ... is applied
54. the conductor of an orchestra is able to determine which one came/comes (?) first → 54. ... which one cames [kejmz] ...
55. when I was much younger → 55. when I were much younger
56. I don't want to part with this book too long → 56. ... to part this book with too long
57. a boy who I know has hair down to here → 57. a boy who I know a boy has hair down to here
58. she'll do it/ she does it (?) → 58. she'll [duwz] it
59. aren't you going to telephone her/call her up (?) → 59. ... to telephone her up
60. she was waiting for her husband → 60. she was waiting her husband for

Z. Negation

1. people agree that it is not well formed → 1. people don't agree that it's well formed
2. I wasn't plugged in for a second → 2. I was unplugged in ...
3. I regard this as imprecise → 3. I disregard this as precise
4. he had no idea → 4. he had an idea – a no idea – that is – he had no idea
5. I know he's not going to Valley College → 5. I don't know he's going – I know he's not going ...
6. children with no tongue/children without a tongue → 6. children not without – children with no tongue
7. the vowels are unrestricted → 7. the vowels are not stricted – are unrestricted
8. don't you know why he's going → 8. do you know why he's not going – I mean ...

9. I tell you he's insane   → 9. I tell you he's not crazy – I mean, he's insane

10. Not that Paul's done anything inadequate   → 10. ... anything adequate – inadequate

11. the electric blanket that we have now isn't working   → 11. ... that we don't have now is working

12. he asked me to write back if there was anything that was unclear   → 12. ... if there was nothing that was clear

13. she can't tell me anything about it   → 13. she can tell me anything about it – can't tell me ...

14. the bonsai died because I didn't water it   → 14. the bonsai didn't die because I watered it

15. there's no way of doing it   → 15. there's a way of not doing – no way ...

AA. Miscellaneous

1. some campaign posters   → 1. some [pæstejn] coasters
2. prepositional phrase nodes   → 2. ... fraid nose
3. my hypothesis   → 3. my [pajθás] – hypothesis
4. can, could, will, and would   → 4. can, can, cal [kæl] ... [wɪld]
5. the third of December   → 5. the [dijsərd] of [θɛmbər]
6. Athabaskans   → 6. [æskəbæθkənz]
7. thought provoking   → 7. [prɔtfəðowkiŋ]
8. when the Japanese attacked Pearl Harbor   → 8. ... the Jakanese attapped Curl Harbor
9. Tim said you should call him in the lab   → 9. Kim said you should call him in the tab
10. room and board   → 10. bood [buwd] and [rɔrm]
11. salt and pepper shakers   → 11. salt and shecker papers
12. whole second half   → 12. soul hecond path
13. I hate long hair in hot weather   → 13. ... hot wair in long heather
14. loose leaf notebook   → 14. [nows nijf luwf] book
15. metamorphoses   → 15. [mɔrtəmɛtəfijz]
16. turn the heat on   → 16. hurt the team on
17. path of least resistance   → 17. leaf of past ...
18. distinguished teaching award   → 18. disteaching tingwer award
19. Airforce Cambridge Research Lab   → 19. ambridge [ejmbrɪdʒ] careforce – uh – Cambridge Airforce – Airforce ...

20. Black policemen   → 20. [bəlæk plijsmən]
21. butterfly and caterpillar   → 21. butterpillar and caterfly

22. non-binary features   → 22. non-[vʌrnij] features
23. it's my banana   → 23. it's banaymana [bənájmənə]
24. during the first blue book   → 24. deering the foost blur book
25. if we juxtapose   → 25. if we juxtapapose
26. union meeting   → 26. union méetowing
27. San Francisco   → 27. fran anísko
28. Richard's going to be at the computer → 28. rooter's going to be ...
    center
29. familiar with Professor Miller → 29. ... professor miliar [míljər]
30. I keep getting a busy signal → 30. ... keep gizzing a busy ...
31. Death Valley   → 31. [fɛθ ðælij]
32. thumb-sucking   → 32. thump sucking
33. it's now middle class whites → 33. it's now whittled clad whites
34. linguistically significant   → 34. significally linguisticant
35. redundant rhetoric   → 35. redunderant rhetic
36. the whole department knows   → 36. the dewhole partment knows
37. if there's no further speaker on the → 37. ... no furker speeder on the
    question   question
38. she'll be here on March first → 38. ... on March firth
39. a three day thing   → 39. a three way thing
40. conjectures   → 40. conjestures
41. a transformation rule   → 41. a transpormation rule
42. other committees of that sort → 42. ... of that hort – sort
43. on a trumped up rape charge   → 43. ... rape karge [kardʒ]
44. in resplendent evening dress → 44. ... evening guess
45. stuck out in the sticks   → 45. ... out in the hicks
46. a lot less expense   → 46. ... wess expense
47. Jack or Jenny   → 47. Jack or Venny
48. books for Viet Nam   → 48. bomb for Viet Nooks
49. during the M.A. exam [ɛm èj ɛgzǽm] → 49. ... the [ɛ̀mɛ̀ks] minátion
50. in his phonology seminar   → 50. in his seminology phominar